POSITIVE INTERVENTION

FOR SERIOUS BEHAVIOR PROBLEMS

**Best Practices in Implementing
the Hughes Bill (A.B. 2586) and the
Positive Behavioral Intervention Regulations**

by

**Diana Browning Wright,
Harvey B. Gurman,**
and the California Association of
School Psychologists/Diagnostic Center,
Southern California
Positive Intervention Task Force

Task Force Members
Nancy Gronroos
Bill Knight
Jocelyn Finn Mayer
Kimble Morton
Marie Kanne Poulsen, Ph.D.
Tom Weddle

Special Consultants
Eva Mauer, M.D.
Joanne Weigel, M.D.
Shiela Wolford, OTR

Publishing Information

Positive Intervention for Serious Behavior Problems: Best Practices in Implementing the Hughes Bill (Assembly Bill 2586) and the Positive Behavioral Intervention Regulations was developed by Diana Browning Wright and Harvey B. Gurman, school psychologists, Diagnostic Center, Southern California, and the California Association of School Psychologists/Diagnostic Center Positive Intervention Task Force. The task force's members were the following:

NANCY GRONROOS
School Psychologist
Arcadia Unified School District

BILL KNIGHT
Teacher, Preschool Program for Students with Visual Impairments
Arcadia Unified School District

JOCELYN FINN MAYER
School Psychologist
Montebello Unified School District

KIMBLE MORTON
Motor Assessment Program Specialist
Diagnostic Center, Southern California

MARIE KANNE POULSEN, PH.D.
Director of Education, University Affiliated Program
Childrens Hospital, Los Angeles

TOM WEDDLE
Teacher, Severely Disabled Program
Spokane, Washington

It was originally edited and prepared by Resources in Special Education (RiSE), a special project of California State University, Sacramento, with the California Department of Education, Special Education Division. The production staff included Patricia Winget, editor; Elissa Cullison and Jim Merk, assistant editors; Thora Chaves, graphic designer; and Sandra Cosner, graphic artist.

This updated revised edition of *Positive Intervention* was published by the California Department of Education, 721 Capitol Mall, Sacramento, California (mailing address: P.O. Box 944272, Sacramento, CA 94244-2720). It was distributed under the provisions of the Library Distribution Act and *Government Code* Section 11096.

ISBN 0-8011-1555-8

Ordering Information

Copies of this publication are available for $14 each, plus shipping and handling charges. California residents are charged sales tax. Orders may be sent to the Publications Division, Sales Office, California Department of Education, P.O. Box 271, Sacramento, CA 95812-0271; FAX (916) 323-0823. See the back of this book for complete information on payment, including credit card purchases, and an order blank. Prices on all publications are subject to change.

An illustrated *Educational Resources Catalog* describing publications, videos, and other instructional media available from the Department can be obtained without charge by writing to the address given above or by calling the Sales Office at (916) 445-1260.

Notice

The guidance in this document is not binding on local educational agencies or other entities. Except for the statutes, regulations, and court decisions that are referenced herein, the document is exemplary, and compliance with it is not mandatory. (See *Education Code* Section 33308.5.)

Prepared for publication
by CSEA members.

DEDICATION

To all the children, parents, and staff who have struggled with poorly understood behavior. To all the professionals and parents who have worked, and continue to work, to see positive behavioral interventions in place throughout California.

CONTENTS

APPENDICES

FIGURES

FOREWORD

The State of California has continually sought to provide an appropriate and meaningful educational program in a safe and healthy environment for all children regardless of possible physical, mental, or emotionally handicapping conditions.

Teachers of children with special needs require training and guidance that provide positive ways for working successfully with children who have difficulties conforming to acceptable behavioral patterns.

Procedures for eliminating maladaptive behaviors should never cause pain or trauma.

When behavioral interventions are used, they must be used in consideration of the pupil's physical freedom and social interaction and be administered in a manner that respects human dignity and personal privacy and that ensures a pupil's right to placement in the least restrictive educational environment.

Behavioral management plans should be developed and used, to the extent possible, in a consistent manner when the pupil is also the responsibility of another agency for residential care or related services.

Training programs need to be developed and implemented in institutions of higher education that train teachers. In-service training programs need to be made available as necessary in school districts and county offices of education to ensure that adequately trained staff members are available to work effectively with the behavioral intervention needs of students with exceptional needs.

Teresa P. Hughes
Senator

PREFACE TO
THE UPDATED
REVISED EDITION

*M*ore than a decade has passed since passage of the pivotal Hughes Bill and enactment of *Education Code* sections related to positive behavioral interventions and functional analysis assessments. What has California achieved in this decade? Two key achievements stand out:

- Every school district in California is now aware that serious behavior problems cannot go untreated, that assessment must occur to determine the "function" of the behavior, and that a positive behavioral intervention plan must be developed that is directly related to the functional analysis assessment.

- Every special education local plan area (SELPA) has defined who is qualified to be a behavior intervention case manager (BICM) and thus qualified to conduct or supervise a functional analysis.

With the reauthorization of the Individuals with Disabilities Education Act (IDEA) of 1997, behavioral assessment has entered a new phase across the United States:

- Whenever a student is determined to have behavior that impedes the student's or his or her peers' learning, strategies, including positive behavioral interventions and supports, must be considered. This consideration is for any and all behaviors an individualized education plan (IEP) team believes warrants this attention, not just for serious behavior problems.

- Additionally, if a student with an IEP violates a code of conduct that results in a district-initiated request for involuntary placement change or expulsion, a functional behavioral assessment of that behavior, often occurring only once, must be conducted.

With these changes, functional assessment and behavior planning has moved out of the arena of serious behavior problems, often occurring most frequently in students with severe disabilities, to wider applicability in schools. Existing *Education Code* requirements for severe behavior problems and the new federal IDEA mandates necessitate that we clearly differentiate when a behavior plan should be developed for a broadened range of behaviors and what depth of analysis should occur prior to developing the plan. Appendix Q has been added to this manual to aid the reader in this differentiation.

It is an exciting time to be serving students with exceptional needs. Accountability for outcomes is infused in all our educational reform movements. IDEA clearly points the way to a high level of accountability for outcomes. For example, consider the following statement:

"The public agency shall ensure that each teacher and provider is informed of his or her specific responsibilities related to implementing the child's IEP and the specific accommodations, modifications, and supports that must be provided for the child in accordance with the IEP." (*Federal Register* 300.342(b)(3)).

Filing written plans without implementing them clearly is not to be tolerated. Behavior plans of any type developed for a student with an IEP become a part of the IEP process and are subject to the same ongoing review and evaluation by the team as would occur for any IEP component. Thus, behavioral goals and objectives related to a behavior plan will be reviewed frequently because of the strengthening of accountability for outcomes.

The decade of experience since publication of the first edition of this manual has taught us that successful students whose needs are met rarely engage in challenging behavior. Students with behavior problems can be taught alternative acceptable ways of getting their needs met; and environments, instructional practices, and curriculum can be tailored to fit the individual student. With this proactive focus, educational success is often achieved, and a substantial reduction or elimination of problem behaviors typically follows.

At long last we have mandates that challenge us to enact best practices in educating our students with problem behaviors. If we can determine the most time-efficient analysis of behavior to use in a given situation and develop the least intrusive, yet effective, interventions at early stages when "behavior is impeding learning," we may not often need to resort to a more detailed analytic process described in this manual.

Diana Browning Wright and Harvey B. Gurman, co-editors
on behalf of all contributors and readers

PREFACE TO THE REVISED EDITION

This revised edition of *Positive Intervention for Serious Behavior Problems* reflects modifications in the California Education Code made during the four years since the first edition was published. These include changes as to when a behavior intervention case manager must join the Individual Education Plan team, when a functional assessment is required, when a positive behavioral intervention plan may be necessary, and other procedural changes. Updated medical information and a streamlined data collection form have been included, as well as revisions in forms and flow charts to adhere to new Education Code language.

The continuing need for proactive problem-solving approaches to address serious behavior problems is reflected in our media and in the increasing number of requests for assistance received by support staff from teachers and parents in school districts throughout the nation. On the national level, the Individuals with Disabilities Education Act (IDEA), reauthorized in 1997, embodies ideas about discipline, functional behavioral assessment, and positive behavioral interventions from the same paradigm that grounds California's Education Code on behavioral interventions. The use of this paradigm, which is the subject of this manual, is becoming more widespread in California and elsewhere as an effective means to assist students with severe and difficult-to-change behaviors. It is our hope that all of us can become better "behavior interventionists," improving both the satisfaction of the families we serve and, most importantly, the long-term outcomes for all of our students.

Diana Browning-Wright, Harvey B. Gurman, and Nancy Gronroos
on behalf of all task force members, consultants, and readers

PREFACE TO THE FIRST EDITION

*P*rofessionals who work with children and adults with significant handicaps have long struggled to find techniques that are effective in remediating serious behavior problems. Aversive behavioral interventions have often been used as a tool for eliminating unwanted behavior. However, agencies and professionals have disagreed about where effective measures end and abusive measures begin. The need for a clear and organized policy defining and regulating the use of aversive behavioral interventions, as covered in the Hughes Bill, has been a long-standing one in California. For years, a number of organizations have attempted to pass legislation protecting the rights of persons with disabilities, but for many reasons they were never successful.

Over the years, because of the lack of a clear, workable, universal policy, people in schools and care facilities have too often suffered due to aversive procedures. These aversive techniques, perhaps used by frustrated and frightened adults, were surely applied in the best interest of the child and without malice or intent to harm; nevertheless, children treated with these procedures have experienced pain, humiliation, and, tragically, even death.

A policy regulating the use of aversives has been difficult to establish because there is disagreement on the necessity for and effectiveness of aversives. There are also justifiable concerns over various statewide regulatory approaches regarding cost, local control, and training of personnel.

In the early 1970s, California laws left the decision on the use of aversives to professionals. Around that time, as a result of court cases (*Wyatt v. Stickney*, 1972; *Knecht v. Gilman*, 1973), institutional and care facilities in California took the lead in addressing clients' rights efforts. Some state legislation and regulations grew out of these efforts. Title 22, California Administrative Code, Section 80341, protects patients receiving services in community care facilities from corporal or unusual punishment, humiliation, and mental abuse. The Lanterman Act (Assembly Bill 3802) established the right of people with developmental disabilities to be free from harm, including physical restraint or isolation, excessive medication, abuse, and neglect, as well as a right to be free from hazardous procedures.

In 1977, legislation introduced by Assemblyman Gary Hart of Santa Barbara attempted to bring education into the effort (Section 67 of Chapter 1247, California Statutes of 1977). Many people in the field thought that this was finally the time to address the use of aversive procedures and develop one consistent policy encompassing all state agencies involved in education and treatment of all people with disabilities. Therefore, in 1978 a joint Department of Education and Department of Health task force was formed, as required by the Hart Bill, to establish guidelines for the legislation. A draft was completed by January 1979 for distribution and public review. The guidelines did not, however, have the California Department of Education's backing. Educational field personnel were concerned over the workability of the guidelines and the heavy demands placed on the schools' resources. The State Department of Education then decided to write separate but "compatible" guidelines for use only in public schools. Once they were written, the State Advisory Commission on Special Education held statewide hearings on the draft guidelines.

In July 1979, the guidelines recommended by the Commission were presented to the State Board of Education. A variety of experts, including Assemblyman Hart himself, made comments to the board pointing out the weaknesses in the application of the guidelines (e.g., lack of qualified staff and too few training programs in colleges and universities to meet staffing needs). They raised a number of other unresolved issues, including disagreement on such basic items as the definition of "aversives." Finally in September 1979, the State Board of Education elected not to adopt the guidelines. Following this, the Board released a policy statement alerting school districts of their potential tort liability if they did not treat students with disabilities carefully, reminding them of the existing state laws governing corporal punishment.

Despite ongoing professional discussion and some political activity, the issue essentially lay dormant for several years. Then in 1987, following the death of a child in a private facility during a behavioral intervention, Assemblyman Richard Katz introduced new anti-aversive legislation. The California Department of Education and various advocacy groups tried to create a bill that was comprehensive and complete in its regulation of aversives. However, the bill died when issues such as expense and local control proved too difficult to surmount.

Following this, the Advisory Commission on Special Education picked up the torch in the next legislative session and sponsored an effort that ultimately led to development of the Hughes Bill (Assembly Bill 2586) and its implementing regulations. This landmark legislation, introduced by Teresa Hughes, was passed by the legislature and signed by Governor Wilson on September 12, 1990. The bill calls for the Department of Education to develop implementing regulations. Once again, the Department proposed a set of implementing regulations and the Advisory Commission on Special Education sponsored a series of public hearings throughout the state from the fall of 1991 through spring of 1992. Following the hearings, a final draft of the proposed regulations was presented to the State Board of Education in September of 1992 and received more public input. The final version of the regulations was adopted by the Board in January 1993. Implementation of the regulations became effective on May 20, 1993, following final review by the Office of Administrative Law.

Positive Intervention for Serious Behavioral Problems is one of the most impressive documents I have reviewed regarding special education for many years. It is not only well written and accurate, it is extremely comprehensive and demonstrates that the authors had a clear understanding of what information the field would need to effectively develop behavioral management plans.

Joyce O. Eckrem, Esq.

Deputy General Counsel, Legal Office, California Department of Education

A MESSAGE FROM THE SPECIAL EDUCATION AND STATE SPECIAL SCHOOLS AND SERVICES DIVISIONS

*I*n the spirit of providing statewide leadership for special education programs and services, we extend our commendations and appreciation for the exemplary work provided by Diana Browning Wright, Harvey B. Gurman, and all the other individuals who contributed to this manual from conception to publication.

We are pleased that our two divisions within the California Department of Education jointly worked to complete the release of this important and long-awaited revised manual, *Positive Intervention for Serious Behavior Problems—Best Practices in Implementing the Hughes Bill (A.B. 2586) and the Positive Behavioral Intervention Regulations*. With funding and contractual oversight provided by the Special Education Division, the State Special Schools and Services Division was afforded the opportunity to revise the original publication to reflect current federal and state laws and regulations.

The California Department of Education receives requests daily from parents, professionals, and paraprofessionals who seek up-to-date, well-founded, and beneficial resources for working with students who require positive behavioral interventions to fulfill their potential in high-quality programs. We are confident this manual will again be received by the field as a highly valued, comprehensive, and often-used resource.

We congratulate each of you for the important work you do each day in providing our most important customers, California's students, with successful educational opportunities and services.

ALICE D. PARKER

Director, Special Education Division

RONALD S. KADISH

Director, State Special Schools and Services Division

ACKNOWLEDGMENTS

This manual is the product of a wonderfully collaborative effort on the part of many dedicated and talented individuals.

We gratefully acknowledge the encouragement of Al Casler, former member of the Advisory Commission on Special Education, and Loeb Aronin, California Association of School Psychologists (CASP) liaison to the Commission, who encouraged school psychologists to take on an active role as child advocates in helping the education community implement this landmark legislation. Their input at the outset of the regulation development process was the catalyst for forming the joint task force.

We are greatly indebted to our task force members, who gave many hours of their time to the development of this manual. Over pizza dinners and spirited discussions, a framework for elaboration was developed. Through both collaborative and individual efforts, the members of this diverse group became a team that wrote, rewrote, and provided anecdotes and examples from personal experiences. For all of your efforts for the children of California, thank you, Nancy, Bill, Jocelyn, Kim, Marie, and Tom.

We thank Deborah Holt, director, and Betty Bollier, assistant director, Diagnostic Center, Southern California, for their shared belief in the importance of this manual, their valuable suggestions, and their encouragement throughout the project.

Marcia Boden and Betty Henry, presidents of CASP during the 1991 and 1992 terms; Pauline Theodore, current CASP president; Joe Platow, CASP chief executive officer; and the entire CASP Executive Board and staff deserve special recognition for their invaluable assistance and good-humored flexibility throughout the two-year development process.

Likewise, Ronald Kadish, director, State Special Schools and Services Division, California Department of Education; John Flores, former State Special Schools director; and Shirley Thornton, former deputy superintendent, California Department of Education, deserve special recognition for their roles in the formation of this uniquely collaborative joint task force and their belief in the importance of this legislation for California's children.

We are indebted to Kendra Rose, past co-chair of the Advisory Commission on Special Education, for her invaluable input, support, and encouragement.

We are especially grateful to the following professionals, who formed an indispensable part of the team effort. They gave generously of their time as reviewers to ensure that this manual is practical, that it is theoretically sound, and that it captures the intent of, and meets the legal mandates provided in, the Hughes Bill (Assembly Bill 2586) and the subsequent implementing regulations:

GREGORY ARMSTRONG, M.S.
School Psychologist
Oceanside Unified School District

LOEB ARONIN, ED.D.
Director, Psychological Services
Los Angeles Unified School District

LOIS CARBONE, M.A.
School Psychologist
Ventura County Superintendent of Schools

KAREN T. CAREY, PH.D.
Coordinator, School Psychology Program
California State University, Fresno

BRUCE DAKE, ED.D.
School Psychologist, San Diego City Schools
Project Coordinator, Interwork Institute
(San Diego State University)

MICHAEL DEYOUNG, PH.D.
School Psychologist
Ramona Unified School District

LARRY DOUGLASS
Educational Specialist
California State University, Sacramento

V. MARK DURAND, PH.D.
Associate Professor of Psychology
State University of New York at Albany

JOYCE O. ECKREM, J.D.
Deputy General Counsel
California Department of Education

ROBERT WILLIAM ELLIOTT, PH.D.
Psychologist
South Bay Union High School District

REBECCA FOX, M.A.
School Psychologist
Ventura County Superintendent of Schools

ELLEN S. GOLDBLATT, J.D.
Managing Attorney
Protection and Advocacy, Inc.
(Bay Area office)

NANCY HARRIS
Coordinator, Member Services and Publications
California Association of School Psychologists

JUDITH KAHN-DEMOSS, M.S.
School Psychologist
Los Angeles County Office of Education

SCOTT W. KESTER, PH.D.
Professor of Education and Director of
School Psychology
Loyola Marymount University, Los Angeles

G. ROY MAYER, ED.D.
Professor of Education
California State University, Los Angeles

MARCIA S. MCCLISH, M.A.
Director, Santa Barbara County
Special Education Local Plan Area

JOSEPH A. PLATOW, PH.D.
Chief Executive Officer
California Association of School Psychologists

KENDRA ROSE, M.A.
Program Specialist
Whittier Area Cooperative Special
Education Program

GARY SEATON, M.A.
Director, North Inland Special Education Local
Plan Area
San Diego County Office of Education

ROGER TITGEMEYER, PH.D.
Supervisor, Psychological Services
Orange County Department of Education

CAROLYN URBANSKI, PH.D.
School Psychologist
Oakland Unified School District

Our medical and occupational therapy consultants freely gave of their time and expertise to provide important information and counsel that added to the thoroughness of this document. Thank you, Eva Mauer, M.D., Joanne Weigel, M.D., and Shiela Wolford, OTR.

Numerous individuals and organizations shared their unique talents and insights:

JACKI L. ANDERSON

KATHRYN BISHOP

DISABILITY RIGHTS AND EDUCATION DEFENSE FUND

K. BRIGID FLANNERY

MIKE FURLONG

BILL AND JENNIFER GLENNON

CAROLYN GURMAN

REBECCA HOLLWEDEL

LEE HUFF

PAM HUNT

STEVE JOHNSON

OFFICE OF CIVIL RIGHTS

MARGARET PETERS

JOSI PRECIADO

PAT RAINEY

JEFF SPRAGUE

LINDA STEIGER

DALE WRIGHT

We are thankful for the talented partnership of Valerie Reyes, administrative assistant and computer wizard extraordinaire, as well as the skillful and cheerful assistance provided by the entire clerical team at the Diagnostic Center, Southern California. Thanks to Hortense Jurado, Antoinette Lopez, Leticia Rodriguez, and Susan McKinney.

For their editing and graphic expertise and their commitment to this project, we thank the following staff members at Resources in Special Education who worked on the first edition: Patricia Winget, editor; Jim Merk, assistant editor; Elissa Cullison, assistant editor; Sandra Cosner, graphic artist; Thora Chaves, graphic designer; Annette Ostertag, program assistant; and Katherine Shea, resources assistant.

Finally, and most deeply, we thank Ronald Kadish for his unwavering enthusiasm, his sense of humor and balance, and his many hours of assistance. Without his collaboration, this manual would not have been possible.

Diana Browning Wright and Harvey B. Gurman
School Psychologists
Diagnostic Center, Southern California

Chapter 1

Introduction

On September 12, 1990, Assembly Bill (A.B.) 2586 (Hughes, Behavioral Interventions) was chaptered into California law, ensuring the rights of special education students to have behavioral intervention plans that are designed to bring lasting, positive changes in their behaviors without application of interventions that cause pain or trauma. This law brought to fruition many years of effort on the part of parents, educators, and concerned citizens throughout the state.

Although the legislation was prompted by tragic events in the public and private education systems, it is rooted in the most hopeful of our premises: that all children can be provided with educational opportunities and environments that respect their dignity and privacy and that promote the full development of their human potential. If a student's difficulties are so serious or intractable that the commonly used interventions are ineffective, the individualized education program (IEP) team now has guidelines for developing a behavioral intervention plan infused with positive behavior principles. The new regulations present opportunities for the best practices seen across California and the nation to become the norm in serving children with serious behavior problems.

Prevention as a Best Practice

The classroom environment is vitally important in providing an atmosphere in which students can learn to manage their own behavior. Students may cope with situations in the classroom that they are unable to manage on the playground or school bus, in the cafeteria or community. As appropriate behavior is established in the classroom, introducing the behavior to other environments can be addressed.

Although the topic of establishing overall school climate is beyond the scope of this manual, it is important to recognize that the district philosophy and leadership skills of the school superintendent and of school board, district special education, and, special education local plan area (SELPA) administration affect the functioning of the individual school sites. At the school site, the principal's leadership informs the overall school climate, which affects teacher morale, enthusiasm, and treatment of students. If the teacher feels nurtured and supported, the students will also. School climate affects staff cohesiveness, feelings of empowerment and ability to affect change, the desire to exert effort and try new methods or approaches, and the ability to approach challenging behavior in positive ways. Frequently, the behavioral intervention case manager (BICM)/IEP team may need to involve school staff (including, when appropriate, school secretaries, lunch and playground duty supervisors, custodians, and so on) beyond the classroom teacher to motivate and support new ways of working with the student who has challenging behaviors. Active involvement of the site administrator, starting with the IEP process to implement a new behavior plan, may be a critical feature of a program's success or failure. Ongoing frequent and systematic support of the teacher's efforts to change behavior will enhance outcome. Understanding the district's unique support structure from district office to individual classroom will be important as the BICM designs programs and builds in needed support for change.

When school climate difficulties arise, the principal, teacher, BICM, and others on the IEP team must strive to create a positive environment. This can be, in some circumstances, a difficult task. If friendliness and acceptance do not permeate the environment, will the students learn to trust it? If general education staff and students are not familiarized with the needs and behaviors of students with exceptional needs on their campus, can they be supportive? If school discipline policies are primarily punitive, will the students learn to acknowledge and grow from their mistakes? Tackling these and other systemic problems is critical in establishing the desired positive environment to ground individual programs for change.

Although the new regulations are written to address individual students who have exceptional needs and their individual problems, the underlying philosophy and principles of functional analysis and positive programming apply to educating *all* students.

Philosophy Guiding the Manual

The positive behavioral intervention regulations were established to ensure that all California students receive educationally oriented behavioral interventions that are proactive, effective, respectful, and positive and that focus on teaching appropriate replacement behaviors. The underlying philosophy of this manual is as follows:

- Behavior is communicative and goal directed.
- Settings and environments should be capable of meeting the student's needs before behavioral interventions are used. Behavioral interventions should not be used to force conformity in inappropriate settings.
- The primary goal of any classroom is to educate and teach effective interpersonal skills, not to manage or suppress behavior.
- Behavioral interventions should consider the developmental level and chronological age of the student.
- Behavioral interventions should be developed collaboratively.
- Behavioral intervention plans should be efficient and minimally intrusive in terms of time, labor, and complexity.
- Interventions should focus on teaching appropriate behavior to replace maladaptive behavior.

Knowledge Base

This manual is a guide to issues and skills needed to effectively implement the Positive Behavioral Intervention regulations. Although professionals who consider assuming the role of BICM may already possess considerable skills in each of the five following domains, each professional will need to assess his or her own preparation. University course work, advanced on-the-job supervision and training, extended workshops, and a diligent program of self-directed study are possible avenues to augment previous training. A thorough study of this manual will help professionals to understand what they already bring to the task and the potential direction for augmenting weak areas.

In addition to possessing a respect for the dignity of students with disabilities, a successful BICM must have a good understanding of five bodies of knowledge:

1. general and special education systems and the interface between them, to include knowledge of the instruction process, teaching techniques, and national reform trends;

2. theory and practice of behavioral analysis, including positive interventions based on functional analysis;

3. unique characteristics of students with serious behavior problems and assessment issues;

4. consultation skills necessary to develop and maintain successful consultant/ consultee relationships in education settings and knowledge and experience in teaming; and

5. procedures and components in the California Education Code, Title 5, and corresponding SELPA policies related to positive programming and emergency interventions.

Ethical Underpinnings

As in all branches of the field of human service, ethical practice is a critical issue in designing and implementing programs for behavior change. A careful review of California education regulations yields the following ethical implications, which should be considered throughout the case management of a student with a serious behavior problem:

- Interventions should be constructive and proactive rather than suppressive and reactive.

- The primary positive gain should be for the student with the serious behavior problem.

- Interventions should provide both immediate and long-term benefits for the student.

- As a result of implementing the behavioral intervention plan, the student should have the potential for increased independence and access to more activities of interest.

- The behavior goals that are developed as a result of the functional assessment should be reasonable and attainable for the student, and the IEP team should be able to implement them within the context of meaningful instructional activities.

- Any changes required to provide a meaningful, accessible, and appropriate curriculum and environment should be made before an attempt is made to directly modify the student's behavior.

- Emergency procedures should protect the safety *and* personal dignity of all parties.

- Emergency procedures should be applied only when safety requires them, and they must not be used as either consequences or punishment or in lieu of a systematic positive behavioral intervention plan.

Chapter 2

Procedures Required by Law and Regulations

The Hughes Bill (Chapter 959 of the 1990 statutes; California Education Code Section 56520 et seq.) and its implementing regulations (California Code of Regulations, Title 5, Education; herein cited with the symbol §)provide a framework to guide educators and parents in developing positive behavior plans and interventions. Although the regulations are complex, they describe clear decision points at which those working with a student can and must determine which of various options are most appropriate. Figure 1 (the flowchart on p. 10) is designed to assist educators in visualizing this process through a simplified decision-tree approach.

Each member of the individualized education program (IEP) team and any other personnel involved must understand the underlying definitions and governing regulations. To this end, each term on the flowchart is briefly addressed below in a question-and-answer format, with references to the applicable sections of the law and regulations cited with each answer. The reader is thus given a quick overview of each step in the process, with direction as to where to find the applicable section of the regulations or the law itself, both of which are included as Appendices A and B.

Students Affected

What is the definition of a "serious behavior problem" under the Hughes Bill?

A "serious behavior problem" is defined by the regulations as "the individual's behaviors which are self-injurious, assaultive, or cause serious property damage and other severe behavior problems that are pervasive and maladaptive for which instructional/behavioral approaches specified in the student's IEP are found to be ineffective."

Which students are covered by the Hughes Bill and implementing regulations?

The law "applies to any individual with exceptional needs who is in a public school program, including a state school for the handicapped . . . or who is placed in a nonpublic school program pursuant to Sections 56365 to 56366.5, inclusive" [California Education Code Section 56521(a)].

Are nonpublic schools and agencies serving pupils pursuant to Education Code Section 56365 covered by the Hughes Bill and implementing regulations?

Yes. The law applies to all individuals with exceptional needs (IWENs) in public and nonpublic school programs. Additionally, nonpublic schools and agencies must "develop policies consistent with those specified" in the regulations relating to emergency procedures [§3052(i)], and they are specifically prohibited from using the procedures outlined in the response to the next two questions [§3052(k) and (l)].

Behavioral Interventions

What is the definition of "behavioral intervention" under the California Code of Regulations?

"'Behavioral intervention' means the systematic implementation of procedures that result in lasting positive changes in the individual's behavior. 'Behavioral interventions' are designed to provide the individual with greater access to a variety of community settings, social contacts and public events; and ensure the individual's right to placement in the least restrictive educational environment as outlined in the individual's IEP. 'Behavioral interventions' do not include procedures which cause pain or trauma. 'Behavior Interventions' respect the individual's human dignity and personal privacy. Such interventions shall assure the individual's physical freedom, social interaction, and individual choice" [§3001(d)].

What behavioral intervention techniques are expressly prohibited in the law and its implementing regulations?

To protect the child from abusive physical or emotional trauma, the regulations specifically identify which types of techniques may not be used by any public or nonpublic school or agency. The interventions prohibited in the regulations are:

(1) "any intervention that is designed to, or likely to, cause physical pain;"

(2) "releasing noxious, toxic or otherwise unpleasant sprays, mists, or substances in proximity to the individual's face;"

(3) denial of "sleep, food, water, shelter, bedding, physical comfort, or access to bathroom facilities;"

(4) procedures such as "verbal abuse, ridicule or humiliation" or others that can be expected to cause "excessive emotional trauma;"

(5) physical restraint by "a device, material or objects that simultaneously immobilizes all four extremities," including "prone containment or similar techniques," unless it is used by personnel who are "trained" in the technique and it is used only as an "emergency intervention;"

(6) "locked seclusion," unless it is used as an emergency procedure and then *only* in a facility licensed or permitted by state law to use a locked room;

(7) any intervention that leaves a student without "adequate supervision;" and

(8) "any intervention which deprives the individual of one or more of his or her senses" [§3052(l)(1-8)].

Functional Analysis Assessment

Do special education due process procedures apply to functional analysis assessments and the development of behavioral intervention plans?

Yes. In addition, the regulations state, "No hearing officer may order the implementation of a behavioral intervention that is otherwise prohibited by this section, by SELPA policy, or by any other applicable statute or regulation" [§3052(m)].

Is the IEP team required to meet to initiate the functional analysis assessment?

Not necessarily. A functional analysis assessment can be started after informed parent consent is obtained. As with any other special education assessment of a student with an existing IEP, this can be accomplished with or without a formal IEP meeting [§3052(b)].

When is a functional analysis assessment required?

"A functional analysis assessment shall occur after the individualized education program team finds that the instructional/behavioral approaches specified in the student's IEP have been ineffective. Nothing in this section [of the regulations] shall preclude a parent or legal guardian from requesting a functional analysis assessment pursuant to the provisions of Education Code 56320 et seq."

Who can conduct a functional analysis assessment?

A functional analysis assessment is "conducted by, or . . . under the supervision of a person who has documented training in behavior analysis with an emphasis on positive behavioral interventions" [§3052(b)]. Further, the regulations indicate that "if the IEP team determines that changes are necessary to increase program effectiveness, the teacher and behavioral intervention case manager shall conduct additional functional analysis assessments . . ." [§3052(f)(5)]. Finally, the regulations indicate that "behavioral intervention case managers . . . will coordinate and assist in conducting the functional analysis assessments . . ." [§3052(j)(2)(A)]. Please see Chapter 3 for more in-depth discussion of this area.

What are the required components of a functional analysis assessment procedure?

Information must be gathered from "direct observation, interviews with significant others and review of available data such as assessment reports prepared by other professionals and other individual records." The assessment procedure must include "systematic observation of the . . . targeted behavior" and of antecedent and consequent events surrounding the behavior, "ecological analysis of the settings in which the behavior occurs," a "review of records for health and medical factors," and a "review of the history" to determine "effectiveness" of previous interventions [§3052(b)(1)(A-F)]. Please see Chapter 3 for more in-depth discussion of this area.

What are the required components of a functional analysis report?

The "written report of the assessment results . . . shall include all of the following: a description of the nature and severity of the target behavior(s)," including "baseline data and an analysis of the antecedents and consequences . . . across all appropriate settings," the "rate of alternative behaviors, their antecedents and consequences; and recommendations for consideration by the IEP team, which may include a proposed plan as specified in Section 3001(f)." [§3052(b)(2)(A-D)]. Please see Chapters 3 and 4 for more in-depth discussion of this area.

Behavior Intervention Case Manager

Who can serve as a behavioral intervention case manager (BICM)?

Anyone who is "a designated certificated school/district/county staff member or other qualified personnel . . . contracted by the school district or county office who has been trained in behavior analysis with an emphasis on positive behavioral interventions." The responsibilities can be performed by existing staff members. There are no "new credentialing or degree requirements." "The duties . . . may be performed by any existing staff member trained in positive behavior analysis with an emphasis on positive behavioral interventions, including, but not limited to, a teacher, resource specialist, school psychologist, or program specialist" [§3001(e)]. Please see Chapter 7 for more information.

Who defines the qualifications of the behavioral intervention case manager?

Each SELPA is responsible for defining "the qualifications and training" needed by the BICM. The qualifications are to be spelled out in the SELPA local plan. The regulations stipulate that the qualifications "shall include training in behavioral analysis with an emphasis on positive behavioral interventions" [§3052(j)(2)(A)].

What are the responsibilities of the behavioral intervention case manager?

The BICM's job is to "coordinate and assist in conducting the functional analysis assessments" and to develop the subsequent behavioral intervention plan. The BICM also consults with staff members implementing the plan and with the parents of the student, as specified in the IEP [§3052(j)(2)(A) and §3001(f)].

If the IEP team determines that the behavioral intervention plan is not effective, the BICM and the teacher "shall conduct additional functional analysis assessments." Based on the outcomes of those assessments, they "shall propose changes to the behavioral intervention plan" [§3052(f)(5)].

Behavioral Intervention Plan

What is a behavioral intervention plan and when is it required?

"The 'behavioral intervention plan' is a written document" that is developed by the IEP team, including the BICM and qualified personnel knowledgeable of the student's health needs [§3052(a)(1)]. It "is developed when the individual exhibits a serious behavior problem that significantly interferes with the implementation of the goals and objectives of the individual's IEP." These plans "shall become a part of the IEP" [§3001(f)]. Please see Chapters 4 and 5 for more in-depth discussion.

What are the responsibilities of the IEP team regarding the behavioral intervention plan?

The "IEP team shall facilitate and supervise all assessment, intervention and evaluation activities. . . ." After the functional analysis assessment is completed, "an IEP team meeting shall be held to review results and, if necessary, to develop a behavioral intervention plan . . ." If a plan is developed, it shall become "a part of the IEP and shall be written with sufficient detail so as to direct the implementation of the plan" [§3001(f)].

What must be included in a behavioral intervention plan?

The behavioral intervention plan must include the following information:

(1) "a summary of relevant and determinative information gathered from a functional analysis assessment;

(2) an objective and measurable description of the targeted maladaptive behavior(s) and replacement positive behavior(s);

(3) the individual's goals and objectives specific to the behavioral intervention plan;

(4) a detailed description of the behavioral interventions to be used and the circumstances for their use;

(5) specific schedules for recording the frequency of the use of the interventions and the frequency of the targeted and replacement behaviors; including specific criteria for discontinuing the use of the intervention for lack of effectiveness or replacing it with an identified and specified alternative;

(6) criteria by which the procedure will be faded or phased out, or less intense/frequent restrictive behavioral intervention schedules or techniques will be used;

(7) those behavioral interventions which will be used in the home, residential facility, work site or other noneducational settings; and

(8) specific dates for periodic review by the IEP team of the efficacy of the program" [§3001(f)(1-8)].

Must the behavioral intervention plan include consideration of multiple school and nonschool settings?

Yes. The behavioral intervention plan shall specify "those behavioral interventions which will be used in the home, residential facility, work site, or other noneducational settings" [§3001(f)(7)]. "A copy of the plan shall be provided to the person or agency responsible for implementation in noneducational settings" [§3001(f)]. Further, "To the extent possible, behavioral intervention plans shall be developed and implemented in a consistent manner appropriate to each of the individual's life settings" [§3052(a)(6)]. Finally, in evaluating a behavioral intervention plan's effectiveness, preintervention and postintervention measures of the occurrence of "the targeted behavior shall be taken . . . across activities, settings, people, and times of the day" [§3052(f)(1)(2)].

How does the IEP team determine the effectiveness of the behavioral intervention plan?

Program effectiveness is determined through "baseline" measures of the targeted behavior "across activities, settings, people and times of the day" during the functional assessment, which are then compared with similar measures of the targeted behavior after the plan is implemented. These measures "may record the data in terms of time spent acting appropriately" (thus focusing on the rate of replacement or adaptive behaviors) "rather than time spent engaging in inappropriate behavior." Documentation of program implementation and periodic review also are required [§3052(f)(1-5) and §3001(f)(8)].

How can a behavioral intervention plan be modified by the IEP team?

The IEP team shall schedule appropriate intervals for the "teacher, BICM, parent or care provider," or other appropriate persons to measure and review program effectiveness. "If the IEP team determines that changes are necessary to increase program effectiveness, the teacher and behavioral intervention case manager shall conduct additional functional analysis assessments and, based on the outcomes, shall propose changes to the behavioral intervention plan" [§3052(f)(4) and (5)].

Can minor modifications be made in a behavioral intervention plan without the need for an IEP team meeting?

Yes. Working together, the BICM (or a "qualified designee") and the parent or parent representative can make minor modifications to the plan, as long as the parent can review the data that any changes are based on, and the parent is "informed of their

FIGURE 1.

Positive Behavioral Intervention Procedural Flowchart

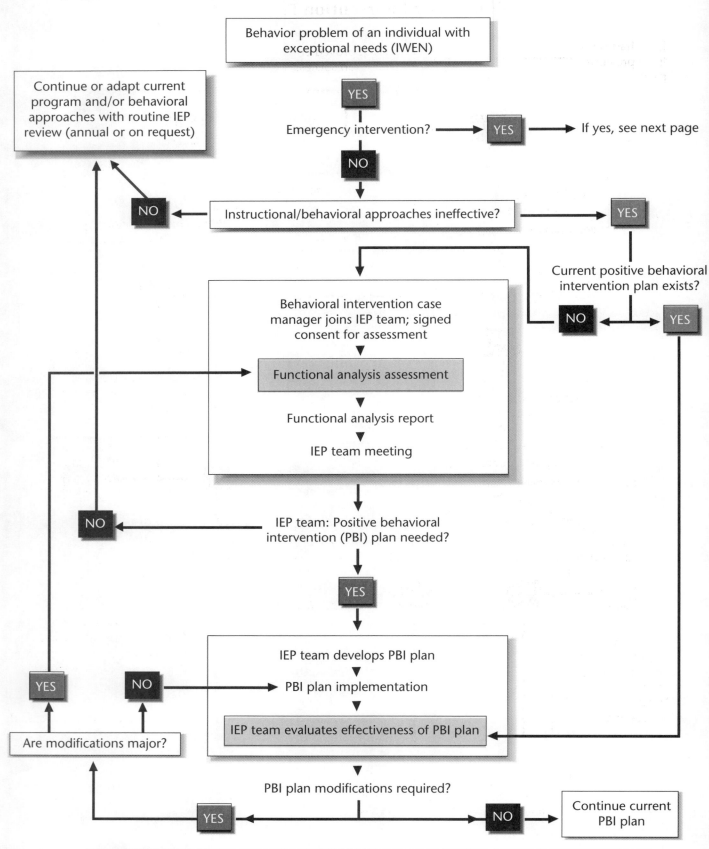

Positive Behavioral Intervention Procedural Flowchart
Emergency Intervention Procedures

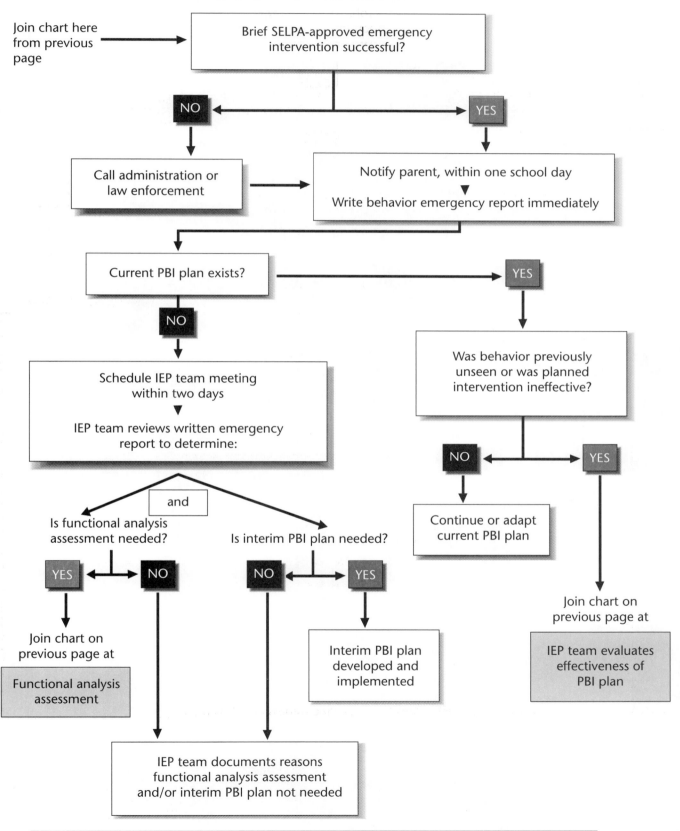

Join chart here from previous page

Brief SELPA-approved emergency intervention successful?

NO

YES

Call administration or law enforcement

Notify parent, within one school day

Write behavior emergency report immediately

Current PBI plan exists?

YES

NO

Schedule IEP team meeting within two days

IEP team reviews written emergency report to determine:

Was behavior previously unseen or was planned intervention ineffective?

NO

YES

Continue or adapt current PBI plan

and

Is functional analysis assessment needed?

Is interim PBI plan needed?

YES

NO

NO

YES

Join chart on previous page at

Functional analysis assessment

Interim PBI plan developed and implemented

Join chart on previous page at

IEP team evaluates effectiveness of PBI plan

IEP team documents reasons functional analysis assessment and/or interim PBI plan not needed right to question any modification to the plan through the IEP procedures" [§3052(g)]. Additionally, the IEP team can initially develop "the behavioral intervention plan in sufficient detail to include schedules for altering specified procedures, or the frequency or duration of the procedures, without the necessity for reconvening the IEP team" [§3052(h)].

Emergency Interventions

What is the role of the IEP team following an emergency intervention, and what timelines apply?

If the student does not have a behavioral intervention plan, "the designated responsible administrator shall, within two days, schedule an IEP team meeting to review the emergency report, to determine the necessity for a functional analysis assessment, and to determine the necessity for an interim behavioral intervention plan. The IEP team shall document the reasons for not conducting an assessment and/or not developing an interim plan" [§3052(i)(7)].

If the student does have a behavioral intervention plan, the IEP team may review the situation to "determine if the incident constitutes a need to modify the plan" [§3052(i)(8)]. Parents and/or residential care providers "shall be notified within one school day whenever an emergency intervention is used" [§3052(i)(5)]. Please see Chapter 6 for further discussion.

What is a "behavioral emergency report" and when is one required?

A behavioral emergency report is a document that contains specific demographic information about the pupil and clear descriptions of the emergency invention and any injuries. It must be written "immediately" following the application of an emergency intervention. [§3052(i)(5)(A-E)]. Please see Chapter 6 for more in-depth discussion of this area.

What are SELPAs required to include in their local plan regarding emergency procedures?

The regulations require that each SELPA's emergency plan include procedures governing the use of behavioral interventions and emergency interventions. Each SELPA must specify the "training that will be required" by anyone responsible for implementing emergency procedures and "the types of interventions requiring such training," as well as what are "approved behavioral emergency procedures" [§3052(j)(2)].

Chapter 3

Functional Analysis Assessment

The first and often most challenging step in developing a successful behavioral intervention plan is to pinpoint both the environmental factors prompting or supporting the problem behavior and the function the behavior serves for the individual. The regulations explicitly require that a functional analysis assessment be completed to obtain this information [§3052(b)(2)]. This chapter gives an overview of the basic concepts involved. Worksheets that may be helpful in completing the analysis are included in Appendix C.

Serious behavior problems require positive behavioral intervention plans when the IEP determines that these problems interfere with achievement of the student's individualized education program (IEP) goals and objectives, or it is determined that the instructional behavioral approaches specified in the student's IEP have been ineffective. These problems might include self-injurious behaviors, assaultive behaviors, or other pervasive maladaptive behaviors (Figure 2). (Refer to Chapter 2 definitions.)

FIGURE 2.

SAMPLE SERIOUS BEHAVIOR PROBLEMS THAT ARE LIKELY TO REQUIRE FUNCTIONAL ASSESSMENT[1]

Self-injurious behaviors	Biting hands; banging head on walls; cutting, stabbing self with pencils, paper clips
Assaultive behaviors[2]	Punching peers, throwing chairs at peers, stabbing peers with pencils
Other pervasive maladaptive behaviors	Running out of classroom into street in front of vehicles, tearing clothing into shreds, prolonged screaming, repeatedly taking off clothing and throwing it out bus window, withdrawing into fetal posture during loud noises
Behaviors causing serious property damage[2]	Setting a fire resulting in serious damage to the school; destroying expensive school property (e.g., computers, lab equipment); significant vandalism or major damage to vehicles

[1]These behaviors are from specific writer's files and appear to meet the definition of a "serious behavior problem." This listing is not exhaustive, but is provided to illustrate the variety of behaviors that require behavioral intervention plans. Typical IEP goals, objectives, and behavior plans will address many behavior problems without the necessity of a functional analysis and accompanying positive behavioral intervention plan. However, when a behavior problem is serious and the student has not responded to more typical classroom approaches, the IEP team will enlist the BICM to proceed with the functional analysis and plan development.
[2]If the behavior results in a disciplinary hearing, federal regulations and IDEA reauthorization require "functional behavioral assessment," even though this may be the first time the behavior has occurred.

The goal of functional assessment is to determine the function of behavior by identifying the antecedent and consequent events that accompany and maintain a problem behavior, as well as any positive replacement behaviors the student has or can develop. This has frequently been termed the "A-B-C analysis of behavior" (antecedent, behavior, consequence).

By direct, structured observation; interviews with significant others; and review of school records and medical and other data, the consultant develops hypotheses about the *function* the behavior of concern has for the student. The behavior is viewed as accomplishing *something*, as a way for the student to meet certain needs or desires, even when others disapprove and the behavior is considered inappropriate by the caregivers. If one knows the purpose of the behavior from the student's perspective, one can design a behavioral intervention plan that teaches an alternative adaptive behavior. Additionally, often environmental factors can be altered so that the student's need to use the undesirable behavior is eliminated.

Analysis: Behavior

The A-B-C analysis begins with a clear description of the problem behavior and any existing incompatible positive behaviors. An incompatible positive behavior is defined as any alternate positive behavior that will achieve the same purpose or serve the same function as the problem behavior. These behaviors must be defined so specifically that any observer could recognize and measure their occurrence. This operational definition is used for the remainder of program development and effectiveness review.

The following are examples of inadequate versus usable, operationalized definitions:

Inadequate description: Student engages in self-abusive behavior.
(Ambiguous because the behavior could be expressed in many ways.)

Operational description: Student bangs forehead on the floor with increasing speed and force until restrained by an adult.

Inadequate description: Student is belligerent and aggressive.
(Ambiguous because belligerent and aggressive may be defined differently by different people.)

Operational description: Student becomes red in the face, clenches his fist, increases his vocal volume, and moves closer and closer to people, frequently culminating in hitting them repeatedly with little attempt to aim the strikes.

As soon as the behavior is defined clearly enough to create a mental picture of how it looks, the behavioral intervention case manager (BICM) is ready to design a baseline data collection system through systematic observation of its frequency, duration, and intensity. Because baseline data consist of repeated measures of the behavior as it *typically* occurs, it is important to allow the student time to adapt to the observer's presence. A variety of methods may be used in data gathering, depending on the nature of the behavior. (Please refer to Appendix C for samples of recording forms and worksheets.) Although some behaviors can be understood with minimal observation time, others may require the BICM to observe for a longer period and then enlist someone else to gather enough data to support or refute initial hypotheses about what is supporting the problem behavior. Skillful consultation is required if the BICM is to be confident that the teacher, aide, or other personnel keeping records on the frequency, duration, and intensity of the behaviors is committed to doing so accurately and consistently. Periodically, the BICM may choose to cross-validate the recording accuracy by having different observers record data simultaneously. (Refer to Appendix C, Worksheet 4 and accompanying guide, for further information.)

Additional Behavior Description Variables

Behavior Frequency (How often does the behavior occur?)

"Frequency" refers to the number of times a behavior occurs in a given time period. High-frequency behavior is examined by dividing the day into intervals as small as necessary (e.g., 9:00-9:15, 8:05-8:10) to capture both the intervals in which the behavior *is* occurring and those in which it *is not* occurring and then recording the presence or absence of the behavior.

Behavior Duration (How long does the behavior last?)

"Duration" refers to the length of time that the behavior is expressed from beginning to end. Some behavior has a very easily observable beginning and end, while other behavior is less discrete. When duration is an essential element in defining the behavior, enough time must be devoted to developing accurate methods of recording because without an adequate baseline, the behavior will not be understood well enough to design a successful intervention. For example, does screaming last only a brief moment or for 20 minutes without interruption?

Behavior Intensity (How forcefully is the behavior expressed? For instance, how insistent, loud, or hard is the behavior?)

The intensity of verbal and physical protest can vary from mild to extremely challenging. By carefully describing and recording baseline intensity, intervention team members can note increases and decreases in response to environmental changes. Specificity in defining the behavior's intensity is helpful in developing criteria for recognizing when the behavior is transitioning to a severity level that requires emergency interventions to contain it and, in contrast, when emergency procedures should be phased out. Good description of the intensity of the behavior also allows early recognition that behavior is escalating and that interventions to redirect it should be used. These criteria are essential for uniform treatment of the student across settings and with different care providers.

Analysis: Antecedent

The "antecedent" portion of the A-B-C model requires the development of as full an understanding of the context that leads to the expression of a behavior as possible. Through an ecological analysis of settings in which the problem behavior and any replacement does and does *not* occur, knowledge of the following variables is obtained: typical interactions between individuals (both those involving the student directly and those that the student observes); specific environmental variables present or absent (e.g., lighting, noise, curriculum components, number of persons present); and periodically occurring events that often change the typical responses of a student (e.g., missing the bus, having an argument, experiencing a sleep shortage the night before). An ecological analysis also includes assessing the nature and variety of activities and instruction; scheduling issues, including the degree to which a student is cognizant of the schedule; quality of communication between staff and students; amount and quality of social interaction; and the degree of the student's participation, independence, and choice. Also part of the antecedent context to be examined are internal variables affecting the student (e.g., medical diagnoses, medication levels, sleep cycles, health, diet, previous interventions).

Professionals in the field of behavior analysis find that mismatches between environments and people are often the major reason that severe behavior problems develop or continue. Therefore, a thorough and systematic ecological assessment is of critical importance before pursuing further functional assessment or behavioral intervention design. Intervention planning should determine needed environmental changes before addressing direct strategies for the student's behavior. This is essential if the natural environment is to provide the discriminative stimuli (i.e., the proper conditions) for useful, positive behaviors to occur routinely and be maintained. Please refer to "Educational Environment Assessment Scale" in Appendix J.

The environment must foster and promote the student's socially acceptable control over his or her surroundings, encourage expansion of interests, and provide options for choice making. When this does not occur, maladaptive behaviors are likely to abound. One of the major needs of a student is for increasing independence; frustration declines with greater control over the environment and oneself. This is true of students at every developmental level and with every disabling condition. It is true even though students with serious behavior problems are a heterogeneous group, frequently learning in idiosyncratic, unpredictable, and nonfunctional ways. It is true even though hypersensitivity or hyposensitivity to sensory stimuli, rigidity of thinking, limited language skills, and limited insight are common and reduce availability for learning. Higher levels of adaptive behavior have been shown to result from altering the instructional environment to accommodate the student's needs and goals, which are identified through functional analysis. When a student enjoys the curriculum and staff, feels successful at tasks, and feels able to exert choices, behavior problems decrease rapidly in most cases.

Analysis: Consequences

Consequence analysis in the A-B-C model considers two elements:

1. Specific environmental outcomes produced by the behavior. This might be removal from the group, reactions from peers or staff members, escape from unwanted attention, and so forth.

2. Specific physiological outcomes produced by the behavior. Examples include increased physical contact during a restraint procedure; opportunity to leave an area or room where stimuli, such as noise, is aversive to the individual; release of natural opiates in the brain due to self-injury; and so forth.

The communicative intent of the behavior is considered. The word "intent" can be misleading because it implies that the student understands his or her behavior and uses it purposefully. In this context, the significance or "intent" is assigned by others to form an understanding of the behavior's potential purposes. Depending on the student's metacognitive skills (awareness of his or her own thinking processes), the student may not be aware of why the behavior is performed. Nevertheless, the student intends, anticipates, expects, or desires a particular result to occur as a result of the behavior chosen for expression. By forming an understanding of potential purposes, the BICM can begin to understand the direction to take in teaching more adaptive ways for the student to achieve his or her purpose.

Evans & Meyer (1985)[1] summarize several functions that behaviors might have:

- *Social communicative:* These behaviors clearly are related to social interactions. The behavior seems to be a method of nonverbal communication and might involve the following different types of messages in different individuals or at different times: (1) "Leave me alone" or "I don't want to do this" (maybe the task is too difficult, or the person is tired or does not like the other person); (2) "Pay attention to me!" (the staff person might be spending time with someone else); and (3) "I want that!" (maybe someone just asked the student to stop an enjoyable activity, or the student wants someone else's sandwich).

- *Self-regulatory:* Behavior serving this function varies with environmental circumstances and perhaps how the person feels physically (e.g., tired, overstimulated, overmedicated, sexually aroused). The behavior seems to be a strategy to adjust arousal level, facilitating the paying of attention to something that is very interesting (when there are distractions) or very boring (when the person is tired).

- *Self-entertainment or play:* This behavior may be related to social situations (i.e., it looks like an attempt to play with others) or may occur only when the person is alone. It might be, for example, a way for the person to entertain himself or herself when left alone or waiting for something, or a strategy for playing with others, even when the behavior is actually regarded as negative by others. This can explain the otherwise confusing situation when a learner seems to prefer to tease or even hit a peer whom he or she is known to like. Initiating, attending, or terminating a play interaction with a peer may be the communicative intent of many puzzling maladaptive behaviors.

Analysis: Baseline Data Collecting

Having interviewed teacher(s) and other significant others who have an understanding of the student and his or her behaviors, and having observed the student in his or her environment(s), the BICM will no doubt have an idea about what supports the problem behavior and what might support increased expression of an alternative behavior. The behaviors will have been fully operationalized and described in such a way that all who observe will recognize the beginning and end of each expression of the behavior. At this point, if baseline data have not already been gathered, the BICM will collaborate with the staff available in each environment to develop a system to record the prevalence and severity of the behavior. This baseline data are critical features of behavioral plan development as described in the Education Code and in the literature on behavior change.[2] Often the function of the behavior will not be fully understood unless this systematically collected data are analyzed.

The BICM will want to consider what is known about the behavior before baseline data collection and what remains to be identified. It is important to understand *where* the behavior occurs and does not occur, with *whom*, and under *what conditions*. It may also be important to understand how frequently the behavior occurs, for what duration, and with what intensity. The point of baseline collection is twofold: to figure out *why* the behavior is occurring (the function) and to obtain data for future comparisons, which are essential to determine and document the success or failure of the behavioral plan.

Selecting a Recording System

There are essentially four basic methods of collecting data (plus a variant of one of the methods) useful for measuring serious behavior or the alternate positive replacement behavior: permanent product, event/frequency, duration, and interval recording. (Refer to Appendix C, Worksheet 4 and guide.)

Permanent Product Recording. This method may not be as useful as the following three recording systems in understanding the behavior and providing a baseline against which future change would be measured. This method entails counting a visible, permanent effect created by the behavior, such as number of finished assignments, number of broken windows, number of torn pieces of clothing or books, and so forth. One advantage of this method is its reliability. The permanent nature of the outcome of the behavior presents little ambiguity; either the product exists or it does not. Also, the permanent product can be counted at any time.

Event/Frequency Recording. This method is used to count how often the behavior occurs and then to convert the data to a rate. The rate is determined by dividing the number of occurrences by the duration of observation. Frequency counting can be expressed in rate per week, per day, per hour, per minute, and so forth. This method is used for low-frequency behaviors or when it is important to know exactly how often the behavior occurs.

FIGURE 3.
A GUIDE TO SELECTING BEHAVIOR-RECORDING TECHNIQUES

Type of Measure	Definition	Example	Advantages and Disadvantages
Permanent product recording	Records the enduring outcome of the behavior	Number of completed math problems, windows broken, pieces of clothing torn	Readily assessed for reliability of measurement
Event/frequency recording	Records the number of times a specific behavior occurs over a specific interval	Punching another person, turning over desks	Appropriate for behaviors that have clearly definable beginnings and endings May be recorded on a checklist, wrist counter, or hand counter, or through transfer of objects (e.g., pennies) from one pocket to another
Duration recording	Records the length of time a behavior occurs	Temper tantrums, high-pitched whining, length of time to complete an assignment	May be recorded with the aid of a wall clock or stopwatch
Interval recording	Records the presence or absence of a given response within a time interval	Thumb-sucking or sideburn pulling	Records behaviors that are not clearly discrete Useful for behaviors that occur at least once every 15 minutes
Whole-interval time-sampling	Records the response when it is emitted throughout the entire interval	On-task behavior	Tends to underestimate the occurrences of the behavior Useful when it is important to know that the behavior is not interrupted
Partial-interval time-sampling	Records the response when a single instance of the response occurs in the interval	Swearing or bizarre gestures	Used to record behaviors that may occur in fleeting moments. Tends to overestimate the occurrence of the behavior
Momentary	Records the response if emitted at the moment the interval terminates	In-seat behavior, frequent stereotypic behaviors	Useful to record behaviors that are apt to persist for a while

Reprinted with adaptations, by permission of Sulzer-Azaroff & Mayer, 1991.

Duration Recording. This method is selected only when it is important to know how long a behavior lasts, and it is used only for behaviors with a clearly observable beginning and ending. Data can then be presented in percentage of observation time during which the behavior occurs. If the behavior lasts more than 5 minutes, this collection technique may be practical.

Interval Recording. This method is used to note the time intervals in which a behavior occurs at least once. The total observation period is divided into equal time segments, and the observer notes whether the behavior is present or absent during each interval. Generally, this method is used to record behaviors that occur frequently.

Time sampling is a variant of interval recording. This method involves dividing the day into equal time segments and randomly collecting data for one or more of the segments. This method can be useful when quantifying behaviors that have a very high frequency or duration, or both, and when continuous data collection by other methods would interfere with classroom functioning. See Figure 3, page 18, "A Guide to Selecting Behavior Recording Techniques."

Analysis: Developing Hypotheses

The BICM and others on the IEP team will generate baseline data across all appropriate settings,[3] interviewing significant others, and conducting an ecological or environmental assessment. Then the BICM and others on the IEP team generate hypotheses about the function of the problem behavior. It will be important to include information on medical factors influencing behavior as hypotheses on functions of behavior are developed. Refer to Chapter 9 for information on how to facilitate gathering this information. Probing to determine which hypotheses should receive the most scrutiny can then occur before the behavioral intervention plan is developed. To understand the functionality of behavior, the team will want to examine daily behavioral logs that objectively measure specific behaviors at different times; use instruments such as a contingency analysis format (Goodwin, 1969), the Motivation Assessment Scale (Durand & Crimmins, 1992)[4] or a scatter-plot analysis (Touchette et al., 1985); possibly look at emergency incident reports; and encourage staff and parents to make suggestions about the possible function the behavior serves.

Consider the following example:[5]

When entering the classroom each day, 9-year-old Mark, a nonverbal individual with autism, walks around the room knocking everyone's things onto the floor.

Hypotheses:

1. Mark enjoys watching/hearing objects fall on the floor and is seeking a sensory experience (play or sensory function).

2. Mark needs more physical exercise and activity and is seeking this experience (sensory or protest function).

3. Mark enjoys the peer/adult attention that results from the behavior and is seeking attention (social communicative function).

4. Mark has no clear understanding of what is supposed to occur when he enters the room (i.e., no sense of the schedule) and is "protesting" this situation (protest function).

5. Mark enjoys play and interaction with a nonhandicapped peer in his classroom and is seeking to initiate interaction (play or social communication function).

6. Mark is protesting an environment or curriculum that does not match his needs (escape or protest function).

If the teacher states, "He just does it to be annoying," hypotheses should be developed about possible maintaining factors, such as negative attention, lack of alternative activities (boredom), and the possibility of an inhospitable environment (possible teacher-pupil rapport problems).

After hypotheses are generated, methods are used to focus on the most likely reason(s) for the behavior. Regarding the example above, one might test the hypotheses by using the following methods:

- Test the "peer/adult attention request hypothesis" by setting up a probe situation where, first, peers are not present in the room and, second, the staff totally ignores the behavior. If this hypothesis is valid, the BICM should note that Mark decreases this behavior or tries other methods of getting the remaining adult's attention.

- Test the "schedule awareness protest hypothesis" by having the staff greet the student at the door with a picture schedule of the day to review together. If this hypothesis is valid, the BICM should note a decrease in this disruptive behavior and Mark's developing interest in reviewing his schedule each morning.

- Test the "seeking interaction hypothesis" by having the staff and peers specifically teach more appropriate methods Mark might use to enlist interaction, reinforcing successful use of the alternative method.[6] If this hypothesis is valid, the BICM should note Mark increasing his appropriate methods of interactions.

Differences Between Intervention Based on Functional Assessment and Commonly Observed Behavioral Interventions

A careful review of behavioral interventions in school settings shows that frequently a behavioral intervention is tried because the person using it has had success with another student or group of students in the past using a particular technique or plan. There is no attempt to determine the behavioral relevance of the intervention to the student receiving the intervention. In fact, frequently rewards are used (e.g., stickers, treats, certificates) without any knowledge about the effect these consequences have on a student's behavior (i.e., does the student find them personally reinforcing?). Instead of attempting to encourage the individual to develop an alternative means of meeting his or her needs, the intervention focuses on eliminating a maladaptive behavior without regard to the purpose it may have served for the student. Often the primary benefit is for the people teaching or supervising the student, with only *secondary* benefits to the student.

Functional assessment, on the other hand, attempts to understand the motivation for the behavior to determine functionally equivalent or related behavior or coping behaviors to take the place of the problem behavior. Suppression or elimination of a behavior without substitution of a socially acceptable behavior is not the primary focus of a behavioral intervention plan generated from a functional assessment. Our primary goal is to educate and teach effective personal skills that may be used in multiple settings rather than just to eliminate a problem behavior.

Part of this education process involves determining the extent to which the student already has positive replacement behaviors that meet the same function as the problem behavior and that will then be used in the behavioral intervention plan. The same functional analysis assessment techniques used for understanding the problem behavior are used to identify the conditions under which these positive replacement behaviors may be occurring and the functions they serve in these situations.

At that point, a functional analysis-driven intervention plan is developed to delineate how the student will be instructed to use the positive replacement behavior, when it will be used, and what reinforcers may be used to strengthen that behavior. The instruction process uses systematic prompting strategies and techniques, such as modeling, shaping, and chaining. (Refer to Chapter 8 for sample useful strategies for students with severe disabilities that are also applicable across populations.) Without preexisting or further training in the instruction process—training that is beyond the scope of this manual—the intervention plans are not likely to be effective. The BICM working in conjunction with special education teachers skilled in the instruction process can be an effective team. Please refer to the Bibliography for texts on instructional methodologies and Appendix D for training programs.

Functional Analysis Example: Protesting Physical Proximity

CHRIS *A 10-year-old child with a mild learning disability served in a Resource Specialist Program (RSP) 10% of his day*

Chris began physically attacking peers in any line-up situation on the playground during the first week after transferring to the school. He dissolved into rages and aggression that resulted in adults and peers getting hit if they got too close. Suspensions for the problem behavior and rewards for alternate positive behavior had been attempted by both the parents and the teacher before the consultation. Chris was in individual and family counseling; he was an adopted boy whose adoptive father and his new wife had just gained custody after a long legal battle from the adoptive mother. The analysis revealed that Chris could tolerate no close physical proximity at this time and viewed even casual "bumping" as premeditated and hostile. Analysis revealed that Chris wanted to be with peers, enjoyed ball games, and was interested in being friends with several of his classmates. His aggressive behavior appeared to be his attempt to express his discomfort with being touched or having close contact with others ("Social Communicative" Protest function," Meyers & Evans model or "Escape function," Durand & Crimmins model). In-class behavior was good, and Chris was very anxious to "be successful" in this new school, he told the counselor.

The successful intervention consisted of continuing therapy, increasing parent/school communication, and implementing a specific behavioral intervention for Chris that temporarily removed him from settings where being touched or having close contact with others was likely. In the morning, he went directly to class to allow extra time to copy assignments from the board. At recesses and lunch, when the bell rang, signaling line-up time, Chris went directly to the office and got his self-charting book. Without adult assistance, he rated his behavior and then returned to class. This was reviewed by the counselor and Chris twice per week. Physical proximity was reintroduced successfully after an 8-week period. At that time, Chris was taught verbal methods of expressing his discomfort with being touched through systematic modeling and role-playing with reinforcement of success provided. His counselor also taught Chris to discriminate touching that was aggressive from accidental touching through similar modeling and reinforcement procedures. In this situation both counseling and a behavioral intervention plan focusing first on removal from the environment, followed by teaching an alternative behavior, were employed to successfully resolve the problem.

1   Evans & Meyer (1985). *Non-Aversive Intervention for Behavior Problems: A Manual for Home and Community.* p. 55. Baltimore, MD: Paul H. Brookes Publishing Co., P.O. Box 10624, Baltimore, MD 21285-0624.

2   The reader is urged to develop a thorough understanding of data collection procedures. This is available in many university courses and texts on behavior analysis. One excellent resource for this purpose is Sulzer-Azaroff & Mayer (1991) *Behavior Analysis for Lasting Change,* Holt, Rinehart & Winston, Inc. New York. Also please refer to Appendix I.

3   Questions often arise regarding whether functional analysis must be done in the home. The regulations state, "To the extent possible, behavioral intervention plans shall be developed and implemented in a consistent manner appropriate to each of the individual's life settings" [§3052(a)(6)]. "The 'behavioral intervention plan'. . . shall describe the frequency of consultation to be provided by the behavioral intervention case manager to the staff members and parents who are responsible for implementing the plan. A copy of the plan shall be provided to the person or agency responsible for implementation in noneducational settings." [§3001(f)]. "The plan shall include the following: . . . those behavioral interventions which will be used in the home, residential facility, work site or other settings . . ." [§3001(f)(7)]. "A functional analysis assessment procedure shall include all of the following: . . . ecological analysis of the settings in which the behavior occurs most frequently" [§3052(b)(1)(D)]. If the IEP team feels data from environments other than the classroom are necessary, the BICM can directly gather that data or appoint or coordinate data collection from other service providers, caretakers, parents, and so forth using agreed-on data collection procedures. Analysis, plan development, and consultation are required to occur under IEP team direction. Collaboration and consensus on "appropriate settings" for data collection or plan implementation appear then to be an IEP team function with the BICM playing an active role.

4   In the Motivation Assessment Scale conceptual model, behaviors are identified as providing "Escape, Sensory, Tangible or Attention" functions for the student. This analysis parallels the Evans & Meyer model and assists in developing hypotheses.

5   This example is an adaptation of one provided in Evans & Meyer (1985) that is a rich source of further information on hypothesis development.

6   Research is showing that the vast majority of interactions for students both with and without disabilities is with their peers in general education environments and integrated settings. Thus, interaction with peers is critical to examine in any analysis of functions of target behaviors in these settings. Initiating, extending, and terminating interactions with peers are important areas to examine in determining communicative intent of a behavior. Please refer to the work of Pam Hunt, Ph.D., cited in references.

Chapter 4

Procedural Overview of Plan Development

C hapter 3 summarized the functional analysis assessment process that forms the foundation of positive behavioral intervention plans. In this chapter, an overview of the complete process, from functional analysis to plan implementation, is presented based on the actual language contained in the Education Code regulations. Both the required components and the possible components of positive programming have been summarized from the regulations. In the following chapters, more in-depth material is presented on how to translate the functional analysis assessment into positive behavior plans. This chapter is intended to provide the reader with the streamlined summary of what is more fully developed later in the manual. It may prove helpful in presenting inservice overviews on the new regulations and in explaining the process to administrators, parents, and other interested parties.

Essentially, after it is determined that a functional analysis assessment should be conducted for an individual with exceptional needs (IWEN), Education Code regulations mandate the following:

- Interviews must be conducted with significant others.
- Information must be gathered from a variety of sources, including, but not limited to, school and medical records and previous intervention plans.
- The student must be observed directly.
- The ecology of the environments where the behavior problems occur must be analyzed.
- Baseline data for both the targeted maladaptive behavior and the positive replacement behavior must be collected.
- The functional assessment phase must provide the foundation of the intervention phase.
- After all the information is gathered, a functional analysis assessment summary must be presented to the IEP team to determine the necessity of a positive behavioral intervention plan. A proposed plan may be presented to the IEP team at that time. It is the IEP team's responsibility to develop the positive behavioral intervention plan if needed.
- The behavior intervention case manager (BICM) is the consultant member of the IEP team who supervises and provides consultation for functional assessment, plan

development, and ongoing monitoring of the plan after it is implemented. The BICM also may participate in the assessment and implementation phases.

- Plans must be modified or redeveloped if they are not proven to be successful through a comparison of current and baseline data.
- The IEP team oversees the entire process, from referral for functional analysis assessment to plan development to plan effectiveness review.

In reviewing the material in this chapter, please note that all language directly taken from the regulations [§3052(b)(1)(A- F)] is in sans serif print. Regular print is used to provide explanatory text or clarification.

Conducting the Functional Analysis Assessment When Instructional/Behavioral Approaches Specified in the IEP Have Not Been Effective

After the IEP team determines that the instructional/behavioral approaches specified in the student's IEP have not been effective, they may consider whether a positive behavioral intervention plan is necessary. A functional analysis assessment must be made if the IEP team is to develop the plan, which is based on the results of that assessment. The functional analysis assessment must be conducted by, or under the supervision of, a person who has documented training in behavior analysis with an emphasis on positive behavioral interventions, i.e., the BICM.

This assessment begins by using three sources of information:

- Direct Observation
- Interviews with Significant Others
- Review of Available Data

Using these three sources, a Functional Analysis Assessment procedure shall include:

A. Systematic observation of the occurrence of the targeted behavior for an accurate definition and description of the frequency, duration, and intensity.

B. Systematic observation of the immediate antecedent events associated with each instance of the display of the targeted inappropriate behavior.

C. Systematic observation and analysis of the consequences following the display of the behavior to determine the function the behavior serves for the individual, i.e., to identify the specific environmental or physiological outcomes produced by the behavior. The communicative intent of the behavior is identified in terms of what the individual is either requesting or protesting through the display of the behavior.

D. Ecological analysis of the settings in which the behavior occurs most frequently.

This includes the following:

- physical setting
- social setting
- activities and nature of instruction
- scheduling
- quality of communication between the individual and staff and other students
- degree of independence
- degree of participation
- amount and quality of social interaction

- degree of choice
- varieties of activities

Earlier this manual stated that the IEP team must design intervention plans for individuals when it has been established that the educational environment either currently meets the individual's need for a meaningful, appropriate, and accessible education experience (see the following guidelines and the Environment Assessment Scale in Appendix J) or can be adapted to meet those needs.

E. **Review of records for health and medical factors which may influence behaviors.** Chapter 5 provides information to assist in understanding these variables. These variables include the following:

- **medication levels** (check for side effects, effect of varying time of administration, dosage variables, and so forth),
- **sleep cycles** (an individual's requirement for sleep, need for periodic nap or rest, impact of family lifestyle, and scheduling are examined),
- **health** (factors are analyzed that may affect behavior, such as seizures, lead poisoning, infections, and so forth), and
- **diet** (diet-related factors are analyzed, such as restrictions, need for periodic snacks, effect of timing of meals on acting out behaviors, and so forth).

By reviewing records and seeking further information from parents and/or medical providers when appropriate, it is possible to determine whether health and medical features are influencing the frequency, intensity, or form of a maladaptive behavior. Making accommodations to health factors or, occasionally, adjusting variables such as sleep quantity or timing of food intake, can reduce the likelihood that a problem behavior will be expressed.

F. **Review of the history of the behavior, to include the effectiveness of previously used behavioral interventions.** Time can be saved during the program planning and needless duplication of ineffectual programs and nonviable hypotheses on functionality can be avoided by reviewing records. Where appropriate, contacting previous service providers to gather information may be helpful to determine what worked, what did not work, what the previous hypothesis was on the functionality of a behavior, what additional positive behaviors have been observed in the repertoire of the individual, what the similarity and differences are between former and current environments, and so forth.

Developing the Positive Behavioral Intervention Plan Based on the Functional Analysis

The regulations state that the eight following items must be included in the intervention plan:

1) *A summary of relevant and determinative information gathered from a functional analysis assessment.* This summary will become part of the IEP and will reflect the outcome of the functional assessment. It will describe what appears to be prompting and reinforcing the problem behavior, as well as a positive replacement behavior. It will also describe what appears to be interfering with, inhibiting, or stopping the goal and problem behavior.

2) *An objective, and measurable description of the targeted maladaptive behavior(s) and replacement positive behavior(s).* The targeted behaviors must be described in observable terms. For example, the word aggressive is open to interpretation, but the phrases, "hitting others hard enough to leave bruises," "biting hard enough to break the skin,"

and "screaming for 15 seconds" are far more descriptive. If Freddy[1] had a hard time making it through the school day without dissolving into rages that included punching other children, and the functional analysis revealed that he engaged in this behavior only to express protests, the following illustrates a written measurable description of both the problem behavior and a positive replacement behavior:

➤ Description of maladaptive behavior:

Freddy responds to frustration by screaming angry statements and hitting others hard enough to cause bruises in all environments (playground, classroom, cafeteria), on an average of two times per day.

➤ Description of positive replacement behavior:

In response to situations he finds frustrating, Freddy will verbally protest with statements such as, "I don't like that" or "I want something different."

3) *The individual's goals and objectives specific to the behavioral intervention plan.* An appropriate goal and objective for Freddy would involve appropriate behavior in each setting. As with all plans, there must be a goal and objective for *both* the problem behavior and the replacement behavior:

➤ Goal: Freddy will not use maladaptive behaviors to meet his needs on the playground.

➤ Objective: Freddy will not engage in verbally threatening behavior or hit another person on the playground during recess. (This example specifies the behavior, tells where it will be measured, and indicates it is to be reduced to the level of zero.)

Similarly the goal and objective for the positive replacement behavior could look like this:

➤ Goal: Freddy will use positive behaviors to meet his needs on the playground.

➤ Objective: Each time Freddy feels frustrated or angry and chooses to protest at recess, he will either tell the student he does not like what is causing him frustration and seek to negotiate a solution, or he will ignore the behavior, or, if the situation is unresolved, he will inform the supervising adult and seek resolution.

(Again, the behavior is specified: The plan tells where it will be measured and indicates that it is to occur every time a situation becomes frustrating to Freddy. It will, of course, be essential to describe frustrating situations and provide ecological analysis as well as teach the positive alternative behavior rather than assume Freddy will be able to do this behavior without training.)

4) *A detailed description of the behavioral interventions to be used and the circumstances for their use.* This description should provide enough detail to clearly convey to the reader: (1) an idea of the different teaching techniques that are to be employed to teach alternative positive behaviors based on the functional analysis assessment, (2) how the environment will be changed to facilitate positive behaviors, and (3) how direct treatment strategies are to be used and what reinforcers are suggested to increase or maintain alternative positive behaviors.

It will be important to specify when the interventions are to be used and in what settings.

➤ Inadequate description: Freddy will be taught appropriate ways to handle frustration. Staff will reinforce Freddy's use of these techniques.

This description is inadequate because it does not specify teaching methods, it provides no suggestion as to what potential reinforcers will be used and the frequency of reinforcement, and it does not specify the circumstances in which intervention is to occur.

➤ Adequate description:[2] Freddy will be instructed in specific procedures to follow when he feels frustrated and has a need to protest actions occurring at recess and during outside activities. These instruction techniques will include modeling and role-playing activities for 2 weeks during his regularly scheduled social skills group, with participation of the recess supervising aide. Freddy will earn additional free time activity tokens during this instruction period.

During and following the instruction phase of the intervention, the aide will prompt and cue Freddy and his peers to use the new behaviors they have learned in specific recess activities. Good behavior tickets will be distributed to students using the alternative instructed language scripts or requesting adult mediation of disputes without resorting to aggression. The recess environment will be changed to include a specific ball checkout procedure and swing set turn-waiting procedure to prevent situations in which frustration is likely to result in aggressive behaviors.

5) This plan component and the following one are presented in the regulations as one item [§3001(f)(5)]. For clarity of discussion, they have been separated into two items here.

a. *Specific schedules for recording frequency of use of the interventions and the frequency of the targeted and replacement behaviors*[3] . . . The written intervention plan must include when and how measurement data will be collected. For example, if part of the intervention for Freddy is to have a supervising adult praise him every time he either ignores frustrations or leaves the situation, tells the student he doesn't like what is going on, or tells the adult when he needs assistance, the supervising adult could self-record his or her praise statements to Freddy during each recess. In addition he or she could count the instances of Freddy's hitting or verbally threatening protest behavior, as well as his replacement behavior during each recess. These data will provide the information necessary for determining if the intervention plan is successful or in need of modification.

➤ Example of a schedule for recording the frequency and use of interventions after the plan is in place: Using event recording, Freddy's instructional aide will collect information on problem behavior on the playground at recess daily for 2 weeks. In addition, the aide will self-record the specific praise statements given when Freddy is frustrated and he responds by either ignoring the student or using other specified coping strategies, telling the adult on duty, or using a learned script, such as, "I don't like that."

b. *. . .including specific criteria for discontinuing the use of the intervention for lack of effectiveness or replacing it with an identified and specific alternative.* As discussed earlier, the frequency data collected will enable those involved to see if change in the right direction is occurring. Some features to consider are the following:

• Is the problem behavior decreasing?

• Is the positive replacement behavior maintaining or increasing?

• Are the instructional techniques used to teach positive behavior effective? Do they need modification?

• Are the reinforcers working to either lower the rates of problem behavior or meet criteria for a gain in positive replacement behavior? Do reinforcers need change or expansion?

• How much time would be appropriate for the intervention to have had an effect? For example, if extensive teaching of new behaviors is a part of the intervention plan, one would expect the problem behavior to remain until the new behaviors are learned (which include coping strategies); therefore, enough time would have to be scheduled before a determination could be made on the effectiveness of the plan.

As part of the initial intervention plan, a statement must be made regarding when the desirable change will be fully present. When that has been determined, other statements must be made regarding how a reexamination of the intervention plan will take place.

➤ **Example of criteria for discontinuing the use of intervention due to lack of effectiveness:** If Freddy's verbally aggressive protests or hitting behavior has not substantially decreased (to not more than one hit per week) after 2 weeks of the implementation phase, further analyses will need to occur. The BICM will consult with the implementer at that time as part of the further analyses. If a minor change is needed, the IEP team does not have to meet. If a major change is to occur, the IEP team will need to convene. A minor change is defined for Freddy's plan as small changes in teaching techniques or reinforcement system.

6) *Criteria by which the procedure will be faded or phased out, or less intense/frequent restrictive behavioral intervention schedules or techniques will be used.* As the maladaptive behavior decreases and the positive replacement behavior maintains or increases, specify criteria for fading prompts and phasing out intrusive reinforcers. This will enhance the probability of maintaining the behavior and the generalization to other situations.

➤ **Example of criteria for phasing out the use of intervention:** The gradual phasing out of the treatment program will begin when Freddy has gone 2 weeks without hitting in response to teasing or name calling. The instructional aide will phase out his or her presence at recess. The aide will begin to phase out by standing farther away from Freddy and by gradually reducing praise statements.

➤ **Example of criteria for discontinuing use of intervention:** The intervention plan for Freddy will be considered to be completed when Freddy has been successful at using the replacement behaviors instead of hitting to manage frustration in all settings for 20 consecutive school days.

7) *Those behavioral interventions which will be used in the home, residential facility, work site or other settings.* If the IEP team feels that data from environments other than the classroom are necessary, the BICM can directly gather that data or appoint or coordinate data collection from other service providers, caretakers, parents, and so forth using agreed-on data collection procedures. Analysis, plan development, and consultation are required to occur under IEP team direction. Collaboration and consensus on appropriate settings for data collection or plan implementation are an IEP team function, with the BICM playing an active role.

In summary, after the functional analysis has taken place for both the problem behavior and the positive replacement behavior, a hypothesis will be made regarding the function of the behavior. It is important to note that the description of what will be done differently in the child's environment is to be as clear as the description of both the problem behavior and the positive replacement behavior. The intervention phase of the plan will incorporate the proactive or positive programming strategies that have been found to promote the positive replacement behavior. These include such things as appropriate curriculum materials; clear sequencing of daily activities and instruction to understand the sequences, including transition times; accommodating to ecological factors, such as sensory overload to noise or touch; and specific teaching techniques to teach important skills necessary for the student to learn positive replacement behavior. The intervention plan also will address appropriate reactive strategies for both the positive replacement behavior and the problem behavior. What reinforcers have been identified? What schedule of reinforcement is the most appropriate? In what settings will the intervention be used? When appropriate, will the intervention be applied consistently in all IEP-determined relevant environments? Who will implement the plan? Does the plan require interagency agreement and coordination? If so, how will this occur? Is the behavior serious enough to require an emergency plan? If yes, what is the point of transfer to emergency procedures? Are the emergency procedures of choice specified in the special education local plan area (SELPA) guidelines?

Essentially, the BICM ensures that every behavior intervention plan has satisfied the who, what, where, when, how, and why elements of the plan design:

- Who will implement and monitor the change?
- What positive programming and reactive strategies are going to be used?
- Where will implementation occur?
- When and how frequently will the components of the plan be implemented?
- How will the plan be implemented? How will the new behaviors be taught?
- Why is the behavior occurring? (This information has already been obtained from the functional assessment.)

8) *Specific dates for periodic review by the IEP team of the efficacy of the program.* When the IEP team convenes to develop the behavioral intervention plan, a schedule for reviewing the effectiveness of the program shall become part of the plan. The frequency of the periodic review is determined by the type of plan and the support needed by on-site staff. For example, if the agreed-on methods are ones the implementer has demonstrated skills in using in the past, the review demands will, of course, be less than if the implementer needs step-by-step assistance.

This periodic review will make use of the ongoing measurement data in determining the appropriateness of the intervention. Obviously, if the data reveal that the problem behavior has not decreased and the positive replacement behavior has not increased, then either further modifications need to be made, or additional functional assessments must take place.

This review process does not have to occur only at a convened IEP meeting, but rather may be through contact by telephone conversations, notes to parents, or other means, as long as the method and time schedule has been agreed on by the IEP team members.

Minor modifications to the intervention plan can be made without parent participation, provided that the parent is informed of the right to dispute the changes. However, if major changes need to be implemented, the IEP team must convene and develop the changes or determine that a new functional analysis is necessary. As a member of the IEP team, the parent has a right to question any modification to the plan at the IEP meeting. As with all parent rights, clearly describing team member roles and legal rights is required.

➤ **Example of periodic review of the program's efficacy:** The BICM will be in telephone contact a minimum of once a week to both Freddy's teacher and his custodial grandparent regarding the success of the program. If minor modifications are going to be made, they will be communicated and agreed to through these conversations.

In addition to requiring that the eight items described above be included in every intervention plan, the regulations also make suggestions regarding what may be included in a behavioral intervention plan, depending on the nature of the student's individual functional level, handicapping condition, and the function of his or her behavior. Positive programming for behavioral intervention may involve the following four techniques:[4]

1. **Altering the identified antecedent event to prevent the occurrence of the behavior**

   Examples include the following:
   - Providing choice
   - Changing the setting
   - Offering variety and a meaningful curriculum
   - Removing environmental pollutants such as excessive noise or crowding
   - Establishing a predictable routine for the individual

   > ### Case examples of altering antecedents:
   >
   > - Karley was no longer required to sit under the school bell in the cafeteria.
   > - David was moved to a setting with more appropriate peer models.
   > - Mike's schedule was made more predictable than it had been before the intervention.

2. **Teaching the individual alternative behaviors that produce the same consequences as the inappropriate behavior**

   Examples include the following:
   - Teaching the individual to make requests or protests using socially acceptable behaviors
   - Teaching the individual to participate with alternative communication modes as a substitute for socially unacceptable attention-getting behaviors
   - Providing the individual with activities that are physically stimulating as alternatives for stereotypic self-stimulatory behaviors

   > ### Case examples of teaching alternative behaviors:
   >
   > - Amy was taught to verbally state her displeasure.
   > - George was taught to use a photo communication system to make his needs known.
   > - Claire was taught to bite on her plastic key container during periods of frustration.

3. **Teaching the individual adaptive behaviors . . . which ameliorate negative conditions that promote the display of inappropriate behaviors**

   Examples include the following:
   - Choice making
   - Self-management
   - Relaxation techniques
   - General skill development

> *Case examples of teaching adaptive behaviors:*
> - Mary learned to chart her task completion behavior herself.
> - Stephanie learned to seek the quiet music corner when feeling restless.
> - Alex chose his learning activity during language arts.

4. Manipulating the consequences for the display of targeted inappropriate behaviors and alternative, acceptable behaviors so that it is the alternative and other acceptable behaviors that more effectively produce desired outcomes

Examples include the following:

- Positively reinforcing alternative and other acceptable behaviors
- Ignoring or redirecting unacceptable behaviors

> *Case examples of consequence manipulation:*
> - When Martha stopped screaming and looked at the refrigerator door, a staff member gave her a sip of juice; when she screamed, no attention was given.

Case Studies: Alex and Randy

Descriptions of Alex and Randy's functional analysis are provided to assist the reader in developing an understanding of how a behavioral plan was developed out of the functional analysis of these two students. The law allows some flexibility for those preparing case studies. All legal mandates must be met, but variability in approach and analysis (as shown in the following case studies) is acceptable. The case studies on Alex and Randy are based on real cases with changes made for clarity and to ensure the anonymity of the parties involved.

Following the case studies, a reinforcer inventory used as part of Randy's functional analysis is provided (Figure 4, pg.44) to illustrate the extent to which investigation can lead to identification of reinforcers not obvious without a thorough assessment.

Following the narrative on Randy, the forms from Appendix C are provided to illustrate how the information on Randy is encoded on the forms. This may help to illustrate the step-by-step development process of a functional analysis and behavioral intervention plan.

Behavior Analysis Case Study Summary: Alex

Following is the case summary of a functional assessment and behavior intervention preliminary plan for an individual with a diagnosis of emotional disturbance (ED). It is the belief of the authors that many different writing styles and formats can convey the analysis and planning necessary to implement the new regulations. This case study is offered to convey one form of the analytical process of functional analysis and plan design rather than provide an invariant model for readers to follow in length, complexity, or style. Each BICM will develop his or her own style of writing and oral presentation method to convey assessment and program planning ideas.[5]

Background

> ### Alex
>
> He is a lean 8-year-old boy who is facing the challenges of emotional disturbances. He is on no medications, and his hearing and vision, according to school records, are within normal range. His cognitive ability and academic skills are average. He has been in five foster placements and two residential programs since his removal from the home 1 1/2 years ago. He is currently placed in a special day class and spends approximately 30% of his school day in a general education second grade program.
>
> He was diagnosed as ED by Ms. Jane Psychologist, Jones City School District psychologist, in a report dated November 20, 1991. In that report, Alex was described as a student in constant need of teacher attention and experiencing difficulty conforming to classroom expectations. He was exhibiting threatening behavior, damaging property, and having violent temper tantrums that resulted in bruises for peers and teachers. This behavior had been occurring for over two years, according to school reports. He frequently teased, bossed, and manipulated others; was inconsiderate; and used angry language. As a result of this assessment, he was placed in a special day class in the Jones City School District in January 1992. He remained in that placement until June 1992.

Alex's current IEP focused on improving his behavior and work habits by encouraging him to:

- use words rather than physical actions for problem-solving with peers,
- remain in his seat when asked,
- raise his hand without calling out,
- follow a direction by the count of five,
- select an option when given two options before the count of five,
- complete a task within a specified amount of time, and
- participate in a small group instruction without interfering with the other students, and
- use a quiet voice.

Functional Analysis of Presenting Problems

Because instructional/behavioral approaches in Alex's IEP were ineffective, a functional analysis was conducted for the following noncompliant behaviors: hitting others, screaming, and running out of the building. This analysis endeavors to identify the events that control the emission and nonemission of these problem behaviors. This evaluation is divided into five specific areas of analysis:

- *Description of the problem:* This analysis attempts to describe the presenting problem in such detail that it can be measured objectively. It presents topography of the behavior (what it looks like), the cycle (beginning and ending) of the behavior (if applicable), and the strength of the behavior (i.e., frequency, rate, duration, intensity).

- *History of the problem:* This analysis presents the recent and long-term history of the problem. The purpose here is to better understand the client's learning history and the historical events that might have contributed to the problem(s).

- *Antecedent analysis:* The antecedent analysis attempts to identify the conditions that control the problem behavior. Some of the specific antecedents explored include the setting, specific persons, times of the day/week/month, and specific events that may occur regularly in the client's everyday life.

- *Consequence analysis:* The consequence analysis attempts to identify the reactions and management styles that might contribute to and/or ameliorate the presenting problems. It also focuses on the effects that the behaviors might have on the immediate social and physical environment, on the possible function(s) served by the problem behaviors, and on the possible events that might serve to maintain or inhibit their occurrence.
- *Analysis of meaning:* The analysis of meaning is the culmination of the above analyses and attempts to identify the functions served by the problem behavior.

Noncompliance/Oppositional Behavior[6]

1. Description of Behavior and Operational Definition

   a. Topography. After a direction is given to Alex or the class, Alex does not begin to follow the direction within 30 seconds following the stating of the direction and remain involved with the task for at least 2 minutes or until the task is complete.

   b. Cycle. A noncompliance event begins 30 seconds following the statement of the direction if Alex does not attempt to follow the direction. Even though Alex may be asked more than one time to follow a direction, this is still considered as one noncompliance event.

   c. Course. When Alex or the class is asked to follow a direction, he may ignore the request or begin to talk to the person making the request about making adjustments to the request or discuss a topic unrelated to the request. He then may ask if he could delay his compliance while he completes another task. He usually waits until he is given a choice of activities. One of these choices is usually considered a negative consequence, such as a visit to the principal.

   d. Strength. With the exception of reading activities, Alex participates in activities that other students are doing between 8% and 10% of the time.

   e. Severity. Alex has exhibited these current types of problems since his enrollment in September 1991.

2. History of the Problem

   Alex has exhibited the specificied noncompliance/oppositional serious behaviors, which often culminate in physical acting out behaviors, since his enrollment in school. According to school records these behavioral issues have been reported consistently from the home setting. Alex has been removed from the home and his current foster placement has been for less than 1 week.

3. Antecedent Analysis

   Alex exhibits noncompliance in both regular and special education settings. He generally is noncompliant when he is asked to leave an activity he finds desirable, when he is worried that the situation may not be in his favor, when he is asked to join a group activity other than reading, or when he thinks that he is in trouble. He is more likely to comply when told to perform a desirable activity, when coaxed by the classroom aide, or after 5 minutes of thinking time. He seems to be more noncompliant after 1:00 p.m. and during transitions from one activity to another. When given imprecise statements, such as, "You need to return to your seat," Alex has more difficulty complying than with precise directions. He seems to respond better to directives such as, "Go to your seat now. I expect you to be in your seat by the count of five, working on page 18 in your math book."

4. Consequence Analysis

Generally, Alex is given time to comply with the direction. Sometimes, the direction is repeated and Alex offers up options or continues to do what he was doing before the request. If Alex does not comply, he then is offered choices of activities. The directives are usually given in a relaxed manner and allow him time to comply. Adults often get engaged in a dialogue with Alex, often negotiating so that Alex changes the intent of the direction. Other students often do not appear to react to these situations unless Alex's behavior escalates to running or assaults. However, on the playground, the students in his general education class do not often volunteer to play with him. On some days, Alex does not comply and runs around, runs out the door, or begins attacking others with his fists if confrontational interactions or physical containment procedures occur with adults.

5. Impressions and Analysis of Meaning

The hypothesized function of the noncompliance appears to be to establish control over the situation. Some of Alex's records suggest that he has been controlled by intimidation by his father in the past, or poorly controlled by his subsequent caretakers.

Alex has been in seven other living situations since his removal from his parents. It is hypothesized that he has a need to control the situations to make sure that adults keep involved with him. If he complies readily, he may fear losing adult attention, which he enjoys.

Alex does not readily engage in social interactions with peers. He is a very talkative boy who wants to have dialogues with adults. Some of his noncompliance may be related to his need for social interaction.

Additionally, Alex does not readily join groups of children unless the activity is highly desirable. When asked to do what others are doing, Alex may be fearful of performing poorly in front of others. Therefore, he avoids the interaction.

Motivational Analysis

The results of a reinforcement analysis (see Figure 4) showed several events that could be used effectively as positive reinforcement in a well-designed behavior support plan to reduce the identified behavior problems. Alex appears to enjoy reading and looking at books, playing games on the computer, playing board games, and playing with building toys. He especially enjoys chess with adults.

Mediator Analysis

A mediator analysis was conducted to identify those people who might be responsible for conducting behavior intervention. This analysis also explored the constraints imposed by the specific settings and existing motivation and interest in implementing behavior intervention procedures as recommended. This analysis showed the following:

- Mrs. Smith, Alex's general education teacher, enjoys Alex in her classroom even though at times she becomes frustrated with his behavior. She has a class of approximately thirty students and will not be able to closely monitor a behavioral program.

- Alex's special education teacher, Mrs. Adams, is a long-term substitute. Alex will start with a new teacher, Mrs. Brown, in 2 weeks. She has observed Alex working in the classroom and is eager to meet the challenges of working with him. Mrs. Jameson, special education classroom aide, appears to have established a good relationship with Alex. She is often the one who coaxes him to work.

- Alex's current foster placement is of unknown duration.

Recommended Intervention Plan

A. Long-Term Goal

The long-range goal for Alex is to establish enough self-control over his problems that he will be increasingly able to participate in the least restrictive setting possible that is capable of meeting his developmental and behavioral needs. Specifically, the goal is to provide him with the skills necessary to meet his needs while eliminating those behaviors that tend to stigmatize and isolate him from his environment. Additionally, the goal is to transfer the control of Alex's behavior from external mediators (staff) to internally generated controls.

Alex should be able to develop the social skills that will assist him in becoming a productive member of a general education program. The focus of this program is to have Alex understand that group membership can be gratifying and can meet his needs much more effectively than drawing negative attention to himself.

B. Short-Term Behavioral Objectives

These objectives were selected as being most reflective of Alex's priority needs and as being the most realistic given his level of functioning at this time. Further objectives may be established as a function of the success or failure of the recommended intervention procedures, such as:

- increasing the time Alex participates in classroom activities from a rate of 8%-10% per day to 50% per day in both regular and special education settings.[8]
- increasing the frequency of compliance/nonoppositional behavior and reducing behaviors that are precursors to behaviors requiring emergency intervention. Baseline rates will be determined following the arrival of Alex's new teacher.
- increasing Alex's use of alternative positive methods to meet his need for attention and to protest tasks he is reluctant to perform.

C. Observation and Data Collection Procedures

Procedures

a. *Duration Recording Strategy for Time Participating in Classroom Activities. At least one time per week, Alex will be observed in special and general education settings. The observer will time how long Alex participates in a classroom activity. Specifically, Alex will be timed while sitting at his desk working on an assignment, working in a small group activity, and listening to a story being read to a class. (These activities will be performed by the behavior interventions assistant.)*

Event Sampling Recording. Every 10 minutes, Alex's activities will be observed for 10 seconds. If he is engaged in an appropriate classroom activity, it will be indicated on the chart as "participating." If he is engaged in an activity that is not part of the classroom routine, then the chart will indicate that he is "not participating." This recording will occur primarily in the special education class.

D. Intervention Procedures

In the following paragraphs, a summary of possible intervention strategies to ameliorate the target behaviors is presented. These are by no means meant to be comprehensive or exclusive of other procedures. They simply represent a set of preliminary idea statements that would be elaborated and modified as the intervention takes place. Intervention is organized around four themes: ecological strategies, positive programming, direct treatment strategies, and reactive strategies.

1. **Ecological Strategies.** Many behavior problems reflect conflicts between the individual needs of a person and the environmental or interpersonal context in which the person must live, work, or behave. As part of the above evaluation, several possible contextual (ecological) conflicts were identified. By altering these contextual conflicts, Alex's behavior may change, thus eliminating the need for consequential strategies. Four "ecological manipulations" are presented with the intention of providing a better mesh between Alex's needs and the environment in which he must behave:

   a. *School Setting. Unfortunately, Alex has had two school changes and five teachers this school year. He is about to have another teacher change. It is recommended that no changes in Alex's teacher or school be instituted for the remainder of the school year.*

   Alex has been showing improvement since his new schedule was established. This should remain the same until the end of the school year.

   Alex most often participates with the group in reading activities. As much as possible, reading lessons should be done in the group format, and Alex should be encouraged to participate in these activities.

   b. *Alex in Leadership Roles. Teaching staff should give Alex opportunities to be a leader when he is involved in group activities. He could tutor other students, listen to students read, or be a group leader in cooperative group activities.*

   c. *Staff Directives to Alex. Directives to Alex should be quite specific. If a teacher wants him in a group, the teacher should tell him specifically to join the group. After giving the directive, the teacher should wait 30 seconds before initiating the reactive strategy if he has not begun to comply.*

   d. *Daily Schedule of Activities. Alex's schedule of activities during the school day should be more precisely defined than the current schedule. The times that he is supposed to be in a general education class should be identified clearly so that everyone knows where he is supposed to be at all times. This schedule should be distributed to Alex, his teachers, the school-based coordinator, and the principal.*

2. **Positive Programming.** Behavior problems frequently occur in settings that lack adequate opportunities for and instruction in adaptive, age-appropriate behavior. It is our assertion that environments that provide programs to promote the development of functional, domestic, vocational, recreational, and general community skills are procedurally important in our efforts to ameliorate problematic behaviors. To the extent that Alex exhibits a rich repertoire of appropriate behaviors that are incompatible with the undesired behavior, the latter should be less likely to occur. Positive programming, therefore, should be effective not only in developing his functional skills, but also in reducing the occurrence of the problematic behaviors. At the very least, a context of positive programming should make it feasible to design effective interventions for

managing his behavior problems. Positive programming strategies are organized around four major thrusts: teaching general constructive skills, functionally equivalent skills, functionally related skills, and coping skills:

a. **General Constructive Skills.** This evaluation indicates that Alex has a wide range of skills deficits. As a result of these deficits, he must rely on those around him to satisfy daily needs. The purpose of teaching these skills is to empower the person with greater independence. By doing this, Alex will have less need to depend on others to meet his needs and will be less likely to come in conflict with an instructional/prompting/monitoring environment that very often can be aversive. It is recommended that the following skill be selected for training:

   (1) *Outdoor Recess Games. To facilitate inclusion more successfully during recess, Alex should be taught the procedures and rules for games played on the playground. Examples include tetherball, handball, and jump rope. Alex also needs to learn how the students enforce the rules of the game and how to enter and exit these games in an appropriate fashion.*

b. **Functionally Equivalent Skills.** People engage in seriously challenging behaviors for perfectly legitimate reasons. They use these behaviors to communicate important messages, to assert themselves, to manage unpleasant emotions, to escape unpleasant events, and to gain access to events and activities. One strategy for helping people overcome their challenging behaviors is to provide them with alternative ways to achieve their objectives, alternative ways to satisfy their needs. These alternatives are defined as functionally equivalent skills because they achieve the same goal as the challenging behavior. One functionally equivalent skill and methods for its teaching are described:

   (1) *Developing Social Participation Skills. Currently, Alex rarely joins a group unless the group is performing a highly desirable activity, such as reading. Alex will be taught to be a member of a group in gradual steps. First, Alex will learn to remain in a group activity for longer and longer times. He will then be taught the interactions to use in a group that will help the students remain interested in having him as a participant. Assistance will be provided to the classroom teacher for curriculum development in this area.*

c. **Functionally Related Skills.** Many other behaviors, if learned by the person, may have a direct impact on the person's behavior. For example, a person who is taught the difference between edible and inedible substances may stop eating inedible substances; a person who is taught to make his own snacks may stop stealing food. The purpose of this category of strategies, again, is to empower the person, to give the person greater skills. For Alex, the following functionally related skill is suggested:

   (1) *Appropriate Expression of Emotions. According to assessment results, Alex often uses his repertoire of oppositional behaviors as a means of expressing anger. Alex may need to learn to discuss what feelings he is experiencing and learn management techniques to handle those feelings appropriately. Assistance will be provided to the classroom teacher for curriculum development in this area.*

d. **Coping Skills.** Many seriously challenging behaviors are a reflection of the person's inability to cope with negative emotions (e.g., anxiety, anger, fear, aversion). In the face of these emotions, people may learn ways to cope that are potentially dangerous or stigmatizing. The following is a coping skill that may benefit Alex:

(1) *Teaching Tolerance to Remain in Group Settings. When Alex is involved in groups, he sometimes wants to move to other individual activities. Alex should be reinforced for remaining in his seat when he is involved with group activities. It should be recognized that Alex has an inclination to leave a situation without permission and that he should be rewarded for staying in an area until the adults direct him otherwise. If he needs to leave, and the teacher has granted permission, he can go to a previously agreed-upon place in the classroom.*

3. Direct Treatment Strategies

a. Target Behaviors. Noncompliance/oppositional behavior

(1) *Procedure 1.*
Differential reinforcement of other behavior-momentary (DRO-M)

Using this strategy, the person is positively reinforced for not using the problem behavior during specified periods of time. Because of the high frequency of the behavior, a fixed interval reinforcement schedule will not be used.

Using a DRO-M strategy, Alex should be observed for a period of 30 seconds at the end of each consecutive 10-minute period. If during this 30-second period a noncompliance event was not observed, then a specified reinforcer should be delivered. If the noncompliance occurred during the interval, the reinforcer should not be delivered.

4. Reactive Strategies.[9] If Alex is noncompliant, staff should anticipate his needs, then offer him choices of activities. For example, if he is not participating in a group or classroom activity, he should be given choices of continuing to participate in the group activity or finding another group activity in which to participate. He should be given a specific time limit (30 seconds) to begin his participation. If he continues to be noncompliant, he should be asked if he wants a time away from the classroom activity or if he wants to choose to participate. If noncompliance continues, then the teacher or principal (teacher's discretion) will confer with Alex. At that time, Alex should be asked why he does not want to participate, be reminded that he is not earning reinforcers for this period of time, and be provided choices for him to remain in school or be sent home. At no time should the staff try to move Alex physically unless an emergency procedure is required to protect Alex, staff, or peers. Should this occur, SELPA emergency procedures should be followed. All occasions requiring this conferencing with the teacher or principal, or occasions that progressed to physical acting out or running, must be logged on SELPA emergency forms.[10]

Behavior Analysis Case Study Summary: Randy

The following description of a functional analysis assessment and behavioral intervention plan describes a program to decrease the intensity and frequency of tantrums in a student with very challenging behavior. The method was successful in training Randy an alternative means for expressing his needs. This case study was chosen to exemplify this strategy and to illustrate the principles and procedures contained in the Hughes Bill and regulations. Although based on a real case, numerous additional fictitious details have been added.[11] To illustrate the use of the sample forms contained in Appendix C, the information gained during functional analysis assessment of Randy's behavior is provided using these forms. Additional narrative description is provided below to illustrate the process of teaching alternative replacement behaviors as part of a positive behavioral intervention plan based on a functional analysis assessment. Each student with challenging behaviors will require a uniquely developed plan with specific teaching strategies and reinforcement procedures. However, by reviewing how one functional analysis assessment resulted in an effective intervention plan, the reader may be able to grasp how this process evolves.

Background

> **Randy** He is a 16-year-old individual with autism, newly enrolled in the district. Randy displays severely delayed language and a need for predictability of routines. Adults and peers note that he enjoys physical contact and social interaction with others. Previous assessments noted that he was independent in many domestic skills, such as dressing, preparing his own snack, and hygiene, but relatively unskilled socially, communicatively, and vocationally. He has few leisure interests and skills but likes puzzles and prefers to be with favorite people everywhere they go. He can be very affectionate with these identified favorites. He uses a few signs and words, vocalized in conjunction with pointing and gesturing. Randy leads others to items of interest but is generally unable to express his choices and needs efficiently and comprehensively. He comprehends most verbal one- or two-step requests given in a familiar context, but when he is excited or angry he seems less able to understand requests.

Summary of Personnel and Process Involved in Functional Analysis and Plan Development

After it was determined that Randy had a serious behavior problem that was interfering with his attainment of IEP goals and objectives and that current approaches were ineffective, his IEP team was expanded to include a BICM. Parental consent was obtained, and the BICM was requested to conduct a functional analysis assessment and to present a report of that assessment for IEP team consideration. Randy's IEP team included his parents, a speech/language specialist, a school psychologist (also serving as BICM), school health personnel, classroom teachers (general and special education), a community training aide, a regional center counselor, and a school site administrator.

The BICM and designated IEP team members obtained information from significant others in Randy's life, from a review of his school records and from direct observation. The BICM prepared a functional analysis report and proposed a positive behavioral intervention plan. These data were presented to the IEP team, and a finalized plan was developed for implementation.

Description of Problem Behavior

Randy's parents and his previous school reported that Randy had frequent episodes of intense tantrums that consisted of prolonged, nonredirectable periods of self-abuse, disruptive behavior, or aggression that often required physical restraint. An increase in medication had not been successful in reducing the behavior. He hit himself with his fist but slapped others with an open hand.

For example, Randy had difficulty waiting in a fast-food line to be served. There was no clear way to communicate to Randy that he needed to wait just a few minutes to order his food and wait for it to be prepared. He wanted his food immediately and would attempt to reach over the fast-food counter to grab food or throw a tray. This often resulted in his being physically removed from the restaurant. Randy then would begin to hit others, grab and throw objects, kick, fall to the floor, hit himself, or rip his clothing.

Baseline Data Information

Baseline data during Randy's first 2 weeks in a new program showed him averaging two to three prolonged incidents (averaging 8 minutes) of disruptive behavior per day in the classroom. These episodes were often accompanied by severe outbursts of hitting others and himself that lasted 5 minutes or more.

A contingency analysis as a modified form of a scatter plot analysis (Touchette, MacDonald & Langer, 1985) and a duration recording system were used to record the number of incidents and the duration of the problem behavior. Analysis of baseline data revealed that the behaviors were used across all environments, people, and activities, but the intensity and frequency of the behaviors varied depending on the degree of Randy's frustration. Team members hypothesized that Randy's problem behaviors were intended to protest change in routine, to reject activities or items offered, and to request social attention or desired items from others. Baseline data-gathering techniques supported the hypothesis that Randy's protest and seeking behaviors were likely to occur in situations where he was unable to get his needs and wants met rapidly. In situations where Randy's schedule was predictable to him, or when activities or items were readily available for him or when he was receiving the desired social attention, appropriate goal-directed behaviors were present.

During baseline data collection, physical restraint and timeout procedures were used to protect Randy and other people in the environment. Emergency physical restraint and timeout procedures appeared to anger Randy in that there was a temporary escalation in the intensity of his physically aggressive and self-abusive behaviors when these procedures were used. (See fast-food example above.)

Goals of the Behavioral Intervention Plan

The primary goal of the intervention was to provide Randy with a more socially appropriate means for lessening his anxiety about change and for expressing his needs. Operationally, this goal meant that he and the primary people in his world would be trained in the use of a shared and mutually acceptable and comprehensible system of communication. Secondarily, we hoped to decrease Randy's dependence on, but not his interest in, one-on-one attention from his favorite people.

Materials

Randy was able to use generic photographs or line drawings to symbolically represent items, people, and activities in his world. However, photographs (Polaroid and 35mm) of the actual people, items, and activities that comprised Randy's days were used so that the message would be unambiguous for Randy and everyone involved in his day.

A communication book was made containing the necessary photos and was updated daily to reflect each day's particular sequence of activity and the items and people that would be available. The variety and number of photos grew as Randy showed us more of his interests and abilities. Photos needed in specific settings, such as leisure, were placed in a clear plastic sheet near him when he was in the setting.

Instructional Procedures

Randy's previous educational program had provided an age-appropriate, community-referenced, functional curriculum, with an emphasis on structured choice making. The IEP team had recently determined that this programming continued to be appropriate. It was hypothesized, based on the analysis of both the problem and the replacement behaviors described above, that Randy would increase appropriate goal-directed behaviors if he were given easy access to a new means for communicating his needs.

The first task was to make Randy aware of the daily routine and the choices available to him during his day. This was done by going over the photos of his day with him as soon as he sat at his desk. Then the entire class rehearsed the day's activities through photos on a portable board. Randy indicated his awareness and understanding of the photos by pointing, categorizing, signing, and occasionally verbalizing. His tolerance for such group activities was increased by his enjoyment of the socializing that was done to help pace the content of the lesson.

Each community outing was also rehearsed as a group lesson about the sequence of the coming events. Choices were given based on student preferences. Money and augmentative communication aids (e.g., photo books of the outing sequence) were distributed. The emphasis was always on the sequence of events and the choices that were available. Randy was trained to use the photos to negotiate for desired items and activities.

The group training lessons were augmented by the use of a portable communication book containing the day's photos. This book always accompanied Randy and was a mutually shared, easily accessed, and readily comprehensible communicative mode for Randy and those communicating with him.

The book was used instructionally to provide Randy with information about transitions and choices during the course of the day. Whenever a transition occurred, Randy was given verbal direction to look at and point to a photo of himself participating in that activity. Then he was given appropriate verbal/gestural input, such as, "Look, Randy, we're going to McDonald's." Randy chose to have the book carried by staff, but it was shared with Randy whenever he chose to use it. He used the photos to make structured choices based on preferences at certain times of the day (community training) but was not required to use the photos to satisfy primary needs, such as water or use of a bathroom. For primary needs, his communication skills were effective (e.g., signs, gestures, words).

Randy and his teachers used the photos as a visible referent whenever possible while communicating. Randy's communicative use of the photos was honored whenever possible. This mutual sharing and honoring of the communicative content of the photos encouraged and fostered the development of two-way communication. Randy was more apt to use the photos when his teacher consistently modeled their use and when use of the photos led to reinforcing consequences (e.g., getting a requested object or initiating or extending peer interaction).

The advantage of two-way communication was most clearly illustrated when Randy refused to change activities or to wait for a desired item. During baseline, this situation usually resulted in the described problem behaviors. However, during the plan implementation phase, during the critical transition points, Randy would take or be given the photo book. If he could not find a photo that expressed his need, he was asked to show staff what he wanted. Once Randy's needs and wishes were clear, negotiations began:

1) Randy was shown a photo of the activity he was requested to do.
2) Randy would use the photos or gesturally demonstrate what he wanted to do or get.

3) If his needs could be honored, they were.

4) If he wished an activity or item that was not scheduled for that time, he was again shown the photo of the activity requested, and staff said, "Look, Randy, first you do this."

5) Then the photo of the activity or item he wanted was shown to him and staff would say, "Then you do/get this."

6) Staff would then rehearse this sequence with Randy to ensure that he comprehended the message by having him point to the photos in sequence while they were verbally labeled and/or pointed to by staff. If allowed time to comply and transition, Randy did not become aggressive. He occasionally fell to the floor but generally followed along after a few seconds.

7) If he consistently refused to participate in a particular activity, the activity or demand was analyzed and modified to fit Randy's tolerance or interests.

Program Expansion and Modification

As Randy's problem behaviors decreased and positive replacement behaviors increased, the program was modified to increase his ability to tolerate delays in getting his needs met. During leisure time, there were photos of Randy's teachers, favored activities, and personal needs in a book on the table that he had access to whenever he chose. Initially, any request for an item or another person's company was granted immediately. As Randy's skill in reciprocal communication with photos increased, it was possible to delay Randy's need for immediate gratification. Delay was built in by encouraging more complex and informative communication from Randy. When Randy initiated a request, staff began asking him what he wanted and encouraged him to sign or point to another photo to complete and/or expand on his request. Randy and his teachers and peers used the photo book to initiate and sustain "conversations" about activities and items of interest to Randy after training.

During the program effectiveness review, the BICM, plan implementers, parents, and administrators (Randy's IEP team) determined that the next step in modifying Randy's positive behavioral intervention plan would be to increase independence and generalization to other environments beyond the classroom and community job site. Concurrently, Randy would continue working on his spontaneous appropriate communication because he still requires considerable structure before using his communication photo system. Randy's family has decided to use the same system in the home and community, developing additional photos as necessary. The family will gather data to present at the next IEP meeting using the same charting system used by the school staff. During this expanded implementation phase, the family and BICM have decided that a telephone consultation once per week is appropriate.

Outcome/Results

Training with the photo cards began immediately following the plan development, but it took approximately one month before it was possible to develop all the photos needed to sequence his day.

During the 4 1/2 month period since the plan was developed, the frequency of tantrums decreased from one to two times daily to approximately one per week. During the last three months of this period, the length of his disruptive behaviors averaged 1-2 minutes and only rarely involved hitting himself or others.

By the end of Randy's 4 1/2 months, he could participate in a leisure activity for 5-30 minutes without one-on-one attention. Randy still fell back on his physical "language" when he was in an unfamiliar environment without established routines, when his needs could not be met, or when there was a sudden change in a routine. However, the intensity and frequency of the disruptive behaviors was much reduced when he had readily comprehensible and accessible communicative options and a receptive "listening" audience.

The IEP team determined that the next step in modifying his positive behavioral intervention plan would be to increase independence and generalization. Therefore, the IEP team determined that Randy will participate in the high school swimming class with the goal of a gradual phasing out of assistance from a special education aide. The long-term goal for Randy is that he will use this communication system in all living and working environments. Increased independence and access to activities of choice is the ultimate goal for Randy.

FIGURE 4.

REINFORCEMENT INVENTORY

NAME: ALEX

NOTE: Portions of this instrument are included to assist the reader in understanding the breadth of a necessary reinforcement survey. The charts reprinted below are not the full instrument. "Don't know" coded below represents Alex's answers combined with staff's lack of observing the potential reinforcer's effect on behavior.

REINFORCEMENT INVENTORY

Description of Potentially Reinforcing Events	Not at All	A Little	A Fair Amount	Much	Very Much
A. FOOD ITEMS					
1. Candy — What Kind?					
a. *chocolate*		✓			
b.					
2. Ice Cream — What Kind?	✓				
a.					
b.					
3. Nuts		✓			
4. Potato Chips		✓			
5. Cake		✓			
6. Cookies		✓			
7. Beverages — What Kind?					
a. *Coke*		✓			
b.					
8. Other Foods		✓			
a. *popcorn*				✓	
b. *apples*		✓			
c. *slurpees*		✓			
B. TOYS AND PLAYTHINGS					
1. Racing Cars	✓				
2. Electric Trains	✓				
3. Bicycle	*don't know*				
4. Skate Board	*don't know*				
5. Playing with Dolls	✓				
6. Make-up and Dress-up Toys	✓				
7. Erector Set	✓				
8. Other Toys	*don't know*				
C. ENTERTAINMENT					
1. Watching Television — Favorite Programs				✓	
a. *90210*			✓		
b. *I Love Lucy*			✓		
2. Movies				✓	
3. Listening to Music — Favorite Musician	*don't know*				
D. SPORTS AND GAMES					
1. Playing Football with Kids	✓				
2. Playing Football with Parents	N/A				
3. Swimming	*don't know*				
4. Bike Riding	*don't know*				
5. Skating	*don't know*				
6. Skiing	*don't know*				
7. Horseback Riding	*don't know*				
8. Tennis	*don't know*				
9. Hiking	*don't know*				
10. Checkers		✓			
11. Chess					✓
12. Fishing	*don't know*				

D. continued on next page

Figure 4. continued

Description of Potentially Reinforcing Events	Not at All	A Little	A Fair Amount	Much	Very Much
13. Baseball	don't know				
14. Ping Pong	don't know				
15. Scrabble	don't know				
16. Monopoly			✓		
17. Painting by the Numbers	don't know				
18. Computer Games					✓
19. Video Games				✓	
20. Clue	don't know				
21. Competitive Games	✓				
22. Other? a.					
b.					
E. MUSIC/ARTS/CRAFTS					
1. Playing a Musical Instrument (Type ?)					
2. Singing			✓		
3. Dancing			✓		
4. Drawing	✓				
5. Building Models	✓				
6. Working with Tools	✓				
7. Working with Clay	✓				
8. Musical Group			✓		
9. Other? a.					
b.					
F. EXCURSIONS/COMMUNITY					
1. Ride in Car	don't know				
2. Going to Work with Mother/Father	✓				
3. Visiting Grandparents or Relatives	don't know				
4. Visit to Beach	don't know				
5. Picnic		✓			
6. Vacation (Where ?)	don't know				
7. Airplane Ride	don't know				
8. Going Out to Dinner			✓		
9. Visit a Friend (Who ?)	✓				
10. Visit a City (Where ?)	✓				
11. Visit a Museum	✓				
12. Going to Store (Name: Blockbuster ?)				✓	
13. Going for Walk		✓			
14. Going to Library	✓				
15. Visit Amusement Park				✓	
16. Other? a.					
b.					
G. SOCIAL/INTERACTION					
1. Playing with Others (Whom?)					Adults ✓
2. Being Praised (by Whom?)					
a. father	✓ N/A				
b. mother	✓ N/A				
c. teacher		✓			
d. friends	✓				
3. Being Hugged and Kissed	✓				
4. Being Touched	✓				
5. Group Activities (Girl/Boy Scouts, clubs)	✓				
6. Going to Friend's House (Whom ?)	✓				
7. Having Friends Sleep Over	✓				
8. Sleeping at Friend's House (Whose ?)	✓				
9. Talking with Others					Adults ✓

G. continued on next page

Figure 4. continued

Description of Potentially Reinforcing Events	Not at All	A Little	A Fair Amount	Much	Very Much
10. Kidding and Joking					Adults ✓
11. Party for Friends	✓				
12. Taking Friend Out	✓				
13. Happy Faces, Smiles				Adults ✓	
14. Other?					
H. ACADEMIC/CLASSROOM					
1. Learning a New Language	don't know				
2. Taking Piano Lessons	don't know				
3. Reading			✓		
4. Being Read to					✓
5. Looking at Books				✓	
6. Spelling	✓				
7. Science		✓			
8. Social Studies	✓				
9. Physical Education	✓				
10. Math	✓				
11. Going to School		✓			
12. Riding Bus to School		✓			
13. Doing Homework	✓				
14. Helping Teacher			✓		
15. Helping Others	✓				
16. Cafeteria Helper	✓				
17. Room Proctor/Leader	✓				
18. Line Monitor	✓				
19. Extra Recess, Free Time				✓	
20. Leave Class or School Early	don't know				
21. Visit Activity Center or Corner	don't know				
22. Listen to Records		✓			
23. Read Book of Choice					✓
24. Write Notes	✓				
25. Hall Monitor	✓				
26. Individual Conference or Counseling				✓	
27. Get a Drink		✓			
28. Tutor Another Student	✓				
29. Arrange Bulletin Board	don't know				
30. Other?					
K. OTHER EVENTS AND ACTIVITIES					
1. Staying Up Past Bedtime	don't know				
2. Earning Money	don't know				
3. Having Free Time					✓
4. Having a Pet	don't know				
5. Having or Going to a Party	✓				
6. Taking a Bath or Shower	don't know				
7. Sleeping with Parents	don't know				
8. Feeding the Pet	don't know				
9. Listening to Stories					✓
10. Friends Over to Eat	don't know				
11. Talking into a Tape Recorder	don't know				
12. Decorating Own Room	don't know				
13. Extended Bedtime	don't know				
14. Plan the Day's Activities				✓	
15. Public Display of Work or Progress	don't know				

(Note: Entire Reinforcement Inventory for Children and Adults appears in Appendix N.)

©INSTITUTE FOR APPLIED BEHAVIORAL ANALYSIS, Thomas J. Willis, Ph.D., and Gary W. LaVigna, Ph.D.

Determination Of Need For Functional Analysis or Positive Behavioral Intervention Plan

Student Randy   Date(s)   2/19/93

Administrator/Designee/BICM   BICM

Information Sources Teacher and parent conference. Direct observation.

Behavior (operationalized) Prolonged (more than 5 minutes) of self-injurious (hitting self with fist & aggressively slapping others) behaviors.

"Serious Behavior Problem" as defined in the Education Code?

[ ] No   [ ] Serious Property Damage   [X] Self-Injurious

[X] Serious Assaultive   [ ] Other Pervasive Maladaptive Behavior

Resulted in Emergency Intervention: [X] Yes, date of report 2/19/93

[ ] No

Is the behavior interfering with achievement of IEP Goals?   Yes [X]   No [ ]

Rationale: Randy does not work for longer than 2 minutes on assigned tasks nor does he communicate needs and wants effectively. He hits self and others when asked to change activities or when his needs cannot be immediately met.

Does the IEP team find that instructional behavioral approaches specified in the student's IEP have been ineffective?

[X] Yes   [ ] No

Rationale: Randy has not responded to the staff's attempts to teach him to wait nor to reinforcement for task completion specified in his IEP.

Setting(s) and time(s) when behavior occurs/occurred: School & job site; various times throughout the day, no pattern except slightly more often during transitions.

Extent to which behavior is on-going: Throughout the day - on-going over the last 3 weeks

Consequences which have occurred as a result of this behavior: Timeout, redirection, peers avoid contact, physical contact, physical restraint,

Extent to which instructional/behavioral approaches have been effective: Nothing has worked yet.

Does this behavior require a functional analysis to determine the need for a systematic, positive behavior intervention plan?

Rationale

Yes/No		Yes/No	
	Student performing the behavior is not an identified individual with exceptional needs (IWEN)		Behavior is performed by a student identified as an "individual with exceptional needs" (IWEN)
	Behavior is not a serious behavior problem as defined in the Education Code		Behavior is a serious behavior problem as defined in the Education Code, or, ineffective instructional/ behavioral approaches are being used
	Although a serious problem, the IEP team feels the selected consequences or changes are likely to solve the problem and the behavior is not expected to recur		IEP team believes behavior now requires a functional analysis assessment
	Existing instructional/behavioral approaches are determined to be effective by IEP team		IEP team believes behavior may now require a positive behavioral intervention plan
	The serious behavior is not interfering with achievement of IEP goals. Family referred to: _____		IEP team believes behavior is interfering with achievement of IEP goals

WORKSHEET 2

Interview With Significant Others

Student Randy   **Interview Date(s)** 2/23/93, 2/25/93

Interviewer Mr. BICM   **Title** School Psychologist

Interviewee Mr. Brown   **Relationship To Student** SDC Teacher

What is the problem behavior in operationalized terms?

Prolonged (more than 5 minutes) episodes of self-abuse (hitting his face with his fist) and aggression (slapping others)

Is this behavior a "serious behavior problem" as defined by Title 5, California Code of Regulations?

[X] YES   [ ] NO

Interviewee Analysis of Antecedents & Consequences - Problem Behaviors

Antecedents (immediately prior to the behavior)	Problem Behavior	Consequences
• Changes in routine or transitions to new activity • Required participation in undesired activity (especially at job site) • Delay in receiving food or desired puzzle • Lack of social interactions • Adult not available to moderate the environment	See Operationalized Definition Above	• Rapid presentation of desired object by staff • Peers run away • Adult attempts to verbally redirect Randy • Adult physical interactions • Timeout in designated areas • Physical restraint

continued on next page

Potential Positive Replacement Behavior(s)

Star ✳ any that are incompatible with the problem behavior, which student already demonstrates.   ✔

☑ ✳ 1. Independent in activity of choice (puzzle play) up to 15 minutes

☑ ☐ 2. Follows people around, enjoys being with them

☑ ✳ 3. Follows predictable routines

☑ ✳ 4. Negotiates on selection of activities and timing of delivery

☐ ☐ 5.

Antecedents Currently Present (Antecedent conditions to the positive replacement behavior when the problem behavior is **NOT** occurring)	Incompatible Or Positive Replacement Behavior Selected From Above	Consequences Currently In Effect (Reinforcers, contingent access to a desired activity, opportunity for attention, etc. that occur after the positive replacement behavior)
No change in routine or careful preparation for transitions or transitioning into favorite activity	Number from above ____3____	Randy performs the requested activity and receives adult praise and occasionally a tangible reinforcer (raisins, contingent access to puzzles, contingent participation in school site recycling

Tentative Hypotheses of Function of Problem Behavior (to be validated or rejected during direct observation).

Randy's seeking of desired items or social interactions is frustrated by his lack of effective communication and choice-making systems. Randy is protesting not receiving his choice immediately.

Direct Observation

Student: Randy   **Observation Date**(s): 2/19/93

Observer: Mr. BICM and Mr. Chavez   Title: BICM and Special Education Aide

Observation Setting(s): Classroom

Problem Behavior (operationalized terms): Prolonged tantrums (more than 5 minutes) including self-abuse (hitting self with fist) and aggression (slapping others)

Positive Replacement Behavior (operationalized terms): Using photo communication book to request desired objects or understand and cope with changes in routine

Observer's Analysis of Antecedents & Consequences

Antecedents	Operationalized Problem Behaviors	Consequences
Multiple Antecedents: • Change in routine • Delay in teacher attention, especially during wait for bus • Teacher not able to understand "request" for item	See above	Multiple: • Timeout (note: teacher feels this increases rate of problem behavior) • Verbal requests to stop/attention • Physical restraint to prevent hitting • Physical restraint to prevent self-hitting (teacher feels increases rate of problem behavior)
Antecedents (currently present)	**Operationalized Positive Replacement Behaviors**	**Consequences** (currently in effect)
Randy wants an item Randy is required to transition	See above Note: Not observed yet	Currently not expressing, behavior, not yet present

Tentative Hypotheses of Functions of Problem Behavior: Seeking of desired items or social interactions is frustrated by lack of effective communication and choice-making systems. Randy is protesting not receiving his choice immediately.

WORKSHEET 3-CONTINUED

Observation For Potential Reinforcers

What activity does the student frequently select when given a choice?

Being with favored people, lining up toy cars, roughhouse play, puzzles.

What objects or edibles does the student select frequently when given a choice?

Raisins, puzzle pieces, hard candies, geranium leaves, linoleum tile pieces.

What consequences have worked to motivate or increase other positive behaviors?

Adult "attention" (allowing Randy to follow favored adults, especially during the recycling program).

What activities or tangibles have been (or may be) used effectively in an "if-then" contingent reinforcement system for the presence of a positive behavior?

So far only raisins for completing a task, satiates easily, social reinforcers work better.

What activities or tangibles have been (or may be) used effectively in an "if-then" contingent reinforcement system for the absence of a problem behavior (DRO)?

Access to recycling program around campus for no tantruming - could occur 2 times daily.

Data Collection

Student: Randy   **Date:** 2/22/93

Behavior intervention case manager: Ms. BICM

Problem Behavior (operationalized terms): Prolonged (more than 5 minutes) episodes of self-abuse (hitting his face with his fist) and aggression (slapping others).

Hypothesized Function Of Problem Behavior To Be Validated: Randy uses the problem behaviors to express frustration (protest).

Positive Replacement Behavior (operationalized terms): Randy will use his photo communication book to request desired items or understand and cope with transitions (coping).

Projected length of Baseline Data Collection: _____

Will the baseline data gathering affect student's behavior?   Yes ☐   No ☒

If yes, describe accommodations: _____

Proposed Data Collection

Baseline B Post Intervention P	Problem Behavior - Positive Behavior +	Dates(s)	Time(s)	Personnel	Setting(s)	Method(s) Positive Behavior	Method(s) Problem Behavior
B	±	Week 1	9 am to 10 am	Classroom assistant	classroom/recess	Event Freq.	Duration
B	±	Week 1	12 pm to 1:30 pm	Teacher	classroom/lunch	Event Freq.	Duration
B	±	Week 1	2 pm to 3:30 pm	Job Coach	skill center	Event Freq.	Duration
B	±	Week 1	6 pm to 7: 30 pm	Parents	home	Event Freq.	Duration
P	+	Week 2	9 am to 10 am	Classroom assistant	classroom/recess	Event Freq.	– –
P	±	Week 2	12 pm to 1:30	Teacher	classroom/lunch	Event Freq.	Duration
P	±	Week 2	2 pm to 3: 30 pm	Job Coach	home	Event Freq.	Duration
P	+	Week 2	6 pm to 7:30 pm	Parents	same as above	Event Freq.	– –
P	-	Week 3	M W F same times	same as above	same	– –	Duration
P	+	Week 4	M W F same		same	Event Freq.	– –

Note: Attach developed sample data gathering sheet to complete this worksheet.

Review Of Records For Behavioral History

Student: Randy   **Review Date:** 2-28-93

I.   Specify Records Reviewed: Cum file, Special Education and School Nurse File

II.   Individuals Contacted From Previous Settings: Regional Center counselor, former teacher

III.   History of The Problem Behavior: Tantrums of this nature have been present since Randy entered school, with steadily increasing intensity in the past 2 years

IV.   Previous Interventions For Problem Behavior: (Note successful / (unsuccessful))

Edible reinforcers and medication alterations have been ineffective. Timeout and physical restraint prevent harm but have not prevented problem behavior from occurring.

V.   Critical Factors To Include or Avoid In Planning For Current Setting:

Include ways of addressing behavior in the community as job training and community activities are included on IEP. Timeout techniques have not eliminated behavior or helped Randy learn new behaviors.

VI.   Tentative Hypotheses of Functions of Problem Behavior:

Obtaining desired items or social interactions is frustrated by lack of an effective communication system and choice-making ability.

Ecological Analysis Of Settings
Where Behavior Occurs Most Frequently

Student: Randy   **Date:** 2/15/93

Physical Setting: (e.g., noise, crowding, temperature)

Lunchroom very noisy, classroom spacious with clear leisure and task completion activity areas demonstrated

Social Setting: (interaction patterns, with and around student)

Randy likes all his classmates, pats them in greeting, especially enjoys Martha and Sally from ROP program. Dislikes Roger. Especially fond of his job coach. Randy seeks teacher attention, hugs in greetings. Environment supports social interactions among all students and staff.

Activities: (activities/curriculum match learner needs?)

Randy is a willing participant for purposeful activities, enjoys activities at adjacent Boys & Girls Club after school, curriculum matches IEP goals and objectives, Randy may benefit from more activities with peers on campus.

Nature of Instruction: (instructional methods and techniques match learner needs?)

No present use of visuals for communication - physical guidance for instructional purpose is well used, modeling and cueing used appropriately. Randy may be ready for a picture exchange system.

Scheduling Factors: (timing, sequencing and transition issues)

Schedule is predictably used and well organized. Vocal warnings on transitions are appropriate. No schedule instruction is present currently. Randy may be ready for systematic schedule instruction.

Degree of Independence: (reinforcement intervals appropriate to foster appropriate independence)

Randy prefers one-on-one assistance, turns to an adult at each step in a sequence. Independence skills need enhancement.

Degree of Participation: (group size, location, and participation parameters)

Randy prefers one-on-one, likes opening group where he participates, hums the anthem. No experience with nondisabled peers on campus other than recycling program. Site and IEP team state they are interested in expanding Randy's interaction opportunities when slapping behavior is eliminated.

Social Interaction: (social communication needs match instruction and opportunities)

Randy does not "converse" with others. He needs training and opportunities.
He likes "UNO" card game, currently his only opportunity for interacting with a nondisabled student working in his classroom.

Degree of Choice: (amount of choice making and negotiation present in environment)

Randy has little opportunity to choose activities. Contingencies are reduced when Randy is out of control. Randy needs further choice-making opportunities.

Review Of Data On Internal States Which Potentially Influence Behavior

Student: Randy   **Date:** 2/24/93

Behavior Intervention Case Manager: Ms. BICM

Interviewees: Parents, teachers, Randy's doctor

Staff Member Completing This Section: Ms. Couch, School Nurse

I.   Identified Handicapping Condition

Educational handicapping condition(s): Autism

   Does this condition have known behavior features?   Yes [X]   No [ ]

   If yes, describe those the student exhibits: Self-injurious, assaultive, perseverative,

   limited repertoire of social interests, severely delayed language.

II. Identified Health/Biological Conditions

Medical Diagnosis: Autism

Does Diagnosis Have Known Behavioral Features: [X] Yes   [ ] No

If Yes, Describe Those The Student Exhibits: see above.

Review of Vision and Hearing

	Date of Last Exam and Source	Nature of Any Problems	List Any Accommodations Required
Vision	1/9/91 School Screening	None	None
Hearing	10/9/90 School Screening	None	None

continued next page

III. Current Medication Summary

Medication(s) and Dosage(s)	Anticipated Benefit	Possible Behavioral Side-Effects	Source of Information: Parent, Doctor, Physicians Desk Reference, Etc.
Propranolol	Decreased aggression	Drowsiness	Dr. Smith, Randy's Physician Phone Conversation 2/18/93

Note Recent Change(s) In Medication: None.

Potential Effect On Problem Behavior:

Behavior Pattern As Related To Medication: Family reports Propranolol appears to have mild positive effect in reducing aggression.

Variation(s) In Behavior As A Result Of Medication Ingestion Time(s): None noted.

IV. Sleep Cycles And Diet

Current Sleep Pattern: Sleeps from 9pm to 6am.

Potential Impact on Behavior: none hypothesized.

Note Recent Change(s) And Potential Impact On Behavior: Sleeps better since Propranolol therapy began.

Note Any Special Dietary Requirements, Restrictions or Food Allergies: None - Randy will not eat any green foods however.

Potential Impact on Behavior: If presented with green food, behavior protests likely to occur.

continued next page

V. Unusual Responses Or Sensitivity To Environmental Stimuli

Stimuli	Unusual Response	Potential Impact on Behaviors
Tactile	Randy likes chewing on edibles and nonedibles	Seeks chewing, doesn't like interrupting, gets angry if small inedibles are removed from his mouth
Auditory	Randy covers his ears and grimaces to loud noises	Difficulty transitioning from classroom to lunchroom (sits under bell in lunchroom)
Visual	Not observed	
Movement	Randy paces rapidly when anxious	May need more movement in the day
Vibration	None	
Smell and Taste	Grimaces at smell of catsup, broccoli, will not eat green food.	May find lunchroom overstimulating, protests green food if asked to eat it.

VI. Periodic Precipitating Factors

Note periodically occurring events that have led to an increase in problem behavior:

1)   If Randy does not get to have his regular bus seat behind the driver or if the driver is absent he arrives in a bad mood.

2)   If Randy has put away his things for a new activity and an unavoidable change occurs he is likely to be upset.

3)   If he is seated next to Roger he escalates more rapidly.

Functional Analysis Assessment Report Summary

(attach Forms 1-2-3 to complete the report)

Student: Randy   **Birthdate:** 1/06/77

Handicapping Condition(s): Autism

Behavior Intervention Case Manager: Ms. BICM

Serious Behavior Problem:

Randy has prolonged episodes of hitting his face with his fist or slapping others lasting more than 5 minutes.

Severity (from baseline data) Baseline average of 1.5 episodes daily for 2 weeks averaging 8 minutes in duration. Slaps leave red marks, punches are delivered with force.

Identified Positive Replacement Behavior(s):

Randy will use a photo communication book to request desired objects or as a coping strategy to understand his daily sequence of activities.

Current Prevalence (from baseline data) zero - Randy will point to pictures on request but no functional use has been made of this skill yet.

Summary Of Relevant Information From Functional Assessment

What Environmental Features Require Alteration? Provide edible munchies, strive to eliminate loose tile he eats. Move eating location in lunchroom away from bell, incorporate more physical movement. Provide more social interaction opportunities and materials (e.g. UNO) at the leisure table when nondisabled peers are present. Move Randy's seat away from Roger, assign Randy a permanent bus seat.

What appears to be prompting and reinforcing the problem behavior based on analysis of antecedents and consequences?
Randy has little opportunity to make choices, has few skills in conversing with others and reduced opportunities to do so. Randy has no other protest behaviors or legitimate methods to protest.

REPORT FORM-4

What Inhibits the Problem Behavior Based on Analysis of Antecedents and Consequences?

So far nothing has affected the rate of his acting out behaviors. Reaction
strategies aren't teaching him alternatives.

Hypothesized Function(s) of the Problem Behavior

Protesting lack of choice and time delays.

What Appears to be Prompting and Reinforcing the Positive Replacement Behavior Based on Analysis of Antecedents and Consequences?

Randy can only tolerate waiting for short periods of time. Therfore short delays result
in more adaptive behavior.

What Inhibits the Expression of the Positive Replacement Behavior?

Randy has never received direct instruction in using photo communication, never
received reinforcers for waiting appropriately. No photos have been developed.

Summary of Baseline Data[8]
(Attach supportive data such as graphs, charts, logs, or summarize on page 3 of this form)

Baseline of Maladaptive Behavior
18.5 episodes of hitting self or others averaging 8 minutes duration for one week.

Baseline of Positive Replacement Behavior
0 episodes of photo communication book usage.

1 episode of pointing to picture to request snack choice.

REPORT FORM 5
Proposed Positive Behavioral Intervention Plan

(attach Forms 1-4 to complete this form)

Student: Randy   Date: 2/04/93

Behavior Intervention Case Manager: Ms. BICM

I.   All Environments Where Interventions Will Be Used: Classroom, lunch area, job site, community

      outings, on-campus recycling in various classrooms

II.   All Supervising Personnel/Implementer(s) for Above: Teacher, special education aides, job site

      coach. Parent to use if successful in school-based program in 3 weeks.

III. Precise Criteria for Discontinuing Plan, Reconvening of IEP Meeting for Major Revisions: _____

      If Randy hits himself or others more than 3 times per day, more than 3 times per

      week, for 2 weeks, the parent and BICM will be notified to determine need for IEP.

IV.   Possible Minor Revisions not Requiring IEP Meeting: If Randy needs further instruction,

      increase in reinforcement scheduling or reinforcers used.

V.   Schedules for Recording Frequency and Use of Interventions (who, how often, what method)

      • Problem Behavior Data Collection: BICM or designee daily for 2 weeks, then

      3 times per week.

      • Positive Replacement Behavior Data Collection: 3 times aide week for 2 weeks, then

      2 times per week.

VI.   Periodic Review Frequency and Method: Daily home journal to contain brief anecdotal

      information. On Friday when parent is normally on campus, brief conference with

      teacher and/or others.

VII. Ecological Changes Necessary Prior to or During Plan: _____

      Randy's environment is appropriate. Interactions between peers and Randy need to

      increase. Randy will participate in peer leisure activities with specific

      instruction provided to peers on initiating interactions 3 times per week with data

      keeping on number of interactions Randy is engaged in (event recording). Randy

      will not sit next to Roger in class or sit under the bell in the lunchroom.

continued next page

VIII. Direct Treatment Strategies for Positive Replacement Behavior: Randy will receive a "high 5" or verbal

praise or hug for each communication he begins or responds to using his book. For each morning and

afternoon with no self-injury or assault, Randy will earn additional time after the buzzer signal-

ing end of free time (11:00-11:20, 1:45-2:05) with peers in leisure UNO games (which he enjoys).

IX. Reinforcement System for Presence of Positive Behavior, or Absence or Reduced Rates of Problem Behavior:

High 5, verbal praise for each use of communication book (No others at this time - natural

reinforcer of making needs known, engaging others in dialogue expected to maintain behavior).

X. Positive Programming/Teaching Techniques and Strategies
(Describe coping/tolerance instruction, teaching of positive behaviors, etc.)
Randy will receive Independence Training to do more classroom activities following a picture

schedule without need for adult (e.g., preparing snack, loading computer, preparing for recycling

program). Randy will receive specific training 5 days per week (as will peers) on using his

communication book following techniques and strategies discussed in "Conversation Handbook" by

Dr. Pam Hunt. This alternative functional skill will be utilized in 100% of Randy's school and job

site settings and recorded on the behavior tracking log (recording: Duration of instruction daily,

number of spontaneous book use Randy initiates).

XI. Reactive Strategies for Problem Behaviors: (Not to include Emergency Procedures)
Describe when/what additional redirecting strategies are to be utilized.
Removal for short walk if Randy shows increased anxiety (shown by pacing or yelling). Calm, very

slow, low-tone voice used to say "Randy, our job is to . . . now" at start of problem behavior.

Expect 10-second response time due to slow processing skills.

Describe what specific behavior will constitute a need for an emergency procedure (log all emergencies on
other SELPA forms):
Hitting self and failing to respond to verbal redirection within 15 seconds, hitting others and

failing to respond to verbal de-escalation techniques within 10 seconds. Prompts should begin with

physically turning pages and guiding Randy to select pictures. Eventually touching of book by adult

or peer to initiate conversation would be a less intrusive prompt. Randy will be selecting the

pictures himself from a shoebox organized to facilitate finding necessary pictures for his schedule

by the end of this plan.

continued next page

XII. Describe modifications to plan if periodic precipitating factors (Form 3) are present (if any)

1) Bus driver to assign seat to Randy – no problem anticipated now.

2) If change is unexpected, aide or peer tutor will help Randy find the correct picture, insert it in sequence and rehearse PAST - CURRENT - NEXT ACTIVITY with pictures as referents.

3) Roger not to sit next to Randy - no problem anticipated now.

XIII. Criteria for Success Achieved: No self hitting or hitting others for 3 weeks, also 10 or more times Randy initiates photo communication per day as recorded in on-going logs.

XIV. Criteria for Phasing Out of Intrusive Reinforcers and/or Prompts: Randy to continue receiving praise, pats on back and "high 5s" for one month on each occurrence of photo communication. Anticipated reduction to 75% over next month, then reduce to 50%. Further meetings will delineate phase out more fully.

1   For the purpose of explanation, this chapter contains references to one particular student, Freddy. These statements are *not* relevant to other students, and statements regarding frequency of contact, procedures, and so forth, are relevant *only* to Freddy's particular case.

2   For the purpose of this section, a very brief description is provided. For very serious behavior problems, a much more specific and detailed account may need to be provided and more stages delineated.

3   This plan component and the following one are presented in the regulations as one item [§3001(f)(5)]. For clarity of discussion, they have been separated into two items here.

4   The examples provided are by no means complete but illustrate the general principles and are the examples as listed in the Education Code. [§3052(d)(1)]

5   The writers are indebted to Greg Armstrong of Oceanside School District for providing this case. Substantial alterations have been made for the sake of brevity, to include some relevant features, and for the sake of anonymity. This particular style and terminology is a variant of that developed by Dr. Gary LaVigna in his training programs to conceptualize challenging behaviors.

6   Although analysis of the alternative positive behavior is required, and objective data on assaultive behavior frequency was conducted and graphed, for the sake of brevity they are not included in this case description.

7   Although an interview with current guardians was conducted, it is not included here for the sake of brevity.

8   Charts from baseline data collection are not included in this write up for the sake of brevity.

9   Reactive Strategies are discussed in Chapter 5. They must be conceptualized as the positive response option to problem behavior used by implementers in the context of a positive behavioral intervention plan.

10 Although strictly speaking the "conferencing stage" would not necessarily constitute an emergency situation, this site, as well as Alex's family, prefers to log all reactive strategies that are close to an emergency so the staff may later review and evaluate the strategies they used to de-escalate potential crises and parents can notice trends.

11 An earlier variation on Randy appeared in a TASH newsletter dated January 1991.

Chapter 5

Recommended Positive Intervention Procedures

R eaders may recognize that the theoretical underpinnings of the Hughes Bill and California Education Code regulations are rooted in a particular school of thought. Although the specific intervention methodology and procedures contained in the regulations have been used with various populations with disabilities, they have been used most specifically and frequently with people with severe disabilities.

Behavioral intervention case managers (BICMs) with expertise in using interventions from other theoretical frameworks are not prohibited from using those interventions within a positive behavioral intervention plan as long as the following requirements are met:

- Alternative positive behaviors to replace the problem behaviors are targeted for increase based on a functional analysis paradigm with adequate establishment of baseline data.

- Interventions determined by the IEP team to be ineffective are modified or new ones are developed on an ongoing basis as a result of the program effectiveness review, as specified in the behavior plan.

- No prohibited interventions or emergency procedures are used.

This chapter presents an integrated model of both proactive and reactive strategies to be used in designing behavioral interventions. Program design requires an understanding of factors to accommodate or change within the individual as well as factors to change in an environment.[1] As a result of the functional analysis, a hypothesis will have been formed regarding the purpose the behavior serves for the individual. This hypothesis guides selection of more adaptive replacement behaviors through which the student can meet his or her needs. Although it is beyond the scope of this manual to delineate the complete teaching skills that may be necessary to implement behavior plans, it is anticipated that material in this chapter will point the way for implementers requiring further study on how to teach alternative positive behaviors using techniques such as modeling, cueing, shaping, and backward chaining. The reader is referred to the Bibliography and Chapter 7 for available training opportunities.

Clearly, the hypotheses generated during the functional assessment will drive the development of the interventions. Please refer to the programming guidelines in Chapter 8 for additional information if these interventions will be designed for individuals with severe developmental disabilities.

Preliminary Information:
Moving from Functional Analysis to Behavioral Intervention Plans

All positive behavioral interventions follow two guidelines:

- They modify the environmental context. Understanding which features in the environment are present when the behavior does not occur and which features are present when the behavior does occur is critical. Problem behaviors may diminish in frequency when the environment in which they occur is altered to more closely resemble the environment in which they do not. This strategy can produce rapid results if the correct variables have been identified. Environmental features are not randomly manipulated, but rather are carefully identified through data collection and hypotheses generation during the functional assessment phase of program design. Environmental changes (which involve teaching methods, curriculum, the physical environment, and interpersonal interactions), combined with direct teaching/ treatment strategies, can lead to rapid, positive change.

- They teach desirable alternative behaviors and/or apply direct treatment strategies so that a more adaptive behavior achieves the same function as the problem behaviors. This may be the more difficult of the two strategies, but it can have the most positive results by increasing the student's skill repertoire and increasing the possibility of generalization in new settings. An understanding of the student's unique characteristics will be critical for all forms of positive behavioral interventions. (Additional unique intolerances for certain environmental variables are described in Chapter 9.)

First Priority: Addressing Curriculum and Instructional Problems

Having completed the ecological assessment of the context in which the behaviors occur, the BICM may have identified some of the curriculum and instructional problems listed below:[2]

- few opportunities for making choices,
- lack of predictability in schedule,
- inadequate assistance provided to the student,
- unclear directions for completing activities,
- few opportunities for the student to communicate,
- activities that are too difficult or that are not challenging,
- activities that take a long time to complete,
- activities that students dislike,
- activities with unclear completion criteria, and
- activities that the student does not perceive to be relevant or useful.

It will be important to address these problems before or during any attempt to change the student's behavior. (Refer to "Educational Environment Assessment Scale" in Appendix J for further elaboration, as well as Chapter 8.)

In accordance with the philosophy stated in Chapter 1, if any of the above problems are observed, they should be addressed first. Lasting change will not likely occur unless the curriculum and environment are able to meet the individual's needs.

Moving from Assessment to Intervention

Student characteristics and tolerances that were identified during the functional analysis assessment should be addressed if the IEP team determines that a positive behavioral intervention plan is necessary. The BICM will want to propose intervention plans that are developmentally appropriate (refer to Chapter 9 for figures useful in explaining developmental stages and needs to others) and address individual needs that were identified in the functional analysis assessment. Information on the seven factors identified in Figure 5 will have been gathered during the functional analysis assessment and will be important to consider as the IEP team, with BICM participation, develops the behavioral intervention plan. These factors will require careful attention when techniques and strategies are identified to teach positive replacement behaviors or when reinforcers are selected and necessary frequency determined.

After completing the functional assessment, the BICM will have more hypotheses about the source and purpose of the behavior that will provide the direction for designing interventions. These functions and potential directions are described in Figure 6, p. 68.

Precise Criteria for Discontinuance or Modification

Plan developers and implementers need to remember that positive interventions must be responsive to variability in behaviors. In developing the plan, the individualized education program (IEP) team will develop criteria to determine when the occasional outburst of problem behavior is occurring too frequently or with too great an intensity to continue with the conceived plan. At that predetermined point, a new plan or modification will be instituted following guidelines described in Chapter 2. Criteria that are very specific as to when a plan should be

FIGURE 5.

MOVING FROM ASSESSMENT TO INTERVENTION FACTORS AND ISSUES TO ACCOMMODATE

Types of Factors Assessed	Issues to Consider
Environmental	Tolerance for lighting, noise, commotion, temperature, physical crowding, space, over-stimulation or understimulation, disruptions
Social	Difficulties with individual care-giving styles, staffing patterns, types of interactions, peer interactions
Communicative	Student's verbal/gestural facility, interactive capacity, receptive processing, behavioral intent
Physiological	Medical conditions, injury or illness, hunger, fatigue, increased arousal (such as following a fight or other disruption), decreased arousal (such as following a seizure)
Cognitive	Attention, exploratory behavior, representational thinking, concrete thinking, problem solving
Psychosocial	Frustration tolerance, regulation of behavior, impulse control, decision making, trust and attachment, task persistence, family and community values, history of reinforcement
Task related	Frustration thresholds for length, complexity, developmental level, time constraints of the task

FIGURE 6.

CHOOSING DIRECTIONS BASED ON BEHAVIOR FUNCTIONS

Behavior Functions		Directions for Designing the Positive Intervention Plan
Meyer & Evans	Durand & Crimmins	
Social Communicative Function *Protesting*	Escape	Teach other ways to communicate a protest response, remove the need to protest or escape by changing the environment
Attention Seeking	Attention	Teach other ways of getting attention, reduce need for attention by increasing independence skills, increase frequency of positive attention for appropriate behavior
Requesting	Tangible	Teach other ways of getting requested items/activities, teach delayed gratification, change the environment to facilitate independence and choice making
Self-Regulatory Function	Sensory	Teach more adaptive ways to modulate arousal, structure and define acceptable places or methods of self-regulation, remove need for arousal modulation (e.g., boredom, overstimulation)
Self-Entertainment or Play Attempt Funtion		Teach more acceptable ways to entertain oneself, ways to initiate, sustain or end play; provide an environment with more interesting entertainment options

Note: The behavior functions identified in the left columns are drawn from the works of Meyer & Evans and Durand & Crimmins. They are presented together in this table to illustrate the overlap of the conceptual models.

modified or abandoned ensure that ineffective programs are altered or replaced quickly. These criteria should be established as a preliminary step in plan development before intervention design. Over time, during the program effectiveness review, the IEP team will no doubt want to change these criteria. What is acceptable at the beginning of plan development in terms of frequency of problem behavior will no doubt be unacceptable in later stages, when expectations for the student using more alternate positive behavior rise.

Examples of Precise Criteria for Specific Individuals:[3]

Johnny's IEP stated:

> *If Johnny hits his face during four 30-minute intervals per day for 3 out of 5 days in a week, the IEP team will reconvene. If hitting occurs during more than two intervals per day, the implementer, case manager, and parent will confer by telephone.*

Johnny's later IEP stated:

> *If Johnny hits his face during three or more 30-minute intervals per day for 2 out of 5 days, the IEP team will reconvene. If hitting occurs during more than two intervals per day, the implementer, case manager, and parent will confer by telephone.*

Mike's IEP stated:

> *If Mike requires removal from a setting for aggressive behavior more than twice per week, in addition to the each-occurrence filing of an emergency report and communication between the BICM and parent, the IEP team will reconvene. If removals are fewer than the twice-in-one-week level, the parent will receive the incident report copy within 24 hours, and the BICM and implementer will fine-tune the behavior plan without an IEP team meeting, with parental input if requested.*

Choosing Proactive Strategies for a Behavioral Intervention Plan

Three Proactive Strategies and Reactive Strategies

Willis, LaVigna, & Donnellan (1987) propose a conceptual framework of proactive strategies versus reactive strategies that explains the scope and breadth of intervention design (see Figure 7). This framework can be helpful in understanding the continuum of behaviors from adaptive to maladaptive, with interventions also selected on a continuum, from direct to indirect. In this framework, the presence or absence of periodic events that lead to problem behavior outbursts, and thus require additional procedures, can be viewed in proper context.

Proactive strategies in this framework include procedures to decrease the intensity or frequency of the problem behavior over time and increase replacement behaviors. These strategies are ecological manipulation, positive programming, and direct treatment strategies.

FIGURE 7.

PROACTIVE VERSUS REACTIVE STRATEGIES

Proactive Strategies			Reactive Strategies
I. Ecological Manipulation	**II. Positive Programming**	**III. Direct Treatment**	
• Settings • Interactions • Instructional methods • Instructional goals • Environmental pollutants (e.g., noise, crowding) • Number and characteristics of other people	• General skills • Functional equivalent • Functional related • Coping/tolerance	*Behavioral* • Differential reinforcement • Stimulus control • Instructional control • Stimulus satiation *Other* • Neurophysical techniques • Medication adjustments • Dietary changes	• Active listening • Stimulus change • Crisis intervention*

*An emergency plan is required under these new educational regulations.

Source: LaVigna (1986). Used with permission of the author.

Reactive strategies in this framework are procedures used to establish control in a specific situation to prevent injury or damage when the established intervention strategies are not effective. They are not the legitimate focus of a positive behavioral intervention plan but rather constitute staff reactions using safe and positive techniques. If "out of control" behavior goes too far, then the plan has entered the emergency intervention phase. This emergency procedure phase has legal requirements and best practice elements of its own, which are covered in Chapter 6.

Proactive Strategy I: Ecological Manipulation

Ecological manipulations are planned environmental changes to produce a change in behavior (see Figure 8). (Please refer to Chapter 8 for elaboration.)

The following examples are offered to show how ecological manipulations can change problem behaviors. This is not intended to be an exhaustive list of potential manipulations. There are many environmental changes that help individuals with problem behaviors to exhibit alternative positive behaviors.

FIGURE 8:
ECOLOGICAL MANIPULATIONS FOR CHANGE

Areas to Potentially Change	Considerations and Action Requirements
Settings	Mismatch of environment to individual needs can result in protest behaviors; analysis of the environment in relation to individual needs based on handicapping condition, learning history, temperament, age, and so forth determines degree of fit
Interactions	Rapport between individuals can be facilitated or inhibited; acceptable interactions between individuals can be modeled, cued, prompted, and reinforced to achieve goals
Instructional Methods	Many variables require analysis to determine degree of fit; these include problem-solving training needs, hands-on learning opportunities, complexity and frequency of directions given, opportunities for choice-making on pacing or instructional content, and so forth
Instructional Goals	If not appropriate, the student may act out; goals can be too broad, impractical, developmentally inappropriate, not functional for current and future environments, unnecessary, and so forth
Environmental Pollutants	Noise, light, crowding, proximity, and so forth can lead to protest behaviors; refer to Chapter 9 for accommodations
Number and Characteristics of Other People	If student needs don't match this feature, exacerbation of problem behaviors can occur; number of people in the environment, voice tones, degree of affect (either too high and excited, or too low and unconnected, or too harsh) shown by peers or adults, and other characteristics may require alteration

Examples of Ecological Manipulation/Environmental Changes

Instructional Methods/Materials - Learning materials should be of high interest and to some degree determined by the student. Activities that are functionally meaningful (e.g., hand-washing, snack preparation, recess) and materials that are directed to student learning strengths (e.g., visual, physical, rote memorization) and interests (e.g., play) increase motivation.

Instructional Methods: Choices - Frequent opportunities for structured choice allow the student increased acceptable control over his or her environment. It is preferable to introduce available choices in as concrete a manner as possible. Even when the student can respond to verbal choices, using line drawings, photos, written words, or concrete items when offering alternatives reduces the need for adult instruction at each step and increases independence.

Instructional: Within one-to-one or small-group activities, allow the student to make as many choices as is instructionally and socially acceptable. The student with the behavior problem should not be the only one making choices in a small group. Turn-taking in making choices will need to be taught.

Contingently: When rewarding good work, provide a pictorial menu of choices or concretely present more than one potential reinforcer (e.g., "Do you want this checker game or this computer disc, Johnny?").

This pictorial/written or concrete representation of choice increases the student's acceptable and predictable control over the environment, reduces confrontations with staff, and motivates work completion without time-consuming "negotiating" the student might otherwise use.

Instructional Goals - Learning activities may need to be kept short and at a high success level, with gradual introduction of new material interspersed into well-known material as the student demonstrates interest or mastery. Self-esteem is enhanced and maintained through success.

Functional activities can be fun, and when an environment is maintained in which the staff and the student find enjoyment, behavioral problems diminish. Students with serious behavior problems often have perseverative and limited interests. It may be necessary to actively seek and develop additional interests for the student within the classroom curriculum.

Interactions - Many students require considerable direct adult attention for success. The use of nondeprecating humor and an emotionally supportive attitude are important in establishing a bond with the student. This bond will prove useful in de-escalating the student's behavior during stressful moments. If staff members become intrinsically reinforcing for the student's behavior, the student will be more apt to follow directions and learn. Programmatically, a supportive approach requires following a consistently positive and accepting routine when redirecting and refocusing the student on activities or classroom rules. Authoritarian or demanding approaches may be stressful and provoke disruptive outbursts. Mildly disruptive behaviors can be verbally or gesturally redirected. Immediate reinforcement for good listening when the student accepts redirection will play an important part in motivating the student to work hard and to listen to directions.

Proactive Strategy II: Positive Programming

There are four variations in the LaVigna, Willis, & Donnellan conceptualization of positive programming to consider in designing positive behavioral interventions: General Skill Development; Teaching Alternative, Functionally Equivalent Skills; Teaching Alternative, Functionally Related or Pivotal Skills; and Teaching Coping and Tolerance. General principles are given below. The reader is advised to pursue further information in this area, especially if the individual has serious disabilities. Curricula and behavior planning are entwined for all students, but especially students with serious disabilities.

1. Positive Programming Variation One:

General Skill Development

Repetitive, nonmeaningful tasks are often so removed from the needs, interests, and potentials of individuals that boredom, protest, frustration, and anger are natural outcomes. Whether the individual is engaged in core curriculum, functional skills curriculum, or combinations of these, instructional objectives should be functional and give an opportunity for relevant and interesting activities. Lengthy worksheets, barren environments, activities devoid of meaning to the individual, and fragmented "pieces" that appear purposeless to the learner are all precursors for acting-out behavior. Opportunities to both learn and engage in a wide variety of meaningful activities lead to an increase in productive behaviors and a concomitant decrease in unproductive behaviors. This proves the adage, "The best behavior management system is good curriculum."

Adaptations for developmental level (such as prelogical thinking in Piaget's model) must, of course, be present. Refer to Chapter 9 for developmental information. When materials and tasks are both developmentally and chronologically appropriate, the dignity of the individual is respected, and direct and indirect positive results are obtained.

For example, when a fractions unit is being taught in the general education classroom of an individual with serious learning disabilities, an accommodation to developmental level might be providing a cooking and measuring experience. Then the individual doubles the recipe in fact (physically putting 1/2 cup of flour in the bowl twice) rather than solving the problem at the abstract developmental level of most peers (mentally performing an algorithm rather than relying on perception to perform the task).

If a 21-year-old student with serious disabilities is learning to dress herself or himself and does not have object permanence, accommodations to developmental level might entail having all items for dressing in clear view. Chronologically, the self-dressing is an appropriate activity regardless of whether all items are in view.

The critical element of "functionality" should be considered when teaching new behaviors or skills, controlling nonproductive behaviors, and designing an environment for learning for individuals with challenging behaviors. The answers to two questions help determine any task's functionality for an individual: Does the student need this skill now or will he or she need it in future environments? and, If the student doesn't learn this, will someone else have to do it for him or her?

For example, tasks such as attempting to trace a name in large letters or to sound out three-letter words are not functional for an 11-year-old with significantly reduced cognitive processing ability who has not mastered the skills after five years of instruction. Analysis will no doubt show that for this individual, the tasks are not necessary skills in the current environment and not appropriate building blocks for future environments. Therefore, because this individual will not be able to progress in the logical sequence for reading and writing, it is time to look at bypass and compensatory elements. In this case, the function of writing may be to acknowledge the receipt of goods, label work, and so forth. Thus, focus might be put on using a name stamp to perform this function, knowing when to use it, and moving it discriminatively, and without prompting, performing this function independently. The function of reading can be thought of as enabling this individual to get information or enjoyment. The questions become, What information does the student need to obtain in this or future environments? What are other methods of getting information or pleasure from literature? When educators focus on providing meaningful and functional activities that match the needs of the students, acting-out behaviors decline dramatically.

To be functional, the activity must provide some reinforcing feedback in and of itself. Activities that require extensive external reinforcement to maintain behavior must be very carefully programmed and should not constitute a major portion of the individual's program if functionality is desired.

For generalization to succeed, the student should learn in the settings and with the materials that are likely to be used when the skills are mastered. For example, when social skills are practiced one-on-one with the language specialist, the student is less likely outside that context to recognize where, when, how, or with whom to use the skills.

2. Positive Programming Variation Two:

Teaching Alternative, Functionally Equivalent Skills

A student might, for example, be taught to use a handshake to substitute for a hit or to use a communication card to substitute for screaming. Many behavioral intervention systems have been developed that use picture/photo communication to solve long-standing behavior problems. For individuals with severe handicaps, communication skill deficits are often at the root of serious problem behaviors. Frequently, addressing these issues becomes the cornerstone of any behavioral intervention plan. The reader is referred to the Bibliography for a list of sources that address these issues.

Communication and independence training are examples of alternative skills. Many students have problem behaviors that serve as their only communication system. Teaching them an alternative that fulfills the communication function can be an effective and rapidly successful intervention. The case study of Randy in Chapter 4 demonstrates this approach. Also, the example below of Janey has some elements of this approach.

Frequently, individuals act out because they feel dependent on the services or direction of caretakers or teachers. For example, having access to desired goods and instruction in how to use them can eliminate the individual's perceived need to act out to get the necessary attention or item of choice.

| Janey | *A 10-year-old individual with autism and visual impairment* |

Janey enjoyed reciprocal games with friends at recess, helped her mother with chores around the home once a routine had been learned, and looked forward to her one-on-one training sessions twice weekly with vision specialists. Although sensitive to tactile input (unexpected touching from others, using a toothbrush or soap), Janey was able to tolerate textures and touch when warned of their imminent presence. Janey tolerated no deviance from the path her orientation and mobility specialist took either when instructing her in cane skills on the walk to the super-market or in teaching her scanning skills in the supermarket setting. Attempts to alter routine resulted in her screaming or demanding to use the toilet in a loud, forceful manner for an extended time period, thus interfering with her learning. Her IEP team interpreted these actions as pervasive maladaptive behavior.

During the functional analysis assessment, it was discovered that Janey strongly preferred doing things "the same way" for every task, in every environment. The intervention consisted of teaching her the tasks to be performed using Polaroid pictures of herself performing each portion of each task (her vision was adequate for close examination). At each sign of agitation, visually cueing her with the photos as to what had just been done, where she was now, and what comes next served to introduce flexibility in the routes taken to the store and the number of items sought for purchasing and their row location. Ordering the pictures (e.g., today we go by the house with the dog first, then cross the big street) and discussing it before departure increased communication. Janey would "argue" for a particular route by seeking the pictures required and pointing vehemently but would compromise on most days. Janey now had the information necessary for events and routes to become predictable for her, which allowed some flexibility because outcomes were now understandable to her. She became a better communicator, became a better choice-maker, and found adaptive ways of increasing her own control over her life.

3. Positive Programming Variation Three:

Teach Alternative, Functionally Related or Pivotal Skills
Choice-making, rule learning and stimulus control are skills that can be used to limit or eliminate problem behaviors.
Being able to reliably indicate a choice is often pivotal in extinguishing serious problem behaviors. Teaching this skill can be a viable method of addressing protest behaviors.

Rule-learning to change behaviors can be achieved even by individuals unable to communicate verbally, when the task is analyzed and systematically taught in a manner consistent with the communicative skill of the individual. (Refer to p. 75, "Review and rehearse classroom rules.")

Stimulus control can be used to limit a behavior to a very narrowly defined place, time, materials, and manner. For example, a student who shreds all available cloth until his clothes are in tatters can be taught to cut only one specific piece of cloth, at one specific time, with one specific shredding instrument. Stimulus control procedures thus limit the behavior so that it occurs reliably and consistently, only in the presence of a particular discriminative stimuli.

4. Positive Programming Variation Four: Teaching Coping and Tolerance

Using relaxation techniques, becoming desensitized to environmental irritants, learning to delay reinforcement, and learning to tolerate ambiguity and variability can all affect change. See Chapter 9 for further elaboration and some suggested teaching strategies.(Refer to p. 76, "Teaching coping skills.")

Checklist of Programming Elements That Facilitate Positive Behaviors[4]

✓ **Expand and develop appropriate social interactions** - Build on social interactions between staff members and each class member, including the student with problem behaviors. Demonstrate positive regard for him or her beyond the current behavior. The student needs to see herself or himself in the group context. Give additional attention when the student shows interest in a topic or is attempting to engage staff appropriately. When off task, steer the student to more appropriate activities through redirection. Do not feed into inappropriate attention seeking by overreacting to disruptive behaviors because it is probable that these are reinforced by adult interest, negativity, and concern.

✓ **Facilitate appropriate peer interactions** - Use group activities to build positive social interactions among students. Teach appropriate social language, how to reciprocally interact, and strategies for getting attention from others and for getting needs met. Teach appropriate language for social interactions during board games, recess activities, snack time, or group discussions. Please refer to Chapter 8 for elaboration.

✓ **Review and rehearse daily schedule** - Students with significant memory impairments, some learning disabilities, emotional disturbances, autism, or mental retardation are frequently anxious during change or transition. Over time, they adapt very well to consistent scheduling and routine. Eventually, they internalize most of the routines and can be very resistant to changing those routines. This internalization of routine is a means of control, and a student can become quite agitated, act silly, or be disruptive when he or she experiences unexpected change. One means for compensating for this problem and building in functional academic experience is verbal rehearsal of scheduling. At the start of the day, go over the sequence of classroom activities verbally *and* pictorially, if possible. The pictures, icons, logos, and line drawings are kept with the student for continuous reference. Sequence, not time, should be the emphasis of these rehearsals, but as an incidental training activity, the time of a particular activity also could be displayed beside the activity. This technique is a concrete and functional approach to reading and time-telling. In addition, it helps to relieve any anxiety associated with change and transition within a hectic or busy environment. This schedule can become a crutch for the individual when he or she cannot receive adult attention at transition time and can be used in preparing the student for change on any given day. Knowing how long he or she has to wait for playtime or free time is important for many students. Coordinate the use of the schedule with other staff members working with the student so that information on the schedule will be accurate. Do not schedule and rehearse events that cannot be delivered reliably. The schedules allow the student greater awareness, but if they are not followed consistently, they will irritate rather than reassure the student.

✓ **Review and rehearse classroom rules** - Actively teach easily generalized, specific rules. Rule-teaching is a primary strategy for students with difficulties in concept formation and generalization. Rules should be stated as positive and incompatible behaviors, such as "hands and feet to self," rather than "no hitting." They may have to be shown to the student in a very concrete fashion, and they may need to be stated before the student begins work. For example, before beginning the lesson, the teacher might show the student a picture of himself or herself or another student working quietly or point out another student in the class working appropriately. The teacher then would state, "The rule is you must work quietly." The student would then be asked to repeat the rule. The student would be reinforced for following that rule. Initially, only one or two rules should be taught at a time. It is important that the student internalize each rule in turn before others are taught contingently. The student may not always succeed in observing the rule, but the teacher must be emphatic that it should be followed. Reminders of the rule should be given whenever the student does not follow it, but punishment or criticism for disobeying the rule should be avoided. Initially, all work should be judged by the student's ability to follow the rules while working. The quality or quantity of work is not the issue. As the student acquires rule-driven classroom behavior and exhibits an interest in school work, quality and quantity can be re-evaluated. Also, rehearse appropriate rules and strategies before the student begins activities that may be difficult for the student.

Use schedules within activities to enhance structure - It is equally important to build in clear and concrete structure to tasks when asking the student to work independently. Making the student aware of behavioral expectations, task sequence, and duration may be necessary to support focusing on the activity without distraction, undue anxiety, or disruptive and demanding behavior. The use of written or pictorial schedules may be beneficial here. Schedules can be used situationally to show the order of events within an activity, for example:

1.   Use your name stamp on this paper.
2.   Circle what we need for this activity.
3.   Hand in your work.
      or:
1.   Write your name.
2.   Do ten addition problems.
3.   Hand in your work.

Pictures or line drawings are available through many educational resources, especially through speech and language service providers or in critical/functional skills curricula. If the student can read, short, simple sentences will suffice; pictures can be used to enhance communication when possible and desirable.

Teach coping skills - This can be especially effective when the student is having difficulty following rules. Teach rules in motivating settings and activities. When the student is involved in motivating activities, remind him or her of the rules for appropriate behavior. Have the student occasionally state the rule when he or she is in danger of not following it. When the student is not involved in motivating activities or when activities become too stimulating or anxiety producing, teach the student to state his or her need to escape: "It's too hard!" or "I need to leave!" or "I need help!" Any verbal explanation that can serve to allow the student to escape in an appropriate manner will do. When the student is aware that he or she has communicatively appropriate options for escaping difficult tasks or for reducing sensory stimuli, then it will be possible to negotiate with a rule, such as, "Try your best!" If the student is agitated or upset, it may prove helpful to teach the student to use a relaxation area, such as a corner with a mat or pillows. It will be necessary to teach the student to use such an area, but it may prove helpful as an additional coping strategy, if consistently used.

Focus whole class on positive behavior - Use the time at the end of the period to comment on positive achievement of all class members. Allow all students to comment on good things they saw others doing. Help others to participate with prompts, such as "Did you see James try his best this morning in group?" Build a classroom spirit around following the classroom rules. Use stickers, applause, praise, additional playtime, or edibles as appropriate when doing this group activity.

Proactive Strategy III: Direct Treatment

Direct treatment strategies may achieve rapid gains when combined with ecological manipulation and positive programming. See Figure 9 for an overview of these strategies. They are the direct treatment techniques used to establish rapid control while changes in the environment which may be necessary to effect lasting change are made. Specific training is required for their effective use. The following ideas are presented to arouse interest in training for readers wishing to develop their skills. The reader is referred to the Bibliography for more information on other areas.

Introduction to Differential Reinforcement

Sufficiently reinforcing the alternative positive behavior as we teach an individual to use it helps to ensure that the behavior will be repeated. Using differential reinforcement effectively requires an understanding of basic behavioral principles. Critical issues include eventual fading of cues, decreasing frequency and immediacy of the reinforcement, and promoting generaliza-

FIGURE 9:

TYPES OF DIRECT TREATMENT STRATEGIES

(Direct treatment strategies are behavioral techniques and other medical/neurophysical methods that alter the likelihood of a student's emitting the positive behaviors she or he has been taught, rather than maladaptive behaviors.)

Potential Strategies	Components
Differential reinforcement	Providing reinforcement for other behaviors, for behaviors incompatible with the problem behavior, for lower rates or absence of problem behavior, and so forth; immediacy, frequency, and power of the reinforcers are important considerations
Stimulus change	Removing those stimuli that are discriminative for the problem behavior (e.g., moving the desk of the student in whose presence the problem behavior consistently occurs, allowing biting on one object only)
a. **Stimulus control**	Isolating the problem behavior to one environmental stimulus (e.g., allowing biting on an approved object only)
b. **Instructional control**	Using rule-governing behavior to establish rapid control over a problem (see Chapter 8)
Stimulus satiation	Reducing a behavior problem by increasing the noncontingent availability of the maintaining reinforcers (e.g., making water and food continuously present if screaming for them is the problem behavior)
Other direct treatment	• Using neurophysical techniques: relaxation therapy and fear desensitization • Making medication adjustments: by careful record-keeping across settings, a physician is enabled to titrate, add, or discontinue medication more effectively • Making dietary changes

tion and maintenance after the new behavior is being emitted at acceptable levels. *Progress without Punishment* (Donnellan et al., 1988) is a particularly useful overview of differential reinforcement in the instructional process.

Direct Treatment Strategy One:
Differential Reinforcement of Alternative Positive Behaviors

This direct treatment strategy is very powerful. Meaningful, supporting relationships with staff members and peers are the most effective and socially natural reinforcers but are often those least available for a student with challenging and patience-trying behaviors. Although difficult to implement consistently in a hectic classroom, direct reinforcement of appropriate behaviors hastens the development of positive behaviors and leads to more natural reinforcement. When developmentally appropriate, using drawings, charts, or tokens in a program to target and reinforce appropriate behavior for the student is likely to improve the functioning not only of the student with the problem behaviors, but of the class in general. Below are some examples of procedures using this strategy:

➤ Lindsay is allowed a 15-minute board game with her teacher at the end of each day for verbally requesting directions, clarification, or reduction in task requirements each time she needs assistance or anxiety reduction during that day. (Lindsay would put her head down and refuse to work prior to this program.)

➤ Brendan places a checkmark on his desk chart each time he is frustrated with a classmate and verbally requests the student to stop the behavior using the script taught to him and his peers. At the end of each hour, Brendan receives a token for absence of physical aggression (a differential reinforcer for absence of the problem behavior) and bonus tokens for any checkmark (reinforcer for presence of an alternate behavior). These tokens are exchangeable for a rich variety of reinforcers. (Brendan would hit classmates with the slightest provocation or perceived slight before this program was implemented. He has limited understanding of alternatives to expressing his anger physically.)

➤ Kyle receives a token for each recess in which he follows the playground rules of going to the end of the line when his peers say he is "out." He exchanges these for the privilege of sitting near the bus driver on most occasions. His peers applaud his rule-following, which he finds reinforcing. (Kyle previously argued or punched anyone calling him "out.")

➤ Grace is praised *each* time she points to an item she desires, with periodic hugs provided in addition to the verbal praise. She also received instruction and reinforcement in tolerating delays. (Grace screamed to express all wants and needs before receiving instruction in pointing as an alternate positive way of getting her needs met.)

Differential reinforcement may be used classwide. For example, when deemed developmentally appropriate, a drawing of a graduated thermometer may be used with each student. Class rules (target behaviors), posted and illustrated for everyone to see, might include the following:

- Following directions
- Friendly talking
- Trying your best or finishing your work
- Hands and feet to self

The individual's thermometer with his or her name and, perhaps, photo may be posted prominently in the room or near the student's desk. When the student follows directions or talks in a friendly manner (behavior often incompatible with problem behaviors), the teacher gains the student's attention, refers to the posted class rules, and, while filling in a graduated line on the thermometer, states the rule the student was following. This procedure may be done privately or with full class attention, depending on the student's comfort level. Modifications for age, developmental level, frequency of reinforcement, and other individual needs should be made. A menu of highly motivating and readily deliverable activities, developed with the student's input, may be posted and illustrated at the top of the thermometer. When the student fills the thermometer, he or she may choose an activity or item from the reinforcer menu.

The rate at which the thermometer is filled should be determined by the student's success level with the system. Initially, it will take time to buy into the system, so delivery of reinforcers at a relatively rapid rate, perhaps two times per day or even two times per hour to start, is recommended. Targeted frequency at the initial stages will be established as a result of the functional assessment based on current functioning. After the student shows an interest in the system, slowly lengthen the time needed to fill the thermometer. Adjust the number of graduated lines or the frequency of filling in the lines to slow down or speed up the process. The student may find the system more understandable and concrete if a picture of a jar, ticket race, or something else is substituted for a thermometer. (See Appendix K for additional sample behavior charts.) Variety can be important, so the teacher may want the student to choose the next system to use after successfully completing one. It is important to remember the "closure" element described below when choosing what pictorial system to use for some student (see "Closure as a Reinforcer, p. 81").

Direct Treatment Strategy Two:
Differential Reinforcement for Absence or Lower Rates of a Problem Behavior

Many professionals working with students with challenging behaviors have successfully eliminated problem behaviors and increased the occurrence of incompatible positive behaviors using strategies that reinforce absence or lower rates of the problem behavior (termed "DRO," "DRL," and "DRD" in behavior literature) while teaching desired behaviors. These techniques must be used with caution and with the understanding that they do not, by themselves, teach alternative behaviors. To be acceptable in terms of a behavior plan to increase positive replacement behaviors, it will be important to delineate how the student is meeting his or her need without exhibiting the problem behavior. Reinforcement for absence of a behavior or lower rates of a behavior on an interval schedule can be an effective and relatively nonintrusive method of helping the student avoid returning to maladaptive behaviors. The BICM may want to simultaneously reinforce presence of the alternate behavior in many instances. Also, the reinforcers should be gradually phased out when the rate of the replacement behavior has reached the predetermined acceptable level.

Examples of procedures using these strategies include the following:

➤ Mike is allowed to watch his videotape at 5:00 p.m. if he is not involved with any physical attacks on the bus.

(Mike's need for attention from peers has been met through teaching him new oral communication techniques. Reinforcement for absence of attacks helps him avoid reverting to previous maladaptive methods of gaining attention.)

➤ Jane receives a token for every 10-minute interval in which she does not bite her hands. The token is exchangeable for portions of an extra snack her parents send for that purpose.

(Jane has been taught other ways of coping with anxiety and frustration: going to a relaxation corner, telling peers or teacher what the problem is, and rubbing her hand. The reinforcement here helps her avoid reverting to previous maladaptive methods of gaining sensory input and expressing her anxiety.)

➤ Alice put a "golden nugget" in the classroom jug (when full, the whole class got a party) for every reading group meeting in which she does not tear classroom materials.

(Alice has been taught to raise her hand to express frustration or request to leave the group. Reinforcement for absence of tearing behavior helps her avoid reverting to tearing books as a method of meeting her needs.)

➤ Dan screams (baseline: 15 continuous minutes) or emits a high-pitch whine while completing assigned job duties to express his desire to terminate the activity rapidly. Dan marks his chart at 5-minute intervals (when the timer goes off) under job coach direction. If he does not scream or whine in the interval, he scores a "+." When all blank squares on the chart are full, he redeems the chart for a free-time activity or snack.

(Dan knows how long the assignment will take now based on the number of intervals to fill in, which helps him with his need to understand the length of on-task behavior he is to perform. He has been taught to seek reinforcement by saying, "I'm doing well, right?" and to verbally request a break if he cannot complete the full assignment.)

➤ Charlie bangs on his own desk with increasing fury before tipping over other students' desks as a way of seeking attention when tasks become frustrating for him. He receives a token if he is able to interrupt the escalation chain with fewer than two bangs on his desk for attention or if he raises his hand to signal help needed. Verbal praise is given for seeking help appropriately, and prompting is initiated as soon as desk banging begins. ("Charlie, hand up, get token. No bang.") The teacher plans to reinforce only hand raising eventually but feels this procedure is necessary during the training process.

(Charlie has been taught an alternative replacement behavior, and he receives a token redeemable for desired activities for appropriate help seeking and other specific behaviors the teacher is targeting for increase. Tokens in his class are for a variety of behaviors, clearly shown on a picture schedule on the students' desks. Reinforcing approximations to the goal behavior is viewed as an interim procedure during the training process.)

Use of Reinforcement in Direct Treatment Strategies

Direct treatment strategies using differential reinforcement are effective only if the reinforcement procedures match the individual's unique characteristics and needs. Errors in achieving this match frequently sabotage the success of otherwise well-designed intervention plans. The BICM will want to assist the implementer in determining appropriate reinforcers for the student and the frequency and manner in which they are given. The following material on reinforcement is offered in response to frequently encountered problems that often lead to intervention failures.

Reinforcer versus Reward

One of the most common errors in behavior plan development relates to a confusion between reward and reinforcement. Reinforcement is said to have occurred when a consequence to a behavior results in that behavior increasing or maintaining its frequency. Thus, the behavior is reinforced — made stronger and more resistant to elimination because the individual desires the reinforcer and associates the behavior with desirable outcomes.

A reward, on the other hand, is given by an observer to someone for having met some criterion established by the observer. Frequently, the giver assumes the recipient will like the outcome. The reward may actually be hated by the receiver (e.g., "You did that sheet of problems so beautifully that you get to do another one as a reward"). A reward is what you think will work, while a reinforcer is what is proven to work.

Resistance to Reinforcement

As is apparent in reviewing Figure 10, there are many different reinforcers available to maintain or increase behaviors. Frequently, individuals described as "resistant to reinforcement" are simply not responsive to the selected reinforcer at enough intensity to support change from the behavior of concern, which, of course, has its own reinforcer present. For example, although a student may love stickers, especially stickers with unicorns, and express a desire to work to earn them, he or she may find the reinforcer for the problem behavior, such as social attention or release of physical energy, even more enticing. Therefore the BICM needs to understand not only the individual's likes and dislikes, but also the degrees of desirability and the purpose or function of the behavior for that individual. If an individual is noted in previous records to be "reinforcer resistant," a thorough examination of the reinforcers currently observable and potentially available across environments is recommended if direct treatment strategies are desired. Understanding the principles involved in reinforcer selection is as important as knowing what the individual finds reinforcing.

Closure as a Reinforcer

Individuals with severe behavior problems may respond to reinforcers in unique and unpredictable ways. For instance, completing a four-part puzzle may be a powerful reinforcer because the closure element is so desired by the individual. Closure here is defined as finishing the whole, completing a set, arriving at the end. There can even be a somewhat obsessive quality to this closure, such as a person driven to check off every item on a "to do" list. If an individual has a limited number sense because of his or her developmental level, the idea, "When you have five stars you may stop" may not be clear, even if the student's rote counting is much higher. If that same individual has a sheet with five spaces, he or she can clearly see how many squares are left to fill, to "close up."

A form of a closure system can be used during assessment of resistive children. A simple water toy may be employed that releases air when a button is pushed, shooting rings toward pegs. For each ring that lands on a peg, the student gets to answer a comprehension question. As another example, a four-piece inset puzzle may be used with one puzzle piece per question or item. For every completed task (getting a ring on a peg), a result occurs (getting to answer a question). Although answering a comprehension question is definitely not a reinforcer for many children, the element of closure, or completing the entire defined task sequence, has proven irresistible. To make this even more reinforcing, the student can "earn" a play break, time spent with a toy the student selects at the outset, by completing the puzzle or getting all the rings on the pegs. Children who have resisted answering questions vehemently before this procedure often become willing participants after it is implemented.

Reinforcement Continuum

Figure 10 highlights types of reinforcement. The reader is cautioned, however, that although the types of reinforcers are presented in hierarchical order, from bottom to top, frequently more than one reinforcer is present in any situation, and the precise hierarchy of intrinsic and extrinsic characteristics of a reinforcer is open to interpretation.

FIGURE 10.

REINFORCEMENT CONTINUUM

REINFORCEMENT

Examples:

How I feel about myself for earning the certificate I am awarded

What my teacher says, what my peers say, when I get the certificate

I get out of class earlier than my peers to get the certificate; I am recognized as a certificate earner

Whoever has earned a certificate gets first choice of free time activities

First I earn the certificate, then I can use the new computer program I want

The certificate is earned after completing the 10 steps on my chart. I like finishing the chart

I get to chose from the tangible awards box when I get the certificate

Going on stage to get the certificate is *extremely* exciting because of the elevator ride to get to the award room

INTRINSIC   • Self-praise, Self-satisfaction
PRAISE   • from Adults • Parent • Teacher • Staff • Peers
SOCIAL STATUS & RECOGNITION   Peers or Adults
PRIVILEGES   • Choice-making, sense of "power"
CONTINGENT ACCESS   Premack Principle } If-then: 1st___ then ___: Activities-Free time/Free choice
CLOSURE   • Completing a set, finishing a list has compulsive features
TANGIBLES   • Money, stickers, camera, etc.
PRIMARY - EDIBLES, PHYSIOLOGICAL RESPONSES   • Natural/Synthetic Stimulants • Massage   • Repetitive Behaviors (Pacing, Rocking, Nail Biting)

© 1992 Diana Browning Wright

Determining What Feature of an Occurrence Is the Actual Reinforcer

It is important to determine which elements in each "reinforcement act" are found to be reinforcing. For example, if the student is responsive to stickers or other tangibles given by the teacher, is the reinforcer successful because of:

- love of the object itself
- the "closure" element of filling every square on the sheet
- the student's sense of success and positive feelings about self following internal self-talk that praises the accomplishment
- love of getting something peers are not getting
- the desire for touch satisfied when the teacher pats the student on the back when giving the sticker
- some other features

If one understands as precisely as possible what element is reinforcing to the individual, effective procedures to increase positive behaviors can be designed more readily. In general, activities and interests actively sought after by the individual are good areas for inquiry. Interviews with the individual and significant others, as well as observation during the functional assessment, will frequently yield important information as to what reinforces behavior for a student. Many published reinforcer surveys can be helpful in this process.[5] If the individual routinely responds to items listed at the upper end of the reinforcement chart, (see Figure 10) such as praise from significant others, one will not focus on a lower level, such as tangibles, in a direct treatment plan unless the student requests them. Also, verbal praise should be paired with more extrinsic reinforcers so that praise may eventually assume reinforcing properties for the individual. The plan will focus on the higher levels on the chart, if that is where the student responds well, especially in facilitating the student to chart and monitor the acquisition of new behavior himself or herself.[6] Alternatively, if the natural reinforcers in the environment work to support maintenance and generalization of the new behavior when environmental change occurs, external and intrusive reinforcement may not be necessary or desirable after natural reinforcers are shown to be effective.

Expanding Activities to Be Potential Reinforcers

There is an interesting and useful reinforcement principle termed "The Tom Sawyer Effect" after the famous fence-painting scene where Tom convinces his friends that fence painting is the ultimate reinforcing activity. If an adult or peer makes contingent access to an activity or item seem highly valuable, a real privilege, conveying much social status and recognition, the individual may come to seek that experience or item above all else. For example, in Mrs. Jones' class, pounding erasers after school may be deemed extremely desirable by her students, thereby assuming positive reinforcing qualities. In Mr. Wright's adjoining classroom, eraser pounding may be deemed a "punisher" by the class and teacher, thereby assuming aversive stimuli properties.

One extreme example was recently discovered that further illustrates this point. Two students worked very hard to earn the "privilege" of staying in at recess to practice making positive comments to each other, even though they were frequently antagonists. The teacher had billed this activity as one of very high status, and these students were highly responsive to status reinforcers and valued the teacher's opinion.

If the individual is responsive to praise, social status, and recognition and desires privileges, the implementer may be able to develop a vast array of potentially reinforcing activities by using techniques to develop conditioned reinforcers. It must be remembered, however, that not every behavioral intervention plan requires extrinsic reinforcers. Frequently, environmental changes or positive programming changes remove the need to express problem behaviors, or the alternative positive behavior elicits reinforcers natural to the setting that support the behavior.

Problem behavior that responded to a program with minimal extrinsic reinforcers

John *Age 9 with mental retardation and autism*

John became explosive, running around the room, hitting and yelling during transitions between activities. John was given a picture schedule and the rule "find what comes next and get ready." This is a positive programming technique to teach a missing skill, in this case awareness of schedule/routine and tolerating a wait. John was able to focus on what was coming next rather than exploding during the wait through this simple transition aid. No additional reinforcers were necessary to support success; the intervention itself served to meet his need to understand what was coming next; thus, no additional components were necessary.

Using Activities: Premack Principle: First_____, Then_____

In programs for individuals who require systematic reinforcement for increasing positive replacement behaviors, one should consider whether or not a highly successful technique known as the Premack Principle may be useful. This entails contingent, conditional access to some activity routinely chosen independently by an individual, to be delivered immediately after a less frequent behavior that has been targeted for increase.[7] This principle is seen when one rewards oneself with a favorite TV program after completing that report, ice cream after finishing that spinach, Nintendo after finishing that homework, free play after finishing those subtest items, and so forth. Typically, the more complex the reinforcer chosen (activities of interest can have a multitude of potential factors that make them satisfying), the less likely that satiation will occur.

Direct treatment strategies using both tokens and the Premack Principle to control running

Kevin *Age 12 with very poor language skills, and reduced cognitive ability*

Kevin ran out of the classroom and in front of buses and cars to protest boredom. Several near misses occurred, so removal to a more restricted site was imminent. Although program changes and ecological manipulations were viewed as the key to lasting change, immediate elimination of the escape behavior was essential. Kevin had reduced awareness of scheduling and passage of time. Kevin loved music and would use tantrums to gain access to a Walkman but was unresponsive to many other activities or consumables. He required immediate gratification and all token economies had failed, probably because of multiple factors, including the lack of one-to-one counting ability. The reinforcement "tokens" selected for this new plan were portions of the Walkman, culminating in the tape itself, whereupon he was allowed ten minutes of music. Kevin was given each piece for an activity completed, with ten pieces possible (four batteries, headset in three pieces, battery door, tape door, tape = ten pieces or tokens to use in delaying the listening-to-music reinforcer). Kevin earned these "tokens" in each of the three critical 45-minute time periods where flight was possible. The times during which Kevin might flee were identified by a scatter plot analysis during baseline data collection. He did not flee during physical education, during cooking time, or on community outings; therefore, this system was not used during those times. Kevin was taught other ways to communicate his desires during the program.

Factors Affecting Reinforcer Effectiveness

After the BICM has identified potential or current reinforcers that are likely to increase or maintain a desired behavior, the scheduling needs of the individual must be considered. Suggested reinforcers to explore for effect on behavior are found in Appendix M. Reinforcers must:

- be selected for a behavior that the student can proficiently perform or for which instruction will be provided (often including shaping and modeling instruction techniques)
- have enough power to affect the specific behavior
- include sufficient variability to maintain effectiveness in the program
- meet the student's immediacy needs
- meet the student's frequency needs

Each of these factors is discussed below.

Instruction Provided as Needed

Too frequently, behavior plans have been designed that expect the student to perform behaviors that he or she has not been instructed to perform. If the student does not exhibit the behavior in the required form, the implementer will need to provide instruction and reinforcement for closer and closer approximations to the goal.

➤ Example: Angie did not apologize for unintentionally bumping into others, which frequently caused other students to react aggressively. Reinforcement for doing so was unsuccessful until Mrs. Jones specifically taught the skill of apologizing to Angie using modeling, prompting, and reinforcement.

Power of the Reinforcer

There is always an internal cost/benefit analysis going on within the individual to determine, "Is it really worth doing X to get Y?" "Is it worth giving up doing A to do X instead, when A always got B, and B was pretty swell?" "Is B greater than Y?"

➤ Example: For David, getting attention from his big sister may be very powerful at times but may not compete with either attention from a returning parent or the reinforcement that occurs when he escapes a noxious environmental event, such as a lawnmower suddenly appearing.

➤ Example: Kristina's teachers uses contingent access to free time for on task behavior, which may not compete with other reinforcers available in an environment for the competing undesirable behavior of throwing objects to get recognition.

Variability of the Reinforcer

Some students satiate easily; some do not. Some seek extensive variety; some do not. A multitude of reinforcers should be available so that whatever reinforcers are available in the environment, and often uncontrolled by the teacher, do not become more appealing and powerful than the "same old thing" given for desired behavior.

➤ **Example:** Mrs. Browning has found that her students were initially very enthusiastic about the student store available each day for exhibiting particular behaviors she had targeted for increase. After 2 weeks, she noted that students were not as enthusiastic and behaviors were not maintaining. An examination of her reinforcers revealed that all the available reinforcers were tangibles and edibles, coupled with praise. Mrs. Browning revamped her menu of reinforcers, used closure principles on her new charts, and made privileges (e.g., passing out paper, going to lunch first, cleaning the rabbit cage), social status (e.g., earning class president status, earning newspaper editor status), and contingent access to activities (e.g., games with a peer, being read to by the teacher) a part of her new variable menu of reinforcers. Mrs. Browning found that behaviors increased well beyond the initial change when she had first began her token economy program.

Immediacy of the Reinforcer

Frequently, the individual's internal cost/benefit analysis tips in favor of other reinforcers more immediately available, even if they are not quite as desirable. Delaying gratification is difficult for individuals with behavior problems, and acceptable wait lengths are self-determined. Individuals at early developmental stages require reinforcers to immediately follow their actions if they are to understand what specific previous behavior resulted in the reinforcer. If other behaviors occur between the behavior targeted for increase and the reinforcer, the individual may lose sight of the connection.

➤ **Example:** Martha has been taught to point to request an item rather than scream, but the teacher often does not immediately acknowledge this behavior either verbally or by giving her the requested item because she is busy with another student. If this is a new skill for Martha, she is likely to return to screaming behavior because her current immediacy needs are for very rapid delivery. Response fluency (i.e., Martha points very well and has a long history of immediate reinforcement) will need to be well established before targeting and teaching the toleration of delays. Otherwise, Martha is likely to lose her pointing behavior under these delay conditions.

Frequency of the Reinforcer

How many times must the behavior be emitted before a reinforcer is given? This frequency question is closely linked to how rapidly following the emission of the behavior (immediacy element) will the reinforcer follow. Frequency problems can sabotage a program as assuredly as variability, immediacy, and power problems can. The token economy and all its variants are attempts to stretch the frequency of reinforcement needs and introduce acceptable delays as individuals bank the tokens for later redemption.

➤ **Example:** Ms. Maffei decided to use a differential reinforcement system for Nicholas and Angela's recess times when verbal or physical arguments did not occur. She decided that at the end of every week, she would give them each extra free time that they enjoyed as a consequence of their elimination of fighting behavior and ability to talk through differences. Thus, approximately 15 recess times would need to be altercation free to earn the reinforcer. They were taught conflict resolution skills and reinforced for their use. Ms. Maffei was unsuccessful with this system, despite both students' desire to earn free time. When she changed her system so that Nicholas and Angela earned free time at the end of each day, the undesirable behavior decreased. Eventually, Ms. Maffei was able to reduce the frequency of access to the reinforcing activity to approximately every three days.

Checklist of Reinforcement Problems That Lead to Failure

Measurement

✓ Check your measurements on the effect of the reinforcer on behavior. Your measurement may not be correct.

Instruction

✓ Failure to select behaviors that can be maintained by the natural environment over time, coupled with failure to plan for and teach skills necessary for generalization and maintenance.

✓ Failure to reinforce closer and closer approximation to the goal behavior (shaping behavior) and failure to effectively prompt or cue the student to perform the behavior to gain the reinforcer as necessary.

✓ The positive alternative behavior is not being taught in small enough steps. Expecting a fully proficient skill without task analysis and instruction can lead to failure.

✓ A prompt signal is given too often during the teaching process. Give the student a signal only when attention is being directed to the instructor. Give the signal only once. Wait a few seconds. Then either (a) let the student find out that the consequence of failing to perform the behavior is missing the reinforcer or (b) give the signal again and prompt the student through the motions of the desired behavior.

✓ Threats are used as signals. Threats are not positive teaching tools.

✓ The student is helped (prompted) not enough or too much.

Frequency

✓ The reinforcer is given too infrequently to support the behavior (i.e., too many responses are required before reinforcement), often occurring when developmental level is not fully considered in program design or when a student use to receive a rich schedule of reinforcement and it was reduced too rapidly. At the start of any program to change behavior, it is very important that the behavior be rewarded nearly every time it happens, that is, on a continuous schedule. Is the student not continuing to be rewarded every so often for behaviors that were heavily reinforced in the past? Intermittent reinforcement helps make a behavior resistant to extinction.

✓ The shift from continuous schedule to intermittent schedule was made too quickly. For example, as you wean the student from the continuous schedule, instead of rewarding the behavior every time, reward it four out of five times, then two out of three, and so forth.

Immediacy

✓ There is a lengthy (by the student's standards) delay in accessing the reinforcer. These immediacy problems can be a result of reduced ability to delay gratification because of a variety of factors, such as developmental level, emotional disturbance, or lack of experience in receiving reinforcers.

✓ Consequences are not given fast enough and the student fails to recognize what is being reinforced. The behavior just before the reinforcer is the one that was reinforced and is the one that will likely increase. If you wait too long to reward the behavior, the student will have engaged in other behaviors. The reinforcer may then be seen as the consequence of the latter behavior. If the reward is food or a token and the student requires an immediate reinforcer, try giving the student some signal that the reinforcer is forthcoming until you can get there.

Power and Variety

✓ Selected reinforcers are not powerful enough to replace the reinforcer currently present following the problem behavior. Check for other reinforcers available.

✓ The so-called reinforcer is not really desirable to the individual but rather is an item or activity selected by the interventionist because he or she believes it should be effective. Always check the effect of the consequence on the behavior.

✓ Variety or complexity is insufficient; therefore, satiation occurs too rapidly to sustain the behavior at the desired level.

✓ Consequences are given too many times. Satiation occurs when a student has gotten the same reinforcer so many times that it is not a reward any more. Switch between many different kinds of reinforcers. Stop an activity before the child has had enough. As soon as a child is satiated on a reinforcer, do not use it for a long time.

✓ The student may be getting other reinforcers for free (such as attention). If the student already gets a form of whatever you are going to provide, the reinforcer may not have sufficient power to effect change.

Integrating the Positive Plan with Reactive Strategies

After the team has established which proactive strategy or combination of strategies is to be used, and considered which reinforcers are likely to increase positive alternative behavior(s), consideration should be given to handling problem behaviors if they periodically occur in spite of the new approaches.

Figure 11 illustrates the way in which the positive intervention plan interfaces with reactive strategies to contain or redirect problem behaviors if they continue to occur. Staff members will want to discuss and delineate exactly how they will manage the student's escalating behavior should that develop. This plan is based on providing the least intrusive redirection possible (e.g., a verbal challenge is best dealt with verbally — staff members should not select a physical containment procedure before it is necessary). The plan is based not only on established procedures within the special education local plan area (SELPA) and parental input, but also on the staff's knowledge of the unique calming techniques that have worked in the past with that student.

The safety and welfare of staff members and students are protected when implementers clearly understand the plan for positive intervention and how to decide when a disruption is becoming serious enough to require planned reactive strategies beyond the positive strategies in the behavioral plan. A careful review of the figure may identify points of transition for staff to plan how challenging behavior will be handled.

Continued on page 90

FIGURE 11.

BEHAVIOR STAGES: INTEGRATION OF REACTIVE STRATEGIES WITH POSITIVE BEHAVIOR PLAN

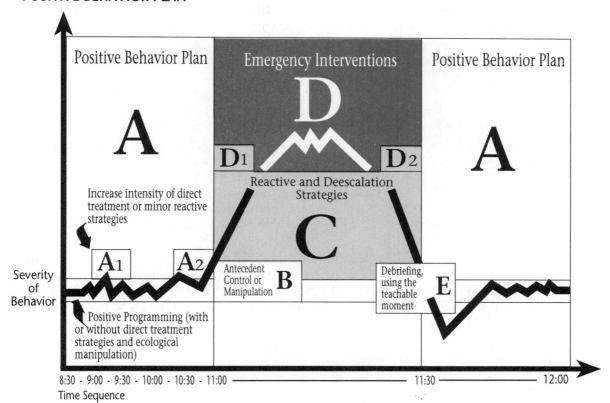

A = The Positive Behavior Plan, which includes all components which address the programming, any ecological changes or direct treatment strategies. This stage also includes minor accommodations to escalating behavior.

A[1] = Increase in accommodations made by staff in response to periodic or minor difficulties the student experiences in expressing the positive replacement behavior; the end result is a successful return to procedures outlined in the positive plan.

A[2] = Same as A[1] only the end result is a transition to reactive and deescalation strategies because the student is unable to return to the positive behavior plan.

B = Staff recognition of the need for systematic reactive and deescalation strategies to prevent the expression of a serious behavior.

C = Specific reactive and deescalation strategies to which staff believe this particular individual will respond positively.

D[1] = Staff recognition that emergency procedures must begin to be utilized for the safety and well being of the student and other peers or staff.

D = Containment procedures approved by the SELPA that constitute the emergency plan and require documentation as such.

D[2] = Staff recognition that emergency containment procedures are no longer required to assure safety of student, peers or staff. Return to C is warranted as deescalation from the crisis is continuing.

E = Staff recognition that the emergency procedures and reactive procedures are no longer required. The student is ready for re-entering the positive behavior plan after the reestablishment of rapport and review of the incident occurs in positive terms. Staff will review success of intervention as part of debriefing.

© MORTON, WRIGHT (1993)

Staff recognized that Sara could not be redirected to her tasks as soon as her arms began flailing and she began pacing the room. This was identified as point A2 on the figure and signaled the need for point B, reactive strategies (see Figure 11). Frequently, Sara would calm down if a calm, steady voice was used to ask her to walk outdoors with the staff person to "cool down." This reactive strategy (C on the figure) normally was effective. D1, recognition
of the need for emergency procedures, was determined by this staff to be when Sara knelt down to initiate severe head banging on the concrete floor. D was determined to be a SELPA approved basket hold (physical containment) in which all staff members had been trained. D2 for Sara was determined to be relaxed breathing and slackening of stiff muscles. After D2, Sara was still not ready to return to activities, but another reactive strategy (C on the figure) that seemed to further calm Sara was relaxation for a few minutes in a specially designed rest area in the room. At stage E, the staff members praised Sara for regaining control, discussed the employed interventions with each other, and helped her rejoin the group activity.

Reactive and De-escalation Strategies

Reactive and de-escalation strategies are specific redirecting responses used by plan implementers to alter an escalating maladaptive behavior. After considering the various proactive strategies, the LaVigna model looks at reactive strategies. Before escalation to an emergency behavioral intervention as the end stage, these brief interventions can be used to disrupt a chain of behaviors or redirect the individual to appropriate behavior (Please see Appendix H, "Management of Antecedents"). These reactive strategies are not the positive intervention plan focus but rather constitute staff planning to manage a behavior crisis that may occur on occasion. They may be included as part of the comprehensive intervention plan. All reactive strategies have significant problems, however, in that although the behavior may be controlled momentarily, the individual may find the strategy reinforcing and therefore may escalate to that level repeatedly to gain that reinforcer. Thus, reactive strategies must be only a small part of the context to achieve change, with proper emphasis placed on the positive programs to develop generalizable, maintainable adaptive behaviors to meet the individual needs.

Problem behaviors often lack consistency. The techniques, strategies, activities, personnel, curriculum, and scheduling that lead to very few problems on one day may be ineffective on another day. One reason for this inconsistency is the role of periodic occurrences that alter the value of different reinforcers and therefore change how typical stimuli are responded to by the individual. Lack of sleep, missing the bus, a "bad morning," and so forth can change reactions to subsequent stimuli. While gathering data on immediate, observable antecedents and consequences are extremely important, every teacher knows that day-to-day fluctuations point to the limits of a strict A-B-C analysis of what can be observed. In many ways, these periodic disruptive occurrences can be viewed as the invisible, internal antecedents to behaviors. In examining the variability of behavior during functional analysis, fluctuations between settings should be examined to identify environmental features associated with adaptive and maladaptive behaviors. The BICM will also look for periodically occurring events that alter the individual's responsiveness to subsequent settings.

One of the most frequent additions to behavioral intervention plans is a contingency plan for what to do when it is obvious that what has worked yesterday, and will no doubt work tomorrow, is not working today. Contingency plans are needed when either of the following situations occurs:

- There is evidence of a stressor likely to alter the student's responsiveness to an existing effective plan. This may be communicated by the student or caretakers. There might be a telephone call from a parent about a sleepless night, returning seizure pattern, "angry morning," or other event from which predictable sequelae are likely to occur at school. Setting up a communication system from setting to setting can frequently prepare the next setting to head off problem behaviors by reducing task demands, changing frequency of reinforcement, increasing choice-making opportunities, providing relaxation techniques, and so forth. This can be an important feature in maintaining behavioral consistency and reducing the likelihood of acting out behaviors.
- Although no stressor has been reported, changes in the student's behavior are noted that may be precursors to an outburst of problem behavior. For instance, tremors, head down, crying, or agitated movements may indicate an escalated state not normally seen in the student and signal a need for reactive strategies.

If the behavior plan is usually effective, temporary accommodations to respond to these periodic events may be sufficient to deal with the occasional off day. If the problem behavior is not meeting the reduction criteria established by the IEP team, new planning is necessary. A new functional analysis of the problem behavior(s) should lead to changes in direct strategies, ecological manipulations, or positive programming components if reactive strategies are increasingly necessary rather than decreasingly necessary.

Activities, educational approaches, and staff responses to the student should be analyzed carefully when the student consistently and predictably refuses to engage appropriately in particular activities. Changes should be made to ensure that the tasks are motivating and educationally appropriate, that the material/information is being presented in a communicatively accessible manner, that the reinforcement is meaningful and effective, and that the student is successful when engaged in the activities. Changes in programming should be based on change in staff approaches, lesson presentation, or activity content rather than on coercing or demanding appropriate behavior from the student.

Reactive Strategy One:
Active Listening or De-escalation Techniques

If adults respond to the escalating behaviors in such a way that the individual no longer feels the need to continue the episode because needs have been met, the behavior will frequently not escalate further. This can be true for both predictable chains of behavior and behavior that occurs unpredictably. If specific events are found to be influencing behavior and account for the periodic outbursts in an otherwise successful program, the BICM may want to specify techniques and strategies to employ when an escalation is observable, yet still well short of a situation requiring an emergency intervention.

Active listening involves listening to the student's comments, observing his or her behavior when upset, and letting the student know that you are aware that he or she is having a difficult time. It requires avoiding nonsupportive gestures or statements when the student is angry. The student is asked what is bothering him or her and then is worked with to solve the problem. This type of interaction can lead to opportunities for teaching rules and understanding the needs of others. Initially, this technique may be a primary method for redirecting the student. Frequently, the student will have an agenda of his or her own. It may be necessary to allow that agenda to be incorporated into the activities that are ongoing within the classroom. For example, it may not always be possible to get the student to make a successful transition from one activity to another. through verbal redirection alone. Active listening in this instance means asking the student what he or she wants. The student may be involved in another activity or with a toy. In such instances, it is possible to use the toy or item that he or she is involved with to ensure that a successful transition is made by saying, for example, "Let's go to lunch, Sally. What do you want to bring with you?" Sally's need to be heard can be satisfied through her holding of the transition object (toy or item with which she was previously involved). Power struggles (e.g., insisting that the student respond to directions on teacher demand) will lead to more frequent episodes of disruptive behavior. It is best to find ways to motivate the student to participate in events, to allow participation at the student's own comfort level, and to maximize the individual's feeling of control while shaping behavior to conform with the routine of the day.

If active listening is not successful, and the student's behavior escalates to classroom disruption or physical aggression, it is advisable to allow a cooling-off period away from the stimuli that are eliciting and/or maintaining the behavior. This should be explained to the student as a time to gain self-control, not as a punishment. Please see Chapter 10 for a discussion of time away procedures. It might entail going with the aide on a brief errand, listening to tapes on a headset, and so forth. Negative attention, as provided by overreacting to acting out behavior, can serve as reinforcement and may increase the frequency or intensity of a difficult behavior. Providing opportunities for success and choice and avoiding dramatic reactions to behavior will maximize a student's interest in participating in a classroom. Examples include the following:

➤ If the student challenges authority, such as by not following rules or direction to stop intolerable behaviors (such as spitting, throwing objects, or striking out at a peer), remind him or her of the rules as they apply to the behavior being demonstrated. If spitting is occurring, the teacher would say, "Grace, remember! Do use your words!"

➤ If the student continues to challenge that rule or is visibly upset, ask directly, "What is wrong?" Active listening becomes your first intervention: "Are you angry?" "Do you want my attention?" "Do you need to rest?" "Do you want to stop doing _____?" If the student is able to respond to this approach, treat the incident as a teaching opportunity on how to get one's needs met.

➤ If the student is unable to respond to a verbal approach to mediating his or her behavior, use stimulus change. Redirect the student to a motivating activity or topic of conversation. Attempt to distract the student whatever means is likely to engage the student (it will vary from person to person and from situation to situation). Redirect the student back into activity as soon as he or she is calm.

➤ If the student cannot be redirected, escort him or her to an area away from the activity. When the student is calm, determine whether he or she is ready to return to the activity by asking "Are you ready?" The student should be allowed to decide his or her willingness to re-engage in the activity.

➤ If the student escalates to out-of-control behavior, follow SELPA guidelines. When the student is calm, ask whether he or she is ready to return to the activity. This is the time to re-establish rapport and review the incident in positive terms. If the behavior was defined as a serious behavior problem that required the use of an emergency procedure, an emergency intervention form and specific procedures described by the SELPA and required in the regulations must be followed. (See Chapter 6 for discussion of emergency procedures.)

➤ Avoid removing the student early in an escalating chain of behaviors, when you know that he or she is attempting to escape the activity itself. Rather, whenever possible, feasible, and safe for all, use those times to teach the student to verbalize a need for support (which may include escape).

Reactive Strategy Two:

Stimulus Change

This technique is best characterized as the sudden and unexpected introduction of novel stimuli that results in the sudden cessation of difficult behavior. One example would be flicking on and off the lights to quiet a classroom that has gotten too noisy and loud. Another example would be to ignore the "issue" of a confrontation, such as a refusal to follow a direction, and to redirect a student in an unexpected manner:

> **Teacher:** *"Guy, finish your activity"*
>
> **Guy:** *"It's too hard!"*
>
> **Stimulus change:** *"Guy, help me finish my activity. I forget how to do it."*
> *After Guy helps you, you then suggest that you help him finish his activity.*

These indirect methods may seem too much like coaxing; however, they do much to remove the stimulus maintaining the oppositional behavior and making a potentially negative interaction a relatively positive one. The danger with such interventions is that they can serve to reinforce oppositional behaviors if used too often or as a first resort, but they can and should be used when the student cannot be redirected through rules and contingent reinforcement.

Other stimulus change examples might be clapping your hands, rattling a candy wrapper, asking everyone to get ready for recess, and so forth. The results are often transitory but do suppress or redirect behavior. For example, Mrs. Harvey, parent of an individual with severe behavioral outbursts of aggression, reports that if the telephone rings, the yelling that precedes physical aggression does not progress further. If students with severe behavior problems who respond to this technique (not all do, of course) are viewed as having train-track thinking, rather than road-map thinking, this is understandable. Derailment ends the behavior temporarily until the individual gets back on the escalation track. If the environment is positive, it may be that the individual will be reintegrated back onto a positive behavioral chain, with very little further staff intervention. Mothers of toddlers report distraction works quite effectively for some problems; the principle is the same.

Stimulus Change for Disruptive Behavior, Increasing Choice-Making Opportunity

Chris *A six-year-old with autism.*

Chris would slide out of his seat at small group activity time, making loud prolonged high pitched noises that disrupted the whole activity for everyone. His teacher trained him so that he did not have to physically leave the group but that his "play behavior" was differentiated from his "work behavior." When he started to make noises, she handed him a small felt heart and said, "Here is your toy. I see play behavior!" He would immediately stop squealing, probably because of the stimulus change. He would then hand back the felt heart (normally within 30 seconds), saying, "Now work time!" The teacher would check for feet on the floor, hands on the table, commenting on those features and praising his "Good working behavior!" before accepting the heart back to signal work time. This reactive strategy allowed Chris to have choice and independence along with systematic training on what constitutes good behavior.[8]

Reactive Strategy Three:
Physical Management Procedures

As a reactive strategy of last resort, physical containment may be used to ensure safety for all involved. Physical containment is governed by the procedural requirements for emergencies outlined in education code regulations and the SELPA plan. Refer to Chapters 2 and 6 for rules and guidelines.

---

[1] The authors are indebted to Dr. Gary LaVigna for permission to use the proactive/reactive model described by him in various books and articles.

[2] Adapted from Foster-Johnson & Dunlap, 1993.

[3] These examples are not meant to be taken as standards for all students. They represent specific statements for a specific child. They are included only to clarify how precisely a criterion should be stated.

[4] Behavior plans are developed based on individual analysis. When these seven elements are present, however, problem behaviors are not as likely to arise.

[5] Alex's case study in Chapter 4 includes a reinforcement inventory that illustrates how the BICM identified potential reinforcers for a positive behavioral plan. A complete Reinforcement Inventory for Children and Adults is included in Appendix N.

[6] Of course, self-charting requires that additional periodic reinforcement, plus considerable student training, be available when the student's chart matches teacher appraisal.

[7] Behavior literature now links the Premack Principle to the Response Deprivation Hypothesis. That is, if access to one of a pair of events is restricted below what the individual is normally accustomed to (baseline), the individual strives to regain the same amount of access. If access to the activity desired by the individual is contingent to performing the less-desired activity, then the less-desired activity is more likely to be performed when requested (Sulzer-Azaroff & Mayer, 1991).

[8] If the heart was available for Chris to select by himself, the strategy might then be viewed as a functional equivalent to protesting or exercising choice and might then be used as a positive behavioral intervention because now a positive alternative behavior is being shaped.

Chapter 6

Emergency Procedures

*T*his chapter focuses on the application of restrictive behavioral interventions in emergency situations, first from the perspective of the requirements of the Hughes Bill and implementing regulations, and then concluding with a discussion of effective practices in this area. The law itself requires the development of Education Code regulations in five areas relating to emergencies. The first part of this chapter identifies those areas and the corresponding regulations. Because the information regarding emergency procedures is found in several sections, they are brought together under the five headings for clarity, with citations provided.

A discussion of several critical elements of the regulations follows. The last section is devoted to general suggestions for best practices in developing and implementing emergency plans and procedures in actual school settings.

The Hughes Bill and Implementing Regulations

Emergency Procedures as Required by the Hughes Bill

The Hughes Bill (A.B. 2586, Chapter 5.5 added to Part 30 of the California Education Code) requires that "the Superintendent of Public Instruction shall develop and the State Board of Education shall adopt regulations governing the use of behavioral interventions with individuals with exceptional needs receiving special education and related services" [§56523(a)]. With regard to emergency procedures, the law requires that the regulations "specify standards governing the application of restrictive behavioral interventions in the case of emergencies. These emergencies must pose a clear and present danger of serious physical harm to the pupil or others. These standards shall include:

" A)   The definition of an emergency.

   B)   The types of behavioral interventions that may be utilized in an emergency.

   C)   The duration of the intervention which shall not be longer than is necessary to contain the dangerous behavior.

   D)   A process and timeline for the convening of an individual education plan meeting to evaluate the application of the emergency intervention and adjust the pupil's individual education plan in a manner designed to reduce or eliminate the negative behavior through positive programming.

E) A process for reporting annually to the State Department of Education and the Advisory Commission on Special Education the number of emergency interventions applied under this chapter" [§56523(b)(3)(A-E)].

Emergency Procedures as Specified in the Implementing Regulations

All citations below refer to Title 5, California Code of Regulations: Amended Section 3001 of Article 1 of Subchapter 1 of Chapter 3 of Division 1 of Title 5, and New Section 3052 added to Article 5 of Subchapter 1 of Chapter 3 of Division 1 of Title 5.

A) "The definition of an emergency"

"'Behavioral emergency' is the demonstration of a serious behavior problem: (1) which has not previously been observed and for which a behavioral intervention plan has not been developed; or (2) for which a previously designed behavioral intervention is not effective. Approved behavioral emergency procedures must be outlined in the special education local planning area (SELPA) local plan" [§3001(c)].

"'Serious behavior problems' are defined as the individual's behaviors which are self-injurious, assaultive, or cause serious property damage and other severe behavior problems that are pervasive and maladaptive for which instructional/behavioral approaches specified in the student's IEP are found to be ineffective" [§3001(y)].

"Behavioral emergency interventions shall not be used as a substitute for behavioral intervention plans" [§3052(a)(4)].

B) "The types of behavioral interventions that may be utilized in an emergency."

"Emergency Interventions. Emergency interventions may only be used to control unpredictable, spontaneous behavior which poses clear and present danger of serious physical harm to the individual or others and which cannot be immediately prevented by a response less restrictive than the temporary application of a technique used to contain the behavior" [§3052(i)].

"Emergency interventions shall not be used as a substitute for the systematic behavioral intervention plan that is designed to change, replace, modify, or eliminate a targeted behavior" [§3052(i)(1)].

"Whenever a behavioral emergency occurs, only behavioral emergency interventions approved by the special education local planning area (SELPA) may be used" [§3052(i)(2)].

"SELPA Plan. The local plan of each SELPA shall include procedures governing the systematic use of behavioral interventions and emergency interventions. These procedures shall be part of the SELPA local plan" [§3052(j)].

"Upon adoption, these procedures shall be available to all staff members and parents whenever a behavioral intervention plan is proposed" [§3052(j)(1)].

"At a minimum, the plan shall include: . . . Special training that will be required for the use of emergency behavioral interventions and the types of interventions requiring such training; and approved behavioral emergency procedures" [§3052(j)(2)(C and D)].

As can be seen from the above, the regulations require the SELPAs to develop and include in their local plans the actual specific details of allowed emergency procedures. The regulations are, however, quite specific regarding interventions that may *not* be employed.

"Emergency interventions may not include:

Locked seclusion, unless it is in a facility otherwise licensed or permitted by state law to use a locked room;

Employment of a device or material or objects which simultaneously immobilize all four extremities, except that techniques such as prone containment may be used as an emergency intervention by staff trained in such procedures; and

An amount of force that exceeds that which is reasonable and necessary under the circumstances" [§3052(i)(4)(A-C)].

C) **"The duration of the intervention which shall not be longer than is necessary to contain the dangerous behavior."**

"No emergency intervention shall be employed for longer than is necessary to contain the behavior. Any situation which requires prolonged use of an emergency intervention shall require staff to seek assistance of the school site administrator or law enforcement agency, as applicable to the situation" [§3052(i)(3)].

D) **"A process and timeline for the convening of an individual education plan meeting to evaluate the application of the emergency intervention and adjust the individual's individual education plan in a manner designed to reduce or eliminate the negative behavior through positive programming."**

"To prevent emergency interventions from being used in lieu of planned, systematic behavioral interventions, the parent and residential care provider, if appropriate, shall be notified within one school day whenever an emergency intervention is used or serious property damage occurs. A 'Behavioral Emergency Report' shall immediately be completed and maintained in the individual's file.

The report shall include all of the following:

- The name and age of the individual;
- The setting and location of the incident;
- The name of the staff or other persons involved;
- A description of the incident and the emergency intervention used, and whether the individual is currently engaged in any systematic behavioral intervention plan; and
- Details of any injuries sustained by the individual or others, including staff, as a result of the incident.

All 'Behavioral Emergency Reports' shall immediately be forwarded to, and reviewed by, a designated responsible administrator.

Anytime a 'Behavioral Emergency Report' is written regarding an individual who does not have a behavioral intervention plan, the designated responsible administrator shall, within two days, schedule an IEP team meeting to review the emergency report, to determine the necessity for a functional analysis assessment, and to determine the necessity for an interim behavioral intervention plan. The IEP team shall document the reasons for not conducting the assessment and/or not developing an interim plan.

Anytime a 'Behavioral Emergency Report' is written regarding an individual who has a behavioral intervention plan, any incident involving a previously unseen serious behavior problem or where a previously designed intervention is not effective should be referred to the IEP team to review and determine if the incident constitutes a need to modify the plan" [§3052(i)(5-8)].

E) "A process for reporting annually to the State Department of Education and the Advisory Commission on Special Education the number of emergency interventions applied under this chapter."

"'Behavioral Emergency Report' data shall be collected by SELPAs which shall report annually the number of Behavioral Emergency Reports to the California Department of Education and the Advisory Commission on Special Education" [§3052(i)(9)].

Critical Elements of the Regulations

Identifying a Behavioral Emergency

Under the regulations, an emergency is defined as "the demonstration of a serious behavior problem: (1) which has not previously been observed and for which a behavioral intervention plan has not been developed; or (2) for which a previously designed behavioral intervention is not effective." Further, the law states, "Emergency interventions may only be used to control unpredictable, spontaneous behavior which poses a clear and present danger of serious physical harm to the individual or others . . ."

Despite the seeming clarity of that definition, occasions will frequently arise when staff judgment will be required to determine if a more restrictive, emergency intervention is required. Unpredicted behaviors that lead to an assault with a weapon with sufficient force to injure the intended victim will clearly fit this definition. So will self-injurious behaviors that clearly may cause harm—for example, head-banging against a window with sufficient force to break the glass. But what if the weapon is a semi-soft ball? Or what if the self-injurious behavior stops when a verbal redirection is given? In these cases, judgment will need to be applied before an emergency intervention is used. School staff members have a positive, legal obligation to protect their students from harm, and clearly this obligation must be considered in the decision whether or not to apply emergency interventions under each circumstance.

Another consideration has to do with considering behavioral problems as part of a potentially escalating cycle. For example, tearing up papers and books may not fit the definition of an emergency even though replacing the materials may be costly. However, this problem behavior may be the initial stage of an outburst that could quickly escalate to a physical assault. Therefore, it will be important for all staff members to have a clear understanding of behavioral patterns and the concept of providing a response that de-escalates rather than aggravates a situation. Additionally, the system needs to be designed to reinforce in staff members the techniques for successfully de-escalating situations and successfully managing emergencies when they occur. This will assist them in identifying the early stages of potential emergencies and intervening with positive options before the need for more restrictive interventions arises. Use of a behavioral emergency reporting form that identifies antecedents to the emergency (and appropriate responses to the early stages of the eventual emergency) will also assist staff in internalizing this positive intervention process. It may be helpful to use such a form to document potential emergencies that were defused before the need for emergency interventions arose as a way of reinforcing the process.

Constraints on the Use of Emergency Interventions

The regulations for this law do not specifically define an emergency intervention. Rather, it gives this responsibility to each SELPA. The regulations do, however, list specific emergency interventions that may not be used.

There are three types of prohibited emergency interventions. The first is locked seclusion. The only exception for this intervention is in a facility that is otherwise licensed or permitted by state law to use such a device. An example of this would be a school that is within a licensed psychiatric hospital or prison facility.

The regulations also prohibit "employment of a device or material or objects which simultaneously immobilize all four extremities," although "techniques such as prone containment may be used as an emergency intervention by staff trained in such procedures...." Prone containment is not specifically described but generally involves physical restraint of one person by one or more people, in a manner that prevents significant movement of all four limbs. This second prohibition would, for example, prevent tying or strapping a student to prevent movement of all four limbs, or rolling the student up in a blanket or rug that immobilized all four extremities.

Also prohibited is "an amount of force that exceeds that which is reasonable and necessary under the circumstances." This may seem somewhat vague to a reader who is not trained in physical crisis intervention. However, a gross example would be using prone containment on a student who was hitting himself on the head with a stick. Removal of the stick would stop the behavior and might necessitate immobilizing one or both arms briefly. However, unless the student escalated and displayed other dangerous behaviors, prone containment (even by trained staff) would seem to constitute an excessive amount of force.

The final constraint on use of emergency procedures involves the duration of any such procedure. The law and regulations state, "No emergency intervention shall be employed for longer than is necessary to contain the behavior." Furthermore, "any situation which requires prolonged use of an emergency intervention shall require staff to seek assistance of the school site administrator or law enforcement agency, as applicable to the situation." This section is meant to make emergency interventions short and to end them as soon as safety permits. Making decisions regarding the length of an emergency intervention will also necessitate staff training in crisis development. Some fairly simple verbal and nonverbal techniques are helpful in enabling the student to regain self-control and signal staff that the emergency intervention is no longer needed. However, practice and coordination among staff members is important in applying these techniques effectively.

Reporting Emergencies

Some checks and balances are included in the regulations to ensure that schools abide by this law, especially when it comes to emergency interventions. Whenever an emergency intervention is used or serious property damage occurs, the parent and, if appropriate, residential care provider must be notified within 1 day. The purpose of this is specifically stated in the regulations: "to prevent emergency interventions from being used in lieu of planned, systematic behavioral intervention. . . ." Furthermore, a "Behavioral Emergency Report shall immediately be completed and maintained in the individual's file," according to these regulations. If an emergency report is written about a student who does not have a behavior plan in place, then the administrator must, within two days, schedule an IEP team meeting to review the emergency report and decide if a functional analysis assessment and/ or an interim behavior intervention plan is needed. The IEP team must also document its reasons if it decides not to perform the functional analysis assessment or develop an interim plan. The specific information required in the behavioral emergency report is also delineated, as mentioned earlier.

SELPAs may want to carefully develop a reporting form that goes beyond the specific information required by this law. A form that also records specific student and staff behaviors and that reiterates the locally approved emergency intervention training method will automatically review procedures for staff. Furthermore, it assists in documenting that the approved procedures were followed. A sample form used by one agency following the procedures of the National Crisis Prevention Institute is included in Appendix E. It not only includes all the information required by the regulations, it also provides space to describe student behaviors and staff responses within the framework of the approved emergency system adapted by the agency. Experience has shown it to be an effective tool both for ensuring accurate, thorough incident reports and for staff review and training.

General Principles and Best Practices

Plan Ahead

Good practice demands readiness with behaviorally difficult students. Have a plan, troubleshoot your plan, practice your plan, revise your plan, and teach your plan to your staff. If not, a real emergency may show you, in the most painful way possible, the weaknesses in your plan. Even if you cannot determine when and where an emergency will strike, you can plan and practice a range of appropriate and effective responses. Advance planning, simulation, practice of emergency procedures, and revision of the plan based on actual and simulated situations are critical to ensuring effective emergency responses. A list of organizations that provide crisis intervention training is included in Appendix E.

Inform Your Staff

Be explicit with your staff regarding the requirements of dealing with behaviorally difficult children. If staff members are not aware that some children are potentially difficult or even violent, they will not be prepared to deal with emergencies effectively. In fact, some emergencies with violent students may be prevented if staff members are prepared properly. If staff members do not feel prepared, they are likely to be shocked by an emergency situation, diminishing the chances of an appropriate, safe, and effective response. When fear is added, unproductive responses may occur, such as freezing and doing nothing, overreacting physically, or using language that escalates the situation.

It is also helpful to provide each staff member with written copies of emergency policies and procedures. Obviously, when an emergency arises, no one has time to look in a book or file. However, the material will provide your staff members with the knowledge they need to prepare adequately ahead of time.

Be Systematic

Use a systematic approach. Train as many staff members as possible in the same system, top to bottom at a site, so you can rely on each other. By definition, an emergency arises without much warning; therefore, if all staff members (teacher, custodian, lunch aide, secretary, principal, and so on) know what is expected, then help will arrive that much sooner. Also, staff members will feel more confident in dealing with difficult children if they know that their colleagues are not only close by but trained and available to help.

Be Philosophically Consistent

Think about, make explicit, and reach consensus on your emergency control philosophy before implementing a training program. If you do not believe in a particular approach or physical containment technique, do not use a system that teaches it; if you do believe in it, use it. Remember, in an emergency, we often act on instinct and training—the obvious reason for the emphasis on preparedness. Therefore, it is preferable to use a system that teaches within your philosophy. Staff will then be able to use the whole approach and will not waste time or be confused thinking about which techniques are "allowed" and which are "forbidden."

Think Prevention

An approach that focuses on prevention and de-escalation may take more time and effort in training but will be much more satisfactory and effective in the long run. Some prevention techniques are easy to implement, such as removing potential weapons or arranging furniture with safety in mind. Other prevention techniques may involve training and practice in observation and verbal and nonverbal communication skills. Prevention is the only way to ensure that injury will not result from a violent outburst or dangerous behavior. Therefore, the more effective staff members are in preventing emergency situations, the less risk there will be for both physical injury and emotional trauma.

Avoid Overreactions

Even though this may be easier said than done in an emergency, it is critical. The natural flow of adrenalin is usually a contributing factor in overreactions. However, the flow may be curbed or reduced by making the situation something at least vaguely familiar through training and practice. This process makes an emergency a less threatening and more understandable event. It enables staff to assess the situation in a systematic manner that provides an effective avenue of action, reducing the chance of an escalation caused by staff overreaction.

Plan for Leadership Roles

Assign leaders for different situations and determine a method to establish new leadership roles quickly in a new situation. For example, assuming emergency training is the same, the instructional aide who supervises a high school student's work experience for 3 hours a day may be a more effective leader of a crisis intervention than the assistant principal who has talked with the student only a few times. Yet an instructional aide is not likely to take a leadership role when teamed with an administrator, unless the appropriateness of it has been discussed in advance.

Emphasize Teamwork

Teams foster support, lower the tendency to overreact, allow for witnesses, diminish fatigue, and can provide for attention to everyone who may be at risk, including bystanders. After an emergency, a teamwork approach to analysis, reporting, and planning for the future is almost always superior to individual work.

Remember Debriefing

The natural lull in activity that follows an emergency provides a window of opportunity for discussing the emergency and planning for prevention of future episodes. This is as important for the person who lost control as it is for staff who intervened. Develop methods and situations in which there is time for staff members to debrief with students and with each other.

Train for Documentation

Use a documentation form that follows the underlying procedural philosophy to enhance the ability of staff members to understand the event. It also enables efficient documentation of critical elements and provides a good reminder and training vehicle for implementers.

Chapter 7

Critical Competencies of the Behavioral Intervention Team

This chapter addresses the issues of qualifications and training for behavioral intervention case managers (BICMs) and other staff members with behavioral intervention responsibilities. It should be remembered that under the new regulations, "'behavioral intervention case manager' means a designated certificated school/district/county staff member(s) or other qualified personnel pursuant to subsection (x) contracted by the school district or county office who has been trained in behavior analysis with an emphasis on positive behavioral interventions. The 'behavioral intervention case manager' is not intended to be a new staffing requirement and does not create any new credentialing or degree requirements. The duties of the 'behavioral intervention case manager' may be performed by any existing staff member trained in behavior analysis with an emphasis on positive behavioral interventions, including, but not limited to, a teacher, resource specialist, school psychologist, or program specialist" [§3001(e)].

This chapter describes both the knowledge base and competencies necessary to perform the BICM role successfully in a school setting, as well as the knowledge and skills needed by all members of the individualized education program (IEP)/behavioral intervention team. The levels of competencies outlined also can be viewed as a framework for training designated BICMs. (See Appendix O.)

Lastly, this chapter describes the critical consultation skills needed by BICMs and all team members.

Knowledge Base of the Behavioral Intervention Case Manager

As mentioned in the initial chapter of this manual, successful BICMs will have a firm grounding in the bodies of knowledge listed below. Descriptors delineating crucial specifics in each area are also provided. This listing is not all inclusive, but it does indicate the fundamental skills and background a BICM needs to successfully assist in the design and implementation of positive behavioral interventions for students with serious behavior problems.

The Education System

- Knowledge of the wide range of curricula available (core curriculum, functional skills, critical skills) and developmentally/chronologically appropriate practices necessary to ensure that the child receives appropriate programming before the further interventions are designed
- Knowledge of teaching strategies
- Knowledge of special education law: eligibility, placement issues, service options, IEP development, and expulsion and suspension as related to special education
- Knowledge of the day-to-day operations in the school setting, constraints on teachers and other service providers, how to engender system support for change

Behavior Analysis: Theory and Practice

- Knowledge of how consequences and antecedents effect the behavior of all individuals
- Knowledge of functional analysis assessment and the "communicative intent" of behavior
- Knowledge of procedures and methodology in effective teaching of new behaviors and assessing for functionality of behavior
- Knowledge of multiple factors affecting behavior change: maintenance and generalization issues; using modeling, cueing, prompting, reinforcement, environmental and internal setting events
- Knowledge of evaluating behavioral programs for needed modifications

Unique Characteristics of Individuals with Serious Behavior Problems

- Knowledge of the importance of antecedents and environmental controls for some individuals
- Knowledge of the effects of medical factors on behavior (e.g., medications, syndromes, seizures, severe migraine, obsessive-compulsive disorders, sensory impairments/differences, and traumatic brain injury)
- Knowledge of the variety of ways individuals with limited language abilities communicate
- Knowledge of different forms of unique communication and how to recognize those students in need of alternative communication modes
- Knowledge of developmental features and needs at different stages

Consultation Skills Necessary to Develop and Maintain Successful Consultant/Consultee Relationships in Education Settings

- Knowledge of collaborative consultation procedures and theory; and how to consult collaboratively with families and other professionals
- Knowledge of how to design programs that use the environment or "the system" to support consultee behavior change; experience and success in working in teams

Procedures and Components in the Education Code Related to Positive Programming and Restrictions on Use of Aversives

- Knowledge of what constitutes a legally acceptable functional analysis assessment and positive behavioral intervention plan
- The role of the BICM in education settings
- The legal procedural requirements and limits on the use of emergency procedures
- Experience in writing and implementing positive, meaningful educational programs for individuals with disabilities

Knowledge Base and Competencies Needed in Members of the Behavioral Intervention Planning Team

The Hughes Bill regulations define a BICM as a person "who has been trained in behavior analysis with an emphasis on positive behavioral interventions" [§3001(e)]. According to the regulations, this role "may be performed by any existing staff member . . . including, but not limited to, a teacher, resource specialist, school psychologist, or program specialist" [§3001(e)]. Each SELPA is responsible for defining "the qualifications and training" required to be a BICM, and each SELPA must delineate those qualifications in its local plan. The specifics in the regulations indicate that the "qualifications and training" for a BICM "shall include training in behavior analysis with an emphasis on positive behavioral interventions." [§3052(j)(2)(A)]. The regulations further require each SELPA to spell out in its local plan "the qualifications and training of personnel who will participate in the implementation of the behavioral intervention plans; which shall include training in positive behavioral interventions" and "special training that will be required for the use of emergency behavioral interventions. . . ." [§3052(j)(2)(B and C)]. Each SELPA will determine which of its personnel meets this criteria.

An IEP team or behavioral intervention planning team capitalizes on the experience and expertise of all its members, including the designated case manager described above. The student's parents, special education teacher, aides, the regular education teacher, the school psychologist, the program specialist, and other interested credentialed staff all have an integral part in the planning and intervention process.

Behavior aides under direct supervision of the behavioral plan implementer (typically a teacher, job site coach, or related professional staff) will have the following knowledge and skills:

- Knowledge of introductory child development
- Training in positive behavioral interventions
- Understanding of individual differences and environmental effects on behavior
- Knowledge of and ability to apply acceptable emergency procedures according to direction, law, and SELPA policy and positive behavioral interventions
- Ability to relate positively to children

Credentialed staff members preparing for implementer level (e.g., regular education teachers or other credentialed staff members) will have the following knowledge and skills:

- Knowledge of child development
- Knowledge of individual differences; impact of medical, emotional, and psychosocial factors on behavior; and various teaching techniques to meet these differences

- Understanding of which emergency procedures are allowed by law
- All the knowledge and skills described for behavior aides

Credentialed staff members transitioning to implementer level (e.g., special education teachers, school psychologists, program specialists, or other interested credentialed staff members) will have the following knowledge and skills:

- Ability to define key concepts and components of behavioral intervention regulations
- Ability to give examples of good practice to each step in developing and implementing a behavioral intervention plan
- Ability to use key concepts to discuss student behavior
- Ability to demonstrate mastery of SELPA-approved emergency behavioral interventions
- All the knowledge and skills described above for other team members

Competent behavioral intervention plan implementers (e.g., special educators or other interested credentialed staff members) will have the following knowledge and skills:

- Completion of supervised experience in positive behavioral interventions with students with disabilities who exhibit maladaptive behaviors
- Ability to collaborate with all IEP team members in positive behavior plan development and implementation
- All the knowledge and skills described above for other team members

In contrast, fully competent BICMs will have all the above-mentioned knowledge and skills plus those outlined below. Recently trained school psychologists, as well as mentor teachers credentialed to teach students with serious emotional disturbances and severe disabilities may have expertise at this level:

- Experience in consulting with behavior plan implementers
- Experience in conducting and supervising functional assessments
- Experience in collaboratively developing positive behavior plans
- Experience in supervising behavioral plan implementers, including the use of emergency procedures
- Ability to use consulting skills to ensure implementation and maintenance of intervention plans
- Ability to provide ongoing assistance to school staff in understanding behavior and procedures

Consultation Skills

The BICM, or other specially-trained professionals, is in the unique position of being able to effect positive change for the student through communicating information, providing support, and providing reinforcement for the implementer. Skillful communication is therefore a key to the effectiveness of positive change for the student. To promote change through consultation, the behavioral intervention team must know how to collaborate with the consultee so that the program is designed jointly. To maximize the team's motivation to follow through on the plan, the BICM must establish in the team members a sense of ownership in the plan.

Because much of the BICM's role is assisting in the development of behavioral intervention plans in a group setting, such as in an IEP team meeting, the ability to collaboratively problem-solve is essential. Understanding what facilitates consensus and how to use group processing skills is an integral part of the consultant role.

Much of the case manager's role involves supervising the gathering of information on environment(s) and analyzing the environment's suitability for the referred individual. The consultee or implementer may feel uncomfortable in this process if this analysis suggests that the consultee, often the person who is organizing the environment, is somehow performing his or her tasks in a faulty manner. It is therefore essential that a collaborative and supportive consultant/consultee relationship be formed and supported by the ongoing interactions initiated by the BICM.

By focusing on the relationship between the individual with the problem behavior and his or her environment, the case manager is able to shift attention to what environmental feature needs to be changed to produce positive changes in the individual.

This focus shifts attention away from inappropriate blaming of the person who designed or maintains the environment for not having provided an appropriate setting, and on to collaborating on how to jointly achieve the desired outcome. Improving the quality of life and available opportunities of the student with the serious behavior problem is the primary focus of the consultation process; this fact should be reiterated frequently.

There is a body of knowledge on the science of behavioral consulting. It involves skillful ways of conferring with the significant people in the student's life regarding the effects of their behavior and the environment on the student. The BICM will need to implement these skills while conducting the functional assessment, preparing the IEP, implementing the plan, and finally ensuring that the student maintains and generalizes the positive behavior change. This brief discussion of consulting skills is provided as an overview.

The case manager may find some behavior problems beyond his or her individual skills or experience. In this case, although emergency short-term assistance may be required, the BICM must consider all available methods of enlisting additional assistance and support. This is necessary if a thorough and ethical functional assessment and intervention plan are to be developed.

It will be important to understand not only the consultation skills required of the case manager for use in the student's different life settings, but also the consultation skills necessary to work with outside medical (or other discipline) service providers.

The act of consulting will take the most time of any of the activities involved in plan development, from the gathering of information through the implementation phase. The consultant, therefore, must fully understand and prepare for the time plan development will take; otherwise, the consultant will encounter frustration and failure. Planning for enough time will be essential for the successful outcome of the intervention plan. The initial time spent will offer many rewards. When the intervention is successful, the teacher will want to experience these same benefits with other students. The consulting model provides for generalization of teacher skills to be used successfully with other students. It cannot be emphasized enough that the time spent in this activity will have a significant bearing on the success of the intervention plan.

Sample Consultation Skills

Establish rapport and a professional relationship with the consultee. This skill is foundational, crucial, and time consuming. After all, this is the person whose motivation to follow through with the plan will most often determine its success. It permeates all consulting and collaboration activities. Spend time with the teacher or other implementer to validate the person and his or her concerns, allowing the person to feel understood. Don't play the "expert" by using technical words. When appropriate, use the consultee's terminology as much as possible.

Answer frequent questions and concerns expressed by the consultee. Validate the implementer. Don't respond defensively to questions and concerns. Don't jump right in to finding solutions. Communicate acceptance and support. Provide a comfortable, collaborative, and reinforcing environment for an exchange of information.

Understand the behavior management skills of the implementer, and build on these existing skills when designing a program. Don't assume that the implementer can start by implementing the "ideal" or "best" program for the student. Recognize that the BICM may need to specifically model and teach some of the suggested program components. Build from the existing program whenever possible, because it will require less disruption to the teacher's programming and will be seen by the consultee as easier to accomplish.

Enhance the consultee's skills gradually. Accomplish program implementation in whatever steps are necessary.

Contact the consultees frequently. Develop a way of providing support that includes reinforcement from the consultee's significant others, such as principal, program specialists, other teachers, district office personnel, parent support groups, and so forth.

Allow for greater consultee independence gradually as program effectiveness becomes obvious to the consultee and as the significant others provide more reinforcement. This promotes greater consultee independence (empowerment) and long-term program maintenance.

Assist in generalizing the consultee's use of the knowledge and skills to other students.

FIGURE 12.

CONSULTATION DO'S AND DON'TS

During interviews with significant others, the BICM must collaborate with others to operationalize behavior, identify record-keeping needs, find out what function the behavior(s) are serving, and develop a collaborative relationship. Figure 12 provides additional guidance for BICMs to remember throughout the ongoing dialogues.

Do Say	Do Not Say
Ask for clarification in nonthreatening manner. "I'm confused. I can't quite picture what the behavior looks like. Can you help me with a few examples?"	"Saying he's lazy is not operational. Tell me what lazy looks like in operational terms."
Communicate understanding and be goal oriented. "I can't believe you've dealt with this so long. I can only try to understand how frustrated you must feel. Just hearing about it makes me frustrated, and I haven't even experienced it yet. Can we explore what has been happening? Then we can try to come up with some ways to understand what is going on."	"Can't you see that you aren't giving him any positive attention? He wants attention, so he sure knows how to press your buttons and get what he wants. Just start praising him for when he's doing his work. I don't understand how you let this get so bad."
Collaborate. It's a team effort. "I have some ideas on the fastest and easiest ways to collect the information on how many times Paula is and is not hitting the other children at recess. Since you are the one who will be doing this additional work, please let me know if this would work for you."	"You will be charting Paula's hitting and not hitting behavior. These are the charts you have to fill out every day, all day. I will pick them up at the end of the week. Just put them in my box all filled out."

Chapter 8

Prevention as a Best Practice

This chapter consists of three parts intended to be free-standing rather than interwoven. Each addresses the issue of prevention from a different perspective and proposes strategies than can be used with classes or smaller groups of students before behavioral intervention plans become necessary.

These three areas are as follows:

"Skills Training Programs to Reduce Aggressive Behavior," discusses using groups to teach decision-making and social skills. Although skills training is highlighted, practitioners using other approaches will find ideas and research on the reviewed models applicable to their own process of organizing groups and enhancing outcomes.

"Programming for Students with Severe Developmental Disabilities," discusses promoting positive behavior by adopting curriculum and teaching strategies that are meaningful, appropriate, and accessible to the student. Strategies, length, and difficulty levels of tasks are matched to the student's learning characteristics; expectations are clear, and schedules are predictable, while tasks are varied. Although the examples presented involve students with severe disabilities, the principles apply or are adaptable to all students.

"Classroom Guidelines," suggests self-study guidelines a teacher can use to evaluate the support for positive behavior present within his or her classroom. The guidelines include those associated with building relationships, recognizing unintentional messages, encouraging self-expression, and creating an atmosphere responsive to the students.

Skills Training Programs to Reduce Aggressive Behavior[1]

In other portions of this manual, measures applicable to students whose disabilities severely affect communication and conceptualization have been discussed. This section addresses group intervention with students having more volitional control over their behavior, greater capacity for verbal communication, and an understanding of cause-and-effect relationships at an intuitive level of reasoning or higher, approximating developmental levels of 4 years or above.

Group interventions to prevent or remediate severe behavior problems are appealing because of the economy of working with several students at once. Group work also offers needed opportunities to develop and practice social skills for students who are in programs that minimize interaction.[2]

The goal of this section is to assist practitioners in selecting effective group skills training programs and to point out some of the pitfalls of using group interventions. The focus will be limited to skills training models because of space constraints and for reasons discussed below. The information provided is supported by research and includes suggestions for assessing which students are likely to benefit from skills training, criteria by which to evaluate programs, and information on resources for further study and program materials.

What are the characteristics of the skills training model?

Two types of skills training were featured in the research reviewed. The interpersonal cognitive problem solving (ICPS) model focuses on teaching reasoning processes that support prosocial behavior, such as thinking of alternatives, anticipating consequences, means-end planning, and taking the perspective of others. The social skills training model emphasizes direct instruction in specific behaviors and behavioral constellations, such as giving eye contact in conversations, complimenting, joining a group, and saying "no" to peer pressure. Because of the complementary features of the two models and their blending in various programs, they will generally be discussed together as "the skills training model."

In contrast with psychoanalytic, humanistic, and other models that assume latent, unused abilities, the skills training model is based on the premise that aggression and other behaviors associated with poor social functioning commonly reflect deficits in specific, teachable skills.

Why is the skills training model selected for discussion?

Although one cannot assume that skill deficiency always underlies severe and persistent behavior problems, the skills training model is highlighted for the following reasons:

- Over the last 20 years, a substantial body of research has supported the hypothesis that social and cognitive skill deficiencies are characteristically found in aggressive and socially withdrawn children.

- Research has identified variables that need to be addressed in refining skills training. Effective programs are available: Shure & Spivack (1980) report results of their own study, while Pellegrini & Urbain (1985) and Goldstein et al. (1987, pp. 22-34) report results of research literature reviews.

- The educational/behavioral emphasis appeals to educators and makes use of and enhances their teaching and classroom management skills.

- Skills training is compatible with the goals of the Hughes Bill. It is nonpunitive in nature and oriented toward preventing and reducing the maladaptive behaviors designated as "serious behavior problems" by the regulations [Title 5, California Code of Regulations, §3001(y)]. The competencies in functional assessment and behavior management planning needed by the behavioral intervention case manager (BICM) are among those supporting successful use of the skills training models.

What are the instructional components of skills training?

Skills training grew out of the work of social learning theorists. Training generally includes verbal instruction in the skills being taught, modeling, rehearsal (through guided practice and role-playing or through verbal recitation or report), and feedback on performance of the skill from the trainer, peers, or self-monitoring. Research has demonstrated the importance of including procedures for transfer of skills to real life and for maintenance, areas of weakness in many programs.

For whom is skills training appropriate?

Skills training has been used with people of all ages, from preschool children through adults. Goals have included prevention or remediation of aggressive or antisocial behavior and improvement in the quality of social interactions of individuals who are shy and withdrawn, socially rejected or neglected, or verbally or physically aggressive. The level of language and cognitive abilities required varies with the program. Among the models reviewed, Shure & Spivack's (1980, 1982) ICPS model addressed the youngest children (4- and 5-year-olds). It involved teaching verbal concepts, such as "different," "not," "because," and "might," and problem-solving skills, such as thinking of alternative solutions to problems, and conceptualizing consequences of actions. Children participating in this type of training would need at least the intuitive understanding of the cause and effect characteristic of Piaget's second stage of preoperational thinking, usually developing in children 4 -7 years of age.

What types of skill deficits are associated with maladaptive social behavior?

In reviewing literature on social skills training with children, Ladd & Mize (1983) found three types of deficits described:

- Lack of knowledge of appropriate social behavior or presence of concepts atypical for peer culture. This includes understanding appropriate goals for social interaction (e.g., winning at all costs versus having fun), knowing strategies for reaching social goals (e.g., knowing how to join a group), and understanding the contexts in which specific strategies can be appropriately used.

- Lack of behavioral skills. Some individuals are able to discuss appropriate behavior but do not apply the skills, perhaps because of a lack of practice or confidence.

- Deficiency in self-feedback. This includes monitoring one's own behavior, picking up cues from others on its effect, and making accurate attributions and inferences about causes of successful or unsuccessful interactions.

Using an expanded information processing model proposed by Dodge et al. (1986), Akhtar & Bradley (1991) reviewed research findings of the last decade on social/cognitive problems of verbally and/or physically aggressive children. In spite of methodological weaknesses in the studies reviewed, Akhtar & Bradley found enough convergence of results to conclude that social reasoning is "an important problem area for aggressive children" and that there were individual differences in the extent to which aggressive children have difficulty with the following skills:

- Encoding. Aggressive children take note of fewer relevant social cues and selectively attend to or recall hostile or aggressive cues.

- Interpretation. Aggressive children tend to attribute hostile intentions to their peers, especially in ambiguous situations.

- Response search and decision. Aggressive children differ from adjusted peers along several dimensions in this area. They tend to generate fewer and lower quality solutions when deciding on a desired goal or social outcome, searching for alternative responses within their behavioral repertoires and selecting a response appropriate to achieving their goal. They are less aware of the individual steps and potential obstacles to be overcome when problem solving. The results of one study cited (Richard & Dodge, 1982) suggest that verbal expressive skills may be a factor in this finding: although they generated fewer solutions, boys with aggressive behavior patterns were able to evaluate as well as popular boys the effectiveness of possible solutions presented to them. Decisions are also affected by behavioral goals, which are likely to differ in the two populations. Some children regard aggression as a means of achieving their ends, avoiding appearing inadequate, and/or increasing self-esteem.

- Enactment. Aggressive children demonstrate a wide variety of social incompetencies. Social approach and response to peer provocation were found to be two particularly difficult areas. Difficulty joining a group of peers seems to be associated with failing to adopt the group's frame of reference. Unpopular boys tend to talk about themselves or make irrelevant comments, possibly reflecting reduced awareness of social cues or problems with taking the perspective of others.

- Evaluation of environmental response. Only two studies were found that evaluated aggressive children's ability to monitor or evaluate their own behavior. The authors concluded that although this appears to be a problem area, evidence was scant. Difficulty imagining the viewpoint of others may be a factor.

How may a student's training needs be assessed?

Among the obstacles in determining treatment effects has been the tendency for researchers to use groups selected on the basis of observed behavior without establishing whether trainees actually lack the skills (Akhtar & Bradley, 1991). Some aggressive students are not only accepted but admired by peers; these students are probably not lacking in social skills, although their goals and values may conflict with school expectations. In addition to observations from school staff, peer ratings of how much they enjoy the companionship of each classmate contributes to understanding a student's social status.

When problem behaviors reflect skill deficiencies, the practitioner must determine what combination of skills should be included in the training. Keeping in mind the types of skill deficits summarized by Ladd & Mize (1983) and by Akhtar & Bradley (1991), student social competencies may be identified through direct observation of peer interactions in natural settings and by interviews with teachers, counselors, and parents. Differences between settings in terms of expectations and sources of reinforcement for aggression may also become apparent through observations and interviews.

Formal rating scales based on skill training models and providing normative data are also available, among them the Matson Evaluation of Social Skills with Youngsters (MESSY) (Matson, Rotatori & Helsel, 1983) and the Social Skills Rating System (SSRS) (Gresham & Elliott, 1990). The rating scales may direct attention to student strengths as well as deficit areas. When raters are asked to estimate frequency of appropriate behaviors, the scales can also assist in discriminating whether specific appropriate behaviors are in the student's repertoire but are underused or are lacking. The SSRS has parallel forms for teachers, parents, and students.

Interviews with potential group members can reveal the presence and strength of belief systems, values, and sources of gratification that maintain problem behaviors and that need to be addressed if skills training is to transfer to real-life settings. A "hassle log,"[3] in which the students record where and with whom conflicts arise and the perceived antecedents of conflicts arising within a time frame, further aids in defining the parameters of target behaviors.

Standardized role-playing tests have been used to evaluate social skills but are inconsistent in correlating with other measures of social acceptance or social skill use (Matson, Rotatori & Helsel, 1983).

Assessment by a language/speech specialist can be used to evaluate a student's ability to recognize problem situations and to verbalize solutions, pragmatic language skills, and language processing abilities affecting behavior and group participation.

What are the components of effective skills training programs?

Review of research results indicates that the following conditions are important for effective skills training:

- The problem behaviors of participating students are attributable to skill deficits in knowledge, enactment, and/or self-feedback. Program components are selected based on analysis of student training needs.

- Programs selected are appropriate for the developmental and language levels of the students.

- Programs are not narrowly focused on a small band of skills. Broad constellations of behavior are addressed rather than microskills or one or two deficit areas.

- Cognitive processes supporting independent and flexible application of skills are taught.

- Issues of motivation, beliefs about the role of aggression in maintaining status or achieving goals, values, and reinforcement of problem behaviors are addressed.

- Activities that promote transfer of skills across settings are an integral part of the program.

- Ladd & Mize (1983) allude to the importance of instructor characteristics, citing studies that suggest the importance of warmth, enthusiasm, and directiveness in working effectively with children. Goldstein et al. (1987) discuss the need to match delinquent youth with the characteristics of the trainers. Among others, they cite Agee (1979), who contrasted expressive and instrumental characteristics in delinquent adolescents and in staff. Expressive youth were described as "overtly vulnerable, hurting, and dependent." Instrumental adolescents were "defended against their emotions, independent, and nontrusting." Agee's research supported matching expressive youth with interveners who were open with their feelings and comfortable working with the feelings of others, and pairing instrumental youth with interveners who were oriented toward behavior rather than working with feelings.

Some programs may be useful but incomplete. Practitioners may need to draw from more than one program or to devise supplementary strategies. This is especially true in terms of transfer and maintenance of skills, which are often insufficiently addressed. Other programs may be too short term and need supplementary lessons for development and consolidation of new behavior patterns.

Factors that promote transfer and maintenance of skills include the following:

- **Working closely with teachers.** Teachers can prompt and reinforce emerging skills and use conflicts arising during the school day for role-playing alternative responses. Teachers may be group trainers or co-trainers when arrangements can be made for students who do not need skills training or whose behavior would be too disruptive to the group process.

- **Working closely with parents and other caregivers.** When parents are trained to prompt and reinforce appropriate behavior or are at least kept informed of the skills being taught, they can encourage transfer of skills to the home environment.

- **Using realistic situations,** preferably those drawn from life experiences and proposed by the students. The "hassle log" (Goldstein et al., 1987) or similar instruments and student, teacher, and parent reports are good sources of suggestions for thinking of alternative solutions and role-playing.

- Assigning use of specific skills for "homework," with discussion of outcomes, self-rating, and rehearsal of any needed changes.

- Using student models. Students who are developing proficiency can practice their skills in scripted role-play for beginning groups, promoting buy-in while serving as models for beginning trainees.

- Inoculating against failure. Students need preparation for unsuccessful interactions. This can include training in evaluating responses to their behavior and making judgments about reasons for success or failure. Pellegrini & Urbain (1985) discuss difficulty in gaining peer acceptance because of rigid friendship networks and negative expectations based on previous behavior patterns as possible obstacles. Modification of peer expectations and behavior may be needed.

PROGRAMMING GUIDELINES FOR STUDENTS WITH SEVERE DEVELOPMENTAL DISABILITIES[3]

The following guidelines are intended to help a teacher or parent promote and/or identify effective educational programming for students with severe developmental disabilities. They are based on three general assumptions concerning effective educational programming: a curriculum must be accessible to the student to ensure comprehension; it must be meaningful so as to motivate the student to participate in the educational process; and it must target skills that are appropriate to the student's educational needs. The challenge for educators who attempt to infuse their curricula with these qualities lies not only in the logistical limitations of time and resources, but also in the understanding of the educational implications of the cognitive, perceptual, and emotional needs of students with severe developmental disabilities. By gathering information from current research on the educational implications of severe developmental disabilities and combining it with current educational practices for students with severe handicaps, we have attempted to create programming that is logistically practical, effective, and designed to match the learning style and educational needs of these students. The programming that resulted was developed over a 3-year period at the Diagnostic Center in Los Angeles. The outcomes for students involved in this programming have been consistently and dramatically positive.

Guidelines for Establishing Meaningfulness

A meaningful educational program is one that fosters and promotes the student's socially acceptable control over his environment and encourages expansion of the student's interests and options for choice making.

1. Choice making should be a targeted skill, and opportunities should be provided within activities and the daily schedule to allow the student to exercise acceptable control within programming.

Allow the student to control one or more factors in task selection or participation. Possible opportunities for choice making and control would include, but are not limited to, the following: duration of task, quantity of work, materials used, reinforcers earned, or type of task. Many students with severe developmental disabilities have limited experience in making choices. Choice making will need to be promoted and supported across all activities and environments if the student is to become an active choice-making individual. Resistance to adult-directed work will decrease as the student gains an awareness of choice making as a means of appropriate environmental control.

2. **The student's attempts at communication should be examined for intent rather than for form.**

The student's language or communication may be adequate in routine situations when the student is comfortable and secure and the language/communication demands are minimal. In settings where the student does not have a routine, where there is sudden change or the language/communicative demands are beyond his capability, the student may not use appropriate communicative forms. The verbal student may resort to gestures, single words, mumbling or turning away under stressful circumstances. The nonverbal student may resort to crying, vocalizing, or screaming when frustrated. Both verbal and nonverbal students are likely to communicate physically (e.g., throw items, hit others, hide, or run away) when they are overstimulated or frustrated. These stress-induced behaviors are communicative in intent but disruptive in form. Interventions for these behaviors should be based primarily on teaching appropriate communicative form to express the communicative intent. Focusing solely on eliminating the disruptive behavior will not address the student's critical need for an acceptable avenue for protest or participation in decision making.

3. **The student's educational activities should be infused with, or based on, the student's interests and preferences.**

Assess the student's interests and preferences through observation, parent report, and direct questioning. The student will attend to and involve himself most appropriately and independently with activities and materials that are directed to his interests and preferences (e.g., snack preparation or cooking, reading and writing on topics of interest, free time play). Actively seek and develop varied appropriate interests for the student within the classroom curriculum, while continuing to provide the student with activities that reflect his interests and preferences whenever possible.

4. **The rapport between staff and the student should be promoted actively.**

For a student with severe developmental disabilities, tantrums may be an indication of anxiety and stress. Stressors for the student can be things as simple and varied as sitting in a group, having to take turns, being required to sit without opportunity for movement, being required to do repetitive tasks, being accidentally touched by another student, being physically prompted to engage in a task/activity, having to stop a preferred activity and begin another activity, or being asked to eat a food item that he or she does not like. At such times, if one attempts to remove the student from a group, to punish or chastise him, or to insist that he continue to participate in a stressful activity, it will only create more stress for the student. Reduce stress when possible, by de-emphasizing aspects of the task/activity that are stressful for him, by teaching and allowing options for escape and calming down, and by giving control, such as choice about interests and preferences. Rapport can be established with the student most quickly by helping him cope with stress through the restructuring of tasks, providing structured choice/negotiations, teaching relaxation techniques, and/or reassuring and comforting the student when he or she is stressed. When the student is comfortable with staff members and knows that they will help him or her to cope rather than punish him or her for failing to cope, the student will become more tolerant of change, new activities, adult direction and instruction. For example, a verbal student who has difficulty sitting and participating in a group activity can be taught to use a scripted phrase, such as "I need to lie down," when he is feeling stressed. A nonverbal student can be taught to use a communication card expressing the same message. Typically, the student might scream or hit another student when stressed in a group setting. Teach the student at those times to use the scripted communication and then allow him to take a break. If the group activities are accessible to him and of interest, this chance to leave the group will result in a calmer, more tolerant student who will willingly return to the group after calming down.

Guidelines for Determining Appropriateness

One of a student's major educational needs is independence in caring for and doing for himself or herself. Greater independence will help to reduce the student's frustration through greater control over his or her environment and self.

1. The student's life skills should be inventoried and targeted for direct and incidental teaching based on current and future work, play, and living environments.

Life skills should be inventoried in the domestic, community, vocational, and leisure domains in all meaningful environments through parent interviews and observations. Those skills that the student lacks and that the student needs to function more independently across all meaningful current and future environments should be targeted for teaching based on usefulness, possibility of acquisition, interest of student, and the immediacy of the student's need for the skill. Skills should be taught in natural environments when possible to maximize functionality of the skill taught.

2. The student's social skills should be targeted for direct and incidental teaching across all environments.

The student should be taught social skills within a natural context as the need arises. Group activities with the teacher as the facilitator can be structured to build positive social interactions with other students. Teach appropriate social language/communication, tolerance for proximity of others, and themes and strategies for getting attention from others and for getting needs met. Game, recess, snack, or group discussion times are excellent times to teach appropriate behavior for social interactions. Making some consequences, such as receiving desired items, contingent on appropriate social interaction is an excellent way to teach effective social behavior. For example, teaching the student to wait and not grab when receiving an item from another person or a turn in a game would be educationally appropriate. The student should be motivated to participate in these activities and not be unduly stressed by these contingencies if targeted goals are to be achieved. All consequences should be positive in nature, and the emphasis of teaching should be placed on the acquisition of socially appropriate skills.

Appropriate role models for a wide range of socially and academically appropriate school behaviors should be available within the student's educational environment. Placement in the least restrictive environment facilitates social growth because of the opportunity for interactions with peers who are not disabled. Therefore, heterogeneous groups within classrooms and schools provide benefits to students with disabilities and provide a diverse community in which *all* students can learn. When an IEP team has recommended a restrictive environment, alternative methods to expose the student to appropriate models should still be explored.

3. **The student's academic skills should be targeted and taught based on the student's age, interests, and abilities.**

In the early elementary years (kindergarten through grade 3), communication, play, and motor skills development through individualized, experiential, and exploratory learning should be the foundation for curriculum development. The acquisition of age-appropriate academic skills should be addressed through high-interest activities. Social skills and age-appropriate life skills should be taught across all pertinent school environments, such as the playground, the cafeteria, and the auditorium.

In the middle elementary years (grades 4-6), the curricular emphasis will be determined as much by the student's demonstrated academic skill and interests as by the student's need for functional skills. Academic capability, if present, should now be infused into high-interest functional activities. If academic capability has not been demonstrated at this point, emphasis should be divided between the continued development of social and communication skills and the development of a wider range of functional skills and leisure interests. Skill training should be moved from the smaller community of the classroom to the larger community of the town, neighborhood, or home in which the skills are normally used. Skills should be practiced across multiple settings to help promote generalization.

In the junior high and high school years (grades 7-12), curricular emphasis should be moved increasingly to the development of vocational, community, and travel skills, practiced in actual community and vocational settings. Other skills (i.e., communication, social, domestic, academic, and leisure) should be infused as needed into functional activities to ensure that the student will be as independent as possible across all potentially meaningful current and future work and living environments.

4. **The student's communication skills should be targeted for direct and incidental teaching in all environments.**

The verbal student may need to be taught the precise language that he or she will need in any given situation. When asked what is wrong, the student may not be able to respond without help. Let the student know that you are willing to listen and to help him or her tell you what the problem is. The student may need to be taught language at specific times that can be used to help him or her cope with stress, such as "I need a break," when overstimulated or tired, or "I'm sick" when not feeling well. Vocabulary and phrase development through drill or repeated out-of-context modeling of language/communicative forms will not produce spontaneous, generalized communication. The nonverbal student will need to be taught the most effective communicative behaviors. Pointing, gesturing, signing, using eyegaze, or using a photo or a written message at the appropriate time all have value, and the student should not be limited to one mode of communication for all purposes and settings. Communication for all students should be taught within a meaningful context by providing the student with the appropriate communicative content and form as he or she attempts to initiate communication. The student's communicative efforts will be gradually shaped through natural contingencies to conform with socially acceptable means for getting one's needs met.

Guidelines to Expanding Accessibility

Students with severe developmental disabilities often have unique and uneven cognitive characteristics. As a result, they frequently learn in an idiosyncratic, unpredictable, and nonfunctional manner. The teacher needs to take each student's characteristics into account when determining teaching strategies and approaches. The following guidelines may be helpful in designing environments that allow these students greater access to learning activities.

1. **Staff members should gain the student's attention and use language that is comprehensible to the student when giving instruction.**

   A student with severe developmental disabilities attends best to verbal instruction when the language used is at his receptive comprehension level and he is visually focused on the speaker. Standing directly in front of the student, gaining the student's attention by touching or calling his name before giving verbal instruction, delivering the instruction at the student's eye level by bending or stooping, and pairing verbal input with gestures and concrete referents will do much to ensure comprehension of verbal instruction.

2. **Individualized teaching strategies, adaptations, and accommodations should be consistently used within and across activities/tasks and settings.**

   No two students will exhibit the same physical, emotional, or cognitive characteristics. As a result, strategies for intervention will vary from student to student. The following information lists potential areas of concern and interventions that have been effective when needed:

   Visual and concrete cues may be needed by the student to attend to and process salient instructional information:

   - The use of a photo communication book containing pictures of the student involved in actual activities will prove very useful in communicating transitions to him or her and as a tool to redirect the student to a task or activity when he or she is distracted.

   - Similarly, play areas and work areas may need to be clearly demarcated for the student. Boundaries can be marked by shelves, masking tape, carpets, or tables so that the student is more visually aware of the intent of each transition around the classroom.

   - Clear and concrete structure should be built into tasks when the student is asked to work independently. Arranging materials so that the student is aware of behavioral expectations, task sequence, closure, and duration may frequently be necessary to ensure that he or she is able to focus on the materials and activity without becoming disinterested, disruptive, and/or demanding. The use of written or picture sequences/directions can be used to show the student the order of events within an activity, as in the following:

     1. *Write your name.*
     2. *Do ten items.*
     3. *Put away your work.*

   Short, simple sentences will suffice. Pictures or concrete items may be needed to enhance this communication.

The rigidity of thought sometimes displayed by the student lends itself well to the use of rule teaching to promote appropriate classroom behaviors. Rules should be stated as positive, very concrete, and incompatible behaviors, such as "hands in lap," rather than "no flapping." They should be taught in a very concrete fashion and within the context to which they apply. For example, before the student begins his or her lesson/activity, the teacher would show the student a picture of himself or herself or another student working quietly and would state, "The rule is you must work quietly!" The student would then be asked to repeat the rule. He or she would be reinforced frequently for following that rule. Initially, only one to two rules should be taught at a time. Allow the student to internalize each rule in turn before others are taught contingently. Remind the student of the rule when he or she does not follow it, but do not punish or criticize the student for disobeying the rule. Negative consequences can destroy gains. Initially, all work should be judged by the student's ability to work independently within rule guidelines. The quality or quantity of the work will not be the issue. As the student acquires rule-driven classroom behavior and exhibits an interest in the work, quality and quantity can be re-evaluated. Rehearsal of appropriate rules before the student begins activities that you know may be challenging for him or her will promote awareness of and promote opportunities for reinforcement of rule-driven behavior. The best behaviors for rule teaching are those that have global impact across settings and activities. Such behaviors are called pivotal behaviors. The acquisition of a pivotal behavior facilitates many other behaviors. For example, "Good listening" is a rule that teaches a pivotal behavior. Listening is a skill that facilitates all areas of instruction. Pivotal behaviors include such things as waiting, turn-taking, and listening.

The student may organize information in a stimulus bound and holistic manner. This cognitive style results in difficulty in generalizing skills and using information or skills flexibly. Provide opportunities to learn and use skills across multiple environments so that the student can acquire flexible use of those skills. For example, if a student is learning to wash hands after using the bathroom, he or she will need to be taught to wash hands in a number of different bathrooms, using a number of different sinks and soap dispensers before he or she will really "know how" to wash hands. The skill will not generalize to other settings just because the student has learned to do it well in one particular setting. The initial teaching should, of course, be taught in one particular bathroom, and the task may need to be task-analyzed and clearly sequenced for the student to learn the task even in one setting. Additionally, teach groups of contextually related skills as a sequential whole, rather than as isolated, out-of-context events. For example, if the goal is to teach the student to set the table, do the training at a regular meal time, at the actual table to be used, and teach other related skills at the same time in their natural sequence. The sequence of skills needed for table setting might include clearing off the table, getting the necessary items for each table setting, setting the table, washing hands, preparing food items, eating appropriately, clearing the table, and washing the dishes. Social and communication skills can be targeted and addressed as needed and appropriate within this chain of contextually, temporally, and functionally related activities.

Instructional cues should be presented in as visual and salient a manner as possible. The use of verbal cues when teaching a sequenced task may result in prompt dependency. The student may learn the task by incorporating the verbal prompts into the chain of task steps. As a result, the student will not be able to do the task unless you perform your "verbal prompts." Task training should rely as much as possible on visual or gestural, within-task prompts with elimination or minimalization of verbal cues. Within-task prompts are often natural prompts or can be faded readily to natural prompts. A natural prompt is a consequence that is a part of the actual behavior chain being taught. For example, when washing hands, the natural prompt for wetting one's hands is the sight of the water pouring from the spigot into the sink. Communication between the student and the teacher is a natural and appropriate activity. One must be careful to distinguish the use of social language and verbal instructional cues. Social language should not be eliminated or minimalized unless it is distracting.

Structuring learning for the student may be difficult because of the student's disinterest in or resistance to direction from others. This "noncompliance," as it is often interpreted, can be mediated through the use of global chaining or incidental teaching strategies. Global chaining allows teaching to be relatively painless for students who do not like to be continuously prompted when learning new skills. Once a task has been task-analyzed and a baseline taken, active instruction is done only during the steps that are relatively easy for the student. All other steps are done for the student. In this way, the student is granted a large degree of independence and freedom from direct and intrusive instruction but still gets to experience the gestalt of the task. Over time, as the student begins to accept the teaching sessions and gets more comfortable with going through the steps of the task with the teacher, the next easiest steps of the task are taught. Eventually, those steps of the task that the student can be reasonably expected to learn can be taught. For example, when teaching dressing, if all steps of the task are very difficult except for getting the pants out of the dresser drawer, then begin instruction at that step. Instruction may consist of nothing more than teaching the student to place the pants on his bed in preparation for the actual dressing. Provide the student with noninstructional assistance with the rest of the task.

Incidental teaching is teaching done at the "teachable moment." Incidental teaching works best when the student is so motivated to perform that he or she will willingly seeks or accepts help. If the student is motivated and the teacher catches the student needing help, learning can proceed rather quickly. Incidental teaching opportunities occur most often in classrooms where activities are built around the interests and preferences of the students.

The "islands" of ability, relative strengths or isolated skills that the student may display, are potential tools for teaching other abilities. A student of eight who reads at the fourth-grade level but cannot independently sequence brushing his teeth can use a written sequence to promote independence. Similarly, this same student can be given written scripts to facilitate social or functional interactions when in the community or within group settings. These scripts can be cued at appropriate times and eventually generalized through their use across settings, people, and time.

The student may have such a dramatic resistance to change or transitioning that it is difficult to get him or her to stop one activity and move onto another. If the student resists a transition after you have communicated as clearly and effectively as possible by using comprehensible language paired with concrete or photo referents, attempt to use closure as a first intervention for prompting the transition. If it is possible to visually end the task (having the student put things away or finish the last item of an activity), do so. If that technique does not work, use one of the items being used by the student as a transition object to the next setting/activity. If that is not possible, engaging the student in an immediately available activity or action (e.g., getting a different toy, a quick tickle, some roughhousing, a drink of water or going for a walk) can serve as a powerful enough stimulus change to allow for an eventual successful transition to the next activity. As the student experiences and is taught the sequence of the activities that comprise his or her day, these transition issues will lessen. Consistent refusal to transition to a particular activity may indicate that the student finds that activity difficult and/or uninteresting. Intervention should then be geared to reducing stress within and/or increasing the motivation for that activity.

When all other strategies fail and a power struggle ensues, switching off (i.e, having another person step in to take over) may have an immediate effect in lessening the power struggle. Switching off may provide an opportunity for successfully redirecting the student to the next activity and should be viewed as a useful crisis strategy.

Shaping of appropriate behavior through incremental approximations may be an important educational strategy for working with the student. Small steps of change allow for frequent reinforcement. For example, a student who screams to gain attention will need many instances of seeing and being reinforced for engaging in appropriate attention-seeking behavior before he or she will stop using screaming to gain attention. To allow for frequent success, it will be necessary to gradually change the shape of the behavior to a more appropriate form of communication, such as seeking out staff and communicating via gestures, an augmentative mode, or appropriate language. It may take many months of gradually teaching the student to use the more appropriate communication. If one insists that all screaming must end before the student has acquired these new behaviors, there will be few opportunities for reinforcing the new behaviors. The screaming behavior will slowly be extinguished as the student is reinforced with attention for attempting to use a different behavior. As the student begins using the new communicative behavior, one can target the frequency, intensity, or volume of the screaming through natural reinforcement contingencies; that is, the student's needs, once they have been communicated appropriately, will be met only if the student stops or reduces the screaming. An ideal program would be to structure the environment, for short periods of the day, so that it is possible to anticipate the student's need for attention, model and prompt the appropriate behavior, if necessary, and immediately reinforce the behavior with the appropriate natural consequence.

Desensitization for new activities, people, or events can be done in the following manner:

1. Allow the student to watch others doing or experiencing the activity.
2. Judge from the student's reaction to the activity or by asking the student directly whether he or she is interested in being involved.
3. If the student says "no," seems fearful or uninterested, do not push. Let the student watch. Try again at another time.
4. If the student says "yes," ask him or her to join you in the activity.
5. Let the student choose to stay for as long or to do as much as he or she likes. Encourage more, but do not push.
6. If the student enjoys the activity, you will know it.

These steps can be modified to fit most situations. Direct contact, in a positive manner, will help the student to accept and adjust to new people and/or new foods. Encourage but do not force the student to be social with someone he or she does not know or to eat food that is new or that he or she does not want.

Desensitization for hypersensitivity to stimuli can be based on giving more control to the student. For example, a student who is afraid of vacuum cleaners can be given a script or pattern of behavior for coping with vacuum cleaners in his environments. A verbal script might involve asking the person running the vacuum cleaner or a staff member to turn off or put away the vacuum cleaner. A patterned behavior might involve having the student see that you are aware of his fear and allowing him to turn off and put away the vacuum cleaner himself. Continued experience with controlling the source of his fear will reduce the student's initial panic reaction, further his or her trust in those working with him, and eventually allow for negotiation when it is impossible to eliminate offensive stimuli as quickly as the student might like.

Repetitive, perseverative behaviors, sometimes referred to as self-stimulatory behavior, "habits," narrow interests, or "stims" may be the student's activity of choice. Self-stimulatory behavior must be judged for acceptableness within the context in which it occurs. Some forms of self-stimulatory behavior, such as fixations on specific toys, can be shaped into appropriate play behavior and within certain settings look quite appropriate. Other self-stimulatory behavior, such as hand flapping or noise making, is often judged inappropriate no matter what the setting. Socially unacceptable or disruptive self-stimulatory behaviors should be shaped or redirected through positive reinforcement into less stigmatizing behavior. For example, hand flapping can be better controlled through teaching "hands down" within specific settings. The student should learn that hand flapping can be done at certain times of the day or in certain settings, but that when he or she is in public it is necessary to put the hands down or to hold onto a high-interest object, such as a radio, to keep the hands occupied. Do not try to completely extinguish a self-stimulatory behavior across all environments. Frequently, attempts at complete eradication of such behaviors lead to increased frustration and/or the appearance of new self-stimulatory behaviors.

Time away from social contact may be a much more powerful reinforcer for the student than social attention from others. Time alone may serve to reduce stress and can be shaped into an appropriate coping mechanism by allowing the student to determine when he or she might need to take a break. Timeout as a means to control inappropriate behavior is sometimes ineffective because of the student's preference for time away from social contact.

Appropriate positioning for participation in an activity is always an issue for students with physical handicaps. When a task requires a specific limb or hand movement or head position for participation, it is important to provide the student with tools and/or positioning devices, such as specialized desks or chairs or supportive standers, that allow for those movements.

3. **The student should be actively taught his or her daily schedule through rehearsal of events both before and during transitions.**

The student may frequently experience anxiety around the issues of change and transition. Over time, he or she may adapt very well to consistent scheduling and routine. Eventually, the student may internalize most of the routines and become very resistive to change in that routine. Internalization of routine is a means of environmental control, and the student may become quite agitated and/or disruptive when he or she experiences unexpected change. One means for compensating for this problem is rehearsing and reviewing daily scheduling. At the start of the day, use pictures of the day's events/items for choice and/or concrete items that represent those events/items to go over the sequence of the classroom activities. Sequence and content should be the emphasis of these rehearsals. Awareness of the day's schedule can help to relieve anxiety about the day's events for the student, and it can be used to prepare the student for change on any given day. Coordinate the use of the schedule with other staff members working with the student so that information on the schedule will be accurate. Do not schedule and rehearse events that cannot be delivered reliably. The rehearsal and review of schedules allows the student greater awareness of routine and change, but this strategy will prove effective only if the schedules are followed reliably and consistently.

4. **The instructional settings and activities should not be perceptually, physically, or emotionally stressful.**

The student may exhibit hypersensitivity to environmental and emotional stimuli. Hypersensitivity can be addressed through desensitization and/or through the direct teaching of coping skills, but there are instances when the stimuli are hindering skill acquisition or simple participation. At such times, it is better to decrease the stressor and increase the motivation for participation in the particular activity. Lighting, sound, overcrowding, poor acoustics, too infrequent reinforcement, hunger, continuous physical prompting, medication, criticism, boredom, confusion, exhaustion, and punishment are all factors that may induce stress within activities. In addition, students who are physically handicapped may experience discomfort and stress because of improper physical handling, positioning, or too-infrequent changing of position.

CLASSROOM GUIDELINES

The Hughes Bill and Positive Behavioral Intervention regulations call for an integrated multidisciplinary team to evaluate students with problem behaviors and to develop a specific plan for remediation. The parents, teacher, BICM and other members of the IEP team all work in a coordinated effort. In the educational setting, it is the teacher (or other instructional support staff) who has most contact with the child and who ultimately makes the plan work successfully.

Working with the type of student whose behavior is covered by the Hughes Bill and implementing regulations is a challenging undertaking even during the best moments. When inappropriate, disruptive, or assaultive behavior erupts, it can seem impossible. The most efficient way to deal with behavior problems is to prevent them from happening. Creating an environment conducive to learning, that is flexible and well-planned enough to anticipate and prevent problem behaviors before they start is a major part of a teacher's job. The following outline offers some ideas and presents some questions to think about when developing a classroom environment aimed at encouraging positive behavior. The ideas are general and certainly are not all inclusive. They are primarily applicable to classrooms with verbal children but can be adapted to classrooms with children of all ages and developmental levels. This is simply a guideline written by teachers for teachers that the authors hope will be helpful in establishing or evaluating their programs.

1. Relevant Interesting Program?

From the students' standpoint, the program needs to be interesting, important, and useful. They need to see the reason for doing things.

2. Clear routines, expectations, and procedures?

This is especially important during the first 3 weeks of class. There are three steps in establishing clear routines, expectations, and procedures:

  a. Present routine to the class — talk through it slowly, and use visuals and prompts to support learners who need them.
  b. Rehearse - practice — demonstrate.
  c. Give lots of feedback — reward or practice again.

In planning for this aspect, there needs to be careful reflection. Anticipate problems and plan for them.

Teachers need to be aware of unintentional messages they send. For example, what does "The first one finished gets to play" convey to students?

3. Material logistics in place?

Are things set up to work best with the developmental needs of the students?
Is ample time allowed for practice?
Are materials interesting? (Ask the students.)
Is there variety? Is it challenging? Are materials changed frequently?
Materials should encourage use — Make sure they are sturdy and safe.
Children need to know how to use the materials.

4. Environment matched to learners' needs?

Check possession — Whose environment is it?
Is it too stimulating or not stimulating enough?
Is there variety? Are there quiet spaces for small groups?
How does environment feel to students?
Have students collect materials for art, science, and so forth.
Check room at different energy levels — How does it feel when the teacher is up, tired, hassled?
Consider the schedule as a part of the environment.
Check difficulty level — Are all activities teacher directed? Child directed? Or are both present?
When planning, check to see if activities are balanced — active and passive.

5. Is ongoing evaluation present?

Student evaluation of your teaching can give accurate feedback regarding pace, clarity, noise level, interest, material, equipment, choices, and control.
Evaluate yourself — Audiotape yourself frequently. With whom do you interact? Are your directions clear? Watch for hidden messages, (e.g., "You're bad," objects are more important than people, there is only one way do things).
Each day for 3 weeks write down your major problem, save your notes, and see if a pattern develops.

6. Is pupils' self-expression encouraged? To teacher and to each other?

Plan opportunities for conversation. Provide mail boxes for messages to each other.
Have bulletin boards for self-expression.
Allow time for journal writing with words or pictures.
Have weekly conference time with each student.
Schedule class meetings to talk about what's going on in the room.

7. Are relationships fostered?

Support and build relationships: child-child, child-teacher, child-environment.
Notice relationships and roles — Is the teacher's behavior locking kids into their roles?
Develop partnerships for students — a peer who can help them, fill them in when they have been out, remind them of rules.
Help students learn to care for each other.
Limit competition and comparison.
Provide time for steam-letting. Then put the lid back on with quiet activities.

8. Crisis response plan in place?

Think of all possible crises, both minor and major.
Think of a whole string of responses.
Plan ahead with other teachers to seek best response.
Instruct students how to respond when a crisis develops.
Practice crisis procedures with students.

Skills Training Programs to Reduce Aggressive Behavior:

[1]   For more information on books and programs, refer to Appendix P.

[2]   In visiting twenty-six programs in thirteen states, Knitzer, Steinberg & Fleisen (1990) found that classrooms serving severely emotionally disturbed students are typically so organized around controlling behavior that students are given little opportunity to develop or use the social skills that would allow them access to regular classes.

[3]   The "hassle log" was developed by Eva Feindler, professor and director of Clinical Psychology, Long Island University, C. W. Post Campus, Brookville, New York, and is described in Goldstein et al. (1987) and Goldstein (1988).

Programming for Students with Severe Developmental Disabilities:

[4]   Although these guidelines were written as a result of experience with individuals with severe disabilities, they are applicable to *all* students.

Chapter 9

Predisposing Conditions, Factors, and Influences

A s is apparent from a review of Figure 13, p. 130, behavior emerges from a confluence of biological and environmental contributors. These contributors vary in their significance for each person, and may include factors such as immediate triggering events, the impact of hormones released just before enactment, the effects of genetic attributes, and the influence of cultural expectations. Narrowly focusing on a single, immediate antecedent to explain behavior may leave the factors most responsible unidentified and interfere with developing effective interventions. A complete functional analysis requires analysis of antecedents that may require an in-depth inquiry to discover factors that support tenacious problem behaviors. To design appropriate behavior programs, the behavior intervention case manager (BICM) must understand the impact of various disabilities, developmental levels, and other variables, and accommodate those needs and characteristics.

This chapter provides useful information for understanding some of the biological, psychosocial, and developmental contributors that differentially affect behavior. The chapter offers approaches and accommodations to consider when these factors are found to be important, along with examples of students who have benefited when these various predisposing conditions were taken into account. It is composed of three parts: Part One, "Overview of Biological, Psychosocial, and Developmental Influences on Behavior;" Part Two, "Program Planning Implications of Some Conditions;" and Part Three, "Medical Intervention as a Component of a Multimodal Approach."

OVERVIEW OF BIOLOGICAL, PSYCHOSOCIAL, AND DEVELOPMENTAL INFLUENCES ON BEHAVIOR

Ecological assessment approaches are based on the premise that assaultive and self-injurious disturbances are not attributable to the individual's behavior alone, but always result from interactions between the individual and the environment. This framework calls for careful study of biological and developmental factors that affect internal controls, as well as analysis of the situations in which the behavior occurs to determine the role of environmental factors, both immediate and previous.

FIGURE 13.

PREDISPOSING CONDITIONS, FACTORS, AND INFLUENCES[1]

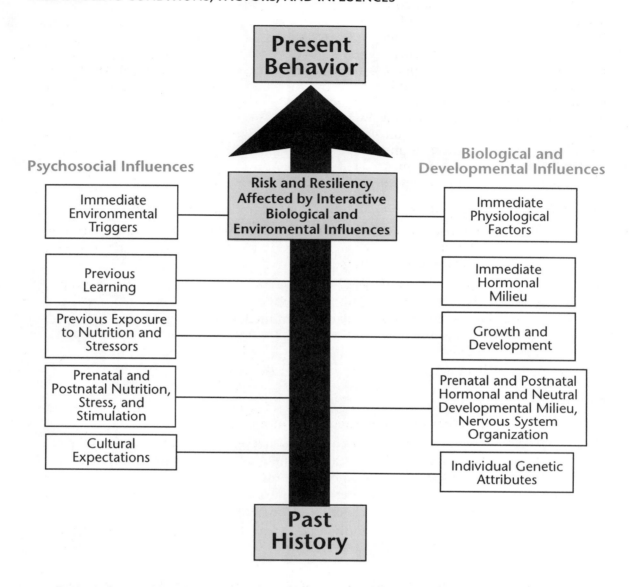

Brain infection or injury or genetic, metabolic, or idiopathic illness may result in difficulties controlling panic or anger, hyperactivity, or restlessness. Anatomical, endocrinological, or biochemical dysfunction, in combination with developmental, environmental, or psychosocial factors, can subject individuals to more stressors than they are able to adaptively manage. Neurological disease may also directly affect the structures that mediate emotional behavior and cause changes in the emotional state. Understanding the impact of both biological and learning history on behavior, and accommodating these factors when designing intervention plans, greatly increases the likelihood of success.

In a significant percentage of children and adolescents, there are many behaviors that may accompany or follow brain injury, illness, or epilepsy. However, the particular expression of a disturbance is more dependent on the individual's developmental level, past history, temperament, or family relationship than on the nature of the condition. There is no brain injury, intoxication, or disease in children that has typical psychiatric sequelae.

Biological Influences

Biological conditions *may* contribute to the manifestations of assaultive and self-aggressive behaviors. The issue of concern and primary focus for the BICM is the *function* of the behavior, however, not the *nature* of the behavior. Regardless of what biological condition may predispose an individual to express a type of behavior, the BICM's task is always to establish the function(s) or purpose(s) the behavior plays for that individual. The following information on influences and predisposing conditions describes the impact a medical condition may have on behavior. Part of the requirement of a complete functional analysis is to examine how a diagnosis or medical factor may influence the behavior observed, but this alone does not fulfill the requirements of the functional analysis. Rather, the student's disability, developmental levels, medical needs, and medication must be reviewed in the context of the functional assessment. There is no substitute for thorough observation and the formation and testing of hypotheses before a behavior plan is developed.

Some biological conditions that have behavioral implications include the following:

- Severe panic reactions or behavior that is violently aggressive and destructive toward self and others may be exhibited by the student with **schizophrenia**. However, most students with schizophrenia do not make such displays.

- Self mutilation has been found to be a characteristic abnormality in some individuals with **Lesch-Nyhan syndrome**.

- Aggressive behaviors are frequently exhibited by individuals with **Klinefelter's syndrome**.

- Assaultive behaviors may be exhibited by individuals with **temporal lobe epilepsy** or **tumors on the hypothalamus or temporal lobes**.

- Behavior dysfunction, including self-mutilation and violent outbursts, may be displayed by individuals with **Fragile X syndrome**, a genetic disorder that is the most commonly inherited cause of mental retardation.

- A behavioral disorder that includes a lack of emotional control, as well as self-injurious (frequently "skin picking") or aggressive behaviors may been seen in individuals with **Prader-Willi syndrome**.

- Aggressive, self-injurious behaviors, and unusual responses to sensory stimuli are frequently seen in individuals with **Autism**.

- Self-injury may be seen in individuals with **Cornelia de Lange syndrome, Rett syndrome, and Riley-Day syndrome**.

- The involuntary, recurrent stereotyped motor movements occurring in individuals with **Tourette syndrome** may become exacerbated under stress, resulting in self-injury or aggressive behavior.

- Catastrophic reactions combined with low impulse control resulting from **traumatic brain injury** may contribute to an increase in aggressive behaviors.

- **Migraine headaches** in some individuals may be immediately preceded by a change of personality, leading to an exacerbation of preexisting aggressive, self-assaultive, or self-stimulatory traits.

Some biological factors may delay or impair the neurodevelopment of the child and influence behavior. A student may exhibit maladaptive aggressive behaviors because of difficulty compensating for a less organized nervous system. It is important to note that these factors *may* influence behavior but that they are *not* necessarily indicators that maladaptive behaviors will develop. Significant biological factors that can influence behavior include the following: lead exposure, poor maternal nutrition, maternal infections or maternal battering during pregnancy, prenatal substance exposure, intraventricular hemorrhage, congenital syphilis, neonatal asphyxia, Respiratory Distress Syndrome, poor nutrition, and inadequate health care.

Psychosocial Influences

In addition, a child *may* exhibit maladaptive, aggressive behaviors because of difficulty coping with psychosocial stressors in the environment. As with biological factors, it is important to note that they may influence behavior but are *not* necessarily indicators that maladaptive behaviors will develop. Significant psychosocial factors that *may* influence behavior are: emotionally unavailable caregivers, lack of consistent primary caregivers, parental substance abuse, domestic violence, homelessness, parental depression, parental mental retardation, chaotic home environment, parental abuse, parental neglect, and parent/child separation.

Developmental Influences and Guidelines

Disturbing behavior must also be understood in light of cognitive and psychosocial development. Individuals with developmental disabilities or emotional disturbance may not function at a single developmental level, but at several levels, depending on the nature of the task demand. For example, a student may be at chronological age expectancy in intellectual abilities but may demonstrate immature attention, concentration, and impulse control. When there is a discrepancy between a student's psychosocial/cognitive competency and the developmental demands of the task presented, one can expect the student to express frustration. Maladaptive behavior may be a reflection of nonspecific cognitive/psychosocial disability rather than a manifestation of a psychiatric disorder calling for medical management. Diminished communication skills or diminished ability to think concretely or abstractly may result in behaviors that are normal when seen in younger children but appear maladaptive in children who are chronologically older. Developmental expectations in classrooms for groups of students without disabilities are important to review. When examining the behavior of a particular student with a disability spending significant time in general education settings, it will be important to understand the expectations peers and adults may have for behavior. Figure 14, pp. 133-135 lists general behavioral characteristics at various developmental levels, providing a helpful guide to the possible need for behavior interventions.

Continued on page 135

FIGURE 14.

DEVELOPMENTAL CHARACTERISTICS OF CHILDREN

	Behavior Characteristics
Piaget: Early Sensorimotor Stages **Erikson: Developmental Task:** **Basic Trust vs. Mistrust** **Typical Developmental Ages:** **0-1 ¹/2 years**	• Attention to persons sporadic. • Self-stimulation • Perseverative behavior. • Focus on objects sporadic. • Preliminary disorganization of behavior in acquisition of new skills. • Specific words are not effective mediators of behavior. • Prosody of language can be an effective mediator of behavior. • Minimal inhibition and control of emotional reactions. • Needs one-on-one interactions. • External person/object important only to extent child's needs are gratified. • No tolerance for delay and minimal frustration tolerance. • Learns action leads to response and therefore will repeat action. • Needs consistent gratifying responses from significant adult. • Needs opportunities to "know" body. • Oral drive to teethe, mouth, bite. • Inward aggression expressed through head banging. • Obeys commands only for duration of command. • Shows distress by crying. • Develops trust in caregiving adult. • Begins to expect response to signals.
Example: *Megan, 14 years old with profound retardation, demonstrates this developmental level and uses prolonged screaming to express all desires and needs.* **Function of behavior:** *communicative, seeking and protesting absence of reinforcers.* **Alternative positive behavior:** *pointing to object of choice.* **Developmentally appropriate interven-tion:** *water and food put always within reach and teaching Megan the adaptive communication of pointing to get her desires met.*	

	Behavior Characteristics
Piaget: Later Sensorimoter Stages **Erickson: Developmental Task:** **Basic Trust vs. Mistrust** **Typical Developmental Ages:** **1+ - 2 years**	• Objects perceived as independent entities. • Outward aggression expressed through temper tantrums. • Exploration of objects. • Attempts goals not immediately attainable. • Uses adults to obtain objects, solace, play. • Attempts trial-and-error problem solving. • Needs one-on-one interactions. • Imitative play emerging. • Responds to vocal, verbal, facial, and gestural cues. • Impulsive in reactions. • Understands means-end relationships. • Rudimentary sense of task completion emerging. • Use of action trial and error. • Awareness of self as separate person. • Feelings need to be identified and labeled. • Seeks to maintain constant relations with a person. • Elementary memory requisites for recognition and recall are established. • Shows jealousy when caregivers attention is directed elsewhere. • Separation fears dominant. • Processes present time only. • Rudimentary sense of direction. • Strong tie to mothering figure.
Example: *Robert, 10 years old with autism and this developmental level, shows these character-istics and tantrums when mother leaves him at school (45-minute duration aver-age, sometimes resulting in assaults on others).* **Function of behavior:** *communicative, protesting separation, based on his ability to process immediate present time only.* **Alternative positive behavior:** *understand daily sequences and when mother will return.* **Intervention:** *photo sequencing training and opportunity to imitate and assist a teacher aide each morning on arrival.*	

FIGURE 14. CONTINUED

DEVELOPMENTAL CHARACTERISTICS OF CHILDREN

Piaget: Preoperational Stage One, Associative Reasoning **Erikson:** Developmental Task: Autonomy vs. Shame and Doubt **Typical Developmental Ages:** 2-4 years	**Behavior Characteristics**

Behavior Characteristics

- Low frustration tolerance.
- Activity level high.
- Rudimentary understanding of mutual rights.
- Adult demands seen as impositions.
- Demands resisted with angry outbursts.
- Frequent emotional outbursts, including temper tantrums.
- Frequent demands for individual attention.
- Short attention span.
- Many separation fears (e.g., departures, nap times, etc.).
- Imitative representational play.
- Pictures/photographs can be used to mediate behaviors.
- Words, signs, and symbols can be used to mediate behavior.
- Doesn't distinguish between fantasy and reality.
- Does not follow rules in game.
- Use of mental trial and error.
- Sense of self-control established.
- Emergence of sense of accomplishment and task completion.
- Persons and objects have separate existences.
- Internalizes prohibition of behaviors.
- Begins to postpone need for immediate gratification.
- Rudimentary internal control system.
- Rudimentary ability to take direction.
- Parallel play prominent.
- Egocentric thinking (e.g., child considers own point of view the only one possible).
- Uses speech for communication.
- Negativism reaches peak in service of autonomy.
- Instrumental aggression (aggression as means to end) is at peak.
- Can follow simple one-step commands.
- Kicking, biting, hitting, temper tantrums are common means of expressing negativism and reflect assertion of an autonomous (vs. passive) will.

Example:

Micah, age 3 with speech language delays, slaps other children frequently in the face, without known provocation.

Function of behavior: *attention seeking to initiate or sustain play.*

Alternative positive behavior: *Micah will use verbal requests to begin or maintain play.*

Intervention: *reinforcing use of verbal scripts taught and modeled to both Micah and her peers.*

Piaget: Preoperational Stage Two, Intuitive Reasoning **Erickson:** Developmental Task: Initiative vs. Guilt **Typical Developmental Ages:** 4-7 years	**Behavior Characteristics**

Behavior Characteristics

- Masturbation reaches first peak.
- Peers/adults viewed as having rights of their own.
- Increased ability to take direction.
- Increased internal control system.
- Rudimentary control of messy aggressive urges.
- Primary adult relationships center on immediate and extended family.
- Cooperative play emerging.
- Thinking is dominated by the configuration/situation perceived at a given moment (e.g., added variables not incorporated).
- Spontaneous exploratory behavior.
- Self-dependence in daily living activities.
- Role-playing is effective mediator for behavior and provides resolution of feelings.
- Rudimentary sense of time and sequence of events.
- Play is process in which solutions to problems are "tried out" in a controlled situation.
- Exacerbated fears of animals, dark, injury, and monsters.
- Dreams conceptualized as external events.

Example:

James, age 6 with a severe emotional disturbance, has periodic rage reactions (which frequently become assaultive) related to any frustrations in his day.

Function of behavior: *communicative, protest using a nonverbal form when he is out of emotional control.*

Alternative positive behavior: *use relaxation techniques to regain emotional control, then use verbal behaviors to protest or negotiate.*

Intervention: *relaxation techniques taught to regain control, frequent reinforcement for emotionally in-control behavior, role-playing and modeling of feeling resolutions taught and reinforced.*

Piaget: Concrete Operational Thinking Stage Erikson: Developmental Task: Industry vs. Inferiority Typical Developmental Ages: 7 years+	Behavior Characteristics
Example: *Alex, age 10 with a severe emotional distur-bance, runs out of the room and school, risking his physical safety in traffic in response to difficult academics.* **Function of behavior:** *escape, avoidance based on fear of failure* **Positive alternative behavior:** *tolerate some challenging tasks, Alex will verbally negotiate if the task is beyond tolerance level.* **Intervention:** *classmates, Alex, and teacher jointly rate the difficulty of a task and assign reinforcer token points accordingly. Bonus points for all tasks over 5 points given, reinforcers earned both for the group and for Alex himself. Verbal praise from teacher and peers for increasing tolerance of difficult tasks. Modeling, teaching, and reinforcing Alex's verbal negotia-tions when his frustration tolerance is reached.*	• Conceptual sense of time, including playtime and work time. • Logical thinking dominant. • Capacity to divert and delay the expression of a given impulse. • Diminution of observable sexuality. • Interest in social relationships broadens to include adults besides parents. • Cooperative team play is prominent. • Thinking can include consideration of more than one variable. • Ability to analyze, classify, seriate, and conserve. • Desires to accomplish something of consequence. • Better impulse control. • Well organized in play.

PROGRAM PLANNING IMPLICATIONS OF SOME CONDITIONS

In program planning for individuals with challenging behaviors, it is important to recognize the biological influences of some conditions and to be knowledgeable of approaches that may accommodate or mediate their effects. The approaches discussed below are not meant to be an exhaustive list of treatment techniques but rather are samples of a few effective interventions the writers have developed repeatedly to address the following behaviors:

- behaviors with obsessive or compulsive features,
- behaviors related to seizure activity,
- behaviors related to bipolar disorder,
- behaviors related to migraine,
- behaviors following traumatic brain injury,
- behaviors related to fears,
- behaviors related to sensory responses,
- stereotypic behaviors, and
- self-injurious behaviors.

Behaviors with Obsessive or Compulsive Features

Some behaviors occur in predictable, almost rhythmic, fashion. Typically, when Obsessive-Compulsive Disorder (OCD) features are present, a behavior (such as repeating a motor act over and over) will be observed for some time, then be replaced by another pattern. On some occasions, these behaviors can fulfill the criteria of being a serious behavior problem (such as repeatedly throwing peers to the ground or hitting others compulsively with a backpack.). When very little reinforcement appears to be earned from a predictably recurring behavior and the function of the behavior is not easily determined after baseline data are collected, the BICM should consider the possibility of OCD features influencing behavior. This probably will require careful analysis and understanding of medical diagnoses and communication with medical providers to seek information and relay observations from data collection. Frequently, the more cognitively able student can describe the compulsion to perform the behavior and the irresistible nature of the urge to do so. A careful interview with significant others and sometimes with the student may assist in determining whether the behavior has these features.

In students with Tourette syndrome, where obsessive-compulsive features are commonly seen, serious behaviors may be a form of tic. Although most students with Tourette syndrome never exhibit tics of this nature, the literature on Tourette syndrome increasingly describes complex motor tics that include behaviors such as kicking others, falling down, throwing, and pinching. Touching of one's own or others' breasts or genitals has been observed in adolescence and typically resolves by age 18.

When OCD features are present, programming must recognize the following:
- the possibility of substituting a less maladaptive "outburst" behavior;
- the possibility of using a stimulus control procedure to contain the behavior within manageable limits;
- the cyclic nature of the behaviors — they may change when they have run their course, regardless of the intervention;
- the individual's often limited ability to control the expression of the urge; and
- the role that environmental factors play in increasing or decreasing the likelihood of the behavior being exhibited and the necessity for manipulating the environment to support control.

Substituting a less maladaptive outburst behavior

Ryan *A 14 year old with Tourette syndrome diagnosis, utilizing the Resource Specialist Program and maintaining a B grade point average.*

Ryan suddenly began screaming daily in his English class, becoming physically aggressive when asked to leave the room. It was noted that Ryan screamed when the teacher paused between phrases. During an interview, Ryan stated that for 3 weeks he had experienced an irrational fear of microscopic spiders, an extension of his knowledge of eye mites and other body parasites. Ryan stated that when he was asked to leave the classroom, he feared that someone might touch him, thus transmitting these mites. He stated that he did not understand why he felt compelled to scream during pauses and was embarrassed after doing so. The family and medical provider concurred that this behavior was likely to be OCD influenced. The school was informed that medications to affect behaviors were not being considered by the medical team because of adverse previous reactions. The intervention consisted of teaching Ryan to whisper a word. On occasions when this was not successful, the teacher used a private hand signal, rather than a verbal request, to ask Ryan to leave for a cooling-off period. He returned when he was ready. He also had permission to go to the hall to vocalize if he felt it was necessary. To reduce disruption of class instruction, his seat was moved next to the door. Thus, the behavior was shaped to a less disturbing form. After 6 weeks, this ideation and compulsion had run its course. By instituting this intervention, Ryan was able to remain in the general education class. His work remained at the B level.

Behaviors Related to Seizure Activity

Although the primary management of seizures is the responsibility of the physician, teachers and parents play an important role in monitoring the frequency and duration of the seizures, giving the anticonvulsant medication as directed by the physician, monitoring the child for the appearance of possible side effects of any medications, and responding appropriately to a seizure if it occurs in their presence. A summary of how to recognize the various types of seizures, as well as information regarding the various anticonvulsant medications frequently prescribed, is included to assist the IEP team in understanding seizure management. Additionally, understanding when certain problem behaviors may indicate potential seizure activity will be important as the team designs programs to address a problem behavior. Clear descriptions and communication with the physician and parent about suspicious behavior can be important to determine the behavior's relationship to seizure activity.

Types of Seizures

Grand mal seizures consist of a loss of consciousness, accompanied by uncontrolled muscle contractions over the whole body. Movements typically consist of jerking of the arms and legs and rolling of the eyes to one side. This is frequently accompanied by loss of bowel and/or bladder control and difficulty breathing. The seizure typically lasts several minutes and is followed by a period of sleepiness and confusion lasting an hour or more.

Petit mal seizures consist of a very brief lapse of consciousness, usually accompanied by eye blinking or other facial movements. Posture is maintained, and the student continues on as if nothing happened. There is a typical brain wave pattern on the EEG. These seizures can be differentiated from daydreaming by attempting to capture the attention of the student by saying a high-interest word, such as "McDonald's" or "Mutant Ninja Turtles." If the student stops staring and can remember what was said, the student was probably only daydreaming. If the student stops staring but does not remember what was said, this may have been a petit mal seizure and should be reported to the family. If this occurs several times in a day, the frequency and duration should be noted and conveyed to the medical providers.

Atypical absence (Lenox Gastaut syndrome) seizures consist of atypical staring spells, sometimes accompanied by violent contractions of one or more muscle groups. This may result in a fall. This type of seizure is very difficult to control and is generally accompanied by mental retardation.

During **simple partial (focal) seizures** there is jerking of one part of the body, but consciousness is unimpaired. This type of seizure may spread and become a grand mal. It is frequently an indicator of severe neurological disease and has a poorer prognosis than many others.

Partial complex (psychomotor) seizures consist of an alteration of consciousness accompanied by a fixed pattern of movements that mimic some natural movements, such as sitting, running, or atypical speech. The automatisms that occur during the period of lost consciousness associated with complex partial seizures can have the appearance of aggressive action. Because the student is unconscious when these occur, however, these behaviors are not under the student's control and are not intended to be harmful. The student will not remember the behaviors after becoming fully conscious. Automatisms occur at some time or other in more than three out of four children with complex partial seizures, particularly those with a temporal lobe focus.

The automatisms that occur during seizures consist of a wide range of poorly coordinated, semi-purposeful activities, and vary widely among students but tend to be stereotyped from one seizure to another in each child. Automatisms have been classified broadly as follows:

- **gestural:** fumbling with or dropping nearby objects, picking at clothes or bedsheets, thrashing, resisting restraint, rocking, and so forth,
- **alimentary:** chewing, swallowing, or lip smacking,
- **mimicking:** displaying facial expressions that suggest an emotion such as fear,
- **verbal:** yelling, laughing, or repetitive speech, and
- **ambulatory:** walking or running.

It is easy to see how a child who is thrashing, yelling, and resisting restraint would be characterized by many observers as demonstrating aggressive behavior. In addition, automatisms can occur during the postictal phase of partial seizures, while the child is still significantly confused. The postictal phase is the period following a seizure when alertness and mental activity is diminished. If the child is physically restrained during this time, he or she may react with aggressive behavior against the restraining person. If left alone, except for maneuvers to protect the child's safety, there will most likely be no directed violence.

Aggressive Behavior Considerations in Seizure Activity

Certain aggressive behavioral outbursts, such as those described above, could actually represent seizure activity and may require medical intervention. When the behavior does not appear to have clear antecedents and consequences observable in the environment, the BICM will want to carefully observe for seizure activity, especially when there are handicapping conditions associated with increased likelihood of seizure development. These include the following:

- Traumatic brain injury increases the possibility of seizure activity, increased irritability, and lower frustration tolerance.
- Autism has an increased risk factor for accompanying seizure activity.
- If other forms of seizure activity are present in the individual, there is an increased likelihood, albeit small, that aggressive behavior seen in this individual is in fact seizure activity.

Observation Guidelines for Suspected Seizure Activity

1. Does the individual become sleepy or actually sleep after an outburst? This is frequently a consequence of seizure activity.

2. During the outburst, are facial grimaces present, especially around the mouth? This can be observed in some seizures.

3. Is eye gaze directed in a fixed manner, especially up or to the right or left? If so, seizure may be suspected.

4. Are clear antecedents or consequences for the seizure-suspect behavior lacking? Is the behavior odd, does it appear not to have a purpose, or does it continue despite efforts to interrupt it? If so, seizure activity possibly is suspect.

5. If an adult says an incongruous word to the student during the outburst, does he or she remember the word later when queried? If not, seizure activity may be suspected. Selected words should be personally relevant and interest-

ing to the individual, such as the name of a favorite person or relative, the family pet, or favorite Nintendo game.

6. Does the student remember what transpired during the outburst with any clarity? If not, seizure may be suspected.

7. If the student is in motion during the outburst, is the quality of movement different from normal movement? For example, is the movement linear with a "pacing" quality or random and atypical for this student? If so, seizure may be suspected.

8. Does the student appear "out of it?" If so, consider the techniques described in guidelines 5 and 6 above. Possibility of seizure activity must be examined further.

(Developed by Mauer & Weigel, 1993)

No one symptom either confirms or rules out the possibility of seizure activity. If the behaviors mentioned above are repeatedly observed and good records maintained, the physician will be better able to determine the likelihood of seizure activity influencing behavior. It is the "preponderance of evidence" that will assist the medical care provider in making a diagnosis.

The importance of adequate baseline data can not be overemphasized. Like a good detective, the BICM must be vigilant and impress on persons assigned to gather data that some small datum may be critical in understanding the source of complex behavior problems. Armed with good observational data on the frequency, intensity, and duration of outbursts; with good descriptive data, and with positive results from one or more of the eight areas of inquiry mentioned above, the BICM will want to collaborate with the family and possibly the family physician. This is a critical part of the functional analysis assessment whenever seizure activity is suspected.

Behaviors Related to Bipolar Disorder

New literature suggests that aggressive behavioral outbursts that occur in predictable cycles, such as once in seven days, may originate from a bipolar disorder. Typically, this disorder is not diagnosed until mid-adolescence to late adolescence. It may be suspected when the behavior is in stark contrast to that exhibited during calmer portions of the cycle and when the occurrence pattern cannot be linked to other antecedents or environmental changes. A good, systematic baseline is needed to determine the predictability of outbursts. This information should be conveyed to mental health or medical providers when bipolar disorder is suspected, because the symptoms of this disorder may improve with medication. The literature suggests that individuals from families with a strong history of panic disorders, various forms of cyclical behaviors, or depression are at increased risk of developing bipolar disorder, especially during adolescence.

Behaviors Related to Migraine

Although aggressive behavior occurs primarily as a reaction to stressors in the environment, internal states related to medical conditions can sometimes be at the root. During the functional analysis, the BICM will want to identify whether or not the parent or caretaker knows of a family history of migraines. Careful observation and data collection can be essential in assisting the physician if migraine-related behavior is suspected. If the outbursts are found to be migraine related, adequate control of migraine through medication may eliminate the aggressive behavior. The importance of a thorough review of medical records for all children with problem behaviors cannot be overemphasized.

Both classic and common migraine are seen in children. Classic migraine can be seen in children as young as 5 years old, but it is not common in the preadolescent child. The major diagnostic features, which are not seen in every patient, include the following:

- personality change preceding onset of headaches;
- visual phenomena (e.g., loss of vision, shooting stars, dots before the eyes);
- pulsating headache, restricted to one side of the head, often including the eye;
- nausea and vomiting; and
- family history of migraine.

The personality change is most often increased irritability or an increase in the problem behaviors of concern, although hypomania (a mild degree of increased psychomotor activity, excitement, rapid change of ideas, distractability) can also occur, as well as aggressive behavior not seen between attacks. Thus, a withdrawn and aloof student with autism may become even more aloof, the hyperactive student may become even more behaviorally disorganized, and the student prone to aggressive behavior may develop even less tolerance before exploding.

In **common migraine**, visual phenomena and clear unilateral distribution of the headache is missing from the pattern described above, while all other features of classic migraine can be present. This is the most frequent variant seen in prepubertal children. If recurrent headaches are occurring in a student with a family history of migraine, migraine should be suspected.

In **complicated migraine**, an association of neurological signs and symptoms is found. During the prodromal or early predictive phase, the individual develops dense hemiplegia (loss of ability to make voluntary movements on one side of the body), a visual field defect, and, if the left hemisphere is involved, aphasia. The headache becomes very severe and is gone within 1-2 days.

In **basilar artery migraine**, vertigo, vague dizziness, and ataxia (loss of coordination) can be present, with some drop attacks, tinnitus, and loss of consciousness reported. A drop attack occurs when a person falls as a result of losing postural tone. Younger children often have the neurological signs without prominent complaints of headache.

In some children, acute confusional reaction accompanies the headache. The reaction consists of confusion, disorientation, and sometimes irritability. Presence of severe headaches or headaches between attacks of confusion, in addition to a family history of migraine, are important clues.

In the **Alice-in-Wonderland syndrome**, sensory perceptions are distorted and cause the student extreme anxiety. Abnormalities of time sense, hallucinations, strange perceptions about the size and shape of body parts, and visual distortions can occur. These changes occur without symptoms of prominent headache, although headaches between attacks are frequently seen.

Behaviors Following Traumatic Brain Injury

Aggressive behavior following traumatic brain injury (TBI) is reported in the literature, especially when left temporal lobe injury has occurred. General irritability, reduced social awareness and understanding of nonverbal communication, and many other features often follow brain injury, leading to distorted perceptions of the environment and low frustration tolerance. Other persons may continue to hold preinjury expectations for the individual with TBI, especially when general recovery is good. Those serving students with TBI will need to become familiar with frequently observed behaviors following head trauma and appropriate behavior techniques. An extensive body of literature exists on assessment and on intervention design for these individuals.[2]

Some students with TBI may experience cognitive fatigue so frequently that "maintaining" for a complete school day is beyond the student's ability, with increased aggression seen as the day progresses. The team will want to consider scheduling to reduce output requirements in the afternoon, perhaps rearranging the student's classes, assigning the student to an "office aide" period, or arranging for a shortened day. Input from the physician providing postaccident care and from family members is important for these IEP team decisions. New medications are being developed to reduce the irritability following brain injury.

Behaviors Related to Fears

Fear reactions may be accompanied by physiological indicators that are not present during most other types of behavior. These may include perspiration not related to temperature, flushing of the face, shaking, movements that seem to be reflexive or automatic, dilation of pupils, high-pitched or loud voice tone, rapid speech, screaming, increased heart rate, fleeting eye contact or darting of the eyes, or increased tolerance of pain. In turn, the desire to escape from the cause of the fear may result in running away or striking out at anything that is perceived to limit an escape. This is commonly referred to as a "fight or flight" reaction.

If escape is the function of the behavior and this is determined to be a fear response, the BICM will want to consider specific techniques to use in behavior intervention planning. These involve both interventions to cope with the fear and relaxation techniques to raise tolerances to anxiety described below.

Effective Interventions with a Person Who is Fearful
Several interventions are available for a student who is fearful:

- Remove the cause of the fear.
- Do not invade the person's personal space or touch the person unless you have the person's permission or are certain the person will view it as helpful. In their own effort to remain in control of the situation, staff members often think that physical guidance, or even a pat on the back or holding hands, will calm an agitated individual (especially a child). When a person is overcome with fear, however, he or she may perceive the contact as hindering escape. Furthermore, students who have been the victim of physical trauma or abuse may be even less likely to view physical contact as helpful. If you find a student striking out at a "helper," it may be important to analyze the situation in terms of personal space, physical contact, and body language.
- Talk calmly, and use simple, clear language.
- Verbalize a fear and talk about ways to control it.
- Give the person who is afraid as much control as possible over the situation; for example, allow the person to close a door or put a barrier between himself or herself and the scary object. Participating in ways to prevent a fear-provoking event may actually reduce the fear reaction because the person feels increased control. Predicting a fear-provoking event may have a similar effect, even if the event cannot be prevented.

- Whenever possible, help the person make a plan for how to react when afraid. This is similar to emergency plans, such as fire drills. For example, running into the parking lot or street may be shaped by practicing running to the classroom next door. This increases safety in several ways: obviously, moving cars are eliminated; staff members do not need to physically restrain or block the student's escape, eliminating injuries that might occur during a struggle; and a clear path is predetermined, which limits the chance of tripping on or bumping into obstacles.

Teaching individualized emergency procedure as a response to fear

---

Greg   *A 10 year old with autism and developmental disabilities.*

Greg frequently ran out of the classroom or school building, with little warning. Sometimes, running was obviously in response to a loud noise, such as a vacuum cleaner or lawn mower, but other times it seemed to have no environmental cause. Greg assaulted anyone attempting to prevent him from leaving the area by hitting or throwing objects. Greg also hit adults who invaded his personal space although he regularly stood too close to adults and peers.

Fear of loud noises and motors was identified as an antecedent. Associated behaviors that occurred as his anxiety began to rise were identified. These included hand flapping, increased whole body movements, rapid breathing, and repeating key phrases. Safe places inside the classroom and just outside each door were developed with Greg's help. Greg was allowed to go to the safe places any time he wanted. Drill sessions were scheduled in which he practiced going to one of the identified safe places. Greg was taught alternate routes on campus to take if he came across a motorized appliance or noise. An adult stayed with him whenever he was outside the classroom but maintained a distance of at least 4 feet. Simple verbal cues were repeated to Greg when the associated behaviors were noticed. These cues involved choices or decisions he could make to keep himself safe and calm (as appropriate to the specific situation), such as, "go to a safe place," "close the door," "go the other way," "take a deep breath," or "hands down." Because these noises were commonly encountered outside the classroom, a plan was reviewed before each trip outside.

Relaxation Training and the Influence of Relative Levels of Tension

People who frequently experience fear reactions may almost constantly be in a state of anxiety or readiness to fight or flee. When the actual number of fear-provoking situations is reduced or eliminated, anxiety and concomitant physiological symptoms are not necessarily eliminated or reduced to the same degree. Relaxation training may be helpful in this circumstance. A variety of relaxation training techniques and programs are available, including Jacobson's (1938) progressive muscle relaxation, and guided imagery. Simple, common sense techniques such as listening to soothing music or sounds in a dim room or taking a few deep breaths at key times may also be very helpful.

Relaxation training can be effective as a prevention and focusing technique. Once specific relaxation skills are taught, they can also be used as a preset immediately before a transition or activity that is likely to provoke anxiety. These learned skills can also be cued as a reactive strategy in the early stages of escalation behaviors.

Using trained relaxation techniques as a reactive strategy

> **Jeff** *An 11 year old, identified as severely emotionally disturbed.*
>
> Jeff persevered on collecting round objects, such as hubcaps, plates, and lids for cups at take-out restaurants. Because he often stole them, he knew that staff members and his parents would try to prevent him from getting one of these objects in most situations. Therefore, he became very anxious when he saw a round object and often assaulted people even before they began to intervene. He knew that trips to the community were contingent on his refraining from stealing round objects, and he was highly motivated to go on community trips, but he rarely was able to resist stealing the objects. Jeff was taught to take three deep breaths when cued by an adult. This was practiced before every transition at school and whenever an adult thought he was beginning to get anxious. Jeff initiated this behavior on his own several times at school when an unusual circumstance arose. Staff members told Jeff that this technique would be used in the community whenever a staff member saw a round object or thought Jeff might be entering an area with round objects. Within a month, Jeff's success at refraining from stealing round objects rose from 10% to 60%.

Progressive muscle relaxation techniques are easy for students and staff members to learn and can be used in several ways. They involve isolating individual muscle groups (such as arms, legs, or face) in sequence and performing a strong contraction or "tensing," followed by complete relaxation. The entire sequence can be performed as a regular activity, or it can be modified so that specific parts are relaxed at key times during the day. When using progressive muscle relaxation training with young children or developmentally disabled individuals, it may be helpful to pair contraction of specific muscle groups with a concrete image. For example, teach facial muscle relaxation by smiling or frowning in a mirror; teach shoulder relaxation by pretending to be a turtle pulling his head inside his shell, then putting it back out again.

Individuals with impaired sensory perception may find some things relaxing that may seem unusual to most people. Refer to the next section of this chapter, "Behaviors Related to Sensory Responses" for a list of calming and alerting sensations.

Using relaxation techniques to reduce anxiety and prevent dangerous behaviors

> **Greg** *(the same 10 year old with autism and developmental disabilities, with fear of loud motors and noises discussed above).*
>
> Greg demonstrated a "fight or flight" reaction whenever he heard a loud noise or motor. Even though effective techniques were developed to shape a safer response to these events, he was constantly anxious and fearful. This concern about the possibility of a noise occurring interfered with his attention to learning tasks.
>
> Relaxation strategies that were effective for Greg included scheduling relaxation time in his "safe place" several times per day; providing items in his "safe place" that were particularly calming for him (a soft brush; quiet, soothing music; pillows; and a flannel sheet), and teaching him a routine of taking three deep breaths and contracting his face, arms, and shoulders before each transition.

Using relaxation techniques to improve on task behavior of a group and to decrease both transition time and afternoon behavior problems.[2]

Special Day Class	A special day class of 12 upper elementary, students with severe learning disabilities.

This class had a significant increase in behavior problems each day after lunch. Most of the students could not stay in their seats; talked out loudly; and were more easily distracted by each other, common classroom objects, and noises that they were able to ignore in the morning. Several times, fights occurred and one student had repeated confrontations with the teacher, requiring her total attention for 10-15 minutes. Positive reinforcement strategies, such as doubling points in the class token economy for the transition period and conducting a special lottery, were somewhat effective, but it was still taking 15-20 minutes for the class to settle down and focus on learning activities.

A relaxation session that took 7-10 minutes was implemented each day as the students returned from the after-lunch recess. Students were given a designated spot on the floor where they lay down with a pillow immediately upon entering the room. Quiet, soothing music was played, and the teaching assistant talked the students through a routine of contracting and relaxing each major body part. Several deep, slow breaths were taken between each contraction. As students came in late they were able to join the activity in progress. Soon the students were able to take turns leading the routine, and the teacher and assistant were free to do individual coaching with students who needed assistance. Increased positive reinforcement strategies were continued.

Teaching relaxation techniques as a method for coping with frustration and fear of failure

Jane	An 8 year old, with multiple mild physical and developmental disabilities, receiving services in a special day class of fifteen, with an academic curriculum.

Jane had little confidence in her reading, writing, and math skills and was easily frustrated. She needed one-on-one adult assistance to do any academic work. She became sullen and withdrawn if her requests for help were not answered immediately. She threw tantrums if her withdrawn behaviors were not addressed within 3-5 minutes. These occurred three to eight times per day and ranged in length from 4 to 30 minutes.

A combination of positive behavior management techniques was used to address this problem because it had multiple causes. However, general anxiety and fear of failure were identified as major variables. Jane was taught a routine of taking deep breaths and identifying and relaxing tense body parts as a way of preparing herself to attempt a task on her own. After using this technique for a month, she initiated its use before attempting to enter a social situation in her special day class and when she participated in a general education class.

BEHAVIORS RELATED TO SENSORY RESPONSES

The BICM, when conducting a functional analysis, may discover that the individual has sensory responses that are either more or less responsive or overloaded by common sensory perceptions in a given environment. Others in the same environment would not respond in similar ways. By understanding how this responsiveness may affect behavior, and by designing plans that accommodate any unusual findings, the likelihood of successful outcomes is increased.

A person's arousal level is affected by sensory input. Various biological, environmental, developmental, and emotional components interact to comprise factors that may cause a person to be underresponsive or overresponsive to sensory stimuli sometime. However, each person has a general state of arousal and responsiveness to sensory stimuli that can be placed on a continuum. Most people have a general arousal level that defines what we call typical responses. The arousal levels of some people, however, fall outside the range of typical responses. These individuals are usually divided into two categories: those with hypersensitivities and those with hyposensitivities.

Hypersensitivities are defined as avoidance of, low tolerance for, or exaggerated responses to sensory stimuli that are considered harmless or nonirritative by most people. This affects behavior because individuals with hypersensitivities quickly learn to avoid or protest the things to which they are sensitive. These avoidance behaviors are easily misinterpreted as oppositional, disruptive, or even aggressive. For example, a young girl's behavior of throwing food every day in school was stopped by providing a very bland diet. The regular school menu contained too many strong tastes for her. Viewing hypersensitivity as sensory-avoidance may make it easier to apply this concept to practical behavior management situations.

Hyposensitivities are defined as a lack of, high tolerance for, or weak response to sensory stimuli on a consistent basis. This is important in understanding behavior because people with hyposensitivities often seek out one or more types of sensory stimulation. This may be done by repeatedly engaging in a behavior, such as rocking or spinning, even when it is inappropriate, it is disruptive, or it interferes with learning. Although behavioral problems related to hyposensitivity are expressed usually in sensory-seeking behaviors, some sensory-avoidance behaviors may be seen. For example, a child with low muscle tone who is hyporesponsive to deep-pressure-proprioceptive input to muscles and joints may exhibit sensory-seeking behaviors, such as bumping into people, slamming doors, and walking on toes. At other times, the same child may exhibit sensory-avoidance behaviors, such as lying on the floor instead of sitting in a chair or giving up on functional tasks that provide resistance, as in pushing a heavy door.

Although any one individual may demonstrate a combination of sensory-avoidance and sensory-seeking behaviors, we will discuss these behaviors as two separate categories in this chapter. When performing the functional behavioral analysis, the BICM needs to be aware that sensory responsiveness occurs on a continuum. One reason for this is that sensory experiences have an accumulating effect over time. As the day wears on, the student may appear more sensitive because of repeated exposure. The accumulating effect can be one way to explain why a student may appear to have inconsistent responses to the same stimuli. During data collection, note the intensity of responses as related to time of day as well as location.

Educators who work with students who have autism are often aware of their students' unusual sensory responses and the problem behaviors that are thought to be related (King, 1990). Students with other disabilities may also demonstrate unusual sensory responses that result in behaviors that seem maladaptive. Additionally, sensory-seeking and sensory-avoiding behaviors may exist without serious behavior problems. When serious behavior problems exist, the possibility of a sensory component should not be overlooked as a possible factor in the analysis. This analysis is important because it leads to three main types of strategies that may be effective in positive behavior planning:

- In the case of sensory avoidance, staff members may be able to make environmental changes that will either reduce the presence of the irritating sensory stimuli or allow the student more appropriate ways of controlling his or her responses.

➤ **Example of reduction:** Reduce extraneous sounds by relocating some activities and installing carpeting.

- ➤ **Example of student control of response:** Provide free access to a "quiet corner" or the use of headphones to listen to music when sounds become too irritating.

- • In the case of sensory-seeking behavior, it may be possible to use the identified stimuli as a reinforcer for a desirable behavior.

- ➤ **Example:** Provide contingent access to Koosh balls and yarn balls for a child who seeks tactile stimulation.

- • Finally, clues regarding specific accommodations may be revealed by considering sensory responses in relation to the function of a particular behavior.

To assist with analyzing sensory-avoidance and sensory-seeking, Figure 15 is offered to exemplify extreme sensory responses in each sensory modality that may indicate a serious behavior problem.

The reader is referred to the appendices for a sensory inventory that may assist the BICM in assessing sensory responsiveness.

The following are summaries of several case studies, exemplifying hypersensitivities and hyposensitivities that were related to serious behavior problems.

Individual and situation specific accommodation to auditory hypersensitivity

Matt *A 7 year old with Tourette syndrome*

On repeated occasions, Matt would suddenly begin throwing food in the cafeteria, screaming, and fighting with peers. Suspension, rewarding good behavior, and parent contact were unsuccessful before the functional analysis. Matt had no insight as to the cause of his behavior; he simply blamed others. Analysis revealed that the cafeteria had reverberating acoustics, Matt's class sat in the middle of the cafeteria, and Matt's parents report that he is hypersensitive to sound. By allowing Matt to choose a friend, go to the cafeteria 2 minutes early, and sit near the door, rather than in the middle, noise was reduced, escape was readily available, and all acting out was eliminated.

Environmental accommodation to tactile defensiveness

Bobby *A 6 year old with Fragile X syndrome*

Bobby consistently resisted sitting in morning group. However, he clearly enjoyed the songs, preparing the photo schedule of the day, and greetings. In fact, he requested these activities almost every day. Various types of chairs, beanbags, and positions were tried, but Bobby insisted on getting up, walking around behind the group of four other students, and yelling to the teacher that he wanted a turn. Bobby entered the group only when it was his turn to put up a picture or lead a song. Making his turn contingent upon sitting in his seat was not effective, because it led to Bobby throwing objects. This was determined to be a serious behavior problem by the IEP team because Bobby was totally unavailable for instruction during this time, the behavior had persisted for many months, and peers were often hit with objects. Bobby was tactilely defensive. He had a particularly strong reaction when someone approached him from behind or from the side and then touched him. He was better able to tolerate tactile stimuli when he could see it approaching. Bobby's seat was moved to the edge of the group, where he had the wall to the side of him and a bookcase in back of him. He was then able to stay in his seat for the entire group time because the natural barriers protected him from being touched without his being forewarned by seeing the approach coming.

FIGURE 15.

ANALYZING SENSORY RESPONSES

Stimuli	Examples of Sensory Avoidance and/or Low Tolerance	Examples of Sensory Seeking and/or High Tolerance
Tactile (touch) Body and limbs	• Wears clothes to cover entire body regardless of weather (resisting unrestricted environmental touch by covering the body) • Wears minimal clothes regardless of weather (resisting touch of garments on body) • Resists physical prompting • Excessive complaints of being bumped and poked • Has unusually large personal space	• Older child who touches everything • Frequently rubs, holds, or manipulates objects of a certain texture • Rubs fingers or body parts constantly • Unaware of substances spilled on body (e.g., glue on hands)
Deep pressure	• Resists tumbling, contact sports, jumping, bouncing • Appears to lack strength for functional tasks but on testing has adequate strength	• Frequently seeks deep-pressure touch such as bear hugs • Will sleep only when wrapped tightly in a sheet or blanket • Frequently bumps into objects and people without apparent reason
Oral/facial	• Primarily eats one type of food texture • Extremely resistant to face washing, tooth brushing, and hair brushing and continues to complain when finished	• Frequently chews or sucks on nonedibles • Appears unaware of touch to face unless there is visual input • Often unaware of food on face or drooling
Pain	• Unusual and prolonged complaints of minor incidents of pain • Complains about or interprets minor body sensations as "painful"	• Unaware of bleeding or swelling of sustained injury • Unusual fearlessness of falling on hard surfaces • Doesn't seem to feel injections • Unaware of sustained burns or sunburns
Temperature	• Consistently comments about temperature changes when experienced • Tends to react to and/or label moderate temperatures as too hot or too cold	• Drinks very hot liquids without complaint • Insists on very warm bath water *continued on next page*

FIGURE 15. *CONTINUED*

Stimuli	Examples of Sensory Avoidance and/or Low Tolerance	Examples of Sensory Seeking and/or High Tolerance
Auditory (sound)	• Covers ears frequently • Notices or comments on quiet background noises, such as normal traffic outside, air conditioning fan, or quiet noises in an adjacent room • Consistently seeks quiet areas away from peers on playground or in classroom • Runs out of room or area in response to sounds • Irrational fear of small appliances such as a blender, vacuum cleaner, or mixer • Hears sirens or oncoming trains before others	• Does not respond to commands without visual cues • Appears to have poor hearing not verified by hearing tests • Seeks unusually loud Walkman sound level (with documented normal hearing) • Puts ear on speakers
Visual **Sight and light**	• Turns off regular household lighting for activities such as eating, watching TV, or playing • Covers eyes or squints frequently • Avoids going outdoors on sunny days • Regularly comments when sun goes in and out of clouds	• Spins brightly colored or reflecting objects, watches light through leaves • Frequently flicks lights on and off • Watches repetitive movements, such as automatic door opening and closing or flipping pages of a book • Manipulates objects close to face although does not have visual impairment
Movement **Body moving through space**	• Fearful and/or resistant during team games, such as basketball, softball, chase/tag • Avoids positions and movements that challenge one's balance • Avoids positions where feet are off the ground • Reacts negatively to head being tipped back in space.	• Not afraid of heights or falling hazards • Excessive seeking of tumbling and wrestling activities • Spins in circles excessively
Reactions to movement forces	• Avoids playground equipment that propels the body through space, such as swings, merry-go-rounds, slides, teeter-totters. • Motion sickness • Fearful of escalators and/or elevators	• Seeks spinning activities for prolonged periods • Consistently assumes unusual positions on playground equipment • Craves fast rides at amusement parks
Vibration	• Fearful of barber's clippers • Refuses to hold food mixer, hair dryers, Dustbuster • Fearful of electric toothbrushes but not normal ones	• Places entire vibrator, or a side of a vibrating appliance, in or near mouth repeatedly • Tolerates vibratory stimuli for extended periods
Smell and taste	• Primarily eats bland foods • Reacts to or comments on normal odors as though they were irritating • Reacts to or comments on faint odors that go unnoticed by others	• Fails to notice noxious smell • Seeks highly seasoned foods

Changing a dangerous self-abusive behavior into one that is safer and more socially appropriate

Sally | *A 6 year old with Down syndrome.*

Sally bit her left hand repeatedly throughout the day and had formed a callous from the biting. The function of her biting appeared to be primarily "sensory" in nature, determined through analysis of the baseline data. Several times, an open wound had developed and had become infected. The infections were prolonged because she continued to bite the wound. Sally was given a small key ring with a plastic float (the type that is usually used for boat keys), which she kept in her pocket. Every time she bit her hand, she was redirected to bite the key ring. This required constant monitoring from an adult for 2 full days. On the third day, Sally began to bite the key ring instead of her hand some of the time. The frequency of her biting the ring increased steadily and her hand biting her hand Sally's biting incidents were on the ring, and the callous on her hand was visibly diminished. An array of hard, raw fruits and vegetables (such as apples, carrots, and celery) were provided by Sally's mother each day for the following 4 weeks. Sally was offered this food each time she bit the key ring. By the end of this 4 week period, biting in general had been decreased by 50% and biting of the key ring had been replaced with biting a carrot. Hard, crunchy food was eventually reduced to three scheduled snack times per day, and Sally was completely independent at getting her snack and eating it quietly without disrupting others. When last observed, she bit her hand only when she became extremely upset or frustrated, and this behavior was beginning to be addressed through other techniques and strategies.[4]

Approach/avoidance behavior during desensitization process

Ryan | *A 7 year old, diagnosed with autism, high functioning.*

Ryan would get into fights in the weekly large group activities, such as assemblies, with peers from all grade levels. During the functional analysis of behavior, it was determined that Ryan got agitated as the noise level increased in that setting and then would hit someone. Relaxation techniques were tried before the assembly and while in the setting. Use of relaxation techniques reduced but did not eliminate the fighting behaviors. Ryan was told that when he got agitated and relaxation techniques did not help, he could leave the area and stand outside until he was calm. The first day, Ryan left three times in 20 minutes. By the end of the month, Ryan was leaving only once per period and had started only one fight. After three months, Ryan often stayed in the setting the entire period, and all fighting stopped. Ryan's IEP team felt increased integration opportunities could now be offered to Ryan.

General Guidelines for Developing Behavioral Interventions Related to Suspected Sensory-Avoidan r Sensory-Seeking Behavior

✓ When the function of a behavior is thought to be the provision of additional sensory stimuli, it is generally helpful to look for a replacement behavior that is less dangerous, less disruptive, and/or more socially appropriate.

✓ In working with individuals with severe behavior problems it may be helpful to be aware of the types of sensory stimuli that are generally calming (instead of arousing or alerting). Hyperarousal is often described as unpleasant or even painful. Therefore, calming stimuli are important to counteract this effect in the hypersensitive individual.

a. Generally, calming stimuli include the following
    (adapted from King, 1986):
    (1) Deep-pressure touch, such as massage, lying between two bean bag chairs, or bouncing. This bouncing may be energetic or slow and rhythmic. Calming effects may differ for different students.
    (2) Neutral warmth, as in retaining the body's heat with a blanket or jacket.
    (3) Chewing, sucking, or licking.
    (4) Vibratory stimulus that is large amplitude and low frequency, as experienced when riding in a car.
    (5) Decreased physical activity.
    (6) Slow, rhythmic movement, such as slow swinging or rocking.
    (7) Quiet music with a definite, predictable rhythm. Instrumental, orchestral music with no vocals may be best.

b. Activities that are alerting generally include the following
    (adapted from King, 1986):
    (1) Light touch, such as tickling, wiping skin with a soft cloth, or light brushing or stroking.
    (2) Cold or chilling activities such as touching ice cubes or standing in a cold breeze.
    (3) Spinning.
    (4) Fast-frequency vibration, as in therapy vibrators (about 300 cycles per second).
    (5) Increased physical activity.

✓ Sensory-seeking individuals may benefit from increased opportunities, throughout the day, to receive the type of sensory input that they seem to seek. For example, a student who rocks a lot may benefit from increased opportunities to use a swing or rocking chair. A student who is seeking proprioceptive stimulation may benefit from regular opportunities to engage in active play, jogging, climbing, pushing, pulling, or lifting.

✓ Alternate active and sedentary tasks to allow for appropriate ways to receive stimulation from movement. Including more varied and functional tasks with more opportunities for choice can be an alternate way of providing the student with increased sensory input.

✓ Provide free time and/or play activities and materials that create appropriate methods for obtaining various types of sensory stimuli.

✓ Consider allowing students to choose their own position for working. In addition to sitting at a table, they could work standing, lying on the floor, sitting in a bean bag chair, or using a chalkboard or easel.

✓ When observing avoidance behaviors, try to identify the specific type or types of sensory stimuli to which the student is sensitive. Attempt to eliminate, soften, or reduce the stimuli. There are many ways to do this, and the appropriateness of a technique will depend on the situation and environment in which it occurs. Examples include dimming lights, reducing background noise, removing extraneous visual stimuli from the classroom or work area, muffling sound with earphones, increasing space between the student and the stimulus, reducing physical/tactile contact with staff and other students, arranging furniture to create a barrier between the student and the stimulus, and positioning the student at the edge of a group of students.

✓ For some students with avoidance behaviors, there is a cumulative effect of exposure to various types of sensory stimuli or repeated exposures to one type. For example, quiet talking in the classroom may not bother a particular student at 9:00 a.m. but may cause an extreme reaction just before lunch. This may be caused by continuous exposure to the background noise of talking, along with a lawn mower motor outside, several vehicles with sirens passing by, background music from the listening center, 15 minutes on a crowded playground at recess, and intermittent verbal instructions by the teacher all morning. Therefore, limiting and controlling some or all types of sensory stimuli in general may be an important environmental accommodation. Using a study carrel or ear phones (without sound) are common classroom techniques to limit extraneous stimuli.

✓ Try not to surprise the student with the unpleasant stimuli. If it can't be eliminated, at least try to prepare the student before it is present. For example, many students who are tactilely defensive are able to tolerate physical guidance if they are warned before it occurs. This may be as simple as approaching them from the front rather than the side or back, or asking if you can help them perform a certain motor task. For students who overreact to sound, it may be helpful to warn them a minute or so before the school bell rings.

✓ For some individuals, stimuli that trigger the memory of overstimulation can cause anxiety and an exaggerated response. For example, the student described earlier, Greg, had the same response to seeing a photo of a vacuum cleaner in a book as he had when a real one was being used in the hallway. Staff members should be aware that some environmental conditions may trigger these memories. The same techniques used when the actual stimuli are present will probably be effective.

✓ Many stimuli cannot be totally eliminated or reduced at all times. Therefore, systematic desensitization may also be effective. It may be helpful to consult an occupational or physical therapist when planning and implementing systematic desensitization; however, the following general guidelines are offered:

   a. After a particular stimulus is identified, allow and encourage the student to approach the stimulus on his or her own terms rather than bringing it to the student. Examples of this include physically approaching an object, turning lights on or off, using a noisy appliance or machine, gazing at a colorful object, or standing at the door of a noisy room.

   b. Expect the student to need many trials of approaching and retreating from the stimulus. Praise or reinforce the student for attempts to approach it, but do not pressure, scold, or punish the student for retreating or not approaching it. The emphasis should be on giving the student control of the situation. Using reinforcers that pair the unpleasant stimulus with one that is calming and pleasant for the student may be helpful in some cases. For example, if chewing or crunching is calming for the student, good reinforcers may be bubble gum, gummie bears, celery, carrots, or apples.

c. Provide regular opportunities for the student to approach the stimulus, even after the student seems to have overcome hypersensitivity to it. In absence of the stimulus, the hypersensitivity may reappear.

d. Desensitization does not necessarily generalize to all materials or situations that cause a certain type of sensory stimulation. For example, a student who is hypersensitive to the auditory and vibratory sensations from appliance motors and is desensitized to a vacuum cleaner may continue to have a severe reaction to a blender, fan, and mixer. This is why both environmental accommodations and systematic desensitization are often used together.

Stereotypic Behaviors

Stereotypic behaviors are similar to, and in some cases may be the same as, self-stimulatory behaviors. As with self-stimulatory behaviors, elimination of stereotypic behaviors (e.g., spinning, rocking, or hand flapping) may not be necessary unless they interfere with learning or safety. The presence of stereotypic behaviors, then, probably should be termed a "serious behavior problem" only if it compromises safety or significantly interrupts learning. Furthermore, high-functioning persons with autism have reported that sensory stimuli are often overwhelming and confusing. One adult with autism related that his efforts to control stereotypic movements left him feeling guarded and anxious (*Autism Research Review International,* 1991). Stereotypic behavior thus may serve to ease anxiety, discomfort, or distraction from a flood of extraneous stimulation. Supportive intervention in these cases would include identifying and reducing environmental stressors.

Another hypothesized function of stereotypic behavior is that of increasing arousal. In fact, this may be another way of looking at sensory-seeking behaviors. When this is suspected, intervention may involve adding activities and materials of interest to the student or teaching recreational skills. Although increasing environmental stimulation sometimes decreases stereotypic behavior, the behaviors sometimes increase or do not change in frequency, according to studies cited in Meyer & Evans (1989).

The same stereotypic behaviors may serve different functions for an individual and vary in their meaning between individuals. Again, if they do not seriously disrupt learning or performance and are not injurious, it may be counterproductive to attempt to alter stereotypic or self-stimulatory behaviors because symptom substitution frequently occurs. For example, Brian regularly squeezed a small block held in his hand. When this behavior was extinguished, flapping his hand in front of his eyes spontaneously emerged.

Self-stimulatory behavior deemed a "pervasive maladaptive behavior" by the IEP team

---

Alice | *An 11 year old with significant visual impairment and other developmental disabilities.*

Alice rubbed her eyebrows with a sweeping motion across her entire face when stressed. This occurred in all settings, including during mobility training, when she was faced with unfamiliar street crossings. Because she has limited field vision and the additional compromise to her safety because of her hand motions, the BICM recommended instituting an intervention plan to teach Alice to tolerate and verbally express her stress more adaptively and to allow Alice to use the same sweeping hand motions on her waist belt (a substitute stereotypic behavior that will not compromise her safety).

Self-Injurious Behaviors

Self-injurious behaviors are repetitive behaviors that can endanger a person's personal safety. All self-injurious behaviors should be given formal consideration. Low-intensity self-injurious behaviors can escalate to serious problems and become prominent habits in a person's repertoire. Common self-injurious behaviors include head banging, scratching, face slapping, finger and hand biting, skin picking, hair pulling, lip biting, eye gouging, vomiting, rumination (a condition usually seen in infants where stomach contents is regurgitated or partially reswallowed), and cutting oneself with sharp objects. Behaviors such as head banging, eye gouging, hand or lip biting, and face slapping can lead to concussions, sensory loss, and body destruction. Interventions for self-injurious behaviors should always be instituted with systematic plans that are formally developed, based on the functional analysis of the behavior and well-monitored.

Self-injurious behaviors are influenced by a variety of environmental, physiological, and communicative factors. **Environmental factors**, such as physical crowding, noise level, bright glaring lights, and temperature may influence the extent to which an individual is able to keep self-injurious behaviors under control. Research has indicated that **physiological factors** may also influence self-aggressive behaviors. Deficiencies in biochemicals, central nervous system damage, and neurological insensitivity to pain are factors contributing to the biological basis of self-injurious behavior. Extreme self-injury may be attributed to frontal lobe seizures (Gedye, 1989), and self-injurious behaviors may increase after puberty (Gillberg & Steffenburg, 1987). Physiological influences on self-injurious behaviors have been attributed to schizophrenia, autism, Lesch-Nyhan syndrome, Fragile X syndrome, Prader-Willi syndrome, Cornelia de Lange syndrome, Rett syndrome, and Riley-Day syndrome. However, self-destruction of organic origin may acquire a **communicative function**, and organic origin does not negate the possibility of behavioral change following intervention (Duker, 1975). Acute physiological factors, such as hunger, fatigue, illness, or injury, may also exacerbate the demonstration of self-injurious behaviors.

Individuals display self-injurious behaviors for a variety of reasons. It is believed that nearly all self-injurious behaviors serve a purpose for the individual. Self-injurious behaviors may result from a need for more sensory stimulation than the environment is providing. When individuals repeat self-injurious behaviors when left alone for long periods of time, it is considered to play a **self-stimulatory sensory function**; that is, it provides the individual with an adequate level of stimulation. However, research has suggested that people use self-injurious behaviors primarily for communicative intent (Durand, 1990). There appears to be a strong relationship between severe communication deficits and the presence of self-destructive behaviors (Shodell & Reiter, 1968). The behavior the student uses is a strategy to achieve a desired end or result—the communicative intent of the behavior. If the behavior occurs primarily after an individual has been asked to perform a difficult or undesirable task, it serves an **avoidance function**, allowing the individual to escape undesired environmental events or activities. **Attention** is considered to be the motivator if the behavior escalates when caregivers leave or ignore the student, pay attention to others in the environment, or pay extra attention to the individual only after observing self-injury. Individuals are considered to use self-injurious behaviors to obtain **tangible rewards** when escalation of behavior is in response to being deprived of a desired toy, object, food, or activity or if the behavior stops when the desired object is provided.

Social and task-related factors also influence behaviors. Self-injurious behaviors may increase in the presence of specific persons or certain classes of persons (e.g., males, nurses, peers) or in response to certain staffing patterns. It is well-documented that self-injurious behaviors tend to decrease when students are provided with an environment in which positive interpersonal interactions are prevalent. Self-injurious behaviors are also known to increase when task demands are too stringent or if a moderately stringent task follows an easier one. In contrast, self-injurious behaviors tend to subside when the moderately stringent task follows a more difficult demand. Thus, conditions just preceding an event in which the self-injurious behavior occurs can affect its occurrence and should be examined carefully.

Because self-injurious behavior addresses various needs among students and even within a single student, a prescriptive intervention approach must be used. Functional analysis of the circumstances in which self-injurious behaviors occur leads to intervention plans based on the conditions that have maintained the behavior. The student can then be taught adaptive "communicative" behaviors to replace the maladaptive ones.

Medications and flexible arm splints may be medically ordered and required to control some extreme self-injurious behavior when it occurs. The flexible arm splints prevent contact between the hands and mouth or eyes without restricting range of motion (Ball, Purna, Rios & Constantine, 1985). Even when medication or splints successfully prevent self-injury, interveners must remember that the behavior was a means of communicating internal states and needs. Efforts should continue to understand, respect, and respond to the needs the behavior served, to teach more adaptive modes of communicating, and to support positive behavior through appropriate changes in the environment. Reduced need for, or elimination of, these medical interventions is frequently observed with appropriate behavioral intervention plan implementation.

Examples of effective intervention strategies include the following:

Teaching words, signs, or symbols to replace the self-injurious behaviors used to obtain desired rewards

Shana *A 12 year old with severe developmental disability.*

Shana habitually slapped her face. Functional analysis determined that her face slapping was more intensive around mealtime and appeared to be used to obtain tangible rewards (food). Teaching her to sign for her favorite foods resulted in a decrease in her self-injurious behavior. Initially, school personnel increased attention to Shana during mealtime to respond promptly when her more adaptive communicative strategy was used.

Teaching requests for help when avoidance of difficult tasks appear to be maintaining self-injurious behavior

Jojo *An 8 year old with moderate developmental disability.*

Jojo became easily frustrated. He responded to difficult tasks by yelling and hitting his head. Jojo was taught the sign and the words for "Help me." Initially, teachers would prompt the request before frustration became evident by asking him if he needed help. Gradually, the teachers stopped prompting him but remained close. Eventually, Jojo learned to go to the teacher and sign, "Help me!"

Teaching requests for social interaction when desire for attention appears to be maintaining self-injurious behavior

> ## Sally | *A 16 year old with severe mental retardation.*
>
> Sally frequently screamed and gouged her eyes. During functional analysis, it was noted that Sally poked her eyes when left alone for more than 5 minutes. She was taught to sign, "I help?" to obtain caregiver involvement in a more appropriate manner. Sally then joined the teacher in a joint task. The intervention plan was set up to ensure that the request could be fulfilled and that someone was always available during training to respond. Sally became increasingly demanding, but all requests were responded to for 2 weeks. Then specific training procedures were instituted to signify that a request would be answered immediately (green card on desk) or a request would be answered in a few seconds or few minutes (red card on desk). Gradually, Sally learned to accept a delay in response to her appropriate attention-seeking behavior.

MEDICAL INTERVENTION IN MULTIMODAL APPROACH

Medications are often prescribed and found to be an effective component of a multimodal approach to the management of psychiatric disorders in children and adolescents. School personnel need to understand this type of intervention. Medications may control symptoms not managed by other techniques and can facilitate other therapeutic procedures. Physicians and parents must weigh the possible side effects of the medication against the potential benefits before a medication is used. Medications, after they are prescribed by the physician, should be monitored regularly so that adjustments or changes may be made. Good medical management dictates that medications should not be used longer than necessary. The physician and parent(s) should investigate the use of medication on the disability and/or behavior disorder. In addition, dosage may be reduced periodically to determine if the symptoms can be controlled with lower levels. Because medications may have a placebo effect that is sometimes equal in benefit to the pharmacological reactions induced, placebos may be prescribed. Teachers are frequently asked to report whether there were behavioral changes with changes of medication or dosage.

A multimodal approach is essential to effective management of behavior problems. Other sections of this manual discuss the importance of school-home communication and development of other behavioral interventions. Many studies have documented the efficacy of behavioral approaches without the use of medication, even for very serious behaviors.

Review of the impact of medication on behavior is an important aspect of functional analysis and may require close coordination among the physician, family, and school personnel. The following critical questions have been reported to be helpful in case management:[5]

- Are the family and/or student aware of anticipated benefits of the treatment and potential side effects?

- Is there an identified medical case manager (most often the pediatrician) overseeing the medical treatment of the student? Care may be provided by a number of specialists for some individuals.

- Are the therapeutic effects of treatment being monitored regularly?

- Is the student being monitored regularly for side effects? Is the family returning the student for regular follow-up?
- Is there a possibility that the current dosage or medication type is no longer optimal?

Figures 16 and 17, pp. 157-159, are provided as a brief guide to some of the frequently prescribed medications for the control of various behavior disorders, along with their potential benefits and possible side effects. These are included to help school personnel understand the desired effects and potential side effects of the medications already prescribed for their students. They are not meant to direct the medical management of any student.

---

1 This chart, adapted by the authors, was developed by Robert Sapolsky, biologist at Stanford University, and presented in his workshop "The Beast Within," 1993.

2 For information on local services and further resources, contact the Southern California Head Injury Foundation, P.O. Box 3955, Downey, CA 90242-4091, (310) 803-4418.

3 It is recognized that off-task behavior is rarely a serious behavior problem. However, this example is included to demonstrate that relaxation training can benefit an entire group, even if only one person in the group specifically requires a formal behavior management plan.

4 Self-abusive behavior frequently is found to have multiple functions for the individual and requires careful analysis. This case is not meant to imply that the function of self-abusive behavior can be determined to be "sensory" without individual functional analysis.

5 The task force medical consultant, Eva Mauer, M.D., suggests that concerns on any of these five points be discussed and/or clarified with the physician managing medications for behavior. In some circumstances, what might appear to be unusual treatment practice is in fact indicated for that particular individual. The BICM can play an important role as a member of both the medical and educational teams providing care for the student. Although reporting observations to the medical care team is the legitimate role of the educational team, changes in medication and medical management in general must occur under the specific direction of the student's physician

Figure 16.
Medications Used in the Management of Disruptive Behavioral Disorders

The following medication chart is provided as a brief guide to some of the medications used in the management of various behavior disorders, along with their potential benefits and possible side effects. It is included to help school personnel understand the effects and potential side effects of the medications already prescribed for their students. It is not meant to suggest medical management for any student. These treatments may or may not be approved by the FDA. A number of them are "off label" treatments, i.e., treatments not specifically approved by the FDA for that drug. Some have been proven effective in double blind studies, others have not. Medication effectiveness and side effects may also vary with the age of the child and other health conditions. Please refer to the footnotes for an explanation of the abbreviations in the "Used for" column.

Medication	ADHD	OCD	Autism	Tourettes	Aggression	Psychosis	Depression	Bipolar	Seizures	Other	Anticipated Benefits	Disadvantages
Stimulant Group												
Ritalin (methylphenidate)	+		A, H	A							• Increased attention span. • Decreased distractibility and motor restlessness. • Decreased impulsivity. • Takes effect within an hour. • May be given daily or used only on school days.	• May decrease appetite. • May cause insomnia. • Can heighten emotional sensitivity. • May lead to headaches, dizziness, abdominal discomfort, skin rash. • Growth problems may occur at high dosages. • Not approved for children under six years. • Excessive dosage may cause decreased attention and lowered academic performance. • May cause or aggravate tics.
Dexedrine (dextroamphetamine)	+		A, H	A								

A = Attention   P = Perseveration   T = Tics   W = Warning   H = Hyperactivity   OCD = Obsessive compulsive disorder
Pa = Panic   Ax = Anxiety   + = Positive effects on general symptoms

Figure 16. Continued

Medication	ADHD	OCD	Autism	Tourettes	Aggression	Psychosis	Depression	Bipolar	Seizures	Other	Anticipated Benefits	Disadvantages
Long-Acting Stimulants												
Ritalin SR, Concerta, Methylin ER, Metadate ER (methylphenidate)	+		A, H	A							• As for Ritalin. • Lasts 8 to 24 hours.	• As for Ritalin.
Cylert (pemoline)	+		A, H	A								• Cylert must be taken daily.
Biphetamine	+		A, H	A								• Cylert may increase lip licking/biting and finger picking.
Dexedrine spansule	+		A, H	A								
Adderal	+		A, H	A								
Antidepressants												
Tofranil (imipramine)	+		A, H	A			+		W	Pa	• Diminish impulsive behaviors. • Decrease hyperactivity. • Treat depression. • Help with mood disturbance. • Improve compulsive and perseverative behavior. • Decrease bed wetting.	• May aggravate a seizure condition. • Cannot be used if there is a risk of psychosis. • Need to be taken daily. • May cause drowsiness, nausea, and constipation. • May cause tremor. • May increase depression. • Tofranil and norpramin can cause heart rhythm disturbances, and death may occur from over-dose.
Norpramin (desipramine)	+	+	A, H	A			+		W			
Anafranil (clomipramine)		+	P				+		W			
Prozac (fluoxetine)	+	+	P				+			Pa		
Wellbutrin (bupropion)	+			W			+		W			
Zoloft (sertraline)	+	+					+		W	Pa		
Paxil (paroxetine)		+					+			Pa		
Luvox (fluvoxamine)		+					+			Pa		

A = Attention   P = Perseveration   T = Tics   W = Warning   H = Hyperactivity   OCD = Obsessive compulsive disorder

Pa = Panic   Ax = Anxiety   + = Positive effects on general symptoms

Figure 16. Continued

Medication		Used for										Anticipated Benefits	Disadvantages
		ADHD	OCD	Autism	Tourettes	Aggression	Psychosis	Depression	Bipolar	Seizures	Other		
Antihypertensives	Catapres (clonidine) tablets skin patch	+	+		A,T	+						• May improve ADHD and aggressive behavior. • May also be used to treat compulsive behaviors and tics.	• May lower blood pressure. • May cause drowsiness. • Skin patch may be removed and swallowed. • Requires monitoring of blood pressure and pulse.
	Tenex (guanfacine)				A, T								
Anticonvulsants Group	Tegretol (carbamazepine)	+							+	+		• May be used in hyperactive patients with seizure disorders. • May be effective when aggression is associated with hyperactivity or organic brain syndrome.	• Requires monitoring of blood levels, and bone marrow and liver functions. • Drowsiness, poor balance, and behavior problems.
	Depakene (valproate)	+						+	+	+			
	Klonopin (clonazepam)	+								+			
Major Tranquilizers	Haldol (haloperidol)			+	T		+					• Reserved for serious disorders characterized by excessive aggressiveness/psychosis. • May have antiaggressive effects.	• Sleepiness. • Involuntary body movements or stiffness. • May decrease mental acuity. • Clozaril may cause bone marrow or liver problems.
	Mellaril (thioridazine)						+						
	Thorazine (chlorpromazine)						+						
	Stelazine						+						
	Orap (pimozide)				T		+						
	Risperdal (risperidone)		?		T		+			W			
	Clozaril (clozapine)						+				W		

A = Attention   P = Perseveration   T = Tics   H = Hyperactivity   OCD = Obsessive compulsive disorder
Pa = Panic   Ax = Anxiety   W = Warning   + = Positive effects on general symptoms

Figure 16. Continued

Medication		ADHD	OCD	Autism	Tourettes	Aggression	Psychosis	Depression	Bipolar	Seizures	Other	Anticipated Benefits	Disadvantages
Minor Tranquilizers	Librium										Ax	• Decreased anxiety. • Decreased agitation. • Buspar may decrease aggression associated with organic brain disorders.	• Sedation. • Risk of psychological dependence.
	Valium									+	Ax		
	Xanax									+	Ax		
	Buspar	+				+					Ax		
	Ativan									+	Ax		
Antihistamines	Benadryl (diphenhydramine)										+	• May decrease anxiety. • May improve sleep. • Antihistamine.	• Dry mouth. • Restlessness.
	Atarax (hydroxizine)										+		
Narcotic Antagonist	Naltrexone			H							+	• May decrease self-injury in children with autism. • May decrease hyperactivity in autism.	• Requires regular liver function screening. • Lethargy. • Irritability. • Loss of appetite.
Other	Lithium Carbonate (in manic-depressive disorder)	?							+	+		• Diminish manic-depressive symptoms.	• Needs monitoring for toxicity.

A = Attention P = Perseveration T = Tics W = Warning H = Hyperactivity OCD = Obsessive compulsive disorder
Pa = Panic Ax = Anxiety + = Positive effects on general symptoms

Figure 16. Continued

Medication		ADHD	OCD	Autism	Tourettes	Aggression	Psychosis	Depression	Bipolar	Seizures	Other	Anticipated Benefits	Disadvantages
Beta Blocker	Inderal (propranolol)					+						• May reduce aggressive acts secondary to brain damage (rage reaction).	• May slow heart rate and lower blood pressure. • Drowsiness. • Aggravates asthma.
Food Supplements	Vitamin B6 with Magnesium			+								• Improved social awareness. • Decreased rage reaction.	• Irritability. • Difficult to administer.
	DMG			+								• Decreased stereotypic behavior.	
	Folic Acid (in fragile X)										+	• Improved attention and behavior. • Decreased activity and impulsivity.	• Paradoxical response of decreased attention and increased activity.

NOTE: This chart represents a sampling of medications and is by no means comprehensive. The chart was developed by Joanne Weigel, M.D., as a summary review of the current literature on medications used for this purpose. The uses of the listed medications are based on medical research and current practice. Some of these have not been specifically approved by the FDA. For more extensive and up-to-date information on any medication or condition, consult the individual's medical provider.

A = Attention P = Perseveration T = Tics W = Warning H = Hyperactivity OCD = Obsessive compulsive disorder
Pa = Panic Ax = Anxiety + = Positive effects on general symptoms

Figure 17.
Antiepileptic Medications

The following chart is not intended to be a comprehensive description of all seizure medications. It is designed to assist parents and educators to identify potential problems arising from a child's anticonvulsant medication regimen. The side effects listed, such as bone marrow suppression, may be rare, and/or related to a specific age range. Drug interactions may be managed appropriately by following blood levels. Consult the child's physician for specific information regarding risks and benefits of a specific set of medications.

Medication Trade name / Generic name	Seizure Types					Side Effects			Interactions with Other Anticonvulsants
	GM	Ab	SP	PC	LG	Neurological	Behavior	Physical	
Luminal phenobarbital	✓		✓	✓		• Drowsiness in 10% • Impairs learning and cognition (worst offender) • Ataxia	• Hyperactivity (worst offender) • Depression	• Rash	• valproate
Mysoline primidone	✓		✓	✓		• Drowsiness • Ataxia	• Depression		• carbamazepine • phenytoin • valproate • clonazepam
Zarontin ethosuximide		✓						• Nausea • Vomiting • Anorexia • Rash	• carbamazepine • phenobarbital • phenytoin
Klonopin clonazepam		✓	✓	✓		• Drowsiness • Impaired balance	• Hyperactivity • Irritability	• Rash • Decreased white blood count	• carbamazepine • phenobarbital • phenytoin
Tegretol carbamazepine	✓			✓		• Drowsiness • Double vision • No intellectual impairments reported • Impaired balance	• Least behavior problems	• Nausea • Headache • Rash in 13% • Chemical hepatitis • Bone marrow suppression	• phenytoin • valproate • ethosuximide • lamotrigine • phenobarbital • felbamate

GM = grand mal or generalized   Ab = absence or petit mal   SP = simple partial or myoclonic
PC = partial complex or psychomotor   LG = Lennox Gastaux

Figure 17. Continued

Medication	Seizure Types					Side Effects			Interactions with Other Anticonvulsants
Trade name Generic name	GM	Ab	SP	PC	LG	Neurological	Behavior	Physical	
Depakene *Depakote* valproate	√	√	√	√	√	• No intellectual impairments reported • Tremor	• Least behavior problems	• Nausea vomiting • Rash • Weight gain • Hair loss • Chemical hepatitis • Bone marrow suppression	• ethosuximide • lamotrigine • phenobarbital • felbamate
Dilantin phenytoin	√			√		• May interfere with learning • Attention problems • Slow mental processing and motor speed • Drowsiness • Double vision • Impaired balance		• Swollen gums • Coarse facial features • Hirsutism • Hepatitis • Bone marrow suppression	• phenobarbital • carbamazepine • lamotrigine • valproate
Felbatol felbamate	√	√	√	√	√	• Limited information	• Limited information	• Bone marrow suppression • Liver failure • Anorexia • Weight loss • Weight loss • Headaches • Insomnia	• phenytoin • phenobarbital • valproate
Neurontin gabapentin		√	√	√		• Dizziness • Ataxia • Drowsiness	• Tantrums • Aggression • Hyperactivity • Defiance	• Weight gain	• No

GM = grand mal or generalized   Ab = absence or petit mal   SP = simple partial or myoclonic
PC = partial complex or psychomotor   LG = Lennox Gastaux

Figure 17. Continued

Medication	Seizure Types					Side Effects			Interactions with Other Anticonvulsants
Trade name Generic name	GM	Ab	SP	PC	LG	Neurological	Behavior	Physical	
Lamictal lamotrigine	√	√	√	√	√	• Double vision • Drowsiness • Ataxia • Insomnia	• Limited information	• Rash in 10%	• valproate • carbamazepine • phenytoin • phenobarbital • primidone
Topamax topiramate	√			√	√	• Impaired concentration • Confusion and "thinking abnormal" • Dizziness and ataxia • Somnolence	• Limited information	• Fatigue	• carbamazepine • phenytoin • valproic acid
Gabitril tiagabine				√		• Dizziness • No effect on cognition		• Headache	• valproate

GM = grand mal or generalized   Ab = absence or petit mal   SP = simple partial or myoclonic
PC = partial complex or psychomotor   LG = Lennox Gastaux

Chapter 10

Timeout in the Context of the New Regulations

The regulations for the Hughes Bill do not address the use of timeout procedures except to prohibit locked seclusion, unless it is in a facility otherwise licensed or permitted by state law to use a locked room. Thus, other than this reference to locked seclusion, timeout procedures are neither forbidden nor specifically addressed within the regulations. This omission has caused numerous local educational agencies to express concern and confusion regarding the use of timeout procedures. This chapter is included to delineate some of the issues, not to endorse the general application of timeout procedures out of context of a complete positive behavior plan and an emergency plan approved by the special education local plan area (SELPA).

In most cases, timeout is a procedure that does not effectively suppress problem behavior in the long run. Additionally, it does not teach a positive alternative behavior and therefore is not a valid component of a positive behavior plan unless used as a time away procedure, as described below.[1]

The education community in general has long recognized the need for more effective techniques to suppress maladaptive behaviors. The new regulations are now helping to more universally disseminate the idea that suppression isn't enough, that it isn't even the correct focus. The legitimate role of education is teaching, and that includes the teaching of adaptive, functional behaviors. Although the regulations recognize the need for emergency procedures in some specific cases to protect the student and others, the clear emphasis of the regulations is not on managing emergencies. Rather, it is in teaching functional alternatives and managing emergencies safely for all.

It seems reasonable that the same principles that govern behavior intervention plans and emergency interventions also may be applied to the use of timeout procedures.[2] These principles are helpful when considering the appropriateness of time away methods as a teaching tool or as one, among many, available emergency procedures.[3]

Timeout from positive reinforcement can be a procedure within the context of a positive environment, but it is not universally effective and requires knowledgeable implementers. The following interpretative analysis is not meant to substitute for necessary grounding in behavior theory; rather, it is an interpretation of the information related to timeout as found in the new regulations.

Timeout Defined

Timeout is a procedure in which access to reinforcement is removed or reduced for a specified time period contingent on a response. Either the student is removed from the reinforcing environment, or the reinforcing environment is removed for a designated time period.

The following are disadvantages of timeout:

- It interferes with the learning opportunity.

- It frequently fails to change behavior because of a variety of interfering variables.

- The stimuli paired with timeout, from the person administering the procedure to the environment itself, may become aversive to the student.

- No positive alternative replacement behavior is being taught; it is not a legitimate positive behavior intervention when used as an aversive consequence.

- There is a strong potential for abuse in that caregivers sometimes apply it more often or more restrictively than necessary. (It is reinforcing to the caregiver to have the aversive behavior removed from the environment.)

Levels of Restrictiveness

Use of timeout with students who exhibit serious behavior problems requires careful consideration[4] as described in Sulzer-Azaroff & Mayer (1991).

There are various levels of restrictiveness: nonexclusionary timeout, exclusionary timeout, seclusion (or isolation), and locked timeout.

Nonexclusionary timeouts include planned ignoring, contingent observation, and use of a timeout ribbon. During planned ignoring (Nelson & Rutherford, 1983), the usual attention, physical contact, and verbal interactions are removed for a short period of time contingent on the occurrence of unwanted behavior. During contingent observation (Porterfield et al., 1976) the student is removed from the group and relocated nearby where he or she can observe but not participate in the activity. A third method, use of a timeout ribbon (Foxx & Shapiro, 1978) involves removing a ribbon the student wears, which signals that that student will not receive the reinforcers given to the other members of the group wearing the ribbon.

Exclusionary timeout involves moving the student to another part of the room or area.

Seclusion or isolation (Sulzer-Azaroff & Mayer, 1991) is another method. Legally, this term applies to removing a client to an isolated room or placing a client behind a barrier. There is case law that applies to this procedure. Essentially, adequate food, heat, light, ventilation, hygiene supplies, and clothing (and bedding if needed) are required. In *Morales v. Turman* (1973), a standard 50-minute maximum duration was established. In the *Wyatt* (1972) decision, seclusion for persons with mental retardation was prohibited unless "legitimate" timeout supervised by a professional in "behavior-shaping programs" was involved. The *Wyatt* decision established that emergency isolation of patients who harm themselves or others must not extend beyond 1 hour.

Locked timeout is an expressly forbidden procedure for agencies without a specific permit to use it. Education settings, public and nonpublic alike, do not have these permits.

Three General Principles

1. **Timeout, as an emergency procedure** for use in addressing a behavior problem demonstrated by a student with a disability, must not be the sole intervention in use to address the problem behavior. That is, there must be a positive behavior plan that is being implemented systematically. Timeout may be designated as a technique to use when less intense methods of intervention have failed to de-escalate an emergency.

2. **Timeout, as a component of the positive behavior intervention plan**, needs to:
   - be a part of a larger program that substitutes increasingly adaptive behaviors for problem behaviors;
   - aim toward increasing the student's independent ability to choose timeout for self-control purposes; and
   - lead to increased independence and access to reinforcers for the student.

     To be considered part of the positive behavior intervention plan, timeout must not be employed primarily as a method of containing or extinguishing the problem behavior. The guiding principle is that positive behavior plans are instructive and focus on developing new and appropriate behaviors.

     Designing programs to teach new adaptive behaviors requires identifying the communicative intent of the problem behavior. That is, it is necessary to determine what the student is seeking or avoiding and then to select and "teach" individually reinforcing and appropriate replacement behaviors rather than focusing exclusively on eradicating problem behavior.

3. **Timeout for behaviors that are not serious and/or timeout** for students not enrolled in special education, are not addressed by the regulations. Therefore, existing Education Code and special education local plan area/local education agency (SELPA/LEA) practices govern these conditions.

Timeout as an Emergency Intervention

Timeout may meet the definition of an emergency intervention when used in response to a serious behavior problem exhibited by a special education student in which less intensive interventions have not diffused a dangerous situation at that specific moment. "'Serious behavior problems' are defined as . . ." those that are ". . . self-injurious, assaultive, or cause serious property damage and other severe behavior problems that are pervasive and maladaptive for which instructional/behavioral approaches specified in the student's IEP are found to be ineffective." [§3001(y)].

An emergency intervention may be used only if the following provisions are met:
- The timeout is administered only after it is determined that no lesser intervention would serve to curtail the problem behavior.
- The behavior plan implementer follows SELPA procedures in documenting the application of the emergency procedure and the SELPA has approved the method of using timeout, as it does all emergency procedures.
- The timeout lasts only as long as is necessary to curtail the behavior.
- The parent is notified within 24 hours.
- No locked, secluded timeout procedure is used.
- A Behavior Emergency Report must be written "immediately," documenting the emergency.

In situations where no positive behavior intervention plan is in place, whenever there is a Behavioral Emergency Report written, an IEP meeting must be scheduled within two days. The IEP team must review the Behavior Emergency Report and determine whether a functional analysis assessment and/or an interim positive behavior plan are needed. For further details regarding the application of the Hughes Bill and its regulations pertaining to behavioral emergencies, the reader is referred to Chapter 6, "Emergency Procedures."

Michael

Michael at chronological age 11 is a student with a severe emotional disturbance in nonpublic school placement (the regulations apply to non-public as well as public school placements). Michael would occasionally become aggressive towards classmates, throwing books and screaming. This has been occurring about three times per month over the last four months, since the behavior plan was developed. Prior to the intervention, Michael had been doing this on the average of four times per week. The positive behavior plan documented steady progress in Michael's ability to verbally, nonaggressively state his needs, an alternate functional equivalent to the maladaptive behavior of screaming and throwing. Michael received additional tokens for the alternative behavior, exchangeable for reinforcers daily as well as aggression replacement therapy in group setting.

In each situation where it was observed that aggression was forthcoming, the team:

1) attempted to use verbal de-escalation strategies to prevent the increase in aggression:
2) filed a written report,
3) contacted the parent within 24 hours if escalation was not stoppable,
4) provided a safe timeout area where Michael could not hurt himself or others,
5) provided a team member in visual contact with Michael the entire time.

Throwing books ended as soon as he went into timeout. As soon as the screaming ended, the discussion phase and readiness for return procedures began. Michael returned to the group when he exhibited a normal pulse rate and had calmly discussed the incident and his intent to return to safe behavior. Loss of points towards a reinforcer occurred as a natural consequence because the classwide program called for the teacher to give points for appropriate behavior to each individual at 15-minute intervals. The explosive behavior episode yielded zero points in every interval in which it occurred. The IEP team had set criteria that would require refining the behavior plan if these outbursts were more frequent than two times per week or if the behavior had not been significantly reduced after six months of intervention (significant reduction defined as less than once per month).

Time Away as Part of a Positive Behavior Intervention Plan

In some cases, a pupil with an individualized education program (IEP) and a positive behavior intervention plan may have a form of timeout in his or her plan as a positive procedure, rather than as an emergency procedure. In this case, the plan implementers may choose to designate the timeout with different terminology, such as *time away*, to clearly differentiate the procedure from the timeout emergency procedure. This terminology change is not contained in the regulations, but rather is a suggestion.

The purpose and method of implementing this time away intervention are different from those of timeout, as described above. A behavior that is being taught, shaped, cued, and/or modeled to replace a problem behavior will be readily observed. The pupil will have a goal of self-determination in choosing this new behavior. At times in the learning process, the teacher may actively encourage the pupil to choose the adaptive behavior over the problem behavior in order to meet the pupil's needs. An observer might see the student making this choice, with the teacher prompting in initial instruction periods, just before an expected exhibition of the problem behavior, based on baseline analysis on the problem behavior. The teacher anticipates the problem behavior (as the end point in an escalating behavior chain) and helps the student develop a more adaptive coping strategy.

Good practice suggests that when the time away is ended, either by teacher or pupil, the re-entry into the group will not have punitive aspects, such as loss of points or taking away of privileges. Furthermore, there may be observable positive aspects, such as verbal praise for the choice and points gained. This form of time away will appear fully described in the positive behavior intervention plan to delineate the exact purpose and form of this procedure. The time away procedure described here is most likely to be in response to the student's need for coping and tolerance instruction and choice-making needs. Thus, the described time away is directly related to the function of the problem behavior in that the time away can be the actual positive replacement behavior we seek to increase as an alternate to the serious behavior. The time away goal is for the student to choose an acceptable escape or an alternative to a nonacceptable escape or protest behavior until he or she can regain the ability to participate in the group. The student retains control of the length of his or her time away.

Joey

Joey at age 16 is an individual with autism. Joey was biting his hand, apparently when the environment was self-perceived as stressful from either lengthy periods of sitting in one position, excitement, boredom, or anxiety during transitions. This information was gained through the functional analysis assessment. As part of his plan, he was taught to say "lie down:" and then go to a designated safe area at the back of the room. Joey re-entered the group when he was prepared to participate appropriately again. The length of self-absenting has grown progressively shorter and the teacher noted that even initially "time away" never exceeded 10 to 15 minutes. At the beginning of the plan's implementation, Joey was assisted/escorted to his safe area when biting occurred and was prompted through some relaxation procedures, Now, Joey is self-initiating leaving stressful situations approximately 80% of the time.

Regular progress has been reported to Joey's parents through the daily logbook, but not each occurrence of the behavior as would be required in an emergency procedure. Joey still chooses to express his anxiety through unacceptable behavior, however the number of times in which he chooses "time away" is increasing. Therefore, the IEP team believes this plan is currently meeting its objectives. Information on Joey's autism proved helpful in designing effective teaching techniques, but functional analysis was still required to understand the behavior and determine the functional alternative.

Timeout for Problems Other Than Serious Behavior Problems

The regulations do not change existing SELPA or school policy on the use of timeout procedures for behaviors that are not defined as serious behavior problems. Good practice suggests that one not continue to use a procedure that has not contributed to positive change.

Craig

Craig at age 10 is a student with a learning handicapped. Craig is required to sit on the bench for the remainder of recess due to his breaking of a rule about where his class should play on the playground and calling classmates names. The behavior does not meet the criteria of being a serious behavior problem (i.e., not leading to suspension or expulsion, not pervasive and maladaptive), and is expressly discussed in the schoolwide behavior plan.

---

[1] If used as a valid component of an emergency procedure applied in the presence of a serious behavior problem, SELPA-approved forms documenting each occurrence will be necessary.

[2] Refer to Chapter 1 on ethical principles for elaboration.

[3] The reader must recognize that "timeout" is a term often used in classrooms of the past where behavior plans were often written in terms of what the student would <u>not</u> do, then went on to specify what would happen to the student if the behavior continued.

[4] The reader is cautioned to consider: Is this procedure definable as a positive behavioral technique? Is it a technique that can be effective in containing an emergency serious behavior broblem? For a particular student, is the technique a viable reactive strategy to consider? Refer to Chapter 5 for further information on positive programming and reactive strategies, respectively.

Bibliography

Agee, V. L. (1979). *Treatment of the violent incorrigible adolescent.* Lexington, MA: Lexington Books.

Akhtar, N., & Bradley, E. J. (1991). Social information processing deficits of aggressive children: Present findings and implications for social skills training. *Clinical Psychology Review, 2,* 621-644.

Albin, J. M. (1992). *Quality improvement in employment and other human services: Managing for quality through change.* Baltimore, MD: Paul H. Brookes Publishing Co.

Alpert, J. L., & Associates. (1982). *Psychological consultation in educational settings.* San Francisco: Jossey-Bass.

Arizona Department of Education. (1992). Incorporating the use of non-aversive behavior management. (AZ-TAS Themes and Issues. Phoenix, AZ) .

Ball, T., Purna, C. D., Rios, M., & Constantine, C. (1985). Flexible arm splints in the control of Lesch-Nyhan victim's finger biting and a profoundly retarded client's finger sucking. *Journal of Autism and Developmental Disorders, 15*(2), 177-184.

Bergan, J. R., & Kratochwill, T. R. (1990). *Behavioral consultation and therapy.* New York: Plenum Press.

Berrol, S., & Rosenthal, M. (Eds.). (1991). School reentry following head injury: Managing the transition from hospital to school. *The Journal of Head Trauma Rehabilitation, 6*(1), 10-22.

Beukelman, D., & Mirenda, P. (1987). Communication options for persons who cannot speak: Assessment and evaluation. In *Proceedings of the National Planners Conference on Assistive Device Service Delivery.* Chicago, IL.

Biklen, D. (1990). Communication unbound: Autism and praxis. *Harvard Educational Review, 60*(3), 291-314.

Bornstein, R. A., & Yang, V. (1991). Neuropsychological performance in medicated and nonmedicated patients with Tourette's disorder. *American Journal of Psychiatry, 148*(4), 468-471.

Bredekamp, S. (Ed.). (1987). Developmentally appropriate practice in early childhood programs serving children from birth through age 8. Washington, DC: National Association for the Education of Young Children.

Brown, L., & Hammill, D. D. (1990). *Behavior rating profile* (2nd ed.). Austin, TX: Pro-Ed.

Budde, J. F., & Summers, J. A. (1991). Consultation and technical assistance. In J. L. Matson & J. A. Mulick (Eds.). *Handbook of mental retardation* (2nd ed.) (pp. 489-502). New York: Pergamon Press, Inc.

Calculator, S. N. (1988). Promoting the acquisition and generalization of conversational skills by individuals with severe disabilities. *Augmentative and Alternative Communication, 2,* 94-103.

Calculator, S. N., & Dollaghan, C. (1982). The use of communication boards in a residential setting: An evaluation. *Journal of Speech and Hearing Disorders, 47,* 281-287.

Calculator, S. N., & Luchko, C. (1983). Evaluating the effectiveness of a communication board training program. *Journal of Speech and Hearing Disorders, 48,* 185-191.

Camp, B. W., & Bash, M. A. S. (1985). *Think aloud: Increasing social and cognitive skills - A problem-solving program for children (grades 1-2, 3-4, and 5-6).* Champaign, IL: Research Press.

Carr, E. G. (1977). The motivation of self-injurious behavior: A review of some hypotheses. *Psychological Bulletin, 84*(4), 800-816.

Carr, E. G. (1980). Generalization of treatment effects following educational intervention with autistic children and youth. In B. Wilcox & A. Thompson (Eds.). *Critical issues in educating autistic children and youth.* (pp. 118-134). Washington, DC: National Society for Children and Adults with Autism.

Carr, E. G., & Durand, V. M. (1985A). The social-communicative basis of severe behavior problems in children. In S. Reiss, & R. Bootzin (Eds.). *Theoretical issues in behavior theory* (pp. 219-254). New York: Academic Press.

Carr, E. G., & Durand, V. M. (1985). Reducing behavior problems through functional communication training. *Journal of Applied Behavior Analysis, 18*(2), 111-126.

Carr, E. G., & Kologinsky, E. (1983). Acquisition of sign language by autistic children II: Spontaneity and generalization effects. *Journal of Applied Behavior Analysis, 16*(3), 297-314.

Carr, E. G., & McDowell, J. J. (1980). Social control of self-injurious behavior of organic etiology. *Behavior Therapy, 11,* 402-409.

Carr, E. G., Newsom, C. D., & Binkoff, J. A. (1980). Escape as a factor in the aggressive behavior of two retarded children. *Journal of Applied Behavior Analysis, 13*(1), 101-117.

Carr, E. G., & Durand, V. M. (1987). See me, help me. *Psychology Today, 21*(11), 62-64.

Carr, E. G., Robinson, S., & Palumbo, L. W. (1990). The wrong issue: Aversive versus nonaversive treatment; The right issues: Functional versus nonfunctional treatment. In A. C. Repp & N. N. Singh (Eds.). *Perspectives on the use of nonaversive and aversive interventions for persons with developmental disabilities* (pp. 361-379). Sycamore, IL: Sycamore Press.

Casey, L. O. (1978). Development of communicative behavior in autistic children: A parent program using manual signs. *Journal of Autism and Childhood Schizophrenia, 8*(1), 45-59.

Cataldo, M. F., & Harris, J. (1982). The biological basis for self-injury in the mentally retarded. *Analysis and Intervention in Developmental Disabilities, 2,* 21-39.

Cautela, J. R., & Groden, J. (1978). *Relaxation: A comprehensive manual for adults, children, and children with special needs.* Champaign, IL: Research Press Company.

Charlop, M. H., Kurtz, P. F., & Casey, F. G. (1990). Using aberrant behaviors as reinforcers for autistic children. *Journal of Applied Behavior Analysis, 23,* 163-181.

Charlop, M. H., & Milstein, J. P. (1989). Teaching autistic children conversational speech using video modeling. *Journal of Applied Behavior Analysis, 22,* 275-285.

Cipani, E. (Ed.). (1989). The treatment of severe behavior disorders: Behavior analysis approaches (Monograph No. 12). Washington, DC: American Association on Mental Retardation.

Cohen, D. J., Bruun, R. D., & Leckman, J. F. (Eds.). (1988). *Tourette syndrome and tic disorders: Clinical understanding and treatment.* New York: Wiley & Sons.

Cole, E., & Siegel, J. A. (1992). *Effective consultation in school psychology.* Lewiston, NY: Hogrefe & Huber Press.

Conoley, J. C., & Conoley, C. W. (1992). *School consultation: Practice and training* (2nd ed.). New York: MacMillan.

Cook, L., Cullinan, D., Epstein, M. H., Forness, S. R., Hallahan, D. P., Kauffman, J. M., Lloyd, J. W., Nelson, C. M., Polsgrove, L., Sabornie, E. J., Strain, P. S., & Walker, H. M. (1991). Problems and promises in special education and related services for children and youth with emotional or behavioral disorders. *Behavioral Disorders, 16*(4), 299-313.

Deci, E. L., Nezlek, J., & Sheinman, L. (1981). Characteristics of the rewarder and intrinsic motivation of the rewardee. *Journal of Personality and Social Psychology, 40*(1), 1-10.

Devinsky, O., & Vazquez, B. (1993). Behavioral changes associated with epilepsy. *Behavioral Neurology, 11*(1), 127-149.

Dodge, K. A., Pettit, G. S., McClaskey, C. L., & Brown, M. (1986). Social competence in children. *Monograph of the Society for Research in Child Development, 51* (2, Serial No. 213).

Donnellan, A. M. (1980). An educational perspective of autism: Educational implications for curriculum development and personnel development. In B. Wilcox & A. Thompson (Eds.). *Critical Issues in Educating Autistic Children and Youth* (pp. 118-134). Washington, DC: National Society for Children and Adults with Autism.

Donnelan, A. M., LaVigna, G. W., Negri-Shoultz, Nanelte, & Fassbender, L. (1988). *Progress without punishment: Effective approaches for learners with behavior problems.* New York: Teachers College Press, Columbia University.

Donnellan, A. M., Mirenda, P. L., Mesaros, R. A., & Fassbender, L. (1984). Analyzing the communicative function of aberrant behavior. *Journal of the Association for Persons with Severe Handicaps, 9,* 201-212.

Donnellan, A. M., Mesaros, R. A., & Anderson, J. L. (1984). Teaching students with autism in natural environments: What educators need from researchers. *Journal of Special Education, 18,* 505-522.

Duker, P. (1975). Behavior control of self-biting in a Lesch-Nyhan patient. *Journal of Mental Deficiency Research, 19,* 11-19.

Durand, M. V. (1982) Analysis and intervention of self-injurious behavior. *Journal of the Association for the Severely Handicapped, 7*(4), 44-54.

Durand, V. M. (1990). *Severe behavior problems: A functional communication training approach.* New York: Guilford Publications.

Durand, V. M., & Crimmins, D. (1992). *Motivational Assessment Scale,* Topeka, KS: Monaco & Associates.

Dyer, K., Dunlap, G., & Winterling, V. (1990). Effects of choice making on the serious problem behaviors of students with severe handicaps. *Journal of Applied Behavior Analysis, 23*(4), 515-524.

Elliott, S, N., & Gresham, F. M. (1991). *Social skills intervention guide: Practical strategies for social skills training.* Circle Pines, MN: American Guidance Service.

Erikson, E. (1963). *Childhood & Society.* New York: W. W. Norton & Co.

Evans, I. M., & Meyer, L. (1985). *An educative approach to behavior problems.* Baltimore, MD: Paul H. Brookes Publishing Co.

Flavell, J. H. (1963). *The developmental psychology of Jean Piaget.* Princeton, NJ: D. Van Nostrand Co., Inc.

Foster-Johnson, L., & Dunlap, G. (1993). Using functional assessment to develop effective individualized interventions for challenging behaviors, *Teaching Exceptional Children, 25*(3), 44-50.

Foxx, R. M., & Shapiro, S. T. (1978). The timeout ribbon: A nonexclusionary timeout procedure. *Journal of Applied Behavior Analysis, 11,* 125-136.

Friend, M., & Cook, L. (1992). *Interactions: Collaboration skills for school professionals.* New York: Longman.

Fuchs, D., & Fuchs, L. S. (1989). Exploring effective and efficient prereferral interventions: A component analysis of behavioral consultation. *School Psychology Review, 18,* 260-283.

Garcia, E. (1974). The training and generalization of a conversational speech form in nonverbal retardates. *Journal of Applied Behavior Analysis, 7*(1), 137-149.

Gaylord-Ross, R. J., Haring, T. G., Breen, C., & Pitts-Conway, V. (1984). The training and generalization of social intervention skills with autistic youth. *Journal of Applied Behavior Analysis, 117,* 229-247.

Gedye, A. (1989). Extreme self-injury attributed to frontal lobe seizures. *American Journal on Mental Retardation, 94*(1), 20-26.

Gedye, A. (1992). Anatomy of self-injurious, stereotypic, and aggressive movements: Evidence for involuntary explanation. *Journal of Clinical Psychology, 48*(6), 766-778.

Gilbert, T. F. (1978). *Human competence: Engineering worthy performance.* New York: McGraw-Hill.

Gillberg, C., & Steffenburg, S. (1987). Outcome and prognostic factors in infantile autism and similar conditions: A population-based study of 46 cases followed through puberty. *Journal of Autism and Developmental Disorders, 17*(2), 273-287.

Golden, G. S. (1987). *Textbook of pediatric neurology.* New York: Plenum Publishing. (See Chapter 26, "Headache.").

Goldstein, A. P. (1988). *The prepare curriculum: Teaching prosocial competencies.* Champaign, IL: Research Press.

Goldstein, A. P., Glick, B., Reiner, S., Zimmerman, D., & Coultry, T. M. (1987). *Aggression replacement training: A comprehensive intervention for aggressive youth.* Champaign, IL: Research Press Co.

Goldstein, A. P., & Kanfer, F. H. (1979). *Maximizing treatment gains: Transfer enhancement in psychotherapy.* New York: Academic Press.

Goldstein, A. P., Sprafkin, R. P., Gershaw, N. J., & Klein, P. (1980). *Skillstreaming the adolescent: A structured learning approach to teaching prosocial skills.* Champaign, IL: Research Press.

Goldstein, H., & Wickstrom, S. (1986). Peer intervention effects on communicative interaction among handicapped and nonhandicapped preschoolers. *Journal of Applied Behavior Analysis, 19*(2), 209-214.

Goodwin, D. L. (1969) Consulting with the classroom teacher. In J. D. Krumboltz & C. E. Thoresen (Eds.). *Behavior Counseling Cases and Techniques,* New York: Holt, Rinehart & Winston.

Gresham, F. M., & Elliott, S. N. (1990). *Social skills rating system.* Circle Pines, MN: American Guidance Service.

Haring, T. G., Roger, R., Lee, M., Breen, C., & Gaylord-Ross, R. (1986). Teaching social language to moderately handicapped students. *Journal of Applied Behavior Analysis, 19*(2), 159-171.

Harris, D. (1982). Communicative interaction processes involving nonvocal physically handicapped children. *Topics in Language Disorders,* 2(2), 21-37.

Heron, T. E., & Harris, K. C. (1987). *The educational consultant: Helping professionals, parents, and mainstreamed students* (2nd ed.). Austin, TX: Pro-Ed.

Hersen, M., & Barlow, D. (1976). *Single-case experimental designs: Strategies for studying behavior change.* New York: Pergamon Press.

Horner, R. H., & Budd, C. M. (1985). Acquisition of manual sign use: Collateral reduction of maladaptive behavior, and factors limiting generalization. *Education and Training of the Mentally Retarded, 20,* 39-47.

Horner, R. H., Dunlap, G., Koegel, R. L., Carr, E. G., Sailor, W., Anderson J., Albin, R. W., & O'Neill, R. E. (1989). *Toward a technology of "nonaversive" behavioral support.* Manuscript submitted for publication.

Hunt, P., Alwell, M., & Goetz, L. (in press). Interacting with peers through conversation turntaking with a communication book adaptation. *Augmentative and Alternative Communication.*

Hunt, P., & Goetz, L. (1988). Teaching spontaneous communication in natural settings through interrupted behavior chains. *Topics in Language Disorders, 9*(1), 58-71.

Hunt, P., Alwell, M., & Goetz, L. (1988). Acquisition of conversation skills and the reduction of inappropriate social interaction behaviors. *Journal of the Association for Persons with Severe Handicaps, 13*(1), 20-27.

Hunt, P., Alwell, M., Goetz, L., & Sailor, W. (1990). *Generalized effects of conversation skill training.* Manuscript submitted for publication.

Hunt, P., Alwell, M., & Goetz, L. (1990). Teaching conversation skills to individuals with severe disabilities and a communication book adaptation: Instructional handbook. San Francisco: San Francisco State University. Conversation and Social Competence Project.

Hunt, P., Alwell, M., & Goetz, L. (1990). *Using a communication book adaptation at home: Informed family members as conversation partners.* Manuscript in preparation.

Hunt, P., Farron-Davis, F., Staub, D., Beckstead, S., Curtis, D., & Goetz, L. (1992). *Evaluating the effects of placement of students with severe disabilities in general education versus special classes.* Manuscript in preparation.

Hunt, P., Haring, K., Farron-Davis, F., Staub, D., Rogers, J., Beckstead, S., Karasoff, P., Goetz, L., & Sailor, W. (1993). Factors associated with the integrated educational placement of students with severe disabilities. *The Journal of the Association for Persons with Severe Handicaps, 18*, 6-15.

Hurtig, R., Ensrud, S., & Tomblin, J. B. (1992). The communicative function of question production in autistic children. *Journal of Autism and Developmental Disorders, 12*(1), 57-69.

Iwata, B. A., Dorsey, M. F., Slifer, K. J., Bauman, K. E., & Richman, G. S. (1982). Toward a functional analysis of self-injury. *Analysis and Intervention in Developmental Disabilities, 2*, 3-20.

Jacobson, E. (1938). *Progressive relaxation: A physiological and clinical investigation of muscular states and their significance in psychology and medical practice.* Chicago: University of Chicago Press.

Jacobson, E. (1964). *Anxiety and tension control.* Philadelphia: J. P. Lippincott.

Karoly, P., & Steffen, J. J. (Eds.). (1979). *Improving the long-term effects of psychotherapy.* New York: Gardner.

Kazdin, A. E. (1987). Treatment of antisocial behavior in children: Current status and future directions. *Psychological Bulletin, 102*(2), 187-203.

Keilitz, I., Tucker, D. J., & Horner, R. D. (1973) Increasing mentally retarded adolescents' verbalizations about current events. *Journal of Applied Behavior Analysis, 6*(4), 621-630.

King, L. J. (1986). *Calming-alerting activities.* Paper presented at a seminar titled "Attention Deficits in Learning Disorders and Autism" with Temple Grandin, Ontario, CA, sponsored by Division of Innovation and Development, Continuing Education Programs of America.

King, L. J. (1990). *The hypersensitive autistic child.* Paper presented at a seminar titled "Attention Deficits in Learning Disorders and Autism" with Temple Grandin, Ontario, CA, sponsored by Division of Innovation and Development, Continuing Education Programs of America.

Knitzer, J., Steinberg, Z., & Fleisch, B. (1990). *At the schoolhouse door: An examination of programs and policies for children with behavioral and emotional problems.* New York: Bank Street College of Education.

Kratochwill, T. R., & Bergan, J. R. (1990). *Behavioral consultation in applied settings: An individual guide.* New York: Plenum Press.

Ladd, G. W., & Mize, J. (1983). A cognitive-social learning model of social-skill training. *Psychological Review, 90*(2), 127-157.

Lancioni, G. E. (1982). Normal children as tutors to teach social responses to withdrawn mentally retarded schoolmates: Training, maintenance, and generalization. *Journal of Applied Behavior Analysis, 15*(1), 17-40.

LaVigna, G. W., & Donnellan, A. (1986). *Alternatives to punishment: Solving behavior problems with non-aversive strategies.* New York: Irvington Publishers.

Lehr, S., & Lehr, R. (1990). Why is my child hurting? Positive approaches to dealing with difficult behaviors. *A Monograph for Parents of Children with Disabilities.* Center on Human Policy, Syracuse University for the Federation for Children with Special Needs, Boston, MA.

Leifer, J. S., & Lewis, M. (1984). Acquisition of conversation response skills by young down syndrome and nonretarded young children. *American Journal of Mental Deficiency, 88*(6), 610-618.

Leonard, H. L., Lenane, M. C., Swedo, S. E., Rettew, D. C., Gershon, E. S., & Rapoport, J. L., (1992). Tics and Tourette's disorder: A 2- to 7-year follow-up of 54 obsessive-compulsive children. *American Journal of Psychiatry, 149*(9), 1244-1251.

Light, J. (1988). Interaction involving individuals using augmentative and alternative communication systems: State of the art and future directions. *Augmentative and Alternative Communication, 4*(2), 66-82.

Light, J., Collier, B., & Parnes, P. (1985A). Communicative interaction between young nonspeaking physically disabled children and their primary caregivers: Part 1 — Discourse patterns. *Augmentative and Alternative Communication, 1,* 74-83.

Light, J., Collier,. B., & Parnes, P. (1985B). Communicative interaction between young nonspeaking physically disabled children and their primary caregivers: Part II — Communicative function. *Augmentative and Alternative Communication, 1*(3), 98-107.

Long, N. J. (1986). The nine psychoeducational stages of helping emotionally disturbed students through the reeducation process. *The Pointer, 30*(3), 5-20.

Lucyshyn, J. M., & Albin, R. W. (1993). Comprehensive support to families of children with disabilities and behavior problems: Keeping it "friendly." In G. H. S. Singer & L. E. Powers (Eds.). *Families, disability, and empowerment: Active coping skills and strategies for family interventions.* (pp. 365-408). Baltimore, MD: Paul H. Brookes Publishing Co.

MacDonald, J. D. (1985). Language through conversation: A model for intervention with language-delayed persons. In S. F. Warren & A. K. Rogers-Warren (Eds.). *Teaching Functional Language* (pp. 21-122).

Martens, B. K., & Witt, J. C. (1988). Expanding the scope of behavioral consultation: A systems approach to classroom behavior change. *Professional School Psychology, 3,* 271-281.

Matson, J. L., Esveldt-Dawson, K., & Kazdin, A. E. (1983). Validation of methods for assessing social skills in children. *Journal of Clinical Child Psychology, 12*(2), 174-180.

Matson, J. L., Rotatori, A. E., & Helsel, W. J. (1983). Development of a rating scale to measure social skills in children: The Matson Evaluation of Social Skills with Youngsters (MESSY). *Behavior Research & Therapy, 21,* 335-340.

Maucherik, D. F., Leckman, J. F., Detlor, J., & Cohen, D. (1984). A new instrument for clinical studies of Tourette's syndrome. *Journal of American Academy of Child Psychiatry, 23* (2), 153-160.

Mayer, G. R., & McGookin, R. B. (1977). *Behavioral consulting.* Los Angeles: Trident Bookstore, California State University, Los Angeles.

McGinnis, E., & Goldstein, A. (1984). *Skill streaming in the elementary school: A guide for teaching prosocial skills.* Champaign, IL: Research Press.

McGinnis, E. & Goldstein, A. P. (1990). *Skill streaming in early childhood: Teaching prosocial skills to the preschool and kindergarten child.* Champaign, IL: Research Press Co.

McNaughton, D., & Light, J. (1989). Teaching facilitators to support the communication skills of an adult with severe cognitive disabilities: A case study. *Augmentative and Alternative Communication, 5*(1), 35-41.

Meisel, C. (1990). *Conversation training pilot study.* Unpublished manuscript, San Francisco State University, Special Education Department, San Francisco.

Meyer, L. H., & Evans, I. M. (1989). *Nonaversive intervention for behavior problems: A manual for home and community.* Baltimore, MD: Paul H. Brookes Publishing Co., P.O. Box 10624, Baltimore, MD 21285-0624.

Mirenda, P., & Iacono, T. (1988). Strategies for promoting augmentative and alternative communication in natural context with students with autism. *Focus on Autistic Behavior, 3.*

Mirenda, P., & Iacono, T., (1990). Communication options for persons with severe and profound disabilities: State of the art and future directions. *Journal of the Association for Persons with Severe Handicaps, 15,* 3-21.

Mizuno, T., & Yugari, Y. (1974). Self-mutilation in the Lesch-Nyhan syndrome. *Lancet,1* (76).

Murray, C., & Beckstead, S. (1983). Awareness Inservice Manual. San Francisco: San Francisco State University, Department of Special Education, Project REACH (ERIC Document Reproduction Service No. ED 242 182).

Nelson, C. M., & Rutherford, R. B. (1983). Timeout revisited: Guidelines for its use in special education. *Exceptional Educational Quarterly, 3,* 56-67.

O'Neil, R. E., Horner, R. H., Albin, R. W., Storey, J., & Sprague, J. (1990). *Functional analysis: A practical guide.* Baltimore, MD: Paul H. Brookes Publishing Co.

O'Neil, Robert E., Horner, Robert H., Albin, Richard W., Sprague, Jeffrey R., Storey, Keith, and Newton, J. Stephen (1997). *Functional assessment and program development for problem behavior: A practical handbook* (2nd ed.). Pacific Grove, CA: Brooks/Cole Publishing Co.

Parker, J. G., & Asher, S. R. (1987). Peer relations and later personal adjustment: Are low-accepted children at risk? *Psychological Bulletin, 102*(3), 357-389.

Pellegrini, D. S., & Urbain, E. S. (1985). An evaluation of interpersonal cognitive problem solving training with children. *Journal of Child Psychology & Psychiatry, 26*(1), 17-41.

Piaget, J. (1970). *Genetic epistemology.* New York: Columbia University Press.

Piersal, W. C., & Gutkin, T. B. (1983). Resistance to school-based consultation: A behavioral analysis of the problem. *Psychology in the Schools, 20,* 311-326.

Piuma, C. (1983). *Project REACH* (USOE Contract No. 300-80-0745): *Final Report.* San Francisco: San Francisco State University, Department of Special Education.

Porterfield, J. K., Herbert-Jackson, E., & Risley, T. R. (1976). Contingent observation: An effective and acceptable procedure for reducing disruptive behavior of young children in a group setting. *Journal of Applied Behavior Analysis, 9,* 55-64.

Reichle, J., Rogers, N., & Barrett, C. (1984). Establishing pragmatic discriminations among the communicative functions of requesting, rejecting, and commenting. *Journal of the Association for Persons with Severe Handicaps, 9,* 21-36.

Richard, B. A., & Dodge, K. A. (1982). Social maladjustment and problem solving in school-aged children. *Journal of Consulting and Clinical Psychology, 50*(2), 226-233.

Romski, M. A., & Sevcik, R. (1988). Augmentative and alternative communication systems: Considerations for individuals with severe intellectual disabilities. *Augmentative and Alternative Communication, 2,* 89-93.

Schuler, A. L., & Goetz, L. (1981). The assessment of severe language disabilities: Communicative and cognitive consideration. *Analysis and Intervention in Developmental Disabilities, 1,* 333-346.

Shure, M. B., & Spivack, G. (1980). Interpersonal problem solving as a mediator of behavioral adjustment in preschool and kindergarten children. *Journal of Applied Developmental Psychology, 1,* 29-44.

Shure, M. B., & Spivack, G. (1982). Interpersonal problem solving in young children: A cognitive approach to prevention. *American Journal of Community Psychology, 10,* 341-356.

Shure, M. B. (1992). *I can problem solve: An interpersonal problem-solving program for children.* Champaign, IL: Research Press Co.

Shodell, M. J., & Reiter, H. H. (1968). Self-mutilative behavior in verbal and non-verbal schizophrenic children. *Archives of General Psychiatry, 19,* 453-455.

Singer, G. H. S., & Irvin, L. K. (1989). *Support for caregiving families: Enabling positive adaptation to disability.* Baltimore, MD: Paul H. Brookes Publishing Co.

Singer, H. S. (1993). Tic disorders. *Pediatric Annals, 22*(1), 22-29.

Singer, H. S., & Walkup, J. T. (1991). Tourette syndrome and other tic disorders: Diagnosis, pathophysiology, and treatment. *Medicine, 70*(1), 15-32.

Snyder, L. S. (1984). Communication competence in children with delayed language development. In R. L. Schiefelbusch & J. Pickar (Eds.). *The Acquisition of Communicative Competence.* Baltimore, MD: University Park Press.

Steiger, L. K. (1987). *Nonviolent crisis intervention: Participant workbook.* Brookfield, WI: National Crisis Prevention Institute.

Stokes, T. F., & Baer, O. M. (1977). An implicit technology of generalization. *Journal of Applied Behavioral Analysis, 10,* 349-367.

Stoner, G., & Green, S. K. (in press). The scientist-practitioner model in school psychology practice: A reconceptualization. *School Psychology Review.*

Stoner, G., Shinn, M. R., & Walker, H. M. (Eds.) (1991). *Interventions for achievement and behavior problems.* Washington, DC: National Association of School Psychologists.

Sugai, G. M., & Tindal, G. A. (1993). *Effective school consultation: An interactive approach.* Pacific Grove, CA: Brooks/Cole Publishing Company.

Sulkes, S. B., & Davidson, P. W. (1989). Self-injurious behavior. In I. L. Rubin & A. C. Cracker (Eds.). *Developmental Disabilities.* Philadelphia: Lee & Febiger.

Sulzer-Azaroff, B., & Mayer, G. R. (1986). *Achieving educational excellence: Using behavioral strategies.* New York: Holt, Rinehart & Winston.

Sulzer-Araroff, B., & Mayer, G. R. (1991). A guide to selecting behavior recording techniques. *Behavioral Analysis for Lasting Change.* New York: Holt, Rinehart & Winston.

Tindal, G., Shinn, M. R., & Rodden-Nord, K. (1990). Contextually based school consultation: Influential variables. *Exceptional Children, 56,* 324-336.

Touchette, P. E., MacDonald, R. F., & Langer, S. N. (1985). A scatter plot for identifying stimulus control of problem behavior. *Journal of Applied Behavior Analysis, 18,* 343-351.

Wacker, D., Steege, M. W., Northup, J., Sasso, G., Berg, W., Reimers, T., Cooper, L., Cigrand, K., & Donn, L. (1990). A component analysis of functional communication training across three topographies of severe behavior problems. *Journal of Applied Behavior Analysis, 23,* 417-429.

Walker, H. M., McConnell, S., Holmes, D., Todis, B., Walker, J., & Golden, N. (1983). *The Walker social skills curriculum - The ACCEPTS program: A curriculum for children's effective peer and teacher skills.* Austin, TX: Pro-Ed.

Walker, H. M., & McConnell, S. R. (1988). *Walker-McConnell scale of social competence and school adjustment: A social skills rating scale for teachers.* Austin, TX: Pro-Ed.

Walker, H. M., Todis, B., Holmes, D., & Horton, G. (1988). *The ACCESS program: Adolescent curriculum for communication and effective social skills.* Austin, TX: Pro-Ed.

Warren, S. F., Baxter, D. K., Anderson, S. R., Marshall, A., & Baer, D. M. (1981). Generalization of question-asking by severely retarded individuals. *Journal of the Association for Persons with Severe Handicaps, 6,* 15-22.

Wilbarger, P., & Wilbarger, J. L. (1991). *Sensory defensiveness in children aged 2-12: An intervention guide for parents and other caretakers.* Santa Barbara, CA: Avanti Educational Programs.

Willis, T. J., LaVigna, G. W., & Donnellan, A. M. (1987). *Behavior assessment guide.* Los Angeles: Institute for Applied Behavior Analysis.

Witt, J. C. (1990). Complaining, precopernican thought, and the univariate linear mind: Questions for school-based behavioral consultation research. *School Psychology Review, 19,* 367-377.

Witt, J. C., & Martens, B. K. (1988). Problems with problem-solving consultation: A reanalysis of assumptions, methods, and goals. *School Psychology Review, 17*(2), 211-226.

Wolery, M., Ault, M. J., & Doyle, P. M. (1992). *Teaching students with moderate to severe disabilities: Use of response prompting strategies.* White Plains, NY: Longman Publishing Co.

Wolpe, J., & Lazarus, A. (1966). *Behavior therapy techniques: A guide to the treatment of neuroses.* Oxford, NY: Pergamon Press.

Wyllie, E., Rothner, A. D., & Luders, H. (1989). Partial seizures in children. *Pediatric Clinics of North America, 36*(2), 343-364.

APPENDICES

Appendix A.

Education Code - Part 30
Chapter 5.5 - Sections 56520-56524
(Hughes - A.B. 2586) Behavioral Interventions

56520.   (a)   The Legislature finds and declares all of the following:

      (1)   That the State of California has continually sought to provide an appropriate and meaningful educational program in a safe and healthy environment for all children regardless of possible physical, mental, or emotionally disabling conditions.

      (2)   That teachers of children with special needs require training and guidance that provides positive ways for working successfully with children who have difficulties conforming to acceptable behavioral patterns in order to provide an environment in which learning can occur.

      (3)   That procedures for the elimination of maladaptive behaviors shall not include those deemed unacceptable under Section 49001 or those that cause pain or trauma.

  (b)   It is the intent of the Legislature:

      (1)   That when behavioral interventions are used, they be used in consideration of the pupil's physical freedom and social interaction, and be administered in a manner that respects human dignity and personal privacy, and that ensures a pupil's right to placement in the least restrictive educational environment.

      (2)   That behavioral management plans be developed and used, to the extent possible, in a consistent manner when the pupil is also the responsibility of another agency for residential care or related services.

      (3)   That a statewide study be conducted of the use of behavioral interventions with California individuals with exceptional needs receiving special education and related services.

      (4)   That training programs be developed and implemented in institutions of higher education that train teachers and that in-service training programs be made available as necessary in school districts and county offices of education to assure that adequately trained staff are available to work effectively with the behavioral intervention needs of individuals with exceptional needs.

56521.   (a)   This chapter applies to any individual with exceptional needs who is in a public school program, including a state school for the handicapped pursuant to Part 32 (commencing with Section 59000), or who is placed in a nonpublic school program pursuant to Sections 56365 to 56366.5, inclusive.

(b)   The Superintendent of Public Instruction shall monitor and supervise the implementation of this chapter.

56523.   (a)   On or before September 1, 1992, the Superintendent of Public Instruction shall develop and the State Board of Education shall adopt regulations governing the use of behavioral interventions with individuals with exceptional needs receiving special education and related services.

(b)   The regulations shall do all of the following:

(1)   Specify the types of positive behavioral interventions which may be utilized and specify that interventions which cause pain or trauma are prohibited.

(2)   Require that, if appropriate, the pupil's individual education plan includes a description of the positive behavioral interventions to be utilized which accomplished the following:

(A) Assesses the appropriateness of positive interventions.

(B) Assures the pupil's physical freedom, social interaction, and individual choices.

(C) Respects the pupil's human dignity and personal privacy.

(D) Assures the pupil's placement in the least restrictive environment.

(E) Includes the method of measuring the effectiveness and interventions.

(F) Includes a timeline for the regular and frequent review of the pupil's progress.

(3)   Specify standards governing the application of restrictive behavioral interventions in the case of emergencies. These emergencies must pose a clear and present danger of serious physical harm to the pupil or others. These standards shall include:

(A) The definition of an emergency.

(B) The types of behavioral interventions that may be utilized in an emergency.

(C) The duration of the intervention which shall not be longer than is necessary to contain the dangerous behavior.

(D) A process and timeline for the convening of an individual education plan meeting to evaluate the application of the emergency intervention and adjust the pupil's individual education plan in a manner designed to reduce or eliminate the negative behavior through positive programming.

(E) A process for reporting annually to the State Department of Education and the Advisory Commission on Special Education the number of emergency interventions applied under this chapter.

56524.   The Superintendent shall explore with representatives of institutions of higher education and the Commission on Teacher Credentialing, the current training requirements for teachers to ensure that sufficient training is available in appropriate behavioral interventions for people entering the field of education.

Appendix B.

Title 5
California
Code of Regulations (CCR)
Behavioral Interventions for Special Education Students

Amend Section 3001 of Article 1 of Subchapter 1 of Chapter 3 to read:
3001. Definitions.

In addition to those found in Education Code sections 56020-56033, Public Law 94-142 as amended (20 USC 1401 et seq.), and Title 34, Code of Federal Regulations, Part 300 and 301, the following definitions are provided:

(a) "Applicant" means an individual, firm, partnership, association, or corporation who has made application for certification as a nonpublic, nonsectarian school, or agency.

(b) "Appropriate education," as in 'free, appropriate, public education,' is an educational program and related service(s) as determined on an individual basis which meets the unique needs of each individual with exceptional needs. Such an educational program and related service(s) shall be based on goals and objectives as specified in an individualized education program (IEP) and determined through the process of assessment and IEP planning in compliance with state and federal laws and regulations. Such an educational program shall provide the equal opportunity for each individual with exceptional needs to achieve his or her full potential, commensurate with the opportunity provided to other individuals.

(c) "Assistive technology device" means any item, piece of equipment, or product system, whether acquired commercially or off the shelf, modified, or customized, that is used to increase, maintain, or improve the functional capabilities of children with disabilities pursuant to Title 34, Code of Federal Regulations, Section 300.5.

(d) "Assistive technology service" means any service that directly assists a child with a disability in the selection or use of an assistive technology device that is educationally necessary. The term includes evaluation of the needs of a child with a disability; coordination of assistive technology devices with other therapies, interventions, or services associated with education programs; training or technical assistance for a child with a disability or, if appropriate, that child's family; and training or technical assistance for individuals providing education services or employers of children with disabilities.

(e) "Behavioral emergency" is the demonstration of a serious behavior problem: (1) which has not previously been observed and for which a behavioral intervention plan has not been developed; or (2) for which a previously designed behavioral intervention is not effective. Approved behavioral emergency procedures must be outlined in the special education local planning area (SELPA) local plan.

(f) "Behavioral intervention" means the systematic implementation of procedures that result in lasting positive changes in the individual's behavior. "Behavioral intervention" means the design, implementation, and evaluation of individual or group instructional and environmental modifications, including programs of behavioral instruction, to produce significant improvements in human behavior through skill acquisition and the reduction of problematic behavior. "Behavioral interventions" are designed to provide the individual with greater access to a variety of community settings, social contacts and public events; and ensure the individual's right to placement in the least restrictive educational environment as outlined in the individual's IEP. "Behavioral interventions" do not include procedures which cause pain or trauma. "Behavioral interventions" respect the individual's human dignity and personal privacy. Such interventions shall assure the individual's physical freedom, social interaction, and individual choice.

(g) "Behavioral intervention case manager" means a designated certificated school/district/ county staff member(s) or other qualified personnel pursuant to subsection (af) contracted by the school district or county office who has been trained in behavior analysis with an emphasis on positive behavioral interventions. The "behavioral intervention case manager" is not intended to be a new staffing requirement and does not create any new credentialing or degree requirements. The duties of the "behavioral intervention case manager" may be performed by any existing staff member trained in behavior analysis with an emphasis on positive behavioral interventions, including, but not limited to, a teacher, resource specialist, school psychologist, or program specialist.

(h) The "behavioral intervention plan" is a written document which is developed when the individual exhibits a serious behavior problem that significantly interferes with the implementation of the goals and objectives of the individual's IEP. The "behavioral intervention plan" shall become part of the IEP. The plan shall describe the frequency of the consultation to be provided by the behavioral intervention case manager to the staff members and parents who are responsible for implementing the plan. A copy of the plan shall be provided to the person or agency responsible for implementation in noneducational settings. The plan shall include the following:

(1) a summary of relevant and determinative information gathered from a functional analysis assessment;

(2) an objective and measurable description of the targeted maladaptive behavior(s) and replacement positive behavior(s);

(3) the individual's goals and objectives specific to the behavioral intervention plan;

(4) a detailed description of the behavioral interventions to be used and the circumstances for their use;

(5) specific schedules for recording the frequency of the use of the interventions and the frequency of the targeted and replacement behaviors; including specific criteria for discontinuing the use of the intervention for lack of effectiveness or replacing it with an identified and specified alternative;

(6) criteria by which the procedure will be faded or phased-out, or less intense/ frequent restrictive behavioral intervention schedules or techniques will be used;

(7) those behavioral interventions which will be used in the home, residential facility, work site or other noneducational settings; and

(8)   specific dates for periodic review by the IEP team of the efficacy of the program.

(i)   "Certification" means authorization by the State Superintendent of Public Instruction (Superintendent) for a nonpublic school or nonpublic agency to service individuals with exceptional needs under a contract pursuant to the provisions of Education Code section 56366(c).

(j)   "Contract" means the legal document which binds the public education agency and the nonpublic school or nonpublic agency.

(k)   "Contracting education agency," as used in this chapter, means school district, special education local plan area, or county office.

(l)   "Credential" means a valid credential in special education or pupil personnel services issued by the California State Commission on Teacher Credentialing.

(m)   "Dual enrollment" means the concurrent attendance of the individual in a public education agency and a nonpublic school and/or a nonpublic agency.

(n)   "Early education programs for individuals with exceptional needs" means the program and services specified by Education Code Part 30, section 56425 et seq.

(o)   "Feasible" as used in Education Code section 56363(a) means the individualized education program team:

(1)   has determined the regular class teacher, special class teacher, and/or resource specialist possesses the necessary competencies and credentials/certificates to provide the designated instruction and service specified in the individualized education program, and

(2)   has considered the time and activities required to prepare for and provide the designated instruction and service by the regular class teacher, special class teacher, and/or resource specialist.

(p)   "Instructional day" shall be the same period of time as constitutes the regular school day for that chronological peer group unless otherwise specified in the individualized education program.

(q)   "Intensive special education and services" means instruction and services, without which the individual would be unable to develop the skills necessary to achieve educational goals appropriate to his or her developmental and cognitive level or potential. Such instruction and services may be provided in any of the program options as stated in Education Code section 56361.

(r)   "License" means a valid nonexpired document issued by a licensing agency within the Department of Consumer Affairs or other state licensing office authorized to grant licenses and authorizing the bearer of the document to provide certain professional services or refer to themselves using a specified professional title. If a license is not available through an appropriate state licensing agency, a certificate of registration with the appropriate professional organization at the national and/or state level or a degree from a regionally accredited postsecondary institution, as specified in Section 3061, may be sufficient to be eligible for certification.

(s)   Linguistically appropriate goals, objectives, and programs means:

(1)   (A) Those activities which lead to the development of English language proficiency through the use of the primary language of the individual with exceptional needs; and

(B) Those instructional systems either at the elementary or secondary level which meet the language development needs of the limited English proficient individual by building on the individual's existing language skills in order to develop English proficiency.

(2) For individuals whose primary language is other than English, nothing in this section shall preclude the individual learning program, as defined by section 52163 of the Education Code, from being included in the individual's IEP.

(3) For individuals whose primary language is other than English, and whose potential for learning a second language, as determined by the individualized education program team, is severely limited, nothing in this section shall preclude the individualized education program team from determining that instruction may be provided in the individual's primary language, provided that the IEP team periodically, but not less than annually reconsiders the individual's ability to receive instruction in the English language.

(t) "Local governing board," for purposes of Section 3080, means either district or county board of education, depending on which agency, district, governing board, or county is alleged to be in violation of a law or regulation.

(u) "Nonpublic agency" means any private, nonsectarian establishment or individual providing related services necessary for an individual with exceptional needs to benefit educationally from the individual's educational program.

(v) "Nonpublic, nonsectarian agency" means a private, nonsectarian establishment or individual that provides related services necessary for an individual with exceptional needs to benefit educationally from the pupil's educational program pursuant to an individualized education program and that is certified by the Department. It does not include an organization or agency that operates as a public agency or offers public service, including but not limited to, a state or local agency, an affiliate of a state or local agency, including a private, nonprofit corporation established or operated by a state or local agency, a public university or college, or a public hospital. The nonpublic, nonsectarian agency shall also meet standards as prescribed by the Superintendent and State Board.

(w) "Nonpublic, nonsectarian school" means a private, nonsectarian school that enrolls individuals with exceptional needs pursuant to an individualized education program, employs at least one full-time teacher who holds an appropriate credential authorizing special education services, and is certified by the Department. It does not include an organization or agency that operates as a public agency or offers public service, including, but not limited to, a state or local agency, an affiliate of a state or local agency, including a private, nonprofit corporation established or operated by a state or local agency, or public university or college. A nonpublic, nonsectarian school also shall meet standards as prescribed by the Superintendent and State Board.

(x) "Nonpublic school" means any private, nonsectarian school enrolling individuals with exceptional needs, and employing at least one full-time teacher holding an appropriate credential authorizing special education services, and certified by the Department. The nonpublic school shall meet those standards as prescribed in Section 3062 herein.

(y) "Nonsectarian" means a nonpublic school or agency that is not owned, operated, controlled by, or formally affiliated with a religious group or sect, whatever might be the actual character of the education program or the primary purpose of the facility. "Nonsectarian" also means that a nonpublic school or agency shall not provide instruction in any particular religion nor solicit pupils to adopt the beliefs of any particular religion, sect, creed, or church.

(z) "Occupational therapy" means occupational therapy as defined in Business and Professions Code section 2570 et seq.

(aa) "Physical therapy" means physical therapy as defined in Business and Professions Code section 2620 et seq.

(ab) "Prescribed course of study," as used in Education Code Section 56026(c)(4), means the course of study that is established by the local board of education pursuant to Education Code section 51000 et seq.

(ac) "Primary language" means the language other than English, or other mode of communication, the person first learned, or the language which is spoken in the person's home. In the case of an individual identified as an individual of limited English proficiency pursuant to Education Code sections 52164 and 52164.1, limited English proficiency shall be defined pursuant to Education Code section 52163(m).

(ad) "Program," when referring to an individual with exceptional needs, means the individualized education program. "Program," when referring to an educational agency, means that system of procedures and resources established by a district, special education local plan area, or county office of education to provide special education.

(ae) "Psychological services, other than assessment and development of the individualized education program," means those services which are authorized pursuant to the issuance of a pupil personnel services credential authorizing school counseling, school psychology, child welfare and attendance services, or school social work pursuant to Education Code sections 44266, 49424, or 49600, or which are within the scope of practice of a marriage, family, and child counselor as defined by Business and Professions Code section 4980 et seq.; a clinical social worker as defined by Business and Professions Code section 4990 et seq.; or a psychologist or educational psychologist as defined by Business and Professions Code section 2900 et seq. "Assessment and development of the individualized education program" means services described in Education Code section 56320 et seq.

(af) "Qualified" means that a person has met federal and state certification, licensing, registration, or other comparable requirements which apply to the area in which he or she is providing special education or related services, or, in the absence of such requirements, the state-education-agency-approved or recognized requirements, and adheres to the standards of professional practice established in federal and state law or regulation, including the standards contained in the California Business and Professions Code. Nothing in this definition shall be construed as restricting the activities in services of a graduate needing direct hours leading to licensure, or of a student teacher or intern leading to a graduate degree at an accredited or approved college or university, as authorized by state laws or regulations.

(ag) "Related services" means services as defined by Title 34, Code of Federal Regulations, Section 300.16.

(ah) "Serious behavior problems" are defined as the individual's behaviors which are self-injurious, assaultive, or cause serious property damage and other severe behavior problems that are pervasive and maladaptive for which instructional/behavioral approaches specified in the student's IEP are found to be ineffective.

(ai) "Specialized physical health care services" are those health services prescribed by the individual's licensed physician and surgeon requiring medically related training for the individual who performs the services and which are necessary during the school day to enable the individual to attend school.

(aj)   "Temporary physical disability" means a disability incurred while an individual was in a regular education class and which at the termination of the temporary physical disability, the individual can, without special intervention, reasonably be expected to return to his or her regular education class.

(ak)   "Valid credential" means any credential, life diploma, permit, or document issued by, or under the jurisdiction of, the Commission on Teacher Credentialing, or issued by the State Board of Education prior to 1970, which entitles the holder thereof to perform services for which certification qualifications are required.

NOTE: Authority cited: Sections 56100(a), (i) and (j), 56366.1(*l*)(5) and 56523(a), Education Code. Reference: Sections 44266, 49424, 49423.5, 49600, 51000, 52163–52164.1, 56026, 56034, 56035, 56320, 56361, 56363(a), 56366(c), 56425, 56520 and 56523, Education Code; Sections 2570, 2620, 2900, 4980 and 4990, Business and Professions Code; and Sections 300.4–300.6, 300.12, 300.16 and 300.550, Code of Federal Regulations, Title 34.

Amend Section 3052 of Article 5 to read:
3052. Designated Positive Behavioral Interventions.

(a)   General Provisions.

(1)   An IEP team shall facilitate and supervise all assessment, intervention, and evaluation activities related to an individual's behavioral intervention plan. When the behavioral intervention plan is being developed, the IEP team shall be expanded to include the behavioral intervention case manager with documented training in behavior analysis including positive behavioral intervention(s), qualified personnel knowledgeable of the student's health needs, and others as described in Education Code Section 56341(c)(2). The behavioral intervention case manager is not intended to be a new staff person and may be an existing staff member trained in behavior analysis with an emphasis on positive behavioral interventions.

(2)   Behavioral intervention plans shall only be implemented by, or be under the supervision of, staff with documented training in behavior analysis, including the use of positive behavioral interventions. Such interventions shall only be used to replace specified maladaptive behavior(s) with alternative acceptable behavior(s) and shall never be used solely to eliminate maladaptive behavior(s).

(3)   Behavioral intervention plans shall be based upon a functional analysis assessment, shall be specified in the individualized education program, and shall be used only in a systematic manner in accordance with the provisions of this section.

(4)   Behavioral emergency interventions shall not be used as a substitute for behavioral intervention plans.

(5)   The elimination of any maladaptive behavior does not require the use of intrusive behavioral interventions that cause pain or trauma.

(6)   To the extent possible, behavioral intervention plans shall be developed and implemented in a consistent manner appropriate to each of the individual's life settings.

(b)   Functional Analysis Assessments. A functional analysis assessment must be conducted by, or be under the supervision of a person who has documented training in behavior analysis with an emphasis on positive behavioral interventions. A functional analysis assessment shall occur after the individualized education program team finds that instructional/behavioral approaches specified in the student's IEP have been ineffective. Nothing in this section shall preclude a parent or legal guardian from requesting a functional analysis assessment pursuant to the provisions of Education Code sections 56320 et seq.

Functional analysis assessment personnel shall gather information from three sources: direct observation, interviews with significant others, and review of available data such as assessment reports prepared by other professionals and other individual records. Prior to conducting the assessment, parent notice and consent shall be given and obtained pursuant to Education Code Section 56321.

(1) A functional analysis assessment procedure shall include all of the following:

    (A) Systematic observation of the occurrence of the targeted behavior for an accurate definition and description of the frequency, duration, and intensity;

    (B) Systematic observation of the immediate antecedent events associated with each instance of the display of the targeted inappropriate behavior;

    (C) Systematic observation and analysis of the consequences following the display of the behavior to determine the function the behavior serves for the individual, i.e., to identify the specific environmental or physiological outcomes produced by the behavior. The communicative intent of the behavior is identified in terms of what the individual is either requesting or protesting through the display of the behavior;

    (D) Ecological analysis of the settings in which the behavior occurs most frequently. Factors to consider should include the physical setting, the social setting, the activities and the nature of instruction, scheduling, the quality of communication between the individual and staff and other students, the degree of independence, the degree of participation, the amount and quality of social interaction, the degree of choice, and the variety of activities;

    (E) Review of records for health and medical factors which may influence behaviors (e.g. medication levels, sleep cycles, health, diet); and

    (F) Review of the history of the behavior to include the effectiveness of previously used behavioral interventions.

(2) Functional Analysis Assessment Reports. Following the assessment, a written report of the assessment results shall be prepared and a copy shall be provided to the parent. The report shall include all of the following:

    (A) A description of the nature and severity of the targeted behavior(s) in objective and measurable terms;

    (B) A description of the targeted behavior(s) that includes baseline data and an analysis of the antecedents and consequences that maintain the targeted behavior, and a functional analysis of the behavior across all appropriate settings in which it occurs;

    (C) A description of the rate of alternative behaviors, their antecedents and consequences; and

    (D) Recommendations for consideration by the IEP team which may include a proposed plan as specified in Section 3001(f).

(c)   IEP Team Meeting. Upon completion of the functional analysis assessment, an IEP team meeting shall be held to review results and, if necessary, to develop a behavioral intervention plan, as defined in Article 1, Section 3001(f) of these regulations. The IEP team shall include the behavioral intervention case manager. The behavioral intervention plan shall become a part of the IEP and shall be written with sufficient detail so as to direct the implementation of the plan.

(d)   Intervention. Based upon the results of the functional analysis assessment, positive programming for behavioral intervention may include the following:

    (1)   Altering the identified antecedent event to prevent the occurrence of the behavior (e.g., providing choice, changing the setting, offering variety and a meaningful curriculum, removing environmental pollutants such as excessive noise or crowding, establishing a predictable routine for the individual);

    (2)   Teaching the individual alternative behaviors that produce the same consequences as the inappropriate behavior (e.g., teaching the individual to make requests or protests using socially acceptable behaviors, teaching the individual to participate with alternative communication modes as a substitute for socially unacceptable attention-getting behaviors, providing the individual with activities that are physically stimulating as alternatives for stereotypic, self-stimulatory behaviors);

    (3)   Teaching the individual adaptive behaviors (e.g., choice-making, self-management, relaxation techniques, and general skill development) which ameliorate negative conditions that promote the display of inappropriate behaviors; and

    (4)   Manipulating the consequences for the display of targeted inappropriate behaviors and alternative, acceptable behaviors so that it is the alternative behaviors that more effectively produce desired outcomes (i.e., positively reinforcing alternative and other acceptable behaviors and ignoring or redirecting unacceptable behaviors).

(e)   Acceptable Responses. When the targeted behavior(s) occurs, positive response options shall include, but are not limited to one or more of the following:

    (1)   the behavior is ignored, but not the individual;

    (2)   the individual is verbally or verbally and physically redirected to an activity;

    (3)   the individual is provided with feedback (e.g., "You are talking too loudly");

    (4)   the message of the behavior is acknowledged (e.g., "You are having a hard time with your work"); or

    (5)   a brief, physical prompt is provided to interrupt or prevent aggression, self-abuse, or property destruction.

(f)   Evaluation of the Behavioral Intervention Plan Effectiveness. Evaluation of the effectiveness of the behavioral intervention plan shall be determined through the following procedures:

    (1)   Baseline measure of the frequency, duration, and intensity of the targeted behavior, taken during the functional analysis assessment. Baseline data shall be taken across activities, settings, people, and times of the day. The baseline data shall be used as a standard against which to evaluate intervention effectiveness;

    (2)   Measures of the frequency, duration, and intensity of the targeted behavior shall be taken after the behavioral intervention plan is implemented at scheduled intervals determined by the IEP team. These measures shall also be taken across activities, settings, people, and times of the day, and may record the data in terms

of time spent acting appropriately rather than time spent engaging in the inappropriate behavior;

(3) Documentation of program implementation as specified in the behavioral intervention plan (e.g., written instructional programs and data, descriptions of environmental changes); and

(4) Measures of program effectiveness will be reviewed by the teacher, the behavioral intervention case manager, parent or care provider, and others as appropriate at scheduled intervals determined by the IEP team. This review may be conducted in meetings, by telephone conference, or by other means, as agreed upon by the IEP team.

(5) If the IEP team determines that changes are necessary to increase program effectiveness, the teacher and behavioral intervention case manager shall conduct additional functional analysis assessments and, based on the outcomes, shall propose changes to the behavioral intervention plan.

(g) Modifications without IEP Team Meeting. Minor modifications to the behavioral intervention plan can be made by the behavioral intervention case manager and the parent or parent representative. If the case manager is unavailable, a qualified designee who meets the training requirements of subsection (a)(1) shall participate in such modifications. Each modification or change shall be addressed in the behavioral intervention plan provided that the parent, or parent representative, is notified of the need and is able to review the existing program evaluation data prior to implementing the modification or change. Parents shall be informed of their right to question any modification to the plan through the IEP procedures.

(h) Contingency Behavioral Intervention Plans. Nothing in this section is intended to preclude the IEP team from initially developing the behavioral intervention plan in sufficient detail to include schedules for altering specified procedures, or the frequency or duration of the procedures, without the necessity for reconvening the IEP team. Where the intervention is to be used in multiple settings, such as the classroom, home and job sites, those personnel responsible for implementation in the other sites must also be notified and consulted prior to the change.

(i) Emergency Interventions. Emergency interventions may only be used to control unpredictable, spontaneous behavior which poses clear and present danger of serious physical harm to the individual or others and which cannot be immediately prevented by a response less restrictive than the temporary application of a technique used to contain the behavior.

(1) Emergency interventions shall not be used as a substitute for the systematic behavioral intervention plan that is designed to change, replace, modify, or eliminate a targeted behavior.

(2) Whenever a behavioral emergency occurs, only behavioral emergency interventions approved by the special education local planning area (SELPA) may be used.

(3) No emergency intervention shall be employed for longer than is necessary to contain the behavior. Any situation which requires prolonged use of an emergency intervention shall require staff to seek assistance of the school site administrator or law enforcement agency, as applicable to the situation.

(4) Emergency interventions may not include:

(A) Locked seclusion, unless it is in a facility otherwise licensed or permitted by state law to use a locked room;

(B) Employment of a device or material or objects which simultaneously immobilize all four extremities, except that techniques such as prone containment may be used as an emergency intervention by staff trained in such procedures; and

(C) An amount of force that exceeds that which is reasonable and necessary under the circumstances.

(5) To prevent emergency interventions from being used in lieu of planned, systematic behavioral interventions, the parent and residential care provider, if appropriate, shall be notified within one school day whenever an emergency intervention is used or serious property damage occurs. A "Behavioral Emergency Report" shall immediately be completed and maintained in the individual's file. The report shall include all of the following:

(A) The name and age of the individual;

(B) The setting and location of the incident;

(C) The name of the staff or other persons involved;

(D) A description of the incident and the emergency intervention used, and whether the individual is currently engaged in any systematic behavioral intervention plan; and

(E) Details of any injuries sustained by the individual or others, including staff, as a result of the incident.

(6) All "Behavioral Emergency Reports" shall immediately be forwarded to, and reviewed by, a designated responsible administrator.

(7) Anytime a "Behavioral Emergency Report" is written regarding an individual who does not have a behavioral intervention plan, the designated responsible administrator shall, within two days, schedule an IEP team meeting to review the emergency report, to determine the necessity for a functional analysis assessment, and to determine the necessity for an interim behavioral intervention plan. The IEP team shall document the reasons for not conducting an assessment and/or not developing an interim plan.

(8) Anytime a "Behavioral Emergency Report" is written regarding an individual who has a behavioral intervention plan, any incident involving a previously unseen serious behavior problem or where a previously designed intervention is not effective should be referred to the IEP team to review and determine if the incident constitutes a need to modify the plan.

(9) "Behavioral Emergency Report" data shall be collected by SELPAs which shall report annually the number of Behavioral Emergency Reports to the California Department of Education and the Advisory Commission on Special Education.

(j) SELPA Plan. The local plan of each SELPA shall include procedures governing the systematic use of behavioral interventions and emergency interventions. These procedures shall be part of the SELPA local plan.

(1) Upon adoption, these procedures shall be available to all staff members and parents whenever a behavioral intervention plan is proposed.

(2) At a minimum, the plan shall include:

(A) The qualifications and training of personnel to be designated as behavioral intervention case managers, which shall include training in behavior analysis with an emphasis on positive behavioral interventions, who will coordinate and assist in conducting the functional analysis assessments and the development of the behavioral intervention plans;

(B) The qualifications and training required of personnel who will participate in the implementation of the behavioral intervention plans; which shall include training in positive behavioral interventions;

(C) Special training that will be required for the use of emergency behavioral interventions and the types of interventions requiring such training; and

(D) Approved behavioral emergency procedures.

(k) Nonpublic School Policy. Nonpublic schools and agencies, serving individuals pursuant to Education Code Section 56365 et seq., shall develop policies consistent with those specified in subsection (i) of this section.

(l) Prohibitions. No public education agency, or nonpublic school or agency serving individuals pursuant to Education Code Section 56365 et seq., may authorize, order, consent to, or pay for any of the following interventions, or any other interventions similar to or like the following:

(1) Any intervention that is designed to, or likely to, cause physical pain;

(2) Releasing noxious, toxic or otherwise unpleasant sprays, mists, or substances in proximity to the individual's face;

(3) Any intervention which denies adequate sleep, food, water, shelter, bedding, physical comfort, or access to bathroom facilities;

(4) Any intervention which is designed to subject, used to subject, or likely to subject the individual to verbal abuse, ridicule or humiliation, or which can be expected to cause excessive emotional trauma;

(5) Restrictive interventions which employ a device or material or objects that simultaneously immobilize all four extremities, including the procedure known as prone containment, except that prone containment or similar techniques may be used by trained personnel as a limited emergency intervention pursuant to subsection (i);

(6) Locked seclusion, except pursuant to subsection (i)(4)(A);

(7) Any intervention that precludes adequate supervision of the individual; and

(8) Any intervention which deprives the individual of one or more of his or her senses.

(m) Due Process Hearings. The provisions of this chapter related to functional analysis assessments and the development and implementation of behavioral intervention plans are subject to the due process hearing procedures specified in Education Code Section 56501 et seq. No hearing officer may order the implementation of a behavioral intervention that is otherwise prohibited by this section, by SELPA policy, or by any other applicable statute or regulation.

NOTE: Authority cited: Section 56523(a), Education Code. Reference: Sections 56520 and 56523, Education Code.

Appendix C.

Introduction to Using the Guide, Flowchart, Report Forms, and Worksheets

Purpose of Forms and Worksheets

The following forms and worksheets are provided as samples to assist the BICM in (1) gathering information from three sources: direct observation, interview with significant others, and review of records and (2) assembling all data for the required functional analysis assessment report to propose or to develop a positive behavior plan. Using forms requires understanding of the concepts and procedures contained in the education regulations (Chapter 5.5 Sections 3001 and 3052).

Flowchart

The flowchart (p. 190) is a visual representation of the guide, provided to assist the BICM in conceptualizing this process in simplified form.

Guide to Functional Analysis and Program Development

The guide is divided into two parts: (1) gathering information and decision making and (2) program development. It provides the step-by-step directions to completing all required tasks, from establishing a need for a functional analysis or developing a positive behavior intervention plan, through implementing the plan. Throughout the guide, references are made to the forms or supportive worksheets. This serves as an interpretive text to each point on the worksheets and forms.

Worksheets

The worksheets provide a framework for performing the functional analysis assessment. Many BICMs will discover streamlined operating methods that do not require the worksheets. Performing these functions is like driving a car. When you first begin, there seems to be a multitude of factors to consider (e.g., distance of cars around you, internal engine integrity, activity of others in the car, traffic signals) that are overwhelming, yet become quite easy and second nature after some practice. BICMs can pick and choose worksheets that are helpful for their particular needs.

Report Forms

The report forms contain the summarized information gathered throughout the analysis that are *required* to be contained in the functional assessment report and the behavioral intervention plan. By referring to the flowchart, the BICM will note that Forms 1 through 3 can actually be filled out *during* the assessment process. Form 4, Functional Analysis Assessment Report Summary Form, and 5, Behavior Intervention Plan, will be used after the entire analysis is completed. The importance of *collaboration* with implementers in developing the plan cannot be overemphasized. The plan should be based on skills the implementer *already* has in: teaching new behaviors, reinforcing behavior, and modifying the environment if the plan is to succeed. Otherwise, the BICM will need to assist the implementer in gaining requisite skills by direct teaching or involvement of others to perform that function, *or* to base the plan on skills that *are* within the repertoire of the implementer. If this cannot be done, than the BICM may determine that this particular environment will not be conducive for this student and that alternatives will need to be located.

Guide to Behavioral Intervention Plan Forms
Flowchart

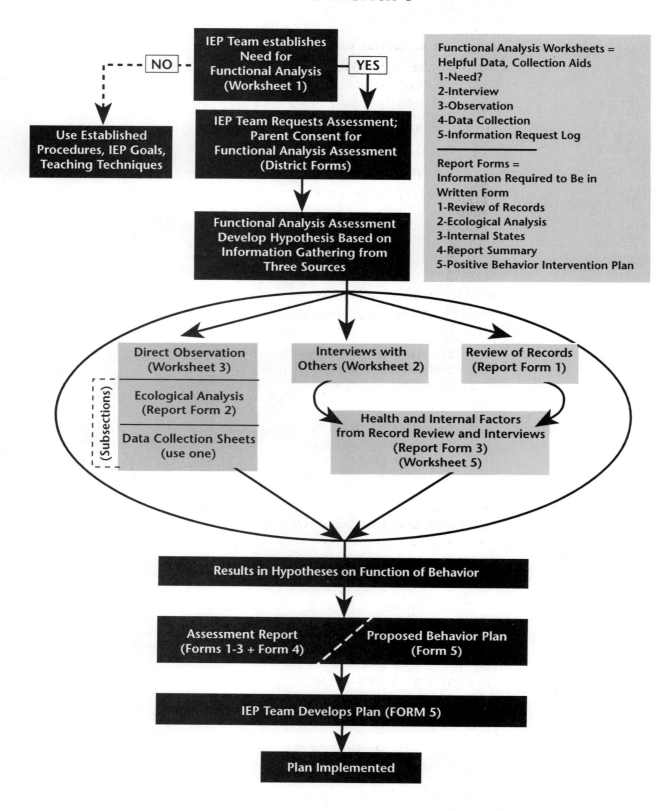

IEP Team establishes Need for Functional Analysis (Worksheet 1)

NO — YES

Use Established Procedures, IEP Goals, Teaching Techniques

IEP Team Requests Assessment; Parent Consent for Functional Analysis Assessment (District Forms)

Functional Analysis Worksheets = Helpful Data, Collection Aids
1-Need?
2-Interview
3-Observation
4-Data Collection
5-Information Request Log

Report Forms =
Information Required to Be in Written Form
1-Review of Records
2-Ecological Analysis
3-Internal States
4-Report Summary
5-Positive Behavior Intervention Plan

Functional Analysis Assessment Develop Hypothesis Based on Information Gathering from Three Sources

Direct Observation (Worksheet 3)

Ecological Analysis (Report Form 2)

(Subsections)

Data Collection Sheets (use one)

Interviews with Others (Worksheet 2)

Review of Records (Report Form 1)

Health and Internal Factors from Record Review and Interviews (Report Form 3) (Worksheet 5)

Results in Hypotheses on Function of Behavior

Assessment Report (Forms 1-3 + Form 4)

Proposed Behavior Plan (Form 5)

IEP Team Develops Plan (FORM 5)

Plan Implemented

Part I:
Guide to Steps in Information Gathering and Decision Making

I. **Determine Need for Functional Analysis** (Refer to Worksheet 1)

1. Student must be an individual with exceptional needs (IWEN).

2. IEP team determines that instructional/behavioral approaches specified in IEP have been ineffective.

II. **Interview with Significant Others** (Refer to Worksheet 2 for steps 2-4)

(Teachers, aides, parents, administrators, and so forth)

1. Develop collaborative relationship(s) with the significant other(s)

- Explain the role of the BICM and clarify expectations.

- Develop plan to gather further information.

2. Operationalize behavior

3. Identify record-keeping needs

- Discuss with teacher and/or other significant person(s) what system of data collection would be best in terms of time and purpose.

4. Focus on the function of the behavior

- Probe for what may be influencing and reinforcing the behavior.

- use questionnaires to begin hypothesizing the functions of the behavior (e.g., the Motivation Assessment Scale [MAS]).

- Complete the A-B-C analysis using record review, interview, and direct observation

    After operationalizing the behavior, it will be important to work collaboratively with the significant other(s) to see the behaviors in terms of their context. When is the problem behavior occurring? What is the context of the positive replacement behaviors? Discover what typically happens right before, or even hours before, the behavior occurs (anteced-ent conditions). Discover clues about the physical setting. Is it something about where he or she is seated? Does time of day make a difference? Does medication, diet, factors in the home, or other ecological factors influence the behavior? Are the instruction materials and/or teaching methods appropriate to the student's functional level? A good detective looks at all the possibilities. (Refer to "Who, What, When, Why, and Where of Behavior," Appendix I.)

    Consequences to the behaviors are just as important to identify. As the detective, you will need to discover the communicative intent of the behavior. What is the student getting when he or she engages in either the problem behavior or the appropriate behavior? Is the student receiving a social consequence (e.g. getting attention)? Is the student's behavior resulting in some self-regulating or sensory stimulation consequence? Does the student's behavior result in his or her being able to engage in a pre-ferred activity or other tangible item? Does the behavior result in the removal of demands or escape?

III. Review of Records

    1.   Review for history of the behavior problem and other intervention plans (Refer to Report Form 1).

    2.   Review for developmental history, handicapping condition, and so forth (Refer to Report Form 3).

IV. Direct Observation (Refer to Worksheet 3)

    1.   Pinpoint operationalized, problem behavior and positive replacement behavior.

    2.   Observe and chart contingency analysis (A-B-C) of problem and positive replacement behavior(s) across all appropriate settings in which the behavior occurs.

    3.   Determine function of both problem behavior and positive replacement behavior (e.g., communicative intent, attention, escape, play, interaction seeking, protest).

    4.   Begin identifying potential reinforcers and observe whether identified "reinforcers" from any surveys are in fact maintaining or increasing desired behaviors.

    5.   Identify all record keepers and methods of data gathering; specify appropriate length of baseline gathering phase (Refer to Worksheet 4).

    6.   Determine other environments where direct observation should take place (if necessary).

    7.   Set up any additional meetings to analyze data.

    8.   Complete functional assessment summary (Refer to Report Form 4)

    9.   Set up date for IEP team to present findings.

V. Designing Data Collection Systems: For measuring baseline and intervention data for both problem and replacement behaviors (Refer to Worksheet 4)

    1.   Determine the length of baseline data collection (This requires enough time to observe a repeating pattern).

    2.   Determine observational method(s) to collect baseline and intervention data most appropriate for both behaviors. (Refer to Figure 18)

    3.   Design data form using a method that probes selected variables (behavior related to who/what/where/when/with whom and for what purpose(s), see Appendix I).

    4.   Measure the frequency of both the problem and positive replacement behavior. The BICM will identify data collectors (working collaboratively with implementers), and when and where the data will be collected. BICMs should ensure that the systems of data collection for baseline and intervention effectiveness reviews are the same or similar enough to render reliable comparisons.

        The most appropriate data-gathering method will be that which clearly demonstrates when, where, under what condition, and with whom, the behavior occurs. This is critical in determining what variables are influencing *both* behaviors. Each data-collecting system must be tailor-made to tap this information based on the developing hypothesis as to the function of the behaviors.

FIGURE 18.
CHOOSING OBSERVATIONAL METHODS

Method	Definition	Example of Behaviors Often Measured by This Method
Event/frequency	Number of occurrences of behavior that has a clear beginning and end, measured over a specified time period	A punch; runs from room; shouts out response, self-injurious acts with a clear beginning and ending
Duration	Length of time from beginning to end of a response	Temper tantrums or any behaviors where duration is an important variable
Permanent product (not often used for measuring serious problems)	Activity with discrete, countable segments	Number of problems completed, (number of assignments completed)
Whole interval time sampling	Response emitted throughout entire interval, for behaviors that continue without interruption	Time on task; time off task; time in seat
Partial interval time sampling	Response emitted any time during an interval, for fleeting behaviors	Eye contact; smiling; skin picking
Momentary time sampling	Frequent behaviors to be counted if response emitted at moment the established interval terminates	In/out of seat; on/off task; eye contact

VI. **Ecological Analysis**

The BICM observes in the environment to determine events or features that increase the likelihood of problem behaviors, and conversely, features that increase the likelihood of positive behaviors. (Refer to Report Form 2 and/or Appendix J.)

Physical Setting: Are there specific settings where the problem behavior tends to occur or tends not to be present? If so, what is different about those settings? Consider presence of environmental pollutants, such as noise, crowding, and so forth, because these may increase the likelihood of problem behavior.

Social Setting: For example, does behavior occur in isolation? On playground? Transition time? Are there any situations or behaviors of others that tend to occur before this student's problem behavior or positive behavior?

Activities: Is the curriculum meaningful? Are success level activities present? Have previous activities resulted in success or failure? Are activities appropriate and accessible to the functional level and chronologically age appropriate? Has appropriate consideration been made to the student's handicapping condition?

Nature of Instruction: Do instructional methods and technique match learner needs? Does student do better in one-to-one situations? Are specific positive behaviors being taught?

Scheduling Factors: Does this behavior occur more frequently at certain times of the day? After or before reinforcement? During transitions? Is the child aware of sequence of his or her day?

Degree of Independence: Is independence encouraged and supported? Is there structured opportunity for successful independent activity? Are reinforcement intervals appropriate to maintain an independent level of on-task performance?

Degree of Participation: When successful or unsuccessful participation takes place, what is the size and location of the group? Are there options for self-removal? Is there adequate structure?

Social Interaction: Are social skills being taught if necessary? Are there specific social situations that promote appropriate social behavior? Are there specific social situations that promote problem behavior? Examine interactions with adults and disabled and nondisabled peers.

Degree of Choice: Does exercising choice affect student behavior? How much opportunity for choice making is present in the student's environments? Is negotiation permissible?

VII. **Reveiw of Data on Internal States** (Refer to Report Form 3)

SOURCES may include a review of records, and interviews with significant others. If you discover a need for further information, this may require the signing of a release of information form. (Refer to Worksheet 5 to log requests.)

1. Handicapping condition(s)

    a. Identify student's educational handicapping condition from records.

    b. Review information on best practices to meet possible needs of individuals with this condition. Does the literature suggest possible approaches to teach alternative positive behaviors?

2. Health and biological conditions

    a. Identify student's medical diagnosis that may affect behavior (e.g., seizure activity, ADHD, identified syndromes, allergies).

    b. Review vision and hearing records.

3. Current medication summary

    a. Complete medication summary with information provided from records or interviews.

    b. Note changes in medication and potential effect on the problem behavior (refer to medication charts in Chapter 9, Physician's Desk Reference, or student's physician).

4. Potential sleep and diet effects on behavior

    a. Describe current sleep pattern.

    b. Note changes and effects of sleep on behavior.

    c. Note special dietary requirements, restrictions, or allergies and potential effects on behavior (either following the diet or not following the diet could affect behavior; timing, amount, hunger, or type of food may affect behavior).

5. Unusual responses to environmental stimuli

    a. Note unusual responses to stimuli (Refer to Appendix G for Sensory Inventory to use in interviews).

    b. Note relationship to behaviors.

6. Periodically occurring events that alter the student's usual behaviors

    a. Note events that have led to problem behaviors increasing (e.g., boredom, rising late, hunger, substitute teachers).

    b. Note methods that have been found helpful.

VIII. Identify Reinforcers that may Maintain or Increase Positive Behaviors in the Behavior Intervention Plan

1. Observe for selected activities in free choice classroom time.

2. Interview student and/or significant others to determine responsiveness to:

    a. Edibles

    b. Tangibles

    c. Closure charts/star charts

    d. Social status and privileges

    e. Contingent access to activities

    f. Praise

Reinforcer surveys seek to identify potential reinforcers to be used in behavior change programs.[1]
Actual questions depend on the student's developmental level and social-cultural environment. However, typical questions included on reinforcement surveys might include the following:

1. What are your favorite foods?

2. If you had _____ dollars to buy whatever you wanted, what would you buy?

3. If you had 30 minutes of free time at _____ (school, work, home), what would you really like to do?

4. What are three of your favorite things to do _____ (at work, at home, at school, with friends)?

5. Who are the people you prefer doing things with at _____ (home, school, work)?

Part II: Guide to Program Development

I. **Summarize all Relevant Information from the Functional Analysis Assessment:**

    1. Attach Form 1 "Review of Records for Behavioral History"

    2. Attach Form 2 "Ecological Analysis of Settings Where Behavior Occurs Most Frequently"

    3. Attach Form 3 "Review of Data of Internal States that Potentially Influence Behavior"

    4. Complete Form 4 "Functional Analysis Assessment Report Summary"

        a. Summarize relevant assessment data on hypothesis of function of behavior, environmental variables affecting behavior

        b. Summarize baseline data

    5. If the IEP team determines that a positive behavioral intervention plan will not be developed, attach Worksheet 1 or other documentation.

II. **Develop a Written Positive Behavioral Intervention Plan** (Refer to Form 5)

1. Attach all information from the functional assessment report (Forms 1-4).

2. Complete Form 5, "Proposed Positive Behavioral Intervention Plan."

   a. Collaborate with implementers who will be implementing this plan to develop the intervention. Without buy-in, the plan is not likely to be implemented successfully.

   b. Identify all environments where the plan will be used and provide copies for all personnel who will supervise use. Frequently, multiple agencies such as regional centers, the Department of Rehabilitation, the Department of Mental Health, or job sites will be supervising implementation, calling for establishment of good communication channels.

   c. Establish criteria to evaluate whether the plan should continue (i.e., is working) or have major revisions (i.e., is not working).

   d. Determine data collection methods and frequency of data gathering to document that the plan is being used and is proving effective.

   e. Establish when communication will occur between implementers, BICM, and parents or other care providers, and how that communication should occur (e.g., phones messages, in person, written notes, weekly or other scheduled observations and dialogues).

   f. Determine if environmental changes are necessary (refer to Appendix J and Form 2)

   g. Determine what specific direct strategies should be employed. Identify the system necessary to reinforce presence of an alternative, positive behavior, or absence or reduction of a problem behavior.

   h. Select any necessary techniques and strategies to teach either functionally equivalent positive behaviors or better coping skills (e.g., shaping, cueing, prompting, physical guidance, aggression replacement strategies, relaxation training).

   i. Identify positive response options for redirecting the problem behavior before instituting an emergency procedure (e.g., reducing contingencies, increasing choice, verbal redirecting) refer to "Management of Antecedents," Appendix H.

[1] *Refer to Bibliography for reinforcer survey included in texts on behavior analysis.*

j.   Specify how implementers will recognize the need for an emergency procedure. What will the behavior look like when reactive strategies short of emergency containment are stopped and emergency procedures are instituted? Carefully stipulating this transition point helps ensure that emergency procedures are not instituted too soon. Reacting too soon leads to a behavior plan that is not emphasizing positive approaches. Conversely, reacting too late may compromise the safety of staff, other students, or this individual. Refer to Appendix F for a suggested emergency report form.

k.   Specify completion criteria of the plan. When has success been achieved and when can phasing out of intrusive reinforcers or prompts begin?

Determination Of Need For Functional Analysis or Positive Behavioral Intervention Plan

Student _____ Date(s) _____

Administrator/Designee/BICM _____

Information Sources _____

Behavior (operationalized) _____

_____

"Serious Behavior Problem" as defined in the Education Code?

☐ No ☐ Serious Property Damage ☐ Self-Injurious

☐ Serious Assaultive ☐ Other Pervasive Maladaptive Behavior

Resulted in Emergency Intervention: ☐ Yes, date of report _____

☐ No

Is the behavior interfering with achievement of IEP Goals? ☐ Yes ☐ No

Rationale: _____

_____

_____

Does the IEP team find that instructional behavioral approaches specified in the student's IEP have been ineffective?

☐ Yes ☐ No

Rationale: _____

_____

Setting(s) and time(s) when behavior occurs/occurred: _____

_____

Extent to which behavior is on-going: _____

Consequences which have occurred as a result of this behavior: _____

_____

Extent to which instructional/behavioral approaches have been effective: _____

Does this behavior require a functional analysis to determine the need for a systematic, positive behavior intervention plan?

Rationale

Yes/No		Yes/No	
	Student performing the behavior is not an identified individual with exceptional needs (IWEN)		Behavior is performed by a student identified as an "individual with exceptional needs" (IWEN)
	Behavior is not a serious behavior problem as defined in the Education Code		Behavior is a serious behavior problem as defined in the Education Code, or, ineffective instructional/behavioral approaches are being used
	Although a serious problem, the IEP team feels the selected consequences or changes are likely to solve the problem and the behavior is not expected to recur		IEP team believes behavior now requires a functional analysis assessment
	Existing instructional/behavioral approaches are determined to be effective by IEP team		IEP team believes behavior may now require a positive behavioral intervention plan
	The serious behavior is not interfering with achievement of IEP goals. Family referred to: _____		IEP team believes behavior is interfering with achievement of IEP goals

WORKSHEET 2

Interview With Significant Others:

Student _____ Interview Date(s) _____

Interviewer_____ Title_____

Interviewee_____ Relationship To Student_____

What is the problem behavior in operationalized terms?

_____

_____

_____

Has the IEP team determined that instructional/behavioral approaches specified in the IEP are ineffective?

☐ YES ☐ NO

Interviewee Analysis of Antecedents & Consequences - Problem Behaviors

Antecedents (immediately prior to the behavior)	Problem Behavior	Consequences
	See Operationalized Definition Above	

WORKSHEET 2-CONTINUED

Potential Positive Replacement Behavior(s)

Star $\boxed{*}$ any that are incompatible with the problem behavior, $\boxed{✔}$ any which student already demonstrates.

☐ ☐ 1. _____

☐ ☐ 2. _____

☐ ☐ 3. _____

☐ ☐ 4. _____

☐ ☐ 5. _____

Antecedents Currently Present (Antecedent conditions to the positive replacement behavior when the problem behavior is **NOT** occurring)	Incompatible Or Positive Replacement Behavior Selected From Above	Consequences Currently In Effect (Reinforcers, contingent access to a desired activity, opportunity for attention, etc. that occur after the positive replacement behavior)
	Number from above _____	

Tentative Hypotheses of Function of Problem Behavior (to be validated or rejected during direct observation).

_____

_____

_____

WORKSHEET 3
Direct Observation

Student:_____Observation Date(s) _____

Observer:_____ Title:_____

Observation Setting(s): _____

Problem Behavior (operationalized terms):_____
_____

Positive Replacement Behavior (operationalized terms): ────────────────────────────
_____

Has the IEP team determined that instructional/behavioral approaches specified in the IEP are ineffective?

☐ YES ☐ NO

Observer's Analysis of Antecedents & Consequences

Antecedents	Operationalized Problem Behaviors	Consequences
	See above	

Antecedents (currently present)	Operationalized Positive Replacement Behaviors	Consequences (currently in effect)
	See above	

Tentative Hypotheses Of Functions Of Problem Behavior:_____
_____

WORKSHEET 3-CONTINUED

Observation For Potential Reinforcers

What activity does the student frequently select when given a choice?

_____

_____

_____

What objects or edibles does the student select frequently when given a choice?

_____

_____

_____

What consequences have worked to motivate or increase other positive behaviors?

_____

_____

_____

What activities or tangibles have been (or may be) used effectively in an "if-then" contingent reinforcement system for the presence of a positive behavior?

_____

_____

_____

What activities or tangibles have been (or may be) used effectively in an "if-then" contingent reinforcement system for the absence of a problem behavior (DRO)?

_____

_____

_____

WORKSHEET 4
Data Collection Sheet

Student:_____ Date:_____

Behavior intervention case manager:_____

Problem Behavior (operationalized terms):_____

_____

_____

_____

Positive Replacement Behavior (operationalized terms): _____

_____

_____

_____

Projected length of Baseline Data Collection:_____

Will the baseline data gathering affect student's behavior? ☐ Yes   ☐ No

If yes, describe accommodations:_____

Proposed Data Collection

Baseline B Post Intervention P	Problem Behavlor – Positive Behavior +	Dates(s)	Time(s)	Personnel	Setting(s)	Method(s) Positive Behavior	Method(s) Problem Behavior

Note: Attach developed sample data gathering sheet to complete this worksheet.

Event Frequency Data Sheet
Multiple Behaviors

Student: _____ Dates: _____

Behavior 1: _____

Behavior 2: _____

Behavior 3: _____

(Use tally marks to note number of occurrences)

Time Period	Behavior 1	Behavior 2	Behavior 3
8:00-8:30			
8:30-9:00			
9:00-9:30			
9:30-10:00			
10:00-10:30			
10:30-11:00			
11:00-11:30			
11:30-12:00			
12:00-12:30			
12:30-1:00			
1:00-1:30			
1:30-2:00			
2:00-2:30			
2:30-3:00			
3:00-3:30			
Total Incidents			
Total time minute/hour/day Time Interval (circle one)			
Rate Per minute/hour/day Time Interval (circle one)			

Reprinted with permission from: Arizona Department of Education, "Incorporating the Use of Non-Aversive Behavior Management, AZ-TAS Themes and Issues (1992)

Duration Data Sheet

Student: _____

Behavior: _____

Date_____ start_____ end_____	Date_____ start_____ end_____	Date_____ start_____ end_____	Date_____ start_____ end_____	Date_____ start_____ end_____
stop_____ start_____ duration_____	stop_____ start_____ duration_____	stop_____ start_____ duration_____	stop_____ start_____ duration_____	stop_____ start_____ duration_____
stop_____ start_____ duration_____	stop_____ start_____ duration_____	stop_____ start_____ duration_____	stop_____ start_____ duration_____	stop_____ start_____ duration_____
stop_____ start_____ duration_____	stop_____ start_____ duration_____	stop_____ start_____ duration_____	stop_____ start_____ duration_____	stop_____ start_____ duration_____
stop_____ start_____ duration_____	stop_____ start_____ duration_____	stop_____ start_____ duration_____	stop_____ start_____ duration_____	stop_____ start_____ duration_____
stop_____ start_____ duration_____	stop_____ start_____ duration_____	stop_____ start_____ duration_____	stop_____ start_____ duration_____	stop_____ start_____ duration_____
Total Minutes Duration				
Total Minutes Observed				
Percent				

Reprinted with permission from: Arizona Department of Education, "Incorporating the Use of Non-Aversive Behavior Management," AZ-TAS Themes and Issues (1992).

Interval Data Sheet

Student: _____ Chart Started: _____

Behavior: _____

Days of the month   ☐ Behavior did NOT occur   ☒ Behavior DID occur

	1	2	3	4	5	6	7	8	9	10	11	12	13	14	15	16	17	18	19	20	21	22	23	24	25	26	27	28	29	30	31
6:30 am																															
7:00 am																															
7:30 am																															
8:00 am																															
8:30 am																															
9:00 am																															
9:30 am																															
10:00 am																															
10:30 am																															
11:00 am																															
11:30 am																															
12:00 pm																															
12:30 pm																															
1:00 pm																															
1:30 pm																															
2:00 pm																															
2:30 pm																															
3:00 pm																															
3:30 pm																															
4:00 pm																															
Total Intervals Observed																															
Percent																															

Notes:

Time Sampling Record Sheet
10-minute intervals

Student: _____ Date: _____

Behavior: _____

	TYPE: 1. Whole Interval	TYPE: 2. Partial Interval	TYPE: 3. Momentary
(Circle 1, 2, or 3) Record + or -	+ = behavior is continuous in interval	+ = single instance is observed in interval	+ = record only if behavior present at end of interval

	+or-	Comments*		+or-	Comments		+or-	Comments
8:00-8:09			11:10-11:19			2:20-2:29		
8:10-8:19			11:20-11:29			2:30-2:39		
8:20-8:29			11:30-11:39			2:40-2:49		
8:30-8:39			11:40-11:49			2:50-2:59		
8:40-8:49			11:50-11:59			3:00-3:09		
8:50-8:59			12:00-12:09			3:10-3:19		
9:00-9:09			12:10-12:19			3:20-3:29		
9:10-9:19			12:20-12:29			3:30-3:39		
9:20-9:29			12:30-12:39			3:40-3:49		
9:30-9:39			12:40-12:49			3:50-3:59		
9:40-9:49			12:50-12:59			4:00-4:09		
9:50-9:59			1:00-1:09			4:10-4:19		
10:00-10:09			1:10-1:19			4:20-4:29		
10:10-10:19			1:20-1:29			4:30-4:39		
10:20- 10:29			1:30-1:39			4:40-4:49		
10:30-10:39			1:40-1:49			4:50-4:59		
10:40-10:49			1:50-1:59			5:00-5:09		
10:50-10:59			2:00-2:09					
11:00-11:09			2:10-2:19					

*   Comments column can be used to describe any prompts or redirections, type of activity, or other variables useful to identify in that interval.

Functional Assessment Observation Form

The Content of the Functional Assessment Observation Form

This Functional Assessment Observation Form has eight major sections (see page 215). A blank copy of the form is included on page 221. Each labeled section is described below. This form combines an event-recording system with hypothesis generation. Once learned, it can provide a streamlined data collection system that implementers value and use consistently[7].

Section A: Identification/dates   In Section A, you show who is being observed and the dates on which the data are being collected. Note that a single page can be used across multiple days.

Section B: Time intervals   Section B is separated into blocks that can be used to designate specific intervals (1 hour, a half-hour, 15 minutes). List here the periods and settings/activities in which observation is taking place. These can be arranged in a variety of ways, depending on a person's daily schedule. For a school student you might list class period times and content (for example, 8:30–9:00, Homeroom; 9:05–9:50, Language Arts; 9:55–10:40, Computer; 11:45–12:30, Lunch; 1:25–3:00, Job Training). For an adult in a less structured home setting, you might simply list time periods (3:00–4:00; 4:00–5:00; 5:00–6:00). Depending on a person's typical pattern of behavior or typical schedule, you may want to use unequal interval sizes within the blocks, such as 15-minute intervals during busy morning routines and 2-hour intervals during the evening when problem behaviors are much less frequent. If targeted behaviors are very frequent during a particular time period or activity, multiple blocks can be used to record data for that period. A row for summarizing total frequencies of behaviors or incidents is labeled at the bottom of the form.

Section C: Behaviors   In Section C, list the individual behaviors you have identified for monitoring during the observations. These targeted behaviors should be the ones identified during your interviews with relevant people. You may also decide to list *positive* behaviors such as appropriate communication responses or attempts that seem important to document or are of interest. The form allows flexibility in monitoring behaviors. For example, if a particular behavior (eye-poking or aggression) occurs in both low-intensity and high-intensity forms, you can list each form as a separate behavior to identify differences or similarities in their patterns of occurrence. When several behaviors occur regularly in combinations, you may monitor them all within a single behavior notation (dropping to the floor, screaming, kicking feet and flailing arms to pound the floor may all be recorded under tantrum). However, be cautious about grouping behaviors together for coding. One of the more useful pieces of information obtained through the FAO is the individual behaviors that tend to occur together and those that do not. Initial perceptions that certain behaviors always go together may not always be supported by direct observation data.

Section D: Predictors   In Section D, list important events or stimuli identified in your interviews as potential predictors for the occurrence of problem behaviors. Such events typically are present or occur just before or at the same time as the problem behaviors. The FAO form already lists several potential predictors that have often been found in the research literature and in the authors' clinical experiences to be

---

[7]Text and forms adapted from *Functional Assessment and Program Development for Problem Behavior* (second edition), by Robert E. O'Neill, Robert H. Horner, Richard W. Albin, Jeffrey R. Sprague, Keith Storey, and J. Stephen Newton (Belmont, Calif.: Wadsworth Publishing Co., 1997, pp. 37-44), by permission of the publisher.

Functional Assessment Observation Form

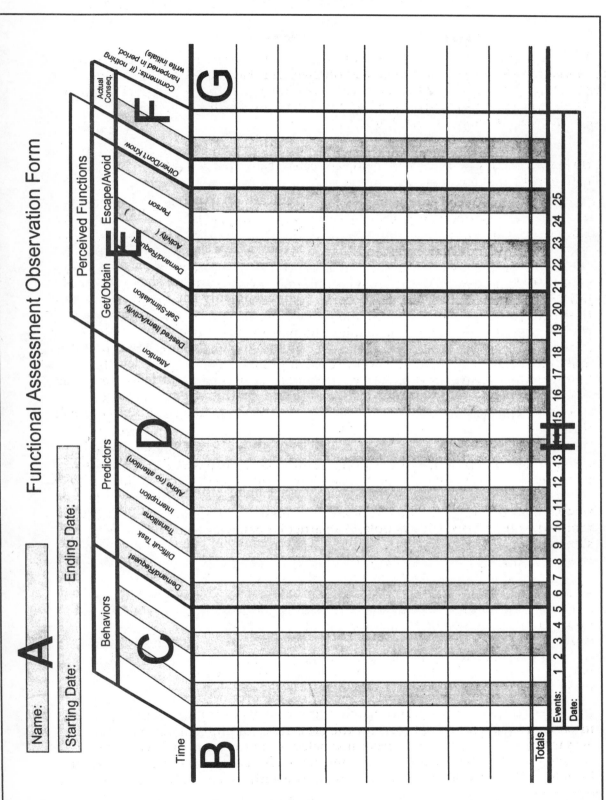

Name:

Starting Date: Ending Date:

A **B** **C** **D** **E** **F** **G** **H**

Time

Behaviors

Predictors

Demand/Request
Difficult Task
Transitions
Interruption
Alone (no attention)

Perceived Functions

Get/Obtain
Attention
Desired Item/Activity
Self-Stimulation

Escape/Avoid
Demand/Request
Activity ( )
Person

Other/Don't Know

Actual Conseq.

Comments: (If nothing happened in period, write initials).

Totals

Events: 1 2 3 4 5 6 7 8 9 10 11 12 13 14 15 16 17 18 19 20 21 22 23 24 25

Date:

Note: The authors have used this form for many cases, and teachers have received it well. We have discovered that the process of filling out the form has given teachers new skills in observing behaviors and designing behavior interventions, often alleviating the need for a more time-intensive plan development.

related to the occurrence of problem behaviors. These are Demands/Requests, Difficult Tasks, Transitions (place to place or activity to activity), Interruptions, and being left Alone (no attention). Additional empty slots are provided for you to list potential predictors specific to the person being observed. These might include the names of different support persons present; particular activities or tasks; conditions such as noise, schedule changes, or confusion; and the presence of particular classmates, housemates, or co-workers. You might also label a column "Don't Know" or "Unclear" to be used when the person recording data cannot identify particular setting events or antecedent stimuli that may be related to the occurrence of problem behaviors.

Section E: Perceived functions   In Section E, we ask observers to make their "best guess" regarding what they perceive as the apparent function of behaviors that occur during an incident. In other words, note why you think the person did what he or she did. This section has two major areas: obtaining desired things and escaping/avoiding undesired things. The specific "things" that would be designated on the form would depend on information gathered during the interview process. However, as in the Predictors section, the form lists several outcomes that individuals have been interested in obtaining or escaping through problem behaviors. These outcomes include obtaining attention, specific items or activities (you might list specific items or activities), and self-stimulation; and escaping or avoiding demands/requests, specific activities, or people. A column for "Don't Know" is included for situations in which observers are unsure of possible functions of the behavior observed.

Focusing on the particular outcome of a behavior and judging its function may be somewhat new ideas for many observers. People are often more accustomed to attributing the occurrence of problem behaviors to a person's "personality traits" or disability labels (for example, "she likes to hurt people because she is mean," "he does that because he is angry," "he does that because he has autism"). Because of this tendency, some observers may need repeated explanations and extra help to understand the important purpose of this section. We believe it is more respectful of a person's dignity to assume that functional reasons exist for problem behaviors rather than to think that such behaviors occur because of some personal trait or characteristic that is unchangeable.

Section F: Actual consequences   In Section F, you record data on the actual consequences that follow problem behaviors—for example, the person was told "no," was put in a time-out area, was ignored, was redirected. This information gives you some idea of the consistency with which certain consequences are being provided. It also provides further clues to the potential functions of problem behaviors. For instance, if a time-out procedure is being implemented with problem behaviors that appear to be escape motivated, then putting the student in a time-out area may actually be reinforcing the behaviors.

Section G: Comments   Observers can write brief comments here regarding behaviors that occurred during the corresponding block of time. We also recommend that observers use this space to write their initials for a block of time in which no targeted behaviors were observed. This practice verifies that observation was occurring and that no problem behaviors were observed. As we noted earlier, knowing when and under what circumstances problem behaviors do *not* occur can be very informative.

Section H: Event and date record   The rows of numbers in Section H are designed to help the observer keep track of the number of problem behavior events that have occurred and the days across which these events were observed. The numbers are used to show each event with one or more problem behaviors.

BOX 2.2

Steps for Setting Up a Functional Assessment Observation Form for Collecting Data

1. Write basic identifying information and dates of observations.

2. List the time intervals and settings/activities down the left side of the form.

3. List the behaviors to be monitored.

4. List potentially relevant setting events and/or more immediate antecedent events in the Predictors section.

5. List any additional possible functions of behaviors, if necessary, in the Perceived Functions section.

6. List the actual consequences that are typically delivered when behaviors occur.

The first time a behavior or incident occurs, the data recorder should mark the appropriate boxes on the form with the number 1 to identify the first recorded event of the behavior. The number 1 in the Events row of Section H would then be crossed off. The next occurrence of problem behaviors and the relevant boxes in each section of the form would be recorded by using the next number in the row (2 indicates the second occurrence, 3 indicates the third, and so on). Each time a number is used, it is crossed off. When recording is finished on a particular day, a slash can be drawn after the last number and the day's date recorded in the Date row below to indicate the date on which those incidents occurred. During the next day's data collection, the first incident would be recorded using the next unused number in the row (such as 5 or 6) and would then continue with the following numbers (7, 8, 9, 10). Using numbers in this way for each incident or occurrence of targeted behaviors enables you to link specific predictors, functions, and consequences with behaviors. If the same data sheet is used across multiple days, notations in the Date row help you see which incidents occurred on which days. Such information can be helpful as you look for patterns across time or try to validate what people tell you about the way a person's behaviors may vary on particular days (for example, "Her behavior is always worst on Mondays"). The steps for setting up the FAO to collect data are summarized in Box 2.2. Page 218 shows a form on which behaviors, predictors, perceived functions, and actual consequences are filled in and ready for use.

A quick analysis and interpretation of the data presented in the completed FAO . . . reveal several pieces of important information. Joe was observed for 2 days (3/16 and 3/17) during which a total of 17 events of problem behavior were coded (see Events row at bottom). Three problem behaviors were observed: slapping others, spitting on the desk, and screaming. Predictors added to the form for monitoring were the three classroom assistants who work with Joe: Marsha, Bill, and John. Actual consequences to Joe were blocking and redirection or having the behavior ignored. The Time column shows the school periods and times during which data were collected.

The observation data show clear patterns in the occurrence of problem behaviors. Look at the very first event involving problem behaviors. It is coded with a 1. This first event included both slapping others and screaming (a 1 in both columns). It occurred

Functional Assessment Observation Form

Name: *Joe*

Starting Date: *3-16* Ending Date: *3-17*

Time	Behaviors			Predictors								Perceived Functions — Get/Obtain				Escape/Avoid			Actual Conseq.		Comments (If nothing happened in period, write initials)
	Scream	Spit (on desk)	Slap others	Demand/Request	Difficult Task	Transitions	Interruption	Alone (no attention)	Martha	Bill	John	Attention	Desired Item/Activity	Self-Stimulation	Demand/Request	Activity ( )	person	Other/Don't Know	Ignore	Block/Redirect	
8:50–9:55 Reading	1, 11	2, 10	1, 11	1, 11			2, 10	2 10 / 1 11				2, 10			1, 11			2, 10	2, 10	1, 11	2-read on own 10-read on own
9:40–10:25 Lang Arts	3 4 5 12 13	12	3 4 5 12 13	3 4 5 12 13				3 4 5 12 13							3 4 5 12 13					3 4 5 12 13	
10:30–11:15 Choice																					
11:20–12:05 Math	6, 7	6, 7	14	6, 7			14	14	6, 7			14			6, 7			14	6, 7	6, 7	M.J.
12:05–12:50 Lunch																					
12:55–1:40 Social Studies	8, 15	8, 15		8, 15					8, 15						8, 15				8, 15	8, 15	14 – seat work B.W.
1:45–2:30 Science	17	16, 17	9	17	16		9	9		16, 17		9			17	16		9, 16	17	17	
2:55–3:20 P.E.	13	4																			J.S.
Totals																					

Events: 1 2 3 4 5 6 7 8 9 10 11 12 13 14 15 16 17 18 19 20 21 22 23 24 25

Date: 3/16   3/17

when a demand/request was made during the reading period (1's are in the row for 8:50 to 9:35). Marsha was working with Joe (see a 1 under Marsha for the period) and she implemented a block/redirect procedure. The perceived function was escape from the demand/request.

In looking for overall patterns, we see that slapping others (which occurred 12 times in the two days) and screaming (9 occurrences) frequently occurred together—but not always (see events 3, 4, and 5). This finding suggests that these two behaviors are members of the same response class and are used for the same function. The perceived function for both behaviors is escape from demands/requests. Note that screaming did occur once by itself during Science on 3/17 (see the event coded with 16). The predictor was a difficult task and the perceived function was escape from the task. This particular screaming incident was ignored. Blocking and redirection were used in the other slapping and screaming events. Spitting on the desk, which was observed four times, was seen as serving an attention-getting function. The predictor noted was that Joe was working alone (no attention). The Comments column provides even further information for events 2, 10, and 14. Despite the perceived function, the spitting was ignored by school staff, at least during the observation period presented here.

Using the Functional Assessment Observation Form

Recording The basic use of the FAO form is straightforward. Recording is event driven, occurring whenever a problem behavior or a behavioral episode or incident involving problem behaviors occurs. When problem behaviors occur during a time interval, place the appropriate number from Section H (1 for the first occurrence or episode, 2 for the second, 3 for the third, and so on) in the appropriate box or boxes in the Behaviors section. Then move horizontally across the rest of the form and place the same number in the appropriate boxes in the other sections, thereby recording the Predictors (setting events and antecedent stimuli) that were present when the behaviors occurred, the Perceived Functions of the behaviors, and the Actual Consequences that followed the occurrence of the behaviors. Finally, cross off the number used in Section H so you can easily see which number will be used next. If a comment is needed or desired, write it in the corresponding Comments box. Also, to facilitate follow-up on observations, observers could write their initials in the Comments box at the end of a time period, particularly if there is no other way to identify who was observing during a period. The example [on page 218] illustrates how several occurrences of problem behaviors might be recorded.

When problem behaviors occur relatively infrequently, information may be recorded for each occurrence of the behaviors. In such a case, an actual frequency count of the behavior can be obtained from the form. However, sometimes problem behaviors will occur in high-frequency bursts (such as several head hits or face slaps in rapid succession), or in episodes that include multiple occurrences of one or more problem behaviors (such as a 5-minute tantrum that involves dropping to the floor, kicking feet, screaming, several hits, and attempted bites). In such cases observers should code the entire burst or episode with a single entry on the form—that is, one number representing the entire episode or burst. Using this method, the frequency of bursts or episodes can be determined but not the actual frequency of each problem behavior.

Finally, for behaviors that occur with high frequency, the form should be used for brief time sample periods in which only a few, or even just one, occurrence or incident is recorded. This approach greatly reduces demands related to data collection but may also result in information being missed. The hope in such a case would be that high frequency behaviors occur so often that a clear picture will emerge even if all occurrences are not recorded.

No matter the recording approach used, support personnel and observers should ensure that the health, safety, and support needs of a person engaging in problem behaviors are met before they shift their attention to recording information on the observation form. *Data collection should not interfere with the delivery of needed support or intervention.* However, the person responsible for collecting data should record information when possible following the occurrence of problem behaviors to ensure accuracy and guard against the loss of information. The copy of the FAO form that is being used for data collection should be located in a convenient, central place where those responsible for observation have ready access for recording, such as on a clipboard or in a file on the teacher's desk.

As noted earlier, knowing where and when problem behaviors are *not* occurring can be very useful. If no problem behaviors occur during a time period, we recommend that the observer write his or her initials in the appropriate Comments column box to indicate that observation was occurring during this period. This eliminates the question of whether the absence of data during a period means that no problem behavior occurred or nobody was observing at that time. Having observers include their initials also allows you to know who was observing during a given time period in case you want to follow up on what was happening during the period. Box 2.3 summarizes the basic steps in the recording process.

BOX 2.3	**Basic Steps for Recording Data on the Functional Assessment Observation Form**

1. If problem behaviors occur during a recording interval:
   a. Recorder puts first unused number (from bottom list, Section H) in appropriate box or boxes in Behaviors section.
   b. Recorder uses the same number to mark appropriate boxes in the Predictors, Perceived Functions, and Actual Consequences sections.
   c. Recorder crosses out just-used number in the list at the bottom of the form.
   d. Recorder writes any desired comments in the Comments column.
   e. At the end of the time period the recorder puts his or her initials in the Comments box.
2. If problem behaviors do *not* occur during a recording interval:
   a. Recorder puts his or her initials in the Comments box for that interval and writes any desired comments.

Initial training   People who will be using the FAO form need to be trained before using the form independently. Training should involve describing the different sections of the form and how they are used, and providing practice on recording on the form before actual observation begins...Training also should include specific information on the logistics of the observation and recording processes to be used. This includes writing on the form the actual time intervals to be employed, identifying the persons responsible for recording data, specifying where the form will be located and stored, and determining the planned schedule for observations. Once actual observation has begun, someone in a supervisory or monitoring capacity should discuss with the observers any issues or problems that arise. It is not unusual to need to revise the observation form or procedures after a day or two of actual recording. For example, behaviors or predictors may occur that were overlooked in the initial interviews and form setup and will need to be added to the form. Behaviors or predictors (difficult tasks, transitions) may need to be more clearly defined for consistent recording. Procedures (such as where the form is kept) may need to be modified.

Functional Assessment Observation Form

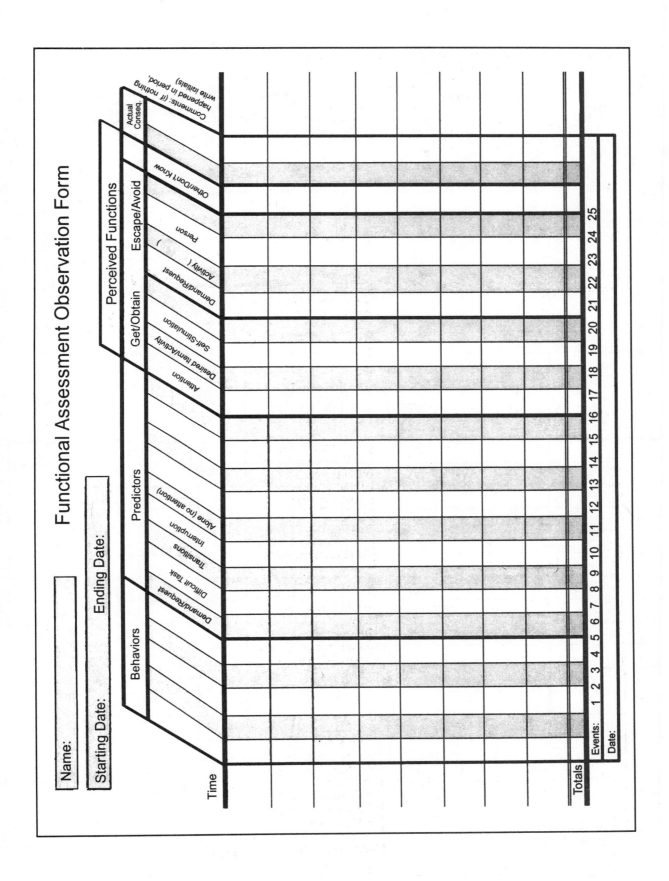

Name:

Starting Date:

Ending Date:

	Behaviors				Predictors							Perceived Functions								Comments: (If nothing happened in period, write initials)
				Demand/Request	Difficult Task	Transitions	Interruption	Alone (no attention)				Get/Obtain				Escape/Avoid				
												Attention	Desired Item/Activity	Self-Stimulation	Demand/Request	Activity ( )	Person ( )	Other/Don't Know	Actual Conseq.	
Time																				

Events: 1 2 3 4 5 6 7 8 9 10 11 12 13 14 15 16 17 18 19 20 21 22 23 24 25

Totals

Date:

Scatter Plot[3] Data Sheet

Student:_____

Date:_____

Behavior:_____

Respondent:_____

■ = more than _____   X̄ = less than _____

Activity	Time (Optional)	Day 1	Day 2	Day 3	Day 4	Day 5	Day 6	Day 7	Day 8	Day 9	Day 10

[3] *A scatter-plot (Touchette et al., 1985) is a frequently used recording system for some behaviors that have discrete beginning and endings. There are many recording methods and variations on methods that can be used. Refer to the Bibliography for additional information.*

WORKSHEET 5
Log of Additional Information Required Prior to Plan Development

Information Needed:	Information Requested From:	Person Responsible for Obtaining:	Date Requested:	Date Received:

Review Of Records For Behavioral History

Student:_____**Review Date:** _____

I.   Specify Records Reviewed:_____

_____

II.   Individuals Contacted From Previous Settings:_____

_____

_____

III.   History Of The Problem Behavior:_____

_____

_____

_____

IV.   Previous Interventions For Problem Behavior: (Note successful/unsuccessful)

_____

_____

_____

_____

_____

_____

V.   Critical Factors To Include Or Avoid In Planning For Current Setting:

_____

_____

_____

VI.   Tentative Hypotheses Of Functions Of Problem Behavior:

_____

_____

_____

_____

Ecological Analysis Of Settings
Where Behavior Occurs Most Frequently

Student:_____ **Date:** _____

Physical Setting: (e.g., noise, crowding, temperature)

_____

_____

Social Setting: (interaction patterns, with and around student)

_____

_____

_____

Activities: (activities/curriculum match learner needs?)

_____

_____

_____

Nature of Instruction: (instructional methods and techniques match learner needs?)

_____

_____

Scheduling Factors: (timing, sequencing, and transition issues)

_____

_____

Degree of Independence: (reinforcement intervals appropriate to foster appropriate independence)

_____

_____

Degree of Participation: (group size, location, and participation parameters)

_____

_____

_____

Social Interaction: (social communication needs match instruction and opportunities)

_____

_____

Degree of Choice: (amount of choice making and negotiation present in environment)

_____

_____

REPORT FORM 3

Review Of Data On Internal States Which Potentially Influence Behavior

Student:_____ Date:_____

Behavior intervention case manager: _____

Interviewees:_____

Staff Member Completing This Section:_____

I.   Identified Handicapping Condition

Educational handicapping condition(s):_____

    Does this condition have known behavior features?   ☐ Yes   ☐ No

    If yes, describe those the student exhibits:_____

_____

_____

II.   Identified Health/Biological Conditions

Medical Diagnosis:_____

_____

Does diagnosis have known behavioral features: ☐ Yes   ☐ No

If yes, describe those the student exhibits: _____

_____

Review of Vision and Hearing

	Date of Last Exam and Source	Nature of Any Problems	List Any Accommodations Required
Vision			
Hearing			

REPORT FORM 3-CONTINUED

III. Current Medication Summary

Medication(s) and Dosage(s)	Anticipated Benefit	Possible Behavioral Side-Effects	Source of Information: Parent, Doctor, Physicians Desk Reference, Etc.

Note Recent Change(s) In Medication:_____

_____

Potential Effect On Problem Behavior:_____

_____

Behavior Pattern As Related To Medication:_____

_____

Variation(s) In Behavior As A Result Of Medication Ingestion Time(s):_____

_____

IV. Sleep Cycles And Diet

Current Sleep Pattern:_____

Potential Impact on Behavior: _____

Note Recent Change(s) And Potential Impact On Behavior:_____

_____

Note Any Special Dietary Requirements, Restrictions, or Food Allergies:_____

_____

_____

Potential Impact on Behavior:_____

_____

REPORT FORM 3-CONTINUED

V. Unusual Responses Or Sensitivity To Environmental Stimuli

Stimuli	Unusual Response	Potential Impact on Behaviors
Tactile		
Auditory		
Visual		
Movement		
Vibration		
Smell and Taste		

VI. Periodic Precipitating Factors

Note periodically occurring events that have led to an increase in problem behavior:

_____

_____

_____

_____

_____

_____

_____

_____

REPORT FORM 4

Functional Analysis Assessment Report Summary

(attach Forms 1-2-3 to complete the report)

Student: _____ Birthdate: _____

Handicapping Condition(s): _____

Behavior intervention case manager: _____

Serious Behavior Problem:

_____

_____

_____

Severity (from baseline data) _____

_____

Identified Positive Replacement Behavior(s):

_____

_____

Current Prevalence (from baseline data) _____

_____

Summary of Relevant Information From Functional Assessment

What Environmental Features Require Alteration? _____

_____

_____

_____

_____

What appears to be prompting and reinforcing the problem behavior based on analysis of antecedents
and consequences?

_____

_____

_____

REPORT FORM 4 CONTINUED

What Inhibits the Problem Behavior Based on Analysis of Antecedents and Consequences?

_____

_____

_____

_____

_____

Hypothesized Function(s) of the Problem Behavior

_____

_____

_____

_____

What Appears to be Prompting and Reinforcing the Positive Replacement Behavior Based on Analysis of Antecedents and Consequences?

_____

_____

_____

_____

What Inhibits the Expression of the Positive Replacement Behavior?

_____

_____

_____

_____

Summary of Baseline Data

(Attach supportive data such as graphs, charts, logs, or summarize on page 3 of this form)

Baseline of Maladaptive Behavior

_____

_____

Baseline of Positive Replacement Behavior

_____

_____

REPORT FORM 4 CONTINUED
Baseline Data Results
PROBLEM BEHAVIOR
Graph of Baseline Data
Observation Date(s): _____

POSITIVE REPLACEMENT BEHAVIOR
Graph of Baseline Data
Observation Date(s): _____

REPORT FORM 5
Positive Behavioral Intervention Plan

(attach Forms 1-4 to complete this form)

Student: _____ **Date:** _____

Behavior Intervention Case Manager: _____

I.   All Environments Where Interventions Will Be Used: _____

_____

II. All Supervising Personnel/Implementer(s) for Above: _____

_____

III. Precise Criteria for Discontinuing Plan, Reconvening of IEP Meeting for Major Revisions:

_____

_____

IV. Possible Minor Revisions Not Requiring IEP Meeting: _____

_____

_____

_____

_____

V.   Schedules for Recording the Frequency and Use of Interventions (who, how often, what method)

Problem Behavior Data Collection: _____

_____

_____

_____

_____

_____

_____

VI. Periodic, Review (Frequency and Method): _____

_____

_____

_____

_____

REPORT FORM 5-CONTINUED

VII. Ecological Changes Necessary Prior To or During Plan:

_____

_____

_____

VIII. Direct Treatment Strategies for Positive Replacement Behavior:

_____

_____

_____

IX. Reinforcement System for Presence of Positive Behavior, or Absence or Reduced Rates of Problem Behavior:

_____

_____

X. Positive Programming/Teaching Techniques and Strategies:
   (Describe coping/tolerance instruction, teaching of positive behaviors, etc.)

_____

_____

_____

_____

_____

_____

XI. Reactive Strategies for Problem Behaviors: (Not to include Emergency Procedures)
   Describe when/what additional redirecting strategies are to be utilized.

_____

_____

_____

_____

_____

_____

XII. Describe what specific behavior will constitute a need for an emergency procedure (log all emergencies on other SELPA forms):

_____

_____

REPORT FORM 5-CONTINUED

XIII. Describe modifications to plan if periodic precipitating factors (Form 3) are present (if any)

_____

_____

_____

_____

_____

_____

_____

_____

_____

_____

XIV. Criteria for Success Achieved:

_____

_____

_____

XV. Criteria for Phasing Out of Intrusive Reinforcers and/or Prompts:

_____

_____

_____

_____

XVI. How Program Implementation will be Documented
     (e.g.,charts, written samples, description of environmental changes, behavioral logs).

_____

_____

_____

Appendix D.

Advanced Training in Positive Behavioral Interventions

As an aid to professionals seeking further education in the field of behavioral interventions, the task force, with the assistance of the School Psychology Education Committee, sought information on where such advanced training could be obtained. Letters requesting information on course work and degree programs in behavior intervention and management were sent to 149 institutions and individual departments of higher education in California. Included were all of the school psychology training programs, every institution that offers a credential in any field of special education, and all the graduate psychology programs in the state. A second request was sent to the school psychology programs that did not respond to the first letter. Of that list, 18 responses were received, and the results of the survey are shown in Figure 19.

Because many institutions change their course offerings from time to time, the reader is encouraged to contact the indicated person for fully up-to-date information. Further, it is assumed that many more institutions offer course work and degree programs than are indicated here. Interested parties would be well advised to contact each school directly for further information, regardless of their presence or absence in Figure 19, on the following page.

FIGURE 19.

UNIVERSITY SOURCES OF ADVANCED TRAINING

Institution	Department	Contact Person Mailing Address Telephone Number	Course Titles
Biola University, Rosemead School of Psychology	Psychology	William M. McQueen, Jr., Ph.D. 13800 Biola Avenue La Miranda, CA 90639 (310) 903-4867	• Basis of Cognitive and Behavior Therapy • Behavior Therapy with Children and Their Families • Behavior Therapy with Adults • Clinical Biofeedback • Cognitive Behavior Therapy • Management Techniques for Parents and Teachers
California Lutheran University	Special Education	Carol J. Genrich, Ph.D. CA Lutheran Univ. 60 West Olsen Road Thousand Oaks, CA 91360-2787 (805) 492-2411	• Application of Behavior Management Strategies
California Polytechnic University, San Luis Obispo	Education	Howard Drucker, Ph.D. CPSU, San Luis Obispo San Luis Obispo, CA 93407 (805) 756-1111	• Behavior Disorders and Classroom Management Strategies
California School of Professional Psychology, Fresno	Psychology	Ennio Cipani, Ph.D. CSPP - Fresno 1350 M Street Fresno, CA 93721-1881 (209) 486-8420	• The Cipani Behavioral Diagnostic System: Assessing, Designing and Writing Functional Behavioral Assessment/ Interventions
California State University, Chico	Education (Special Education Program)	Mary C. Savelsbergh, Ph.D. CSU Chico First and Normal Streets Chico, CA 95929-0222 (916) 898-6421	• Advanced Classroom Management for Individuals with Exceptional Needs
California State University, Chico	Psychology (School Psychology Program)	Neil Schwartz, Ph.D. CSU Chico First and Normal Street Chico, CA 95929-0234 (916) 898-4968	• Psychological Consultation in the Schools
California State University, Dominguez Hills	Psychology	Judith Todd, Ph.D. CSU Dominguez Hills 1000 East Victoria Street Carson, CA 90747 (310) 516-3427	• Behavior Modification
California State University, Fresno	Psychology (School Psychology Program)	Karen T. Carey, Ph.D., NCSP CSU Fresno 5310 North Campus Drive Fresno, CA 93740-0011 (209) 278-2691	• Intervention and Prevention • Consultation and Supervision • Interviewing and Individual Psychotherapy • Cognitive and Behavior Therapy *Continued on next page*

FIGURE 19. CONTINUED

Institution	Department	Contact Person Mailing Address Telephone Number	Course Titles
California State University, Fresno	Psychology (School Psychology Program)	Karen T. Carey, Ph.D., NCSP CSU Fresno 5310 North Campus Drive Fresno, CA 93740-0011 (209) 278-2691	• Assessment of Intellectual Abilities • Assessment of Learning and Developmental Abilities • Internship in School Psychology
California State University, Fullerton	Special Education	Jan S. Weiner, Ph.D. CSU Fullerton P.O. Box 34080 Fullerton, CA 92634-9480 (714) 720-0341	• Nonaversive Classroom Management
California State University, Hayward	Educational Psychology	T.G. Alper, Ph.D. CSU Hayward Hayward, CA 94542 (415) 881-3011	• Principles of Cognitive Behavior Therapy • Curriculum-Based Assessment and Cognitive Behavioral Intervention • Pediatric Psychology
California State University, Long Beach	Deptartment of Educational Psychology and Administration (School Psychology and Special Education)	Thomas J. Kampwirth, Ph.D. CSU Long Beach 1250 Bellflower Boulevard Long Beach, CA 90840-2201 (310) 985-4111	• Diagnosis and Treatment of the Emotionally Handicapped Student • Behavior Management in the Classroom
California State University, Los Angeles *	School of Education (School Psychology, School Counseling and Special Education Programs)	G. Roy Mayer, Ph.D. CSU Los Angeles School of Education 5151 State University Drive Los Angeles, CA 90032 (818) 343-4441	• Applied Behavior Analysis • Behavioral Counseling and Self-Management • Behavior Analysis in School, Home, and Agency Settings • Advanced Behavioral Contingency Management in Schools • Advanced Topical Study in Application of Behavior Analysis to Education • Behavior Management Using Reinforcement in Classrooms
California State University, Northridge	Education (Special Education Program)	Joyce C. Hagen, Ph.D. CSU Northridge 18111 Nordhoff Street P.O. Box 1277 Northridge, CA 91328-1277 (818) 885-2596	• Instruction of Exceptional Pupils: Behavioral Assessment and Positive Behavioral Management

Continued on next page

FIGURE 19. CONTINUED

Institution	Department	Contact Person Mailing Address Telephone Number	Course Titles
California State University, Sacramento *	Psychology	Joseph R. Keller, Ph.D. CSU Sacramento 6000 J Street Sacramento, CA 95819-6007 (916) 278-6011	• Applied Behavior Analysis: Basic Principals • Experimental Analysis of Behavior • Applied Child Psychology • Field Work in Behavior Modification • Principles of Behavior Analysis • Behavior Modification: Operant Theory
Pacific Oaks College	Special Education	Virginia Kennedy, Ph.D. Pacific Oaks College 5 Westmoreland Place Pasadena, CA 91103 (818) 397-1300	• Course on mental health approaches in schools currently being developed
University California, Riverside	Education (School Psychology Program)	Colleen M. McMahon, Ph.D. School of Education UC Riverside Riverside, CA 92521 (714) 787-5228	• Behavioral Assessment • School Psychological Consultation • Principles of Social Behavior Intervention • Principles of Academic Behavior Intervention • School Psychological Consultation • Child Behavior Therapy • Single Case Experimental Design
University California, Santa Barbara	Psychology	A. Robert Sherman, Ph.D. UC Santa Barbara Santa Barbara, CA 93106 (805) 893-3534	• Behavioral Approaches to Psychotherapy • Behavior Modification
University California, Santa Barbara	School of Education, School Psychology Program	Robert L. Koegel, Ph.D. Counseling/Clinical/School Psychology Program Graduate School of Education UC Santa Barbara Santa Barbara, CA 93106 (805) 893-2176	• Behavioral Intervention
University of San Diego	Education (Special Education Program)	Katie Bishop, Ph.D. USD 5998 Alcala Park San Diego, CA 92110-2492 (619) 260-4538	• Positive Behavioral Interventions in Education • Classroom Management and Behavior Change

* *This institution has a specific degree or certificate program in the area of applied behavior analysis, behavioral interventions, or behavior modification.*

Appendix E.

Emergency Intervention Training Programs

It is anticipated that individuals, districts, county offices of education, and special education local plan areas (SELPAs) will seek training programs in physical emergency management techniques. The task force therefore conducted an informal telephone survey of professionals in the field to determine where such training is available.

Three main sources were identified and are listed below. The task force wishes to emphasize that this was an informal telephone survey; this listing is not intended to be comprehensive. The programs listed here are the ones that school personnel and training groups themselves identified as being available in California and in current use by school personnel within the state. Other systems may also meet those criteria but have not come to the attention of task force members. The training groups themselves will be the best source of information on their philosophy, actual techniques and procedures, and locations where their programs are being used regularly.

It is important to restate here a recommendation contained in Chapter 6 on Best Practices in Emergency Procedures. Before adopting any specific training program or approach to physical emergency intervention techniques, individuals and governing bodies must learn which specific techniques are actually being taught. Only then can they determine that the techniques are consistent with the emergency intervention philosophy and policy of the district, county, or SELPA where these techniques will ultimately be used to contain the crisis behaviors of individual students.

This listing does not indicate or in any way imply a recommendation or an endorsement of any particular program. The programs are listed alphabetically:

1.　**National Crisis Prevention Institute, Inc.**

   3315-K North 124th Street
   Brookfield, WI 53005
   (800) 558-8976, (414) 783-5787
   Linda Steiger, Director
   Program Title: Non-Violent Crisis Intervention Direct Training and
   trainer-of-trainers programs available

2. **National Residential Child Care Project**

G-20 MVR Hall
Cornell University
Ithaca, NY, 14853-4401
Martha Hold or Kim McGuire
Program Title: Trainer of Trainers in Therapeutic Crisis Intervention
Trainer-of-trainers program only; referrals for local trainers for
therapeutic crisis intervention are available from above contact persons

3. **Professional Growth Facilitators**

P.O. Box 5981
San Clemente, CA 92674-5081
(714) 498-3529
Lois Johnson, Managing Partner
Program Title: Professional Assault Response Training
Direct training and trainer-of-trainers programs available

Appendix F.

Sample Emergency Intervention Report Form

The form in this appendix is one type of incident report that is offered for use in reporting emergency interventions. It is modeled after the procedures and techniques taught by the National Crisis Prevention Institute (CPI) course in Nonviolent Crisis Intervention. This form includes all required components of an emergency report that are listed in the Hughes Bill and related regulations, while encompassing all four phases of crisis development taught in the CPI course. This form may be most useful if staff members are trained in the CPI model. There is an advantage in using an emergency report that follows the crisis intervention method in which staff members are trained. That is, in addition to meeting legal requirements, it also serves to document and remind staff of specific procedures.

The first copy is a blank copy of the form, and the second includes extra columns with examples of statements that may be used in each section. This appendix is offered as a sample that may or may not meet the specific needs of a particular local education agency (LEA). However, it is hoped that it may provide a starting point for many LEAs in developing their emergency procedure reports.

INCIDENT REPORT

Must be completed in ink / no white out

Must be completed for: (circle one)
Physical Intervention, Major Disruption Threats,
Dangerous Running, Injury, Major Property Damage,
Assaultive or other Serious Behavior Problem

Date: _____   Time: _____   Positive Behavioral Intervention Plan in Effect: Yes No (Circle One)

Setting and Location: _____   People Involved: _____

Student: _____   Age: _____   Person Preparing Report: _____

	Describe Student Behavior/Description of Incident	Check Staff Response Used/Emergency Intervention	
Escalation Stages	**ANXIETY:**	____ proximity ____ counseling ____ restructure routine/environment ____ accommodate materials/expectations ____ referral (to: _____)	**Prevention**
	DEFENSIVE: (question, refuse, vent: intimidate)	____ redirect, restate direction ____ set limits: _____ _____ ____ separate student from group ____ separate the group from student ____ sit out within the group	
Dangerous Behavior	**ACTING OUT:**	Intervention Team: _____ ____ clear area ____ basket hold ____ block ____ team restraint ____ release ____ escort ____ visual supervision ____ call administrator ____ other	**Intervention**
Self Control Reestablished	**TENSION REDUCTION:**	____ review events ____ review schedule ____ make plan: _____ _____ _____ _____ _____	**Debriefing**
	INJURY/MEDICAL:	____ sent to nurse ____ first aid ____ 911 Paramedics ____ CPR	

INCIDENT REPORT

Must be completed in ink / no white out

Must be completed for: (circle one)
Physical intervention, Major Disruption Threats,
Dangerous Running, Injury, Major Property Damage,
Assaultive or other Serious Behavior Problem

Date: _____   Time: _____   Positive Behavioral Intervention Plan in Effect: Yes   No (Circle One)

Setting and Location: _____   People Involved: _____

Student: _____   Age: _____   Person Preparing Report: _____

Examples of observable Behavior	Describe Student Behavior/ Description of Incident		Check Staff Response Used/ Emergency Intervention		Examples of Staff Behavior/ Intervention Techniques
Pacing, shaking, nervousness, change in eye contact, change in facial expression, change in posture, movement to specific area, change in rate of speech	ANXIETY:	Escalation Stages	____ proximity ____ counseling ____ restructure routine/environment ____ accommodate materials/ expectations ____ referral (to: _____)	Prevention	Move close to student w/o invading personal space; Active reflective listening; attend to complaints/ request; simplify work; change directions; offer help; separate from bothersome stimuli; calming techniques; give choices.
Loud (noises or speech); questions, refusals, swearing, name calling, challenging, threatening, increase in breathing and/or heart rate	DEFENSIVE: (questions, refuse, vent, intimidate)		____ redirect, restate direction ____ set limits: _____ _____ ____ separate student from group ____ separate the group from student ____ sit out within the group		Use simple clear language; reasonable, enforceable and understandable limits; restate positive consequences; separate from group; remove dangerous implements; assemble team members; allow venting.
Hit, kick, throw, turn over desks, pounding windows, tearing clothes or materials, running in dangerous area (e.g. street), self injury.	ACTING OUT:	Dangerous Behavior	Intervention Team: _____ ____ clear area ____ basket hold ____ block ____ team restraint ____ release ____ escort ____ visual supervision ____ call administrator ____ other	Intervention	Maintain a safe distance from acting out person; remove bystanders if still in area; plan for team intervention if necessary; implement non-harmful, physical intervention techniques as a last resort.
Reduction of above behaviors; can answer simple questions rationally; can follow simple direction such as "Take a deep breath"; briefly discusses incident w/o reescalation; breathing and heart rate return to resting rate.	TENSION REDUCTION:	Self Control Reestablished	____ review events ____ review schedule ____ make plan: _____ _____ _____ _____ _____	Debriefing	Calm down time; discuss incident, make plan w/acting out person for alternative behavior. For individuals w/ cognitive limitations review rules and return to a successful activity.
	INJURY/MEDICAL		____ sent to nurse ____ first aid ____ 911 Paramedics ____ CPR		

ANALYSIS OF
SENSORY BEHAVIOR
INVENTORY

REVISED

Kimble Morton, MA and Shiela Wolford, MA, OTR

Student or Client:	
Date of Birth:	
Responder:	
Relationship to Student or Client:	
Data Collector:	
Date:	

Copyright 1994 by Kimble Morton and Shiela Wolford

Printed by

Skills with Occupational Therapy

P.O. Box 1785

Arcadia, CA 91077-1785

Analysis of Sensory Behavior Inventory-R

Kimble Morton, MA and Shiela Wolford, MA, OTR

Unusual sensory processing differences are frequently found in combination with a range of disabilities and handicapping conditions but most especially for individuals with severe disabilities and problem behaviors. Analyzing these differences may play a key role in understanding some puzzling behaviors which have proven difficult to change. Behavior interventions which accommodate these individual differences often result in improved adaptive functioning.

The Analysis of Sensory Behavior Inventory-R assesses six sensory modalities: vestibular, tactile, proprioceptive, auditory, visual and gustatory-olfactory. There are sub-sections to allow rating of both sensory-avoidance and sensory-seeking behaviors within each modality. This division allows the identification of clusters of responses within or across modalities. The worksheets at the end are provided to assist in organizing the information and developing both hypotheses and accommodations.

The Analysis of Sensory Behavior Inventory-R is designed to be used for collection of information regarding an individual's behaviors and responses as they are related to sensory stimuli. The information revealed may be a useful component in completing a functional analysis of behavior, leading to a variety of possible interventions. In some cases, the results may lead to development of a hypothesis regarding "sensory seeking" or "sensory avoidance" as the function of a behavior. Additionally, it may contribute to the development of effective intervention strategies, including accommodations or reinforcers for the individual.

The Analysis of Sensory Behavior Inventory-R can be completed by a variety of people who know the student or client. This can be done either as an individual or as a group. It can also be used as an interview guide with parents, teachers, DIS personnel, aides, or, in some cases, the student or client as respondents. However, because various respondents may view a particular behavior differently, it is important for each respondent to provide clear, operationalized descriptions and examples of all relevant behaviors. This will be important to emphasize when giving instructions to the respondent if an interview format is not utilized. Using the inventory as an interview guide may also help in matching differing perceptions of behaviors among respondents.

Once the Analysis of Sensory Behavior Inventory-R information is obtained from all sources, it should be compiled and then analyzed. When analyzing the information gained from the Analysis of Sensory Behavior Inventory-R, several "yes" answers in any single category indicates the student may be seeking or avoiding that type of stimulation or sensory input. The smaller the difference between the number of yes answers and the number of total possible answers, the stronger the indicator. The worksheets will assist in determining strong indicators and possible areas of concern. The analysis (or worksheets) can be done by one person or by reviewing the results in a small group meeting. A group process may maximize the potential for reaching a more complete understanding of the behavior by all parties.

Sensory related factors are only one of many components which influence behavior. Therefore the Analysis of Sensory Behavior Inventory-R should not preclude or exclude relevant medical, developmental, emotional, or environmental factors when planning intervention strategies.

Analysis of Sensory Behavior Inventory-R

Kimble Morton, MA and Shiela Wolford, MA, OTR

Please rate the student in each of the following six areas. A "yes" answer indicates that the student demonstrates this behavior or response in a manner or to a degree that is inappropriate for his or her chronological age. Provide specific examples whenever possible. At the end of each section is a row labeled "other." Use this space to add any other behavior or sensory response that you think might be related to that area.

1. VESTIBULAR STIMULATION (movement & gravity information).

	YES	NO	UNSURE	COMMENTS/EXAMPLES
Behaviors or responses that may indicate AVOIDANCE of this type of sensory stimulation				
a. fearful of heights and/or elevators				
b. protests head being tipped back				
c. avoids or protests positions in which feet are off ground				
d. prefers quiet play as opposed to more active play				
e. fearful of simple challenges to balance (for example, moving in and out of different positions or being bumped)				
f. fearful of moving equipment (for example escalators, swings, merry-go-rounds)				
g. other				
The following behaviors or responses, not necessarily avoidant in nature, indicate hypersensitivity to vestibular stimulation and are often associated with other vestibular avoidant behaviors.				
h. gets motion sickness easily				
Behaviors or responses that may indicate SEEKING of this type of sensory stimulation				
a. rocks while sitting or standing				
b. frequently jumps or bounces				
c. likes being tossed in the air				
d. likes merry-go-rounds or fast rides				
e. frequently spins or whirls				
f. no fear of movement or falling				
g. craves being rocked, now or as an infant				
h. craves wrestling or tumbling activities				
i. other				

2. TACTILE STIMULATION (touch information)

	YES	NO	UNSURE	COMMENTS/EXAMPLES
Behaviors or responses that may indicate AVOIDANCE of this type of sensory stimulation				
a. strongly dislikes hair washing/ brushing, or toothbrushing, and may continue to complain when finished				
b. strongly dislikes having face washed or wiped and may continue to complain when finished				
c. strong likes or dislikes toward certain food textures				
d. avoids or objects to being touched				
e. dislikes or overreacts to unexpected touch (for example, when approached from behind)				
f. disliked being cuddled as infant (or now)				
g. avoids "messy" things (mud/finger paint/etc.)				
h. avoids using hands for extended periods				
i. protests nail cutting				
j. strongly dislikes cloth of certain textures; picky about texture of clothes				
k. excessively ticklish				
l. covers entire body with clothes regardless of weather				
m. wears minimal clothes regardless of weather				
n. excessive complaints of being bumped and poked				
o. walks on toes especially if barefoot				
p. consistently comments about temperature changes when experienced				
q. unusually large personal space				
r. other				

2. TACTILE STIMULATION (touch information) *(Continued)*

	YES	NO	UNSURE	COMMENTS/EXAMPLES
Behaviors or responses that may indicate SEEKING this type of sensory stimulation				
a. seeks lots of touch				
b. examines or explores objects by putting them into mouth				
c. examines or explores objects by touching them				
d. hits or bangs head on purpose (now or in past)				
e. pinches, bites or otherwise hurts self				
f. frequently rubs, holds or manipulates objects of a certain texture				
g. rubs fingers or body parts frequently				
h. chews or sucks on non-edibles frequently				
i. other				
The following behaviors or responses, not necessarily seeking in nature, indicate hyposensitivity to tactile stimulation, and are often associated with other tactile seeking behaviors.				
j. tends to feel pain less than others				
k. unaware of substances spilled on body (for example, glue, paint or food on hands or food or drooling on face)				
l. unaware of scrapes, bleeding, swelling, burns or sunburn				
m. drinks very hot liquids without complaint				

3. PROPRIOCEPTIVE STIMULATION (deep pressure, vibration, muscle and joint information)

	YES	NO	UNSURE	COMMENTS/EXAMPLES
Behaviors or responses that may indicate AVOIDANCE of this type of sensory stimulation				
a. avoids or refuses to hold vibratory appliances such as food mixer, blow dryer, or dust vacuum				
b. fearful of electric barber clippers				
c. tends to give up on tasks that provide resistance such as opening tight jar lids, pushing heavy doors, carrying objects or climbing on playground equipment				
d. avoids crunchy or chewy foods				
e. seems weak performing age-appropriate functional tasks				
f. other				
Behaviors or responses that may indicate SEEKING of this sensory stimulation				
a. places vibrating appliance in or near mouth repeatedly				
b. tolerates vibratory stimuli for extended periods				
c. frequently moves quickly and is unable to move slowly from one position or place to another				
d. craves tumbling or wrestling				
e. frequently gives or requests firm or prolonged hugs				
f. likes to be wrapped tightly in sheet or blanket				
g. frequently bumps people or objects without apparent reason, but does not seem accidental				
h. holds hands and/or body in strange positions				
i. usually walks on toes regardless of footwear				
j. tends to prefer only crunchy or chewy foods				
k. bites or chews on non-edibles				
l. other				

4. AUDITORY STIMULATION (sound and hearing)
(Note: Diagnosed hearing loss or ongoing difficulties with ear infections must first be ruled out)

	YES	NO	UNSURE	COMMENTS/EXAMPLES
Behaviors or responses that may indicate AVOIDANCE of this type of sensory stimulation				
a. protests or over reacts to unexpected or loud noises				
b. seems unable to pay attention when there are other noises nearby				
c. runs out of room or area in response to sounds				
d. serious behavior problem is significantly reduced in quiet environments				
e. irrational fear of noisy appliances such as blender, fan, vacuum cleaner or mixer				
f. frequently seeks quiet areas				
g. notices or comments on quiet background noises such as air conditioners, or normal traffic				
h. hears sirens or oncoming trains before others				
i. covers ears frequently				
j. other				
Behaviors or responses that may indicate SEEKING of this type of sensory stimulation (or high thresholds for sound)				
a. seeks out toys which make sound				
b. appears to be hard of hearing, but loss is not verified by tests				
c. craves music or certain sounds				
d. other				
The following behaviors or responses, not necessarily seeking in nature indicate hyposensitivity to auditory stimulation, and are often associated with other auditory seeking behaviors.				
e. misses hearing some sounds				
f. does not respond to commands or requests without visual cues				
g. needs loud (increased volume) verbal input to respond or comply				

5. VISUAL STIMULATION (sight and light)
(Note: Diagnosed visual loss or uncorrected visual acuity loss must first be ruled out)

	YES	NO	UNSURE	COMMENTS/EXAMPLES
Behaviors or responses that may indicate AVOIDANCE of this type of sensory stimulation				
a. poor eye contact (reduction in amount)				
b. seems to enjoy dark				
c. becomes very excited or overstimulated when there are a variety of visual objects				
d. consistently turns off regular lighting for activities				
e. frequently covers eyes, squints, or rubs eyes				
f. avoids or protests going outdoors on sunny days				
g. regularly comments on changes in lighting such as clouds covering sun or going from lighter to darker room				
h. other				
Behaviors or responses that may indicate SEEKING of this type of sensory stimulation				
a. looks very closely and carefully at pictures or objects				
b. resists having eyes covered				
c. frequently spins bright or reflecting objects				
d. seems to enjoy repeatedly flicking lights on and off				
e. frequently watches repetitive movements such as flipping pages of a book, or an automatic door opening and closing				
f. manipulates objects or moves hands and fingers close to face (but does not have diagnosed visual impairment)				
g. likes to look at things out of the corner of eyes (with peripheral vision)				
h. riveting eye contact (excessive amount)				
i. other				

6. GUSTATORY-OLFACTORY STIMULATION (taste and smell information)

	YES	NO	UNSURE	COMMENTS/EXAMPLES
Behaviors or responses that may indicate AVOIDANCE of this type of sensory stimulation				
a. reacts to or comments on normal odors as though they were irritating				
b. reacts to or comments on faint odors that are not noticed by others				
c. primarily eats bland foods				
d. other				
Behaviors or responses that may indicate SEEKING of this type of sensory stimulation				
a. explores by smelling or licking				
b. likes highly seasoned foods				
c. other				
The following behaviors or responses, not necessarily seeking in nature, indicate hyposensitivity to gustatory-olfactory stimulation, and are often associated with other gustatory-olfactory seeking behaviors.				
d. acts as though all food tastes the same				
e. ignores or does not seem to be bothered by unpleasant odors				

NOTES:

_____

_____

_____

_____

_____

_____

_____

_____

_____

Analysis of Sensory Behavior Inventory-R Worksheet

SENSORY STATE	SCORING Responses yes/poss.		"X" if area of possible concern
VESTIBULAR AVOIDANCE: vertical motion (items a-d)		4	
VESTIBULAR AVOIDANCE: other motions (items d-f, h)		4	
VESTIBULAR SEEKING (items a-h)		8	
TACTILE AVOIDANCE: oral/facial area (items a-c)		3	
TACTILE AVOIDANCE: other body areas (items d-q)		14	
TACTILE SEEKING (items a-h, j-m)		12	
PROPRIOCEPTIVE AVOIDANCE: feeling vibration (items a-b)		2	
PROPRIOCEPTIVE AVOIDANCE: feeling deep pressure (items c-e)		3	
PROPRIOCEPTIVE SEEKING: feeling vibration (items a-b)		2	
PROPRIOCEPTIVE SEEKING: feeling deep pressure (items c-k)		9	
AUDITORY AVOIDANCE (items a-i)		9	
AUDITORY SEEKING (items a-c, e-g)		6	
VISUAL AVOIDANCE (items a-g)		7	
VISUAL SEEKING (items a-h)		8	
GUSTATORY-OLFACTORY AVOIDANCE (items a-c)		3	
GUSTATORY-OLFACTORY SEEKING (items a-b, d-e)		4	

The closer to the number "1" the fraction formed by yes answers divided by possible answers in a sensory state area, the stronger the indicator that an area of possible concern exists. (yes answers)/(possible answers)=1 is the strongest indicator that the sensory state is an area of concern. Clinical judgement, however, must be used in all decision making regarding possible areas of concern and the resultant influence on behavior.

QUESTIONS TO ASK ABOUT AREAS OF POSSIBLE CONCERN:

Do these responses interfere with performance? _____

If yes, list each area of concern where responses interfere with performance in the first column of the chart on next page. Then fill out the chart answering the questions regarding each area of concern.

Analysis of Sensory Behavior Inventory-R Worksheet

AREA OF CONCERN	WHEN do responses interfere?	WHERE do these responses occur?	HOW do responses interfere?	TO WHAT EXTENT is the interference?

Using this information, complete the last page of the worksheet.

Analysis of Sensory Behavior Inventory-R Worksheet

Student or client: _____ Date: _____

Sensory Findings Summary: _____

_____

_____

Implications:

☐ No hypotheses

☐ Hypotheses on relationship of sensory information to function of problem behavior

_____

_____

_____

☐ Sensory information may be useful in developing accommodations or reinforcers

Recommendations (fill in all that apply)

☐ 1. Accommodate by _____

_____

_____

_____

☐ 2. Eliminate or reduce exposure to specific sensory input by _____

_____

_____

_____

☐ 3. Provide opportunities to access specific sensory input by _____

_____

_____

_____

☐ 4. Increase tolerance of specific sensory input by _____

_____

_____

_____

Appendix H.

Management of Antecedents to Escalating Behaviors

Many inappropriate antecedent behaviors can be redirected in their beginning stages by naturally occurring social interactions between staff members and students. The following techniques and strategies are suggested for use in redirecting the student to more appropriate behaviors.[1] It is important to remember that <u>all</u> interventions must be tailored to the developmental level of the student. The following suggestions are *not* intended to be the sole intervention to increase a positive behavior but rather are to be used to de-escalate or redirect inappropriate behaviors, thus avoiding the need for further emergency interventions as behaviors go further out of control:

- **Planned ignoring.** This is more successful if planned before the behavior occurs. It is most effective when a student is trying to get attention or to provoke staff members, as long as other students are not involved. Not calling on the student to run an errand or ignoring the student while telling several other students what a good job they are doing are examples. It is important to provide a positive reinforcer as soon as a correct behavior is exhibited. *Caution*: Be ready to reinforce the correct behavior the moment it appears. Do not use for severe behavior problems when the maladaptive behavior has begun.

- **Signal interference.** These include nonverbal indications to signal to the student when behavior is beginning to be inappropriate, (e.g., snapping fingers, furrowing eyebrows, holding hand up to show "stop." This is most useful for behaviors that are mild in nature when they have just begun to escalate.

- **Proximity control.** When a student's behavior begins to be disruptive or distracting, the staff member moves close to the student while carrying on the activity with the whole group. No punishment or undue attention needs to be given to the student at the time. Generally, the adult's presence at close range is enough to subdue mild inappropriate behaviors.

- **Interest boosting.** When a student's behavior indicates that he or she is drifting away from attending to the task or activity, some additional information related to the student's interests or experiences is helpful to pique the student's attention and interest in the activity. For example, when leading a discussion about music, the staff member might ask the student about his or her personal stereo equipment to boost the child's interest in the discussion.

- **Tension reduction through humor.** Frequently, a problem or potential problem may be defused with a joke, or a light-hearted comment. Many times anxiety, fear, or a challenge will make the student feel obligated or forced to react negatively. Humor can act as a pressure release valve to allow the student to laugh it off without a negative response. This works well when the student has responded instinctively in a negative fashion or appears to be wanting to retaliate but is indecisive of whether or how to do so. *Caution*: Satire and ridicule are <u>not</u> appropriate at anytime. The child must correctly read the affectionate aspect of the interaction. Beware of the unintentional reading of an attempt at humor as "ridicule" and plan your humor attempts accordingly.

- **Hurdle help.** The staff member must provide immediate instruction at the very moment the student gets into trouble, to help the student over the hurdle of dealing appropriately with others. A timely comment at the onset of the problem helps the student to follow the correct course of action. For example, a student who has just bunched up a piece of paper and raised his or her arm to throw it is seen by the staff member, who reminds the student to walk to the trash can to throw it away. Timing is essential to intervene before the misbehavior occurs.

- **Restructuring routine.** Routine has a stabilizing effect on everyone. It is important to have a clear understanding of all that we are expected to do and to feel secure that our schedule or routine will allow it. Young people depend on a routine so they can plan their day in their own minds. However, sometimes it becomes clear that the students tire of the routine. Adjusting to energy level provides an opportunity for the student to be refreshed. This should be an occasional shift in routine so as not to disrupt the orderliness of a planned, sequenced routine. For example, rescheduling TV time to allow students to watch a special program after the group has done chores. *Caution:* Many children with severe behavior problems require visual reminders of routines, such as personal schedules of their activities on their desks. Changes should be explained and integrated to any visual tracking system the child is using.

- **Direct appeal to values.** The student is encouraged to make a decision as to whether his or her behavior is helping the situation. One-on-one conferencing to elicit an understanding of how this behavior may be making matters worse and to discover alternate behaviors that can help the student to focus attention on the problem at hand and his or her part in it. A questioning format is most helpful here, beginning with questions that require a "yes" answer (to develop a positive attitude) and phasing in questions that require a more in-volved answer (e.g., Where did this happen? What did you do then? How do you feel about that? Why do you think he responded that way?). Finally, seek some sort of commitment for continuing a behavior or stopping a behavior next time the problem occurs.

- **The antiseptic bounce.** When a student's behavior indicates a buildup of stress or restless-ness, it is a good idea to remove the student in such a way that attention is not focused on the negative behavior. A pass to the office to run an errand is often enough to defuse a potential problem and allow the student to return fresh to the activity. This allows a few minutes away from the problem area without confrontation about behavior and provides enough of a release and a distraction to enable the student to return to the program in a new frame of mind.

- **Distraction.** When a confrontation or a negative behavior is creating a disturbance, focusing the group's attention and/or the individual's attention on something different can reduce or eliminate the problem. A student who is screaming may stop to listen if the staff member begins discussing a topic of interest to the student (e.g., what's for lunch, special events coming up) or if the staff member begins an activity with the other students that the misbehaving student would enjoy. This helps the student to give up the negative behavior by providing an opportunity for the student to make the choice to do so and prevents the staff member from having to use more restrictive intervention models.

- **Infusion with affection.** Often a very positive, supportive, and appreciative approach may help a student to respond more appropriately. A warm, open, caring response from a staff member may help the student to talk about the problems he or she is experiencing before the problems build into a significant incident. An example might be, "I think you probably feel very sad now, and that makes me feel badly, too. Do you think we might walk and be able to talk about what happened?"

- **Interpretation as interference.** A student may not understand or be aware of a behavior that is occurring. Sometimes it is helpful to describe to the student what the or she is doing by commenting on observable behavior. This serves as a reminder and as a warning that the behavior is unwanted. For example, "When you talk while I am talking, not only is it hard for you to listen, but you make it hard for the others to listen, too."

- **Regrouping.** When a student is having trouble within the group, it is often advantageous to move him or her to another group or space (e.g., classroom, living unit, or subgroup within the unit) to avoid continuing problems. This is not a punishing "kick out" but an attempt to offer the student an environment that will help the student maintain control of his or her own behavior. For example, "I think this new location will be better for you and allow you to be in control of yourself better. I can see you're trying."

- **Limitation of supplies and tools.** When a student begins to misuse, abuse, or otherwise cause a problem with tools or supplies, it is advisable to limit continuing access to the material at this time. This requires a calm voice and a supportive stance if de-escalation is desired.

- **Role-modeling.** The most significant management tool available to staff members is conducting themselves in the manner in which the students are expected to behave. Staff members who maintain self-control, respect for others, good manners and courtesy, honesty, fairness, and good judgment teach by example. Students look to adults for models and for guidance, and they learn every day by watching and listening to every word. Students with serious behavior attend to the emotional tone of the speaker often with more concentration than actual words. Clear, calm words are often modeled by other students and immediately diffuse a tense situation (e.g., "Mrs. Walsh says it's not my job to worry about Johnny. My job is _____ right now.").

- **Pacing indicator.** Some students, especially severely handicapped students, lose the ability to use language when protesting an activity choice. Shifting the student to "break time" and asking the student to rejoin the instructional activity when ready can diffuse escalating behaviors. Giving the student an object that signifies break time to that individual and asking for the object (e.g., a felt heart, puppet, small stuffed animal, magazine) to be returned when the student is ready can be useful to de-escalate behavior and provide for choice making.

- **Relaxation activity.** Sometimes severe behaviors can be avoided by training the individual to choose another behavior to express the same purpose as the maladaptive behavior (e.g., stating "I need to lie down" rather than screaming in protest). At first, the student may need modeling, prompting, or guidance to select the alternate relaxing activity. The student should return to the regular routine when he or she determines readiness. Examples include: music, rhymic movement in a rocking chair, covering up with a blanket, and flipping through a magazine.

---

[1] Note: Adapted from material developed by Sidney Monroe, Diagnostic Center, Southern California

Appendix I.

Analyzing Behavior
Who, What, When, Why, and Where?[1]

Who   Who is present when the problem behavior occurs? How many people? Who was about to come in or who was about to leave? Who were the adults, children, teachers, parents? Were people present who ordinarily would not have been (e.g., strangers or people in unusual attire)? Who was not present who ordinarily would be present? Does the problem behavior occur more often when a particular person is present? To whom was the behavior directed? Answers to these questions will help determine if a particular person or grouping of people is related to the problem behavior.

What   What was the behavior? What was happening when the problem behavior occurred? Was the student being asked to do something? Was the task too hard or too easy? Was the student playing freely, or were the tasks and time more structured? What were other people doing? Was the event or task almost over? Was it about time to move on to something else? Did the problem behavior occur at the beginning, middle, or end of the event or task? What is happening when the problem behaviors do not occur or are less likely to occur?

When   This question is complex because it also relates to when the behavior does not occur. Are problems (or no problems) more likely to occur in the morning, before lunch, bedtime, free play, going out, Mondays, Fridays, and so on? Within an activity, does the behavior occur at the beginning, middle, or end?

Where In what location does the problem behavior happen most often? Does it occur in the kitchen, bedroom, hallway, classroom? What other locations? Even more specifically, does it occur in a particular part of a certain location (e.g., near the window or door, close to a closet where a favorite toy is kept) Where does it not occur?

Why   What is the purpose of the behavior? This question, obviously, is the most difficult to answer. But after the information has been gathered from the other questions (e.g., who, what, when, where) the answer to this question may be more apparent.

With this question, you are trying to determine what function the behavior serves for the student that is, why does he or she behave this way (what is happening), at this time (when), in this location (where), and among these people (who)?

---

[1] Based on an excerpt that appeared in *Why is My Child Hurting? Positive Approaches to Dealing with Difficult Behaviors,* A monograph for Parents of Children with Disabilities by Susan Lehr, Center on Human Policy, Syracuse University (1989) for the Federation for Children with Special Needs, Boston: MA.

EDUCATIONAL ENVIRONMENT ASSESSMENT SCALE
by Tom Weddle, M.A.

Each assessment item is to be scored using the following guidelines and the worksheet on page 3:

RARELY = Occurring in less than 25% of observed opportunities/possibilities

OCCASIONALLY = Occurring in more than 25% of observed opportunities/possibilities but in less than 50% of observed opportunities/possibilities

OFTEN = Occurring in more than 50% of observed opportunities but in less than 75% of observed opportunities/possibilities

CONSISTENTLY = Occurring in more than 75% of observed opportunities/possibilities

1. **Is choice allowed or possible for this child during activities/tasks? (Is child allowed to control one or more factors concerning an activity/task, such as duration of task, type of task, quantity of work, when to work, which materials or items to use, reinforcers, etc.)**
   1. Items and opportunities for choice are **rarely** available during activities/tasks
   2. Items and opportunities for choice are **occasionally** available during activities/tasks
   3. Items and opportunities for choice are **often** available during activities/tasks
   4. Items and opportunities for choice are **consistently** available during activities/tasks

2. **Are the life skill domains (leisure, integration, vocation, domestic, community) included in this child's goals and objectives?**
   1. Life skill domains are **rarely** included in this child's goals and objectives
   2. Life skill domains are **occasionally** included in this child's goals and objectives
   3. Life skill domains are **often** included in this child's goals and objectives
   4. Life skill domains are **consistently** included in this child's goals and objectives

3. **Do staff communicate clearly to this child? (Staff gain child's attention and provide instructional language at the child's comprehension level and/or additional communicative cues, such as gestures, photos, objects, etc., as needed)**
   1. Staff **rarely** communicate clearly to this child
   2. Staff **occasionally** communicate clearly to this child
   3. Staff **often** communicate clearly to this child
   4. Staff **consistently** communicate clearly to this child

4. **Is communication promoted and supported for this child ? (Child is allowed to communicate at own level as needed; staff listen to communicative content and respond to communicative intent)**
   1. Communication is **rarely** promoted or supported for this child
   2. Communication is **occasionally** promoted or supported for this child
   3. Communication is **often** promoted or supported for this child
   4. Communication is **consistently** promoted or supported for this child

5. **Are social skill needs of this child being met? (Social skills, such as turn-taking, waiting, seeking attention and assistance are taught and social interactions, such as parallel and interactive play are promoted during classroom activities)**
   1. Social skill instruction for this child **rarely** occurs
   2. Social skill instruction for this child **occasionally** occurs
   3. Social skill instruction for this child **often** occurs
   4. Social skill instruction for this child **consistently** occurs

Reprinted with permission of Tom Weddle, MA.

6. **Are teaching strategies and adaptions which accommodate to this child's learning strengths and weaknesses being utilized? (Learning is maximized through effective instructional ratios and through accommodations to motoric, cognitive, emotional or perceptual strengths and weaknesses)**

    1. Accommodative teaching strategies and adaptations are **rarely** utilized
    2. Accommodative teaching strategies and adaptations **occasionally** utilized
    3. Accommodative teaching strategies and adaptations are **often** utilized
    4. Accommodative teaching strategies and adaptations are **consistently** utilized

7. **Do teaching materials and activities include this child's interests? (Does child exhibit an interest (is focused and/or enthusiastic) in the items, materials, topics or themes used in instructional activities/tasks)**

    1. Teaching materials and activities **rarely** include the interests of this child
    2. Teaching materials and activities **occasionally** include this child's interests
    3. Teaching materials and activities **often** include this child's interests
    4. Teaching materials and activities **consistently** include this child's interests

8. **Are academic skills being taught within functional or high interest activities?**

    1. Academic skills are **rarely** taught within functional/high interest activities
    2. Academic skills are **occasionally** taught within functional/high interest activities
    3. Academic skills are **often** taught within functional/ high interest activities
    4. Academic skills are **consistently** taught within functional/high interest activities

9. **Are successful classroom transitions between activities/events promoted for this child? (Staff follow a consistent schedule, discuss changes beforehand in daily schedule and instruct or prompt awareness of sequence of activities either during or before transitions)**

    1. Successful classroom transitions are **rarely** promoted for this child
    2. Successful classroom transitions are **occasionally** promoted for this child
    3. Successful classroom transitions are **often** promoted for this child
    4. Successful classroom transitions are **consistently** promoted for this child

10. **Is programming designed to promote and support rapport between staff and this child? (Staff view disruptive behavior as a sign of stress or lack of skill and attempt to promote coping skills and alternative skills as a means to eliminate the need for disruptive behavior)**

    1. Rapport building is **rarely** promoted for this child
    2. Rapport building is **occasionally** promoted for this child
    3. Rapport building is **often** promoted for this child
    4. Rapport building is **consistently** promoted for this child

11. **Is communication/language instruction being done for this child within instructional environments? (Child is receiving instruction in communication/language skills within all environments to satisfy personal needs)**

    1. Communication/language instruction is **rarely** done for this child
    2. Communication/language instruction is **occasionally** done for this child
    3. Communication/language instruction is **often** done for this child
    4. Communication/language instruction is **consistently** done for this child

12. **Is this child physically at ease in this environment? (Child does not exhibit stress due to perceptual, emotional or physical factors in the classroom)**

    1. Child is **rarely** at ease in this classroom
    2. Child is **occasionally** at ease in this classroom
    3. Child is **often** at ease in this classroom
    4. Child is **consistently** at ease in this classroom

WORKSHEET

Circle a number to indicate that criteria were met during an observed activity or event. Put an "X" over a number to indicate that criteria were not met during an observed activity or event. Obtain a minimum of 5 observations per question. Refer to assessment questions above for detail concerning criteria standards.

QUESTION 1: CHOICE WITHIN ACTIVITIES AND TASKS (Assess each activity for presence or absence of opportunities and materials for choice)

    1   2   3   4   5   6   7   8   9   10

QUESTION 2: GOALS INCLUDE LIFE SKILL DOMAINS (Assess each activity to see if fits into one of the four following life skill areas (integration, community, leisure, domestic or vocational))

1   2   3   4   5   6   7   8   9   10

QUESTION 3: STAFF COMMUNICATE CLEARLY (Assess instructional directions for clarity does child seem confused or unaware of the instruction(s)

1   2   3   4   5   6   7   8   9   10

QUESTION 4: COMMUNICATION IS PROMOTED AND SUPPORTED (Assess staff response to child's communicative acts)

1   2   3   4   5   6   7   8   9   10

QUESTION 5: SOCIAL SKILLS ARE TAUGHT (Assess each activity for teaching of social skills)

1   2   3   4   5   6   7   8   9   10

QUESTION 6: ACCOMMODATIONS ARE BEING MADE (Assess each activity for the presence of accommodations or adaptations)

1   2   3   4   5   6   7   8   9   10

QUESTION 7: CHILD'S INTERESTS ARE INCLUDED (Assess each activity for interest from child)

1   2   3   4   5   6   7   8   9   10

QUESTION 8: ACADEMIC SKILLS ARE TAUGHT WITHIN FUNCTIONAL OR HIGH INTEREST ACTIVITIES (Assess each activity that requires or targets pre-academic or academic skills.)

1   2   3   4   5   6   7   8   9   10

QUESTION 9: SUCCESSFUL TRANSITIONS PROMOTED (Assess each transition between activities as to whether the activities are scheduled and the schedule is consistently followed)

1   2   3   4   5   6   7   8   9   10

QUESTION 10: RAPPORT PROMOTED (Access each behavioral intervention to see if staff maintain a consistently positive educational approach)

1   2   3   4   5   6   7   8   9   10

QUESTION 11: COMMUNICATION INSTRUCTION BEING DONE (Assess communicative interactions between student and staff to see if staff are actively teaching the student to communicate)

1   2   3   4   5   6   7   8   9   10

QUESTION 12: CHILD IS AT EASE (Assess each classroom activity)

1   2   3   4   5   6   7   8   9   10

SCORE SHEET

SCORE EACH NUMBER BELOW AS "1", "2", "3" OR "4" POINTS CORRELATING WITH THE NUMBER OF THE ANSWER CIRCLED FOR EACH ITEM OF THE QUESTIONNAIRE ON PAGES 1 AND 2.

MEANINGFULNESS	APPROPRIATENESS	ACCESSIBILITY
1.	2.	3.
4.	5.	6.
7.	8.	9.
10.	11.	12.
Total: _____	Total: _____	Total: _____

Rating Scale

Less than 8:   Need for improvement.

Between 8-12:   Adequate. Improvement still desirable.

Between 12-16:   An area of strength.

Appendix K.

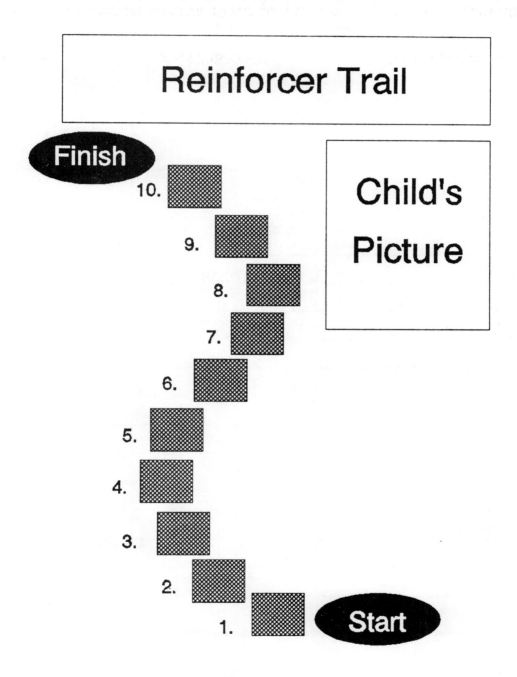

SAMPLE STAR CHART FOR CLASSROOM

NAME: _____ Date: _____	Stay In Seat	Follow Directions	Hands and Feet to Self	Finish Work	Friendly
8:55 - 9:00					
9:00 - 9:15					
9:15 - 9:30					
9:30 - 9:45					
9:45 - 10:00					
10:00 - 10:15					
10:15 - 10:30					
10:30 - 10:45					
10:45 - 11:00					
11:00 - 11:15					
11:15 - 11:30					
11:30 - 11:45					
11:45 - 12:00					
12:55 - 1:00					
1:00 - 1:15					
1:15 - 1:30					
1:30 - 1:45					
1:45 - 2:00 Clean up/Stars					

NEED:_____

EXAMPLE: 80 ★'s = (specific reinforcer)

SAMPLE STAR CHART FOR CLASSROOM - 2

NAME: _____

DATE: _____

			WORK COMPLETED	HANDS FEET	FRIENDLY TALKING	GOOD LISTENING	FOLLOWING DIRECTIONS
	8:00 a.m. 8:15 a.m.						
Library Computer	8:15 a.m. 9:00 a.m.						
Task	9:00 a.m. 9:30 a.m.						
Puzzle	9:30 a.m. 10:15 a.m.						
Recess Snack	10:15 a.m. 10:45 a.m.						
Math	10:45 a.m. 11:00 a.m.						
Listening	11:00 a.m. 11:30 a.m.						
Art	11:30 a.m. 11:50 a.m.						

Appendix L.

Positive Environment Checklist

The following Positive Environment Checklist was designed for use in the federal project, "Building Positive Behavioral Support Plans."[1] When used to evaluate settings in which persons with severe disabilities live, work and go to school, in the context of a complete analysis and plan development process, it can play an important role in understanding how environmental features impact behavior. Refer to Appendix E for information on further training in this model.

The table, Process of Building a Positive Behavioral Support Plan, outlines the entire process involved in developing a plan for individuals challenged by severe disabilities in this model. Please note the Positive Environment Checklist is included in step 4, "Conduct Assessments" stage in this framework.

Positive Environment Checklist

The Positive Environment Checklist (PEC) is designed for use in evaluating whether the settings in which persons with severe disabilities live, work, and go to school are structured in a manner that promotes and maintains positive, adaptive behaviors. The PEC looks at whether settings provide the conditions that support positive behaviors and do not present conditions that make negative behaviors more likely. It also addresses several concerns related to the ways in which program staff support and interact with the people with disabilities in the setting.

The checklist should be used as part of a proactive, preventive approach to addressing problem behaviors. Positive environments will help to minimize the occurrence of problem behaviors. The checklist can be used as a general tool to provide an overall assessment of a setting. Also, when a particular individual is targeted, it can be used as part of a comprehensive analysis of an existing problem behavior(s) to determine whether environmental conditions are contributing to the problem.

The Positive Environment Checklist focuses on the physical, social, and programmatic structure of the environment. Checklist questions are divided into 5 sections: (1) Physical Setting, (2) Social Setting, (3) Activities and Instruction, (4) Scheduling and Predictability, and (5) Communication. Responses to questions in each area should be based on direct observation of the environment, on review of written program documents and records, or on responses obtained from questioning program personnel. Three response options are provided for each question: YES, NO, and UNCLEAR. The term "staff" applies to paid and volunteer personnel who provide support and services in the setting. The term "people" refers to the people with disabilities who live, work, or attend school in the setting.

Scoring the completed Positive Environment Checklist is simply a matter of determining which questions received a YES response, and which received NO or UNCLEAR responses. NO responses indicate areas or issues that should be addressed to create a more positive environment. UNCLEAR responses indicate the need for further analysis, perhaps by extended observation or by questioning a larger number of program personnel.

---

1 The Positive Environmental Checklist is from: Albin, R. W., Horner, R. H., & O'Neill, R. E. (1993). Proactive behavioral support: Structuring and assessing environments. Eugene, OR, Specialized Training Program, University of Oregon.

SECTION 1: PHYSICAL SETTING			
1. Is the physical setting clean, well lighted, and Odor free?	YES	NO	UNCLEAR
2. Is temperature regulation in the setting adequate?	YES	NO	UNCLEAR
3. Is the physical setting visually pleasant and appealing?	YES	NO	UNCLEAR
4. Does the arrangement of the setting promote easy access for all individuals within the setting?	YES	NO	UNCLEAR
5. Is the setting arranged in a manner that facilitates needed staff support and supervision?	YES	NO	UNCLEAR
6. Does the setting contain or provide interesting, age-appropriate items and materials for people to use?	YES	NO	UNCLEAR
7. Is the setting located and structured in a manner that promotes and facilitates physical integration into the "regular" community?	YES	NO	UNCLEAR
SECTION 2: SOCIAL SETTING			
1. Is the number of people in this setting appropriate for its physical size and purpose?	YES	NO	UNCLEAR
2. Are the people who share this setting compatible in terms of age, gender, and support needs?	YES	NO	UNCLEAR
3. Do the people who share this setting get along with each other?	YES	NO	UNCLEAR
4. Is the staff ratio in this setting adequate to meet the support needs of all of the people here at all times?	YES	NO	UNCLEAR
5. Do staff actively work to develop and maintain a positive rapport and relationship with the people here?	YES	NO	UNCLEAR
6. Do staff promote and facilitate opportunities for social integration with people who are not paid to provide service?	YES	NO	UNCLEAR

SECTION 3: ACTIVITIES AND INSTRUCTION			
1. Do people in this setting regularly participate (whether independent, supported or partial participation) in activities and tasks that are useful and meaningful to their daily lives?	YES	NO	UNCLEAR
2. Do people participate in a variety of different activities?	YES	NO	UNCLEAR
3. Do people participate in activities that occur irregular community settings outside of the home, school, or work place?	YES	NO	UNCLEAR
4. Do people in this setting receive instruction on activities and skills that are useful and meaningful to their daily lives?	YES	NO	UNCLEAR
5. Is the instruction that people receive individualized to meet specific learner needs?	YES	NO	UNCLEAR
6. Are peoples' personal preferences taken into account when determining the activities and tasks in which they participate and receive training?	YES	NO	UNCLEAR
SECTION 4: SCHEDULING AND PREDICTABILITY			
1. Is there a system or strategy used to identify what people in this setting should be doing and when?	YES	NO	UNCLEAR
2. Is there a means to determine whether the things that should be occurring actually do occur?	YES	NO	UNCLEAR
3. Do people in this setting have a way of knowing or predicting what they will be doing and when?	YES	NO	UNCLEAR
4. Do staff prepare people in this setting in advance for changes in typical schedules or routines?	YES	NO	UNCLEAR
5. Do people in this setting have opportunities to exercise choice in terms of what they will do, when, with whom, and what rewards they will receive?	YES	NO	UNCLEAR

SECTION 5: COMMUNICATION			
1. Do people in this setting have "acceptable" means to communicate basic messages (e.g., requests, comments, rejections) to staff or others in the setting?	YES	NO	UNCLEAR
2. Do staff promote and reward communication?	YES	NO	UNCLEAR
3. Are effective, efficient communication strategies being used by or taught to the people in this setting?	YES	NO	UNCLEAR
4. Are staff familiar with the receptive language levels and skills of the people in this setting?	YES	NO	UNCLEAR
5. Do staff have "acceptable" means to communicate basic messages to the people in this setting?	YES	NO	UNCLEAR

This instrument is designed to be used in the context of a complete process of building positive behavioral support plans.

Process of Building a Positive Behavioral Support Plan

1. Describe the learner and the contests in which the learner spends his/her time
   - Begin personal futures planning process

2. Identify and operationally define the behavior(s) or behavior class(es) of concern.
   - Collect baseline data

3. Implement behavioral supports as needed while conducting assessment
   - Life Style Enhancements I
     - Integration - school, work, living, environment
     - Enhanced interactions, participation, independence, choice, variety, predictability
   - Positive Procedures I
     - Stimulus change
     - Differential Reinforcement of Alternative (desirable) Behavior(s)
   - Crisis prevention and intervention procedures I (if necessary)

4. Conduct Assessments
   - Quality of Life
     - e.g., Resident Life Style Inventory, Person Centered Assessments, Social Network Analysis, PQI, Quality of Life Cue Questions
   - Ecological/Environmental Systems
     - e.g., Positive Environment Checklist, Interaction Observation Form, Curricular Activity Profile
   - Functional Assessment of target behavior(s) or behavior class(es)
     - Interviews - e.g., Communication Interview, Functional Analysis Interview
     - Checklists/rating scales - e.g., Motivation Assessment Scale
     - Direct observation - e.g., A-B-C (S-R-C) Analysis, Functional Analysis Observation Form, Scatter Plots, Anecdotal Records, Behavior Maps, Communicative Functions Analysis
   - Communication Repertoire Assessment
   - Learning Characteristics Assessment

5. Analyze Results of Assessments
   - Generate hypotheses regarding function(s) of behavior(s) or behavior classes

     In reference to
     - Ecological variables
     - Setting events
     - Immediate antecedents and maintaining consequences
     - Potential competing behavior(s)/functional equivalents
     - Communication repertoire and communicative functions
     - Quality of life
   - Construct a competing behavior analysis

- Conduct functional analysis manipulations to test hypotheses (if necessary)
  - Antecedent/consequence manipulations

6. Articulate new and ongoing questions and strategies for continued assessment

7. Design hypothesis driven Comprehensive Behavioral Support Plan
   - Life style enhancement II - (same categories as I but specific to assessment/hypotheses)
   - Setting and immediate antecedent modifications (e.g., alter antecedents/triggers, remove environmental pollutants, alter grouping arrangements)
   - Changes in curriculum and instruction strategies (e.g., clarify expectations, meaningful tasks, task difficulty, variation, and length, predictability, instructional strategies matched to learning characteristics)
   - Functional equivalence training/instructional programs
   - Communication, social skills instruction
   - General skill building across skill areas
   - Positive Procedures II. (DRO, DRL, stimulus control, etc.)
   - Self Regulatory Strategies
   - Emergency Management Procedures

8. Outcomes of Support Plan Implementation and Evaluation Criteria
   - Improvements in quality of life
   - Effectiveness of instruction
     - functional equivalents developed and/or increased
     - general skills developed and/or increased
     - communication and social skills developed and/or increased
   - Basic health and safety improved (e.g., decreases in visits to emergency room, injury from SIB, etc.)
   - Target behavior(s) reduced or eliminated (and replaced)

9. Establish process and schedule for ongoing positive behavioral support
   - Team of friends, co-workers, family members and service providers to provide ongoing support
   - Long range goals/Personal future plans
   - Evaluation of effects on intervention and subsequent adjustments
   - Evaluation of lifestyle, social networks, personal preferences and process for facilitating changes over time
   - Mechanism for cycling back through the functional assessment intervention process as new behavior, needs and/or situations arise

Anderson, J. L., Albin, R. W., Mesaros, R.A., Dunlap, G. & Morelli-Robbins, M. (in press) Issues in providing training to achieve comprehensive support. In J. Riechle & D.P. Wacker, (Eds.) Communicative approaches to the management of challenging behaviors. Baltimore: Paul H. Brookes.

Appendix M.

Possible Reinforcers

The following list of reinforcers are provided as possibilities to help implementers begin to brainstorm other ideas available in the students' environments. It will be important to remember that some children may find a reinforcer listed here highly aversive rather than truly reinforcing. Developmental level, chronological age and unique likes and dislikes must always be considered in selecting potential reinforcers to validate by either discussing it with the student or caregivers or provisionally trying it out. Immediacy, frequency, power, and variability needs of the student must be considered equally in selecting reinforcers.

Reinforcers Which are Available in Almost Any Classroom

praise	self-graphing
daily weekly, and monthly good reports to parents	model building
field trips	messenger
party after school	class proctor
nurse's helper	cafeteria helper
library time	lunch counter
stars on paper	papers on wall
get to sit by a friend	class leader to bathroom
class leader to cafeteria	smiles of teacher
pat on back by teacher	happy faces on paper
library passes	chance to help other students
music pass	magazine selection
choose a game	extra privileges
picnic	teacher for the day
game equipment manager	clean chalk board
stamps on hand	read to younger children
listen to records	cross walk patrol leader
flag raiser	first turn
sharpen pencils for class	roll call leader
sit in front of classroom	sit in back of classroom
sit by windows	sit by door
feed classroom animals	turn lights off and on
self-selection of activity	go to locker one minute early

Home Reinforcers

(The teacher may find these useful in developing plans involving multiple environments)

money
gum
pat on back
extra time before going to bed
new clothes
new toys
extra helping at dinner
go to a movie
records
time outside
coloring
get a pet
soda
opportunity to go out for sports at school
choose a TV program
play a game with the parents
making something in the kitchen
washing and drying dishes
choose a gift for a friend or sibling
sleep later on weekends
go out to a special restaurant
choose own clothing to wear
go to summer camp
open the mail
make something for the teacher
use dad's tools
not have to iron own clothes for a week
start a fire in the fireplace
lick stamps or stickers
put things on the wall
select video or Nintendo game

candy
praise (verbal)
extra TV time
watch more TV shows
extra play time
entertain friends
choose a particular food
go to the zoo
swimming
parties
carbons
charting
friend to spend the night
have a friend over for dinner
increase allowance
have a picnic
have breakfast in bed
wrap gifts
fewer chores
go on errands
watch dad shave
choose own hairstyle
buy something for the car
take pictures of friends
put soda in the refrigerator
not have to wash clothes for a week
piggyback ride on dad
work to go to the circus
help dad make a dog house
slide down the banister rail

Activities and Tangibles for Contingent Access in School

storybooks
pictures from magazines
college materials
counting beads
paint brushes
paper mache
book covers
crayons
coloring books
paints
records
flash cards
surprise packages
bookmarkers
pencils with names
seasonal charts
pencil sharpeners
subject matter accessories

pencil holder
stationery
compasses
calendars
buttons
pins
pictures
musical instruments
drawing paper
elastic bands
paper clips
colored paper
pets
flowers
classroom equipment
chalk
clay
computers, software

Individual Activities and Privileges

leading student groups
displaying student's work - any subject matter
putting away materials
caring for class pets, flowers, etc.
choosing activities
show and tell - any level
dusting, erasing, cleaning, arranging chairs, etc.
reading a story
working problems on board
outside helping - patrols, directing parking,
 ushering, etc.
assisting the teacher to teach
making gifts
correcting papers
responsibility for on-going activities during
 school holidays (pets, plants, etc.)
"Citizen of the Week" or "Best Kid of the Day"

representing group in school activities
straightening up for teacher
running errands
collecting materials - papers, work
 books, assignments, etc.
constructing school materials
helping other children with drinking,
 lavatory, cleaning, etc.
answering questions
classroom supervision
first in line
leading discussion
recognizing birthdays
special seating arrangements
decorating room
presenting hobby to the class

Unusual Opportunities to Observe Novel Actions

watch teacher organize material
see teacher in costume
watch teacher riding tricycle around campus
being principal's shadow for an hour
see teacher eat something unusual

teacher playing sports
principal doing work at desk on roof
watch new construction
watch teacher do handstands

Social Reinforcers for Individuals and/or Group

movies
decorating classroom
presenting skits
playing records
puppet shows
preparing for holidays
making subject matter games
visiting another class
field trips
planning daily schedules
performing for PTA

dancing
going to museum, fire station, court house,
 picnics, etc.
participating in group organizations
 (music, speech, athletics, social clubs)
talking periods
recess or play periods
parties
talent shows (joking, reading, music, etc.)
musical chairs
competing with other classes

Expressions - Approval - Facial

looking
smiling
winking
nodding
grinning
raising eyebrows
opening eyes
slowly closing eyes
signaling O.K.
thumbs up
shrugging shoulders

widening eyes
wrinkling nose
blinking rapidly
giggling
whistling
cheering
laughing
chuckling
skipping
shaking head

Playthings *(Use of, or access to, playthings may provide reinforcement to many children)*

toys	stamps
cartoons	whistles
kaleidoscopes	bean bags
flashlight	jumping beans
headdress	masks
rings	straw hats
striped straws	banks
kickball	address books
playground equipment	fans
tape recorder	silly putty
badges	toy musical instruments
pins	birthday hats
ribbons	play dough
balls	dolls
puzzles	dollhouses
combs	make-up kit
comics	trains
jump ropes	stuffed animals
balloons	pick-up sticks
commercial games	cowboy hats
bats	boats
marbles	blocks
toy jewelry	miniature cars
jacks	snakes
yo-yo's	plastic toys (animals, Indians, soldiers)
money (play, real, exchangeable)	class pictures
household inexpensives (pots, cans, cardboard boxes)	

Physical Contact or Proximity

patting shoulder	leaning over
touching arm	straightening clothes
putting face next to child	hugging
tickling	touching hand
cupping face in hands	shaking hands
squeezing hands gently	guiding with hand
patting cheeks	nudging
helping put on coat	eating with students
ruffing hair	sitting on desk near students
walking alongside	standing alongside
combing hair	walking among students
tying shoes	gently guiding
quick squeeze	interacting with class at recess
gently raising chin	

REINFORCEMENT INVENTORIES
for Children and Adults

INSTRUCTIONS

The items in this questionnaire refer to things and experiences that may give a person joy, satisfaction, or pleasurable feelings. Check each item in the column that describes how much the person enjoys the things described.

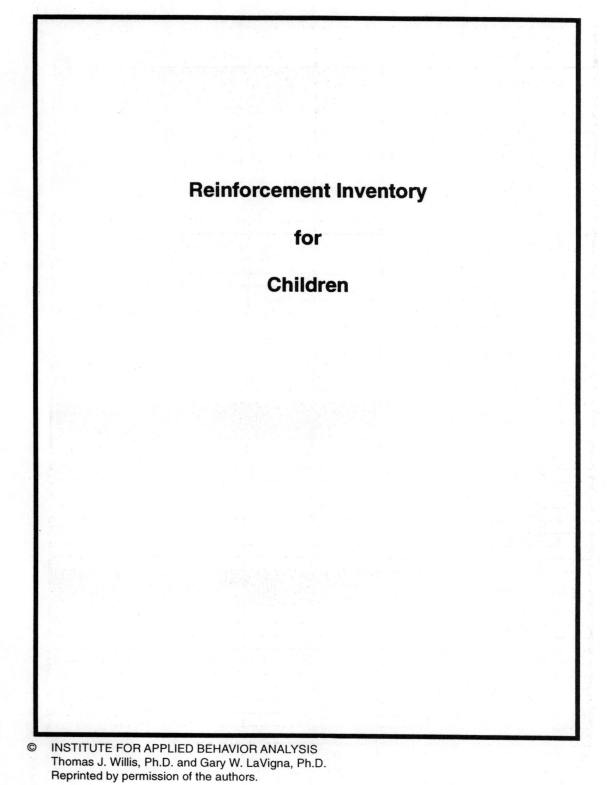

Reinforcement Inventory

for

Children

DESCRIPTION OF POTENTIALLY REINFORCING EVENTS	NOT AT ALL	A LITTLE	A FAIR AMOUNT	MUCH	VERY MUCH
A. FOOD ITEMS					
1. Candy.					
What Kind?					
a.					
b.					
c.					
2. Ice Cream.					
What Kind?					
a.					
b.					
3. Nuts					
4. Potato Chips					
5. Cake					
6. Cookies					
7. Beverages.					
What Kind?					
a.					
b.					
8. Other Foods.					
a.					
b.					
c.					
d.					
B. TOYS AND PLAYTHINGS					
1. Racing Cars					
2. Electric Trains					
3. Bicycle					
4. Skate Board					
5. Playing with Dolls					
6. Make-up and Dress-up Toys					
7. Erector Set					
8. Other toys					
a.					
b.					
C. ENTERTAINMENT					
1. Watching Television					
Favorite Programs?					
a.					
b.					
2. Movies					
3. Listening to Music					
Favorite Program / Artists					
a.					
b.					

DESCRIPTION OF POTENTIALLY REINFORCING EVENTS	NOT AT ALL	A LITTLE	A FAIR AMOUNT	MUCH	VERY MUCH
D. SPORTS AND GAMES					
1. Playing Football with Kids					
2. Playing Football with Parents					
3. Swimming					
4. Bike Riding					
5. Skating					
6. Skiing					
7. Horseback Riding					
8. Tennis					
9. Hiking					
10. Checkers					
11. Checkers					
12. Fishing					
13. Baseball					
14. Ping Pong					
15. Scrabble					
16. Monopoly					
17. Painting by the Numbers					
18. Computer Games					
19. Video Games					
20. Clue					
21. Competitive Games					
22. Other					
a.					
b.					
E. MUSIC / ARTS / CRAFTS					
1. Playing a musical instrument (Type _____ ?)					
2. Singing					
3. Dancing					
4. Drawing					
5. Building Models					
6. Working with Tools					
7. Working with Clay					
8. Musical Group					
9. Other?					
a.					
b.					
F. EXCURSIONS / COMMUNITY					
1. Ride in Car					
2. Going to Work with Mother / Father					
3. Visiting Grandparents or Relatives					

DESCRIPTION OF POTENTIALLY REINFORCING EVENTS	NOT AT ALL	A LITTLE	A FAIR AMOUNT	MUCH	VERY MUCH
4. Visit to Beach					
5. Picnic					
6. Vacation (Where _____ ?)					
7. Airplane Ride					
8. Going Out to Dinner					
9. Visit a Friend (Who _____ ?)					
10. Visit a City (Where _____ ?)					
11. Visit a Museum					
12. Going to Store (Name _____ ?)					
13. Going for Walk					
14. Going to Library					
15. Visit Amusement Park					
16. Other?					
a.					
b.					
G. SOCIAL / INTERACTION					
1. Playing with Others (Whom__ ?)					
2. Being Praised (By Whom____ ?)					
a. by father					
b. by mother					
c. by teacher					
d. by friends					
3. Being Hugged and Kissed					
4. Being Touched					
5. Group Activities (girl/boy scouts, clubs)					
6. Going to Friends (Whom____ ?)					
7. Having Friends Sleep over					
8. Sleeping at Friends House (Whose _____ ?)					
9. Talking with Others					
10. Kidding and Joking					
11. Party for Friends					
12. Taking Friend out					
13. Happy Faces, Smiles					
14. Other?					
H. ACADEMIC / CLASSROOM					
1. Learning a New Language					
2. Taking Piano Lessons					
3. Reading					
4. Being Read to					
5. Looking at Books					
6. Spelling					
7. Science					
8. Social Studies					

DESCRIPTION OF POTENTIALLY REINFORCING EVENTS	NOT AT ALL	A LITTLE	A FAIR AMOUNT	MUCH	VERY MUCH
9. Physical Education					
10. Math					
11. Going to School					
12. Riding Bus to School					
13. Doing Homework					
14. Helping Teacher					
15. Helping Others					
16. Cafeteria Helper					
17. Room Proctor / Leader					
18. Line Monitor					
19. Extra Recess, Free Time					
20. Leave Class or School Early					
21. Visit Activity Center or Corner					
22. Listen to Records					
23. Read Book of Choice					
24. Write Notes					
25. Hall Monitor					
26. Individual Conference or Counseling					
28. Get a Drink					
29. Tutor Another Student					
30. Arrange Bulletin Board					
31. Other:					
a.					
b.					
I. DOMESTIC ACTIVITIES					
1. Setting the Table					
2. Making the Bed					
3. Baking					
4. Repairing or Building					
5. Working in the Yard					
6. Going on Errands					
7. Cooking					
8. Washing or Working on the Car					
9. Sewing					
10. Shopping					
11. Preparing a Menu					
12. Running Errands					
13. Exempt from a Domestic Activity					
J. PERSONAL APPEARANCE					
1. Getting New Clothes					
2. Putting on Makeup					
3. Purchasing Makeup					
4. Wearing Special Clothes					
5. Dressing in a Costume					

DESCRIPTION OF POTENTIALLY REINFORCING EVENTS	NOT AT ALL	A LITTLE	A FAIR AMOUNT	MUCH	VERY MUCH
6. Wearing Others' Clothing					
7. Getting a Haircut					
8. Going to Beauty Parlor					
9. Manicure					
10. Pedicure					
11. Massage					
12. Wearing Perfume or Cologne					
13. Wearing Jewelry					
14. Purchasing Jewelry					
15. Having Picture Taken					
16. Other:					
a.					
b.					
c.					
d.					
K. OTHER EVENTS AND ACTIVITIES					
1. Staying up Past Bedtime					
2. Earning Money					
3. Having Free Time					
4. Having a Pet					
5. Having or Going to a Party					
6. Taking a Bath or Shower					
7. Sleeping with Parents					
8. Feeding the Pet					
9. Listening to Stories					
10. Friend to Eat over					
11. Talking into a Tape Recorder					
12. Decorating Own Room					
13. Extended Bedtime					
14. Plan the Days Activities					
15. Public Display of Work or Progress					
16. Choosing Own Bedtime					
17. Sleeping Late					
18. Chairperson at Meeting					
19. Subscription to Special Magazine					
20. No Nagging by Others					
21. Attention Given in a Group					
22. Period with No Monitoring					
23. Opportunity to Masturbate					
24. Opportunity to Leave Work Early					
25. Opportunity to Select a Job					
26. Work in a Special Setting (office)					

DESCRIPTION OF POTENTIALLY REINFORCING EVENTS	NOT AT ALL	A LITTLE	A FAIR AMOUNT	MUCH	VERY MUCH
27. Other:					
a.					
b.					
c.					
d.					
e.					
L. TOKEN REINFORCERS					
1. Stars on a Chart					
2. Happy / Smiling Faces					
3. Special Badges					
4. Grades					
5. Certificates					
6. Name on Honor Roll					
7. Accumulation of Marbles / Chips					
8. Signatures					
9. "Correct" Marked on a Page					
10. Points					
11. Numbers					
12. Money					
13. Play Money					
14. Theater Tickets					
15. Numbers in Check Book Register					
16. Gift Certificate					
17. Other:					
a.					
b.					
M. OTHER					

© INSTITUTE FOR APPLIED BEHAVIOR ANALYSIS
Thomas J. Willis, Ph.D. and Gary W. LaVigna, Ph.D.
Reprinted by permission of the authors.

List below those event or activities the person does more than:

5 times a day ?	10 times a day ?

15 times a day ?	20 times a day ?

How much time does the person spend in the following activities (e.g., hours, minutes)?

Watching Television?	Sleeping?
Listening to Music?	Along?
Playing with Others?	Reading?
Playing with Toys?	Playing Alone?
Talking on Telephone?	Organized Sports?
Sitting Around?	Eating?
Random Activity?	

What is the person's most favorite thing to do? _____

What is the person's least favorite thing to do? _____

What does the person ask for most often?_____

What does the person complain about most?_____

What does the person seem to try to avoid the most? _____

Reinforcement Inventory

for

Adults

Our appreciation to Linda Fuller for her contribution in developing this inventory, 1985.

Positive Intervention for Serious Behavior Problems

DESCRIPTION OF POTENTIALLY REINFORCING EVENTS	NOT AT ALL	A LITTLE	A FAIR AMOUNT	MUCH	VERY MUCH
ENTERTAINMENT					
1. Watching television					
Favorite programs?					
a. _____					
b. _____					
c. _____					
2. Playing home video games					
Which ones?					
a. _____					
b. _____					
3. Playing community video games					
4. Computers					
5. Movies					
6. Dancing					
7. Listening to music					
Cassette tapes					
Compact discs					
8. Singing					
9. Playing musical instruments					
10. Drawing					
11. Painting					
12. Sculpting/pottery					
13. Latch hook					
14. Sewing					
16. Working with tools					
17. Other _____					
HOBBIES					
18. Photograph					
19. Typing					
20. Collecting Items:					
Specify					
a. _____					
b. _____					
c. _____					
21. Building models					
22. Plants/gardening					
23. Other _____					
FOOD					
24. Fruit					
What kind?					
a. _____					
b. _____					
c. _____					

© INSTITUTE FOR APPLIED BEHAVIOR ANALYSIS
Thomas J. Willis, Ph.D. and Gary W. LaVigna, Ph.D.
Reprinted by permission of the authors.

DESCRIPTION OF POTENTIALLY REINFORCING EVENTS	NOT AT ALL	A LITTLE	A FAIR AMOUNT	MUCH	VERY MUCH
25. Nuts					
What kind?					
a. _____					
b. _____					
c. _____					
26. Cookies					
What kind?					
a. _____					
b. _____					
c. _____					
27. Ice cream					
What kind?					
a. _____					
b. _____					
c. _____					
28. Chips					
What kind?					
a. _____					
b. _____					
c. _____					
29. Snack bars					
What kind?					
a. _____					
b. _____					
c. _____					
30. Hot dogs					
31. Hamburgers					
32. Tacos					
33. Pizza					
34. Popcorn					
35. Pretzels					
36. Bagels					
37. Granola					
38. Other					
a. _____					
b. _____					
c. _____					
BEVERAGES					
39. Fruit juice					
What kind?					
a. _____					
b. _____					
c. _____					

Positive Intervention for Serious Behavior Problems

DESCRIPTION OF POTENTIALLY REINFORCING EVENTS	NOT AT ALL	A LITTLE	A FAIR AMOUNT	MUCH	VERY MUCH
40. Sparkling water					
What kind?					
a. _____					
b. _____					
c. _____					
41. Sodas					
What kind?					
a. _____					
b. _____					
c. _____					
42. V-8 juice					
43. Coffee					
44. Decaffeinated coffee					
45. Hot tea					
46. Hot herbal tea					
What kind?					
a. _____					
b. _____					
c. _____					
47. Milk					
48. Chocolate milk					
49. Beer					
50. Wine					
51. Mixed drinks					
52. Lemonade					
53. Punch					
SPORTS					
54. Aerobics					
55. Jogging					
56. Roller skating					
57. Swimming					
58. Soccer					
59. Running					
60. Football					
61. Baseball					
62. Frisbee					
63. Windsurfing					
64. Skateboarding					
65. Bowling					
66. Golf					
67. Miniature golf					
68. Pool					
69. Boating					
70. Waterskiing					
71. Snowskiing					
72. Tennis					

DESCRIPTION OF POTENTIALLY REINFORCING EVENTS	NOT AT ALL	A LITTLE	A FAIR AMOUNT	MUCH	VERY MUCH
73. Bodybuilding					
74. Weightlifting					
75. Exercise bike					
76. Racquetball					
77. Climbing					
EXCURSIONS					
78. Spectator sports					
a. car racing					
b. olympics					
c. baseball					
d. basketball					
e. horse racing					
f. wrestling					
g. hockey					
79. Car rides					
80. Shopping					
81. Out to dinner					
82. Health club					
83. amusement parks					
84. Going camping					
85. Vacations					
86. Visting beach					
87. Visiting mountains					
SOCIAL					
88. Talking with others					
89. Having others listen					
90. Being praised					
91. Being touched					
92. Being hugged					
93. Visting friends					
94. Group activities					
95. Activity with one other					
MISCELLANEOUS					
96. Looking at magazines					
97. Looking at books					
What kind?					
a. _____					
b. _____					
c. _____					
98. Work jigsaw puzzles					

© INSTITUTE FOR APPLIED BEHAVIOR ANALYSIS
Thomas J. Willis, Ph.D. and Gary W. LaVigna, Ph.D.
Reprinted by permission of the authors.

DESCRIPTION OF POTENTIALLY REINFORCING EVENTS	NOT AT ALL	A LITTLE	A FAIR AMOUNT	MUCH	VERY MUCH
HELPING AROUND THE HOUSE					
99. Setting the table					
100. Making bed					
101. Vacuuming					
102. Washing dishes					
103. Dusting					
104. Going on errands					
105. Yard work					
106. Cooking					
PERSONAL APPEARANCE					
107. Getting new clothes					
108. Putting on makeup					
109. Going to beauty parlor					
110. Getting hair cut					
111. Other					
a. _____					
b. _____					
c. _____					
OTHER EVENTS AND ACTIVITIES					
112. _____					
113. _____					
114. _____					
115. _____					

How much time does the person spend in the following activities (e.g., hours, minutes)?

	Hours	Minutes
Watching television		
Listening to music		
Interacting with others		
Alone		
Reading		
Organized sports		
Working		
Sleeping		

List below those events that the person does or requests more than:

5 times a day? _____

_____

10 times a day _____

_____

15 times a day? _____

_____

20 times a day? _____

What is the person's most favorite thing to do? _____

_____

What is the person's least favorite thing to do? _____

_____

What does the person ask for most often? _____

_____

What does the person complain about most? _____

_____

What does the person seem to try to avoid the most? _____

_____

_____

Appendix O.

Proposed Training Framework

The following framework and worksheet may be helpful for those individuals seeking a structure around which to organize and describe their training and experience. They are provided to the reader as a method of organizing documentation of training in positive behavioral interventions.

It is important to note that the regulations do not establish a separate specified training for a "behavioral intervention case manager" (BICM) other than to require training in positive behavioral interventions. Each special education local plan area (SELPA) will determine which of their personnel meet this criteria.

"Behavioral intervention case manager" is defined in the regulations as

> *a designated certificated school/district/county staff member(s) or other qualified personnel pursuant to subsection (x) contracted by the school district or county office who has been trained in behavior analysis with an emphasis on positive behavioral interventions. The "behavioral intervention case manager" is not intended to be a new staffing requirement and does not create any new credentialing or degree requirements. The duties of the "behavioral intervention case manager" may be performed by any existing staff member trained in behavior analysis with an emphasis on positive behavioral interventions, including, but not limited to, a teacher, resource specialist, school psychologist, or program specialist.*

This proposed training framework is presented to assist individuals in the field to self-evaluate their preparedness to serve as an implementer or case manager and to provide guidance for what training they might need to augment their skills and knowledge. Additionally, it may prove helpful in evaluating whether or not a course, inservice, workshop, or self-study plan meets one's particular need for further training.

Proposed Training Framework
(Created by the Positive Intervention Task Force)

	KNOWLEDGE BASE	TYPICAL PERSONNEL	POSSIBLE OPTIONS FOR ACHIEVEMENT	REQUIRED COMPETENCIES
A	• Introductory child development training • Training in positive behavioral interventions • Understanding of individual differences and environment effects on behavior • Is receiving on-site training in acceptable emergency procedures & positive behavioral interventions	• **Behavior Aides** under direct supervision of "Behavior Plan Implementor" (typically a teacher, job site coach, or related professional staff)	• District inservices • University or community college coursework • Independent study • On-going training within the setting	• Relate positively to children • Apply positive interventions and follow emergency procedures according to direction, law and SELPA policy
B	• A above, plus: • Child development coursework • Knowledge base includes understanding individual differences, impact of medical, emotional and psycho-social factors on behavior (e.g. seizure disorders, genetic disorders, brain injury, disrupted home life) • Understands which emergency procedures are allowed by law	• **Credentialed staff** preparing for implementator level (e.g., regular education teachers or other credentialed staff).	• University coursework has been completed to credential status • Independent study, and/or workshops beyond credentials as needed • Case-specific consultation • District inservices	• A above, plus: • Varies teaching techniques to meet individual differences • Demonstrates understanding of SELPA approved emergency behavioral interventions
C	• A & B above, plus: • Ability to define key concepts and components of behavioral intervention regulations (functional analysis, positive programming, observational methods, etc.) • Ability to give examples of good practice to illustrate each step in developing and implementing a behavioral intervention plan	• **Credentialed staff** in transition to Level D (e.g., special education teachers, school psychologists, program specialists, or other interested credentialed staff).	• Workshops and inservices • Independent study, correspondence courses or other creative options	• A & B above, plus: • Uses key concepts to discuss student behavior • Demonstrates mastery of SELPA approved emergency behavioral interventions
D	• A B C above, plus: • Completion of supervised experience in positive behavioral interventions with IWENs who exhibit maladaptive behaviors (e.g., self-abuse, aggression, property damage and other pervasive maladaptive behaviors)	• **Fully competent behavioral intervention plan implementors** with training through level C (e.g., special educators or other interested credentialed staff).	• University coursework • Workshops with hands-on behavioral intervention assignments over multiple sessions (e.g., a series of meetings interspersed with assignments culminating in the completion of a project).	• A, B & C above, plus: • Successfully implements positive interventions with IWENs who exhibit maladaptive behaviors • Collaborates with all IEP Team members (e.g., aide, BICM, parent, administrator) in positive plan development and implementation
E	• A B C D above, plus: • Experience in consulting with behavior plan implementors • Experience in functional assessment • Experience in positive behavioral intervention plan development • Experience in supervision of behavior plan implementors including the use of emergency procedures	• **Fully Competent Behavioral Intervention Case Managers** • Recently trained school psychologist may have expertise to this level • School psychologist frequently are at this level after refresher courses, workshops, etc. due to previous experience and coursework • SED mentor teachers and SH mentor teachers frequently are at this level as above	Augmentation of previous training by: • District training (under mentor) • Networking/ consultation on cases with district personnel, or other agencies with specific expertise • University coursework • Multi-day workshop formats which have hands-on assignment in case management and supervision.	• A, B, C & D above, plus: • Conducts and supervises functional analysis assessments • Collaboratively develops positive behavioral intervention plans • Utilizes consulting skills to assure implementation and maintenance of intervention plans • Provides ongoing assistance to school staff in understanding behavior and procedures

NOTE: Level E represents the standards for a fully competent behavioral intervention case manager. Level F is offered in recognition of the fact that some professionals may not be school based employees but have extensive knowledge in the general field of behavior analysis. These individuals will still need to demonstrate the full range of competencies through Level E.

	KNOWLEDGE BASE	TYPICAL PERSONNEL	POSSIBLE OPTIONS FOR ACHIEVEMENT	REQUIRED COMPETENCIES
F	• A B C D E above, plus: • Masters, Ph.D. or other graduate degree in the field of behavioral intervention, or university coursework in a full range of behavioral intervention (management, consultation, research) culminating in a university approved certification.	• **Professionals in the field of Behavioral Intervention** with specific degrees or certifications (This level of training is beyond the requirements of the Education Regulations) to serve as a BICM	• Specific training and supervised experience in a systematic program at the university level.	• A, B, C, D & E above if functioning in a school setting

* The purpose of this framework is: (i) to assist in self-appraisal of one's current expertise (ii) to assist in identifying one's training needs; (iii) for LEA use in determining staff training needs.

Proposed Behavioral Intervention
Background Verification Worksheet
(created by the PBI Task Force)

Proficiency at any stage requires all previous stages to have also been completed.

Stage	Incremental Knowledge Base Criteria Proposed for Behavioral Intervention Aide, Intervention Implementer, and Case Manager	Applicable Experience Category	Documention on Attached Page #
A	❏ Introductory child development training	_____	_____
	❏ Training in positive behavioral interventions	_____	_____
	❏ Understanding of individual differences and environmental effects on behavior	_____	_____
	❏ On-site training in acceptable emergency procedures & positive behavioral interventions	_____	_____
B	❏ Child development coursework	_____	_____
	❏ Knowledge base includes a focus on understanding individual differences, impact of medical, emotional and psycho-social factors on behavior (e.g., seizure disorders, genetic conditions, brain injury, disrupted home life).	_____	_____
	❏ Understands which emergency procedures are allowed by law	_____	_____
C	❏ Ability to define key concepts and components of behavioral intervention regulations (functional analysis, positive programming, observational methods, etc.)	_____	_____
	❏ Ability to give key examples of good practice to illustrate each step in developing and implementing a behavioral intervention plan	_____	_____
D	❏ Completion of supervised experience in positive behavioral interventions with students with disabilities who exhibit maladaptive behaviors (e.g., self-abuse, aggression, property damage, and other pervasive maladaptive behaviors)	_____	_____
E*	❏ Experience in consulting with behavior plan implementers	_____	_____
	❏ Experience in functional assessment	_____	_____
	❏ Experience in positive behavioral intervention plan development	_____	_____
	❏ Experience in supervision of behavior plan implementors including the use of emergency procedures	_____	_____
F	❏ Masters, Ph.D. or other graduate degree in the field of behavioral intervention, or university coursework in a full range of behavioral intervention (management, consultation, research) culminating in a university approved certification	_____	_____

Applicable Experience Categories

1	Correspondence course	7	Workshops by consultants
2	University or Community College coursework	8	Case-specific consultation
3	Independent study with or without supervision	9	District inservice
4	On-going training within the setting by non-district staff	10	Multi-day experiential workshop
5	University coursework complete to credential status	11	District training (under a mentor)
6	University coursework beyond credential requirements	12	Networking/consultation with district colleagues/other agencies

*Submit narrative to document activities completed to meet each of the four knowledge base criteria for E. It is suggested that the supporting narrative should be approximately two pages in length.

Provided by:

CALIFORNIA ASSOCIATION OF SCHOOL PSYCHOLOGISTS

BEHAVIORAL INTERVENTION VERIFICATION PACKAGE

Submitted to: _____

Person Submitting Materials: _____

Address: _____

City: _____ Zip: _____

Phone: _____

I verify the accuracy of the information contained in this package.

_____
Signature   Date

This Verification Worksheet is provided to the reader as a method of organizing documentation of training in positive behavioral interventions. The regulations DO NOT establish a separate specified training for a Behavioral Intervention Case Manager (BICM) other than to require training in positive behavioral interventions. Each SELPA will determine which of their personnel meet this criteria. This worksheet may be helpful for some readers in describing their training to others if they are called upon to do so.

Appendix P.

Resources for Skills Training Programs

The following annotated materials dealing with skills training are referenced in the first section, "Skills Training Programs to Reduce Aggressive Behavior," in Chapter 8, "Prevention as a Best Practice." They are available through Research Press, Department G., P.O. Box 9177, Champaign, IL 61826, (217) 351-3273, Fax (217) 352-1221.

I Can Problem Solve: An Interpersonal Problem-Solving Program for Children, by Myrna B. Shure. The ICPS program is available for three levels — preschool, kindergarten and primary grades, and intermediate elementary grades — and is designed for classroom use. It has been used successfully for both prevention and intervention with young children and is based on more than 20 years of research, including follow-up studies at one and two years posttreatment. Before being introduced to problem-solving skills, students are taught needed vocabulary, identification of their feelings and those of others, and consideration of other points of view. Subsequent lessons focus on generating multiple alternative solutions to problems, anticipating consequences of actions, and the means-end thinking involved in selecting goals and problem solutions — three cognitive problem-solving skills investigators have found that consistently discriminate youngsters displaying maladaptive behavior from those who do not (Pellegrini & Urbain, 1985).

Skillstreaming in Early Childhood: Teaching Prosocial Skills to the Preschool and Kindergarten Child, by Ellen McGinnis and Arnold P. Goldstein; *Skillstreaming the Elementary School Child: A Guide for Teaching Prosocial Skills* by Ellen McGinnis and Arnold P. Goldstein, with Robert P. Sprafkin and N. Jane Gershaw; *Skillstreaming the Adolescent: A Structured Learning Approach to Teaching Prosocial Skills* by Arnold P. Goldstein, Robert P. Sprafkin, N. Jane Gershaw, and Paul Klein. Skillstreaming is based on an experimentally supported skills training model called "structured learning."[1] Skillstreaming is designed for students who are aggressive, withdrawn, or socially immature because of skill deficiency. In addition to providing skill lessons, the books describe procedures for assessing skills, developing behavioral objectives, evaluating progress, managing problems, and prompting use of skills in multiple environments.

Aggression Replacement Training: A Comprehensive Intervention for Aggressive Youth, by Arnold P. Goldstein and Barry Glick, with Scott Reiner, Deborah Zimmerman, and Thomas M. Coultry. Designed for delinquent, aggressive adolescents, the program expands upon skillstreaming, providing lessons on anger control and moral reasoning, as well as teaching prosocial behavior skills.

The Prepare Curriculum: Teaching Prosocial Competencies, by Arnold P. Goldstein. This book provides group problem-solving curriculum for preadolescent and adolescent students with behavior on a continuum from aggressive, antisocial to withdrawn, isolated, asocial. It is research-based and draws extensively from and expands on Skillstreaming and Aggression Replacement Training. The program incorporates training to develop students' interpersonal problem solving, situation perception, anger control, moral reasoning, stress management, empathy, ability to recruit supportive models, cooperation, understanding of group pressures, and control over outcomes of group interactions. Organization of groups, assessment of student skill competencies, selection of program components based on assessment, and transfer and maintenance are discussed.

Think Aloud: Increasing Social and Cognitive Skills - A Problem-Solving Program for Children, by Bonnie W. Camp and Mary Ann S. Bash. This program emphasizes use of verbal mediation in cognitive and social problem solving. There are parallel formats for use in small groups with 6- to 8-year-olds having aggressive or other excessive behaviors and for classwide use for children in grades 1 and 2, 3 and 4, and 5 and 6. The programs are research-based and have been field tested in Denver, Colorado, public schools. Followup studies at 6 and 12 months indicated weak evidence of behavioral change. However, in contrast to those in control groups, the cognitive pattern of aggressive, hostile, distractible, and hyperactive young boys generally continued a trend toward normalization, which predicted favorable response to a refresher program resulting in significantly improved teacher ratings of behavior. Boys who continued to show aggressive cognitive patterns at followup did not show significant benefit from the refresher course. The authors conclude that students who are cognitively too high or too low for the program or who are emotionally or motivationally damaged are unlikely to benefit. They conjecture that children whose families are chaotic, abusive, or rejecting; whose attendance is erratic; or whose behavior is too erratic are also among those unlikely to respond significantly.

The following materials are available from American Guidance Service, P.O. Box 99, Circle Pines, MN. 55014-1796, (800) 328-2560, Fax (612) 786-9077:

Social Skills Rating System (SSRS), by Frank M. Gresham and Stephen N. Elliott. This is a research-based, standardized (national sample of over 4,000 children), norm-referenced instrument for assessing prosocial skills, problem behaviors, and, for school-age children, academic competence based on ratings of the student's cooperation, assertion, responsibility, empathy, and self-control. There are forms for ages 3 to 5 years, grades kindergarten through 6, and grades 7 through 12, with parallel forms for parents and teachers at all levels and student forms for grades 3 through 6 and secondary students. Parents and teachers are asked to rate frequency and the importance they attach to the skills they are evaluating.[2]

Social Skills Intervention Guide: Practical Strategies for Social Skills Training, by Stephen N. Elliott and Frank M. Gresham. Designed for use with students in grade 3 through high school, the program provides 43 lesson plans to remediate problems identified by the Social Skills Rating System. The book also includes suggestions for selecting and grouping students, involving parents, and establishing outcome goals.

The following rating scales and program have not been examined by the authors. They are available through Pro-Ed, 8700 Shoal Creek Boulevard, Austin, TX, 78758-6897, (512) 451-3246, Fax (512) 451-8542.

Behavior Rating Profile, Second Edition, by Linda Brown and Donald D. Hammill. This is a battery of six norm-referenced (2,682 students) instruments for use with children ages 6-6 through 18-6 years. Home and school behaviors are rated by the student, teachers, and parents. A sociogram administered to classmates is part of the evaluation of interpersonal relationships. Each of the instruments is normed individually and may be used alone or in any combination.

Walker-McConnell Scale of Social Competence and School Adjustment: A Social Skills Rating Scale for Teachers, by Hill M. Walker and Scott R. McConnell. This instrument was normed on over 1,800 students and consists of a 43-item teacher-rating scale for students in kindergarten through grade 6.

The Walker Social Skills Curriculum - The ACCEPTS Program: A Curriculum for Children's Effective Peer and Teacher Skills; by Hill M. Walker, Scott McConnell, Deborah Holmes, Bonnie Todis, Jackie Walker, and Nancy Golden. This program is designed for children in kindergarten through grade 6 and provides lessons for individual, small group or large group direct instruction in specific social skills, such as listening to the teacher, taking turns, sharing, and good grooming.

The ACCESS Program: Adolescent Curriculum for Communication and Effective Social Skills, by Hill M. Walker, Bonnie Todis, Deborah Holmes, and Gary Horton, is designed for secondary-level students. The 30 social skills that make up its curriculum were identified by teachers and students as critical for social competence. They include skills such as making and keeping friends, disagreeing with adults, and using self-control. Both programs are appropriate for use by regular and special education teachers.

[1]   Goldstein et al. (1987, pp 22-34) summarized research results from their own group and 30 other studies on outcomes of skills training with chronically aggressive or delinquent youngsters. They found that use of skills training with aggressive adolescents reliably resulted in skill acquisition, but that studies frequently failed to provide transfer training. Research on the effects of their structured learning model, which includes transfer training, indicated that over 90% of the trainees learned the skills taught. Approximately 45-50% applied them in other settings, in contrast with average transfer rates of 15-20% for varying types of psychotherapies and psychopathologies reported by other studies (Goldstein and Kanfer 1979 and Karoly and Steffen 1980).

[2]   Interpretation of scores yielded by standardized rating scales requires understanding of basic principles and limitations of educational and psychological testing. When these instruments are used as part of an evaluation of a student's need for skills training, further assessment, including interviewing the student, is required to determine whether problem behaviors or low rates of specific prosocial skills are attributable to skill deficiency or other factors.

Appendix Q.

Contrasting Behavior Support Plans and Positive Behavioral Intervention Plans

by Diana Browning Wright

The following series of questions and answers may help in clarifying the difference between the extensive analysis and plan development described in this manual and a less data-driven approach to behavior change as described in the 1997 reauthaorization of the Individuals with Disabilities Education Act (IDEA).

Why are behavior support plans developed?

- A behavior support plan is developed to implement certain strategies when the individualized education program (IEP) team believes that a student exhibits behavior that impedes his or her learning or the learning of other students or peers.

The federal reauthorization of the Individuals with Disabilities Education Act stipulates that the IEP team shall consider the use of strategies, including positive behavioral interventions, if a student's behavior impedes learning. If the use of these strategies is considered and found to be necessary, a statement to that effect must be included in the IEP. This statement must be conveyed to each teacher and provider and must delineate his or her specific responsibility to implement the new strategic plan. This plan can be designated by any name, including *behavior support plan (BSP)*.

Differentiating a behavior support plan from a positive behavioral intervention plan is important in California. These two types of plans differ in their comprehensiveness. A behavior support plan is an IEP team's best effort, based on information that is immediately available, to support a student and to eliminate or reduce the effects of his or her problem behavior on learning. On the other hand, the development of a positive behavioral intervention plan is based on the extensive data collected during a functional analysis assessment that is conducted or supervised by a designated specialist—the behavioral intervention case manager (BICM).

- A behavior support plan is developed to implement behavioral or instructional approaches that are specified in the IEP before a functional analysis assessment of serious behavior problems is deemed n ecessary because these approaches were unsuccessful.

The *California Code of Regulations (CCR)* stipulates that a functional analysis assessment shall be conducted whenever "instructional/behavioral approaches specified in the student's IEP have been ineffective" (5 *CCR* 3052[b]). Therefore, it can be concluded that initial approaches to changing serious behavior problems may be specified in the IEP and that these instructional and behavioral approaches may be termed a *behavior support plan*. If these approaches are found by the IEP team to be ineffective for a serious behavior problem, the next step must be taken, and a functional analysis assessment must be conducted.

- A behavior support plan is developed to assist a public agency in meeting its mandate that each teacher and provider is informed of his or her specific responsibility to accommodate, modify, and support (34 *Code of Federal Regulations [CFR]* 300.342[b][3]).

Positive behavioral interventions, strategies, and supports that IEP team members determine are necessary must be specified in the IEP. It then becomes the school district's responsibility to ensure that each teacher and provider is informed about the approaches that the IEP team members have determined will support the student in receiving a free and appropriate public education (FAPE) in the least restrictive environment (LRE). A behavior support plan that delineates the teacher's responsibilities to implement specific strategies, to make certain environmental changes, and to provide behavioral supports is now considered one of the "supplementary aids and supports" (34 *CFR* 300.28) available to students in the pursuit of adequate educational progress.

- A behavior support plan delineates services designed to help ensure that the dangerous behavior of a student who has violated a conduct code does not recur (34 *CFR* 300.522[b][2]).

The Individuals with Disabilities Education Act provides for involuntary removal of a student who has committed a code of conduct violation that involves drugs, weapons, or dangerousness "beyond a preponderance of evidence" (34 *CFR* 300.521[e]). A 45-day removal to an interim alternative placement ensures the student's absence from his or her current placement during due process procedures. This provision helps in securing a school's safety. During the 45-day interim period, the student must receive services to ensure that the behavior doesn't recur in the alternate placement (34 *CFR* 300.522[b][2]). These provisions may be spelled out in a behavior plan that is not yet based on a full functional analysis assessment, that is, in a behavior support plan.

- A behavior support plan is developed to serve as the interim behavior plan while the functional analysis assessment is being conducted following the use of an emergency intervention to contain a student's behavior.

If an emergency containment procedure was used, a functional analysis assessment is mandatory. During the collection of data to complete the assessment and before the development of the positive behavioral intervention plan, an interim behavior plan must be in effect. A behavior support plan can fulfill that requirement.

Is it necessary to collect data before developing a behavior support plan?

It is unnecessary to collect data extensively before developing a behavior support plan. The plan can often be developed during the IEP meeting in which it is determined that such a plan is warranted. The development of the behavior support plan is based on observations that have already been gathered about the student and the environment in which the student exhibits the behavior.

Is it necessary to have an assessment plan before developing a behavior support plan?

Having an assessment plan is unnecessary if the development of the BSP is based on a review of existing data occurring during an IEP meeting. As in all IEP functions, it is important to involve the parents and the student, when appropriate, in the process of developing the plan. If new data need to be collected (e.g., through testing or through specific individual observations by someone other than the teacher), an assessment plan for collecting these data would need to be developed.

What are the best practices for developing a behavior support plan?

A behavior support plan must address both the match between the student and the environment and the reason (also referred to as the *function*) of the student's behavior. A behavior support plan should specify:

- The environmental and instructional changes that may reduce the student's need to exhibit the problem behavior and reduce or eliminate the triggers or predictors of the behavior

- The strategies that should be used to teach, elicit, and reinforce other behaviors that fulfill the same need for the student as the problem behavior

- The persons who are responsible for implementing each component of the plan

- The process for the coordination between other plans and between all the persons who are implementing the plans

- The reactive strategies that all implementors of the plan will employ if the student's challenging behavior recurs

This appendix contains a sample behavior support plan and instruction sheet. A blank sample may also be downloaded from <*http:www.calstat.org/blank_plan.pdf*>.

For which students are behavior support plans developed?

Behavior support plans are developed for students who exhibit behaviors that impede their learning or the learning of others or for students who require behavioral and instructional approaches in their IEPs.

- If the student has an IEP, the IEP team develops the BSP.

- If the student has a 504 plan, the specified interventions could become a part of the 504 service plan to ameliorate adverse effects of a mental or physical disability on a major life activity, learning.

- Prereferral interventions that are specified in the behavior support plan may be made during the student success team process and before the student is considered for special education evaluation.

- If the student receives only general education services, the school can elect to provide any student with behavioral interventions as a part of that school's regular procedures. This approach is optional, but it embodies research-based best practices for school sites attempting to address the needs of at-risk youth.

When is a positive behavioral intervention plan developed?

After the functional analysis assessment has been conducted and when the IEP team deems that a positive behavioral intervention plan (PBIP) is warranted based on this assessment, such a plan must be developed.

- Whenever a student's behavior has not responded to behavioral or instructional approaches that are specified in the IEP and the IEP team has determined that these approaches are ineffective for a serious behavior problem, the IEP team must request that a functional analysis assessment be conducted or supervised by a behavioral intervention case manager (BICM).

- If an emergency intervention has been used to contain a student's behavior, a functional analysis assessment must be conducted. Based on the findings of the assessment, the IEP team determines whether a positive behavioral intervention plan is warranted.

What are the differences between the PBIP and the BSP?

- The degree of specificity regarding assessment and intervention components, accountability, generalization, and maintenance is much greater for a positive behavioral intervention plan than it is for a behavior support plan.

- The degree of training needed to develop a positive behavioral intervention plan is much greater than the degree of training needed to develop a behavior support plan. During the meeting in which the positive behavioral intervention plan is developed, the IEP team must include a behavioral intervention case manager who has conducted or supervised the conducting of a functional analysis assessment. In contrast, any IEP team may develop a behavior support plan.

- Any behavior, no matter how minor, that interferes with learning may be addressed in a behavior support plan. In contrast, the positive behavioral intervention plan specifically targets serious behavior problems for which specified behavioral or instructional approaches, such as a behavior support plan, have not yet been successful.

- The positive behavioral intervention plan is very dependent on data. It is based on a full review of all current data that were collected during the functional analysis assessment, including information about the effects of all medical conditions and medical treatment and a review of all previous attempts to change the student's behavior.

- The positive behavioral intervention plan must be based on a functional analysis assessment. The functional analysis assessment must be conducted or supervised by a behavior intervention case manager who has been deemed by a special education local plan area (SELPA) to have had sufficient training to assume this role.

- An assessment plan is necessary for conducting the functional analysis assessment because new data will be collected. In addition, a full report of the results of the functional analysis assessment must be provided before a positive behavior intervention plan can be developed. The report must delineate the methods used to collect the new data and describe the specific antecedents and consequences of a student's difficult behavior. In contrast, an assessment plan is not required before developing a behavior support plan during an IEP meeting because new data have not been collected before the meeting.

What are the similarities between the PBIP and the BSP?

- Parents may request that a functional analysis assessment be conducted and that a positive behavioral intervention plan be developed for serious behavior problems. The school district then conducts the assessment or declines to conduct it. If the district declines to conduct the assessment, it gives parents the reason for this decision, proposes alternative options, if necessary, and provides due process procedural rights. Similarly, parents may request that interventions be included—through a behavior support plan—as a regular part of the IEP process if the student's behavior that is impeding learning is identified. All due process safeguards apply in the development and implementation of both plans.

- Efforts to change a student's behavior should follow the same best practices for both types of plan: identify the function of the behavior; teach alternative behaviors; make instructional and/or environmental changes; specify how to react to challenging behaviors in the future; determine reinforcers for the new behaviors (or for the absence of the old behaviors); determine who should communicate with whom and how often.

Addressing Behavior in Educational Settings in California

Individuals with Exceptional Needs

Additional Expertise/Refinement:

Applied to FAA-based PBI plans not yet effective, under IEP team supervision

Individuals with Exceptional Needs

Functional Analysis–Based Positive Behavior Intervention Plans:

For serious behavior where an emergency intervention was used, or when previous behavioral/instructional approaches (BSP plans) addressing "behavior that impedes learning"(IDEA) are found ineffective by IEP team. An FAA (California *Education Code*) must be conducted by or supervised by a behavior intervention case manager (BICM). Development of a positive behavior intervention plan (PBIP) for individuals with exceptional needs is mandated to follow the FAA if the IEP team deems necessary after reviewing the FAA results.

Individuals with Exceptional Needs

Individualized Behavior Support Planning:

Developed by the IEP/504 team for a student when "behavior is impeding the learning" of the student or peers. (Optional: some schools elect to provide behavior support planning as a pre-referral intervention through the student success team (SST) process, even though special education eligibility determination has not occurred; other schools elect to develop behavior support plans for *any* student who needs one through a team approach with family and staff.)

All Students

Strategies and Supports for At-Risk Students:

Classroom strategies may be necessary emphasizing group problem solving, classroom structuring, reinforcement systems, and the teaching of rule-following behavior. For students with IEP/504 plans, ensuring implementation of curricular accommodations is critical. Special small-group counseling activities may occur at this stage.

All Students

Positive School Environments:

Emphasis on the positive shaping of all students' behavior, reinforcement of progress, family participation, and extension of unconditional positive regard for each student, e.g., schoolwide safe school programs, educational behavioral support (EBS), behavior and environment strategies and support teams (BESST), etc.

Diana Browning Wright, **Behavior/Discipline Trainings**, 2001.

Behavior Support Plan

for Behavior Interfering with Learning of Student or Peers

Student _____ IEP date of this addendum _____

Behavior impeding learning is _____

It impedes learning because _____

Team estimate of need for behavior support plan ☐ extreme ☐ serious ☐ moderate ☐ needing attention, early stage intervention

Current frequency/intensity/duration of behavior _____

Any current predictors for behavior?

IEP team believes behavior occurs because (team hypothesis-behavior function)

What team believes student should do instead of the problem behavior (match to hypothesis)

What supports the student using the problem behavior (in or missing in environment, in or missing in instruction)

Behavioral goals/objectives related to this plan:

To achieve this outcome, <u>both</u> teaching of new alternative behavior and reinforcement is needed.	☐ yes	☐ no
To achieve this outcome, reinforcement of alternative behavior alone is emphasized (no new teaching is necessary).	☐ yes	☐ no
To achieve this outcome, environmental supports or changes are needed.	☐ yes	☐ no
Are curriculum accommodations necessary? ☐ yes ☐ no; Is there a curriculum accommodation plan?	☐ yes	☐ no

BSP to be coordinated with other agency s service plans? ☐ yes ☐ no; Person responsible for contact _____

Teaching strategies and necessary curriculum or materials for new behavior instruction

By whom? _____ How frequent? _____

Environmental structure and supports to be provided (time/space/materials/interactions)

Who establishes? _____ Who monitors? _____

Reinforcement procedures

By whom? _____ Frequency? _____

Reactive strategy to employ/debriefing procedures to use if problem behavior occurs again

Personnel: _____

Communication provisions Daily/weekly reports/record keeping

Between _____ Frequency? _____

Diana Browning Wright, *Behavior/Discipline Trainings*, 2001.

This plan is not a mental health treatment plan nor accommodation plan for disability. This plan should dovetail with other necessary components.

┌─▷ **Behavior Support Plan** ◁─

This is an action plan for what adults will do to shape, model, and cue behavior in conducive environments.

for Behavior Interfering with Learning of Student or Peers

Student **Full name is ok, first name only is best or initials**   IEP date of this addendum _____ **If general education student, delete. If for 504 eligibility, alter to 504 plan date.**

Behavior impeding learning is **Make statement nonjudgmental, observable, and clearly defined.**

It impedes learning because **Describe how this results in less skills learned by student or others.**

Team estimate of need for behavior support plan ☐ extreme ☐ serious ☐ moderate ☐ needing attention, early stage intervention
Current frequency/intensity/duration of behavior **Give reader a sense of severity.**

Any current predictors for behavior? **Those situations you can predict problems such as difficult task, transition time, when not working in group, with specific people, when alone, after a request, etc.**

IEP team believes behavior occurs because (team hypothesis-behavior function) **What student is getting or protest/escape avoiding with this behavior**

What team believes student should do instead of the problem behavior (match to hypothesis) **How will the student get his/her needs met, e.g., how will he/she APPROPRIATELY get something, escape or avoid something when necessary?**

What supports the student using the problem behavior (in or missing in environment, in or missing in instruction) **Think in terms of: 1) eliminating behavior through changing context so student doesn t need to use this behavior or 2) teaching new way to meet function identified**

Behavioral goals/objectives related to this plan: **Brief statement referencing IEP or 504 plan: What new skills will student achieve through this plan (not just what student won t do anymore)**

To achieve this outcome, <u>both</u> teaching of new alternative behavior and reinforcement is needed.   ☐ yes   ☐ no
To achieve this outcome, reinforcement of alternative behavior alone is emphasized (no new teaching is necessary).   ☐ yes   ☐ no
To achieve this outcome, environmental supports or changes are needed.   ☐ yes   ☐ no
Are curriculum accommodations necessary? ☐ yes ☐ no; Is there a curriculum accommodation plan?   ☐ yes   ☐ no
BSP to be coordinated with other agency s service plans? ☐ yes ☐ no **(ex: Depts. of mental health, correction, regional center, private therapists)**; Person responsible for contact **(Identify a school staff member to coordinate actions between agencies.)**

Teaching strategies and necessary curriculum or materials for new behavior instruction
Examples include: better communication skills, anger management, picture exchange system, self-management systems, following schedules and routines, learning new social skills, learning how to negotiate, learning structured choice, learning new scripts, learning notebook organization, learning to use playground conflict-resolution managers, learning how to use classroom meeting structure to solve problems, etc.; i.e., <u>any general or specific skill deficit you hope to correct to change behavior</u>
By whom? **Who will teach this?** _____   How frequent? **Be sure you have consensus from actual providers.**

Environmental structure and supports to be provided (time/space/materials/interactions)
Time pacing techniques, closure systems, completing tasks in parts, having more time/less on tasks, etc.
Space seating, use of masking tape to identify areas, different   work space for different tasks, etc.
Materials tasks in sequencing trays, manipulatives, material organizers, etc.
Interactions Are there specific styles or frequency of interactions or specific supportive words, voice tone quality, etc., that help this student? Who is involved? Peers? Teachers, aides, bus driver, etc.?
Who establishes? **Typically teacher/aide with administrator help**   Who monitors? **Typically teacher w/additional help as needed**

Reinforcement procedures
Consider a range of possibilities: A simple praise statement the student enjoys, privately given specific praise, notes home, contingent access to favorite classroom activities or privileges, high 5." What motivates the student and enhances quality of life <u>right now</u>? Who will give, how frequently? Will reinforcement happen in school <u>and</u> at home or by outside school or community personnel?
By whom? **Maximize sources of reinforcement**   Frequency?   **High frequency for learning new behaviors, reducing as behavior becomes habituated**

Reactive strategy to employ/debriefing procedures to use if problem behavior occurs again
What works to calm the student? How can you best prevent escalation? Will structured choice help? Offering time away to cool off nonemotionally? What series of behaviors should adults employ to return the student to rule-following behavior? (Will consequences be necessary? Who will therapeutically debrief the student after control is achieved?)
Personnel: **Who should interact under what level of crisis? teacher only? Specific support personnel? Outside classroom assistance?**

Communication provisions   Daily/weekly reports/record keeping
What system? Phone calls by whom to whom? Informal notes? Daily report cards? Weekly logs? Consider family, administrators, IEP team, counselors, probation office, other agencies. Report new skills learning rates, not just infractions. Remember, behavioral goals and objectives are reported at least quarterly in the IEP process.
Between **Who needs this information?** _____   Frequency?   **Different people or agencies may require different frequencies.**

Diana Browning Wright, *Behavior/Discipline Trainings*, 2001.

Summary of Behavioral Terms and Correlations in Federal and State Law

Diana Browning Wright, M.S.

Terminology	Assessment Considerations	Source(s) of Mandate, Correlations
"Behavior Impeding Learning" of student or peers	• Assessment components not specified in IDEA or *Federal Register* or state codes—can be any behavior IEP team identifies as impeding.	• IDEA, *Federal Register*.
"Positive Behavioral Intervention Strategies and Supports"	• IEP team must consider these (among other strategies) if behavior impedes learning of student or peers. • Assessment components not specified.	• IDEA, *Federal Register*. • Also same as the intent of California *Education Code*: "behavioral/instructional approaches specified in IEP"—California *Education Code* 56522 (d).
"Behavioral/Instructional Approaches Specified in IEP"	• Assessment components not specified. • IEP team to have developed these approaches to address serious behavior (prior to functional analysis assessment and any positive behavioral intervention plan based on that assessment).	• Terminology is in California *Education Code* only. • Overlaps with *intent of IDEA*'s "behavior impeding learning."
Functional Analysis Assessment *(A specific behavioral assessment that hypothesizes the function of a behavior and systematically manipulates a variable to prove/disprove hypothesis—dbw)*	• Requires use of a specific paradigm, "Applied Behavior Analysis," to comprehensively collect data and analyze antecedents, behavior, consequences (A-B-C) to determine function of behavior and appropriate interventions. Findings must be reported to IEP team who develop positive behavior intervention plan if needed. • Must be conducted by or supervised by SELPA (Special Education Local Plan Area) approved behavior intervention case manager (BICM).	• California *Education Code* only; is not included in IDEA or *Federal Register*). • Required, 1) if an emergency intervention was used to contain a behavior, or 2) if behavioral/instructional approaches specified in the IEP have been unsuccessful.
Functional Behavioral Assessment *(May utilize a variety of assessment methods: review of records, interviews, observations to analyze retrospectively the function of a specific behavior that may have only occurred once—dbw)*	• Not yet defined in California *Education Code* after numerous attempts. • Perform FBA when a behavior has resulted in suspensions beyond 10 cumulative days in a school year. • Also perform prior to involuntary transfer, or expulsion proceedings (in addition to the "manifestation determination" for students with IEPs).	• IDEA and *Federal Register*, but not defined in either. • Occurs with or without elaboration as part of the manifestation determination process in a disciplinary proceeding for an individual with exceptional needs.
Functional Assessment *(What student is "getting"–i.e., positive reinforcement, or "escape/protesting"–i.e., negative reinforcement, removal of an aversive—dbw)*	• Generic term, found in different literature bases, meaning different things. • As applied to behavior, the determination (hypothesizing) of function a behavior serves for an individual.	• Not encoded.
"Positive Behavioral Intervention Plan" *(A specific type of behavior plan that must be based on functional analysis assessment as described in California* Education Code*)*	• Part of a behavioral analysis paradigm with many specified components. • Must be based on a Functional Analysis Assessment, developed by the IEP team based on BICM report following an FAA. • Must include positive strategies among other mandated components.	• California *Education Code* only.
"Behavior Support Plan" *(Proactive action planning to address behavior(s) impeding learning. Delineation of "positive behavioral interventions, strategies and supports," includes: teaching an alternative behavior, making instructional and environmental changes, providing reinforcement, reactive strategies and effective communication—dbw).*	• Assessment components not mandated, but (best practice) should be based on understanding the "why" (function) of the behavior. • Interventions are specified in written form, part of IEP, whenever behavior impedes learning (prior to more intensive assessment, and interventions required in California). • Specifies environmental instructional changes, positive interventions strategies and supports; not just consequences for infractions are included.	• If IEP team specifies interventions necessary because "behavior impedes learning," has IDEA, *Federal Regulations* roots. • If IEP team develops because behavioral/ instructional approaches need to be specified in the IEP for a serious behavior, has California *Education Code* roots. • BSP is a common term for initial behavior plans in place across California. • BSP <u>may</u> or may not in the future be included in California *Education Code*—several bills have passed the House and Senate, but were not finally approved by the Governor. Bills may recur.

Diana Browning Wright, M.S., **Behavior/Discipline Trainings**, 2001. See www.ideapractices.org for IDEA/Fed.Regs.